Fabio Steinbruch

Memories on wheels

THE AUTOMOBILE IN BRAZIL OF THE 1960s

CSN
Companhia Siderúrgica Nacional

BANCO FIBRA

LEI DE INCENTIVO À CULTURA
MINISTÉRIO DA CULTURA

This book was published with the benefit of the Culture Incentive Law n° 8.313, of the brazilian Culture Ministery.

EDITORA ALAÚDE

Dados Internacionais de Catalogação na Publicação (CIP)
(Câmara Brasileira do Livro, SP, Brasil)

Steinbruch, Fabio
Memories on wheels: the automobile in Brazil of the 1960s / Fabio Steinbruch; [English translation Bob Sharp; photographers Cláudio Larangeira and Christian Castanho]. – São Paulo: Alaúde Editorial, 2007.

Título original: Memórias sobre rodas: o automóvel no Brasil dos anos 1960
Patrocínio: CNS - Companhia Siderúrgica Nacional / Banco Fibra.

Bibliografia
ISBN 978-85-98497-67-9

1. Automobilismo - Brasil 2. Automóvel - Brasil - Design e construção - História 3. Automóvel - Brasil - História I. Laranjeiras, Cláudio. II. Castanho, Christian. III. Título.

07-6950 CDD-629.230981

Índices para catálogo sistemático:
1. Brasil: Automóvel: Design e construção: História 629.230981
2. Brasil: Automóvel: História 629.230981

Sponsorship
CSN - Companhia Siderúrgica Nacional
Banco Fibra

Editor
Antonio Cestaro

Editorial Coordination
Lucimara Leal e Marileide Gomes

English Version and Technical review
Bob Sharp

Version Review
Maria Sylvia Corrêa

Illustrations
Estúdio196 Design (Gil Tokio - Pingado)

Fotograph
Cláudio Larangeira e
Christian Castanho (images of Toyota Bandeirante)

Print Production
Rogério de Simone

Graphical Design and Desktop Publishing
Walter Cesar Godoy

Alaúde Editorial Ltda.
R. Hildebrando Thomaz de Carvalho, 60 - CEP 04012-120 - São Paulo - SP
Telefax: 55+ (11) 5572-9474 / 5579-6757
alaude@alaude.com.br
www.alaude.com.br

Presentation

When Fabio Steinbruch told me that he was about to finish one more book about automobiles, I deemed it fantastic. When, however, he told me that he would like me to participate by writing counterpoints at the end of each chapter, I felt very happy. But when I learned that it was the work *Memories on wheels – The automobile in Brazil of the 1960s*, I became exultant.

Fantastic, because I keep a deep admiration for those who write about this wonderful machine called automobile, synonymous of individual freedom like no other when it deals with locomotion.

Happy, for participating in the work of someone I admire and that encompasses true spirit of the automobile enthusiast, nursed since the early years of life, something not arisen suddenly, from nothing, or by mere commercial interest or fashion.

Exultant, because rightly were the 1960s the most important ones of my professional life – my beginning! –, always linked to the automobile in one way or another, and also the years our automotive industry ceased crawling and speeded up for good, thus popularizing the automobile in Brazil.

The reading of this second Fabio Steinbruch book takes us to his world in the optics of a boy who happened to be born in the 1960s, that grew up watching the automobiles of that time, even those not built here. This factor alone has certainly forged his ability to analyze and judge a very few only in the country have.

Way in the late 1970s came the great moment of every youngster, that of getting the driver's license. Later, the adult age, that of responsibility, of professional progress, but, in a certain way, those 1960s remained more strongly present than ever in Fabio Steinbruch's mind.

He could do nothing but to go for this work, it was one of his missions in life. The mission of showing and *interpreting* to current generations and future ones what all those automobiles really represented, how they were like, how they ran, what role they played.

That's what one soon learns by reading this book, a enthusiastic narrative that takes the reader, he or she, to the driver's seat of so many automobiles, built here or imported, that helped to write this beautiful, endless history of ours.

Bob Sharp

Another book by Fabio Steinbruch...

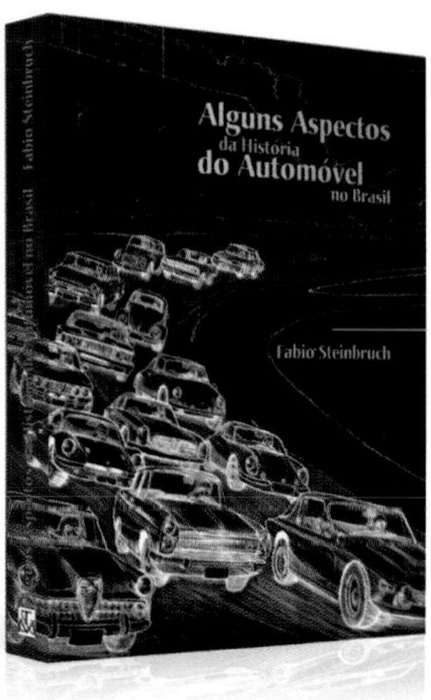

Some Aspects of the Automobile History in Brazil is the work that kicked-off my career as a writer and also the partnership with Bob Sharp.

Acknowledgements

For sure this book is the result of teamwork.

All contained information was confirmed by Bob Sharp beforehand. Cláudio Larangeira's photos are the ones that really illustrate and credit the true visual quality. Additionally, drawings by Estúdio 196 Design came to add extra charm to this work.

Thank you, everybody!

The English version was Bob Sharp's job, who also wrote the boxes where he counterpoints with his point of view what is expressed in the text.

Publishing house Alaúde assigned its best team. Each one did its best! My thanks to Antonio Cestaro, publisher; to Marileide Gomes and Lucimara Leal, both in charge of editorial coordination; to Walter Cesar Godoy, for the graphic production; to Ronaldo Antonelli, for organizing the text; to Rogério de Simone, who helped iconographic research, and to reviewer Maria Sylvia Corrêa. It would render useless gathering the best professionals if there was no competence for desktop work, reviewing text and all other pertaining adjustments during edition.

It is very rewarding to be allowed to count on Brazil's Department of Culture law no. 8,313 for Culture Incentive. My thanks to Wilson Valença, from WV Produções, who knew how to set the guidelines and follow this project up, and to the decisive CSN and Banco Fibra support!

My task was to conceive, to write, to set guidelines and also to coordinate the work.

The exclusively-photographed automobiles were in good working order. An enormous collaboration was provided by those who lent us their rarities in mint condition. Besides the pleasure in owning and conserving these vehicles, their owners have been demonstrating a strong compromise with the History of Brazil, that of the automobile more specifically. My special thanks to Mimo, who lent me the 1960 Dauphine and the 1967 Gordini III; to Léo, for the 1966 Volkswagen Sedan 1200 and several other cars; to João Paulo Ming de Camargo, for the 1967 Aero-Willys 2600; to Leonardo Peixoto, for the 1967 Willys Itamaraty; to Fábio Pagotto, for the 1960 VW Kombi; to Antônio Carlos de Oliveira and André Sanfaz, for the 1967 Ford Mustang GTA; to João Otávio, for the 1970 Alfa Romeo gt 1300 Junior; to Eduardo for the 1970 Rural and the Murads, for the 1958 one; to Luís, for the Candango; to Luiz Francisco Santis Beu, for the Jeep; and to Sérgio Berezovsky, who at *Quatro Rodas* magazine and with photographer Christian Castanho have kindly provided us with photos of the Toyota Bandeirante, and so many, anonymous others. The publicity images was given by Memória da Propaganda or courteously subsided by Celso Luiz de Carvalho da Car Velho – Memorabilia.

Many thanks to Carlos Pina, who closely followed conception and extensively helped in doing it. Even when some health problems arose, he has never refrained from working to make the project feasible. Like him, my cousin Alegria always present. So much dedication!

Special thanks to those who have been helping me to turn my wishes into books.

Thanks also to all that directly participated, my thanks to my sister, who is always around; to my brother, who had started this "automobile stuff" with me; to my father, who even without understanding what "this stuff was about", for sure played an important role; and to my Fabiane, who was the one that gave meaning to all this.

Summary

Foreword

Many dates and one only history
The hour of making it happen

In Brazil, as year 1956 was close to ending, Vemag produced its first automobile, a station wagon. At first the model was christened DKW-Vemag station wagon Universal. Before it, also in 1956, the production of the Romi-Isetta had began, a vehicle with characteristics peculiar enough that, especially for the fact of having only one door, located in the front section, could not be classified as a true automobile according to the government thinking. For such, and officially, the DKW station wagon was considered the first national car. However, much more important than the discussion of pioneering is the fact that something new was happening: it started in Brazil the era of a true industrialization.

The nation's president Juscelino Kubitschek de Oliveira had been elected under a top compromise, publicly assumed, with the development of Brazil. His slogan was "Fifty years in five". Nothing could be more important and attention-drawing than the implementing of an automotive park. Independently of any other implication, the Brazilian auto industry became reality and the automobile was the motor of enthusiasm.

In 1967, or maybe in the end of 1966, there was the kick-off, and it would last approximately two years, a process of change in all the structures implanted at first. It is very difficult to precise the facts and the dates when transformations occur, the evidently do come from nothing of from one moment to another. However, by assuming Simca, in the end of 1966, Chrysler debuts a period of great changes. In this year Volkswagen would acquire Chrysler and, in 1967, Ford would do so regarding Willys-Overland. Three automakers of the pioneering phase where no longer in business. In their places, three out of the four main automakers in the world, one debuting here – Chrysler – and two increasing their playing – Ford and Volkswagen – a fact that by itself signaled the consolidation and a new stage in development.

Automobiles of the 1960s in Brazil, a title that enunciates not always so exact a period, in a story that has its dawn with the invention of the wheel, if not before, a long period yet to go.

The automobiles and I

our early years

Growing together

In 1956 I was not born yet, and in March of 1967 I turned six years old. Therefore, my involvement with cars of those times goes through several discoveries, a lot of magic and an infinite enchantment.

I can feel the emotions I lived together with the many models that circulated in our streets, although I cannot precise the story an, many times, not even localize the exact time. Sincerely, I doubt my memory and I am afraid that many things are fantasy, however it seems real or, at least, as important as it were; after all, I was a child.

The enchantment years

Everything was magic. Automobiles moved as by magic, as well as all the accessories: the speedometer, top star, knew what the speed was; the windshield wipers worked because the switch was pulled; headlights lit when another switch was pulled; the horn honked when "we honked the horn"; and the car moved when it was accelerated. Everything was direct, there were not mechanisms, things just worked when ordered to.

Some data, from this or that model, always arrived and I kept in memory. At that time I learned that: the Gordini "is not worth a cent"; the Simca "only gets stranded"; the Mercedes "is the best car in the world"; "no, the best car in the world is the Rolls-Royce"; the Volks "is small"; the Kombi "rolls over" and many others.

However, all information fell well short of the power, neither so imaginary, I perceived in the automobiles: the Gordini had sympathetic shape and I always saw it painted, especially in advertising, as a racing car; the Simca, with fish-tail among other adornments, could only be possessor of some power from beyond; the Mercedes would not be better than the JK, and a Rolls-Royce, this was a complete strange, perhaps the best in the world; the Volks was cool and the Kombi, very large.

The instrument cluster of the JK enchanted me; the DKW, that passed by making noise and smoking, was different; the big American cars seemed old, yet strong; the Impala, with three little circular taillights and a badge with the jumping deer, seemed very special; the cars of the 1930s were the "jalopies", singed and cultured in my favorite song, "The calhambeque" ("The jalopy"), by Roberto Carlos. These and other impressions were above reason, and I was in love for any car. All of them, with no exception, deserved my admiration.

My cars at the time

My mother, for sure, had two Volkses until 1967. In 1968 came the third one, a beige 1300 model, with "mile" auxiliary lamps.

My father had more than one JK. I remember a gray one, which had a few stains that looked like dirt (they were small dust spots) and one that was green and my sister said it was blue. After my mother mediation, I reached the conclusion that the car was "greenish-blue", a new color name for my vocabulary. Additionally for these cars, I eventually rode in Kombi, when traveling on vacation, or in an another uncle's car

As for driving, I "drove" already! Home, the piano bench served as steering wheel and the stand of an ashtray, long enough, the gearshift. At the amusement park, my favorite play was the cart. I sit in the miniature-car that, in a round line, kept going round and round. I preferred the "cart" to the merry-go-round by a large extent. Better than that, only to drive my blue, pedal-moved car, of indefinite model. I had a perfect adoration for it, which could be driven in the building's garage only, where I and other kids played. Many mother always advised me to not lend it to the taller boys, but a buddy three years older than me and weighing about twenty kilograms more than myself, persuaded me and I let him drive my car. As he sat, the toy made a strange noise that was later diagnosed as "not repairable". Some times I imagined the analysis was forged: that would be my punishment for lending my car or a penalty for using the advantage of the larger body of the "tico-tico" (a kind of pedal tricycle for up to about five-year old children) of a girl neighbor that, upon refusing to pull and give me way, received a "touch" as to learn good manners? Today I believe that the repair technician was very incompetent, after all, if I am not wrong, all it needed was an electric welding, which would be expensive and complicated!

I always missed this toy, although it was later replaced by a bicycle that, at first, was fitted with two small side wheels for not flipping over. With time a wheel was removed and later on the other. That's how I learned to ride bicycles. Nimbler and faster, my imagination had made an automobile out of it. I cannot precise, but I was about seven already.

My favorite standard toys, those I was allowed to play with indoor, were the car miniatures, the little cars I could push while on my knees. They were made of plastic and, in my opinion, "disassembling", for as soon as was given one, I immediately torn its wheels off.

I was still six or seven years old when I discovered the metal miniatures. They were rare, expensive and desired. The brand with more *status* was Matchbox. I won one and tried to take care of it. It was the miniature of a Ford Galaxie (American) in fire department decor. Later I won another one, however my metal car fleet would only grow when my father made his first trip to Europe and brought me some five wonderful models.

In 1966 I discovered the most fascinating of toys: my cousins, and also neighbors, won an Autorama (slot-racing). I worked bad, but it was just great. I won mine in 1968. A few years later I would replace the amusement park carts that went round without my intervention by miniatures powered by internal combustion engines, that reached speeds lower than those of a bicycle, but that I could really drive in a closed circuit. Additionally to this new toy, another little car, called auto scooter, became one of my favorite toys in amusement parks.

Another way of driving, perhaps the coolest of them all, was be at a real-car steering wheel, imagining being the best driver in the world. It is obvious that the key was put somewhere far away and the car remained off, but even so, once, in a slope, I had my first mini-accident. To crash a real car, with engine working, only in 1969, when I stole the car's keys and covered a route less than two meters long until hitting a wall.

School vacation times were the nectar of my childhood. I would rather go to country, but the beach had its enchantments. The amusement park was one of them. My favorite attraction was a car than went round and round without my intervention, yet it pounded my imagination. Before 1970, when I was less than seven years old, my vacation at the beach turned more interesting thanks to a mini-car with an internal combustion engine, throttle and brakes controlled by pedals, and a steering wheel. If I am not wrong, they were Interlagos miniatures. One year later they were replaced by Karmann Ghias, with throttle and braking actuated by a single lever, manually operated. They were a little less amusing and made impossible the partnership between a friend and I, as to make our money to last more: in one turn he throttled and I drove, in the next one we exchanged jobs. As incredible as it may seem, we achieved good results in the rounds.

Therefore, even the bicycle, the metal cars and the Autorama, or powered cars and bumping cars (auto scooter), or yet cars with working engines, became part of my life after 1967 only.

When information starts feeding imagination

Along the following years I kept riding automobiles of the previous period, although I also had contact with recently-launched models.

Home, in 1968, my father traded the JK by a 1963 Mercedes-Benz 220 S, which was replaced in 1970 by a 1965 230 S, which gave place to a Dodge Dart in 1972. My mother, in 1968, went riding a Volks 1300, a car that represented a new generation, in the same way the Kombis that served us, replaced by newer, 1,500 cm^3 models.

Some uncles trade their cars for more recent models, however a very close uncle only traded his 1967 bordeaux DKW-Vemag Belcas S in 1970, as well as another uncle had his Aero-Willys until 1969. Therefore, for at least five more years, all models produced in the period of my first years kept running together with the newly launched ones, integrating the day-by-day scenery and sharpening my curiosity. It was a time when everything seemed to be somewhat magic, but there was certain information already.

Getting close to 10-years old, I found out that my mother could own a Volkswagen Variant or a Ford Corcel. That my father would have to decide between buying Ford Galaxie or a Dodge Dart. It started to become difficult to like all, I had to make a choise. I was almost sure to prefer this or that model, and I did it for few rational reasons. I began to choose my favorite makes, as a kid choose a soccer team to cheer: with no logic at all, but with many explanations.

A long period away from the pioneers

At 12 years old, I started reading regularly about the cars of the period, which interested me more than the previous decade's, about which it would not be possible to find literature. My reading consisted uniquely and exclusively of all the buff magazines then. With this age I started to drive occasionally, in more remote sites, with less risk of meeting a cop.

In 1976 I entered secondary school and began to attend the school's library. There were bound, complete collections of Quatro Rodas and Autoesporte magazines. Whenever I skip classes I went to the library and read about some models I knew well, but I did not have information about their technical and practical aspects. This way, I went on learning about cars I rode in all my childhood. The published advertising in any kind of media also helped.

The caring observation, that conferred the main role to automobiles in films, documentaries, photos, stories where it was exhibited, increased to large extent all the involvement.

Then the adult age would come. I got my driver license and only current models, or those yet be launched, drew my attention, although curiosity about antique automobiles persisted.

In 1984 I obtained my first racing driver license and in 1985 I would enter a race for the first time.

A replica of my Alfa Romeo 2600 Touring Spider like mine, made in "manzipan", was atop my wedding cake, with a red-haired broom and a little blonde princess aboard.

The reencounter with the old automobiles

Time went by. In the late 1980s, just a few samples remained to give life and illustrate history. It was when a started to have contact with antique car world. I was not thirty yet when I entered a group of people over forty years old and that, by majority, also valued the cars they lived their childhood around. Since I was one of the youngest, I cultured models still not collectable. They were deemed "junk", but I was not the only that admired them. My generation had started to integrate to the group.

I had then the opportunity to purchase some samples and restore then, besides being able to daily drive them or going to antique car gatherings, that included speed runs. It was with those cars that I began racing regularly.

Those models, that had awakened my thoughts, took shape and started to integrate my quotidian.

I have discovered the true working of each one and, more than ever, I had the conscience that many of my childhood impressions were correct: the best of them, as with any other automobile, was the magic.

Once more I could prove that hardly an automobile is better than the other. Many times it more adequate to use or taste of someone else, but think that one is better, this is really to fantasy.

As with any other adult, I have a lot to learn with me the child.

Very few just-married couples have the pleasure to leave for the wedding night at the wheel of the "car of the bride".

Ambiance

Brazil

In the beginning of the 20th century, when still a novelty – a toy for grown-ups, yet desired by everyone, but accessible to millionaires only – the automobile started to arrive in Brazil in a most timid and aristocratic way.

Santos-Dumont – the "Father of Aviation" – was the first to bring one. It was a Peugeot (French) model.

At that time the cultural influence, especially on the elites, was clearly European and Santos-Dumont would accomplish the first flight of a heavier-than-air craft (the aircraft) in Paris, not by chance had chosen a car of French origin.

Much more than just go motoring, the "Father of Aviation" was interested studying the application of light and compact internal combustion engines for aeronautical purposes (but this is another story...)

When the 1920s got nearer, the automobile began to be taken more seriously: it was no longer a "mere toy" to become a transport mean.

From then on the Ford model T – of American origin – starter to turn into the most individual transport mean used in Brazil.

Scarce roads and lack of service were the circumstances that privileged Ford cars, which were easy to maintain and apt to go through difficult paths.

The bad income distribution, at that time, enabled that the extremely reduced elite only had access to the best of the world and, although the lack of good roadways was inhibiting to the wealthy Brazilians, a handful of them were enthusiastic – in fact – about bringing the most refined European models. They were a minority that, however, had interesting cars.

Nevertheless, step by step, spaces were being opened.

At this time, Washington Luís (president of the Republic from 1926 to 1930) was elected under the banner "To govern is to build roads".

Roads began to offer a new reality. Road transport started to integrate to the country. The automobile was part of the scenery already and the mainstream of progress.

By then automobiles still looked like what it was later conventionalized to be called a jalopy: fenders were not integrated to body; headlights were not imbedded and there were running boards to enter the car.

The Ford domain would extend and consecrate to almost World War II, however the Chevrolet brand – also American-originated – already showed certain strength, ending, as well as Ford, in assembling imported completely knocked down (CKD) automobiles.

During the war by very little, better yet, not at all, did the national fleet evolve, and due to gasoline shortage it had to be adapted for using a poor gas as fuel, produced on board in a strange and bulky apparatus called gasogene.

From the end of war (1945) to the implementation of the Brazilian auto industry (in the late 1950s), the market was predominantly occupied by American cars, imported used from the United States aging between 2 and 5 years.

Cars from soon after the war still maintained certain jalopy traces. However, in the early 1950s they underwent strong evolution.

In mid-1950s, the American golden years, they went through a sophistication process that included their modernization. Equipments such as automatic transmission, power steering and power brakes became commonplace, as it was so rare to find car equipped with power windows, power-adjusting seats, automatic antenna and many other convenience items.

But sophistication was not present in equipments only, but in size, shape and ostensive decor showing with a lot of chrome work.

Although some cars – like the Volkswagen Sedan and the Jeep – started being assembled in Brazil (also imported CKD), what dominated the market were the used General Motors cars, since, in spite of not featuring the same driveability of their competitors – the Fords – were considered sturdier and more suitable to the precarious driving conditions of the Brazilian land.

The models arrived here usually were of the less sophisticated kind, although, in smaller scale, quite more refined models used to be imported also.

Even before the industries arrived, the Brazilian autoparts industry had started to develop itself. Several parts, especially for General Motors cars, could already be replaced by similar ones produced here when necessary.

The ambiance was favorable for the arrival of the automobile made in Brazil.

The first harvest of the national car consisted of:

- Small: Volkswagen Sedan and Renault Dauphine (made by Willys; it would evolve to the Gordini).

- Medium: DKW-Vemag lineup, a sedan and a station wagon, christened Belcar and Vemaguet, respectively, as of 1962.

- Large: Simca lineup (Chambord; Rallye; Présidence and Jangada); Aero-Willys and FNM 2000 JK (an almost low-scale production Alfa Romeo).

- Prestige: the Présidence version, Simca's most luxurious and the Itamaraty one, competed with the imports in higher *status* e representation segment.

- Sports: Volkswagen Karmann Ghia and Willys Interlagos.

- Mixed used utilities: Volkswagen Kombi and Chevrolet Amazona.

- Off-road utilities: JeepWillys; DKW-Vemag Candando and Toyota Bandeirante.

All these lineups would multiply, resulting in model variants (or sports; or luxury; or popular; or... and certainly they would evolve.

Without exception, any one of them was the owner of a variety of vices and, excepting Volkswagen, had been phased-out – or were to be – in the countries of origin, where they had not achieved success.

When launched: full-synchromesh gearbox, disc brakes, radial-ply tires or even power output adequate to the car's weight were hardly found and the outdated adjective, respectful to what existed the world over, was quite applicable.

However, they evolved!

All gear synchronized, almost all of them soon had, and one speed for the gearbox were also customary improvements. The Gordini, to become Renault's line more common option – although more sophisticated than the Dauphine's – and the Aero-Willys – in 1964 – had four speeds instead of three. Yet the Volkswagen – in 1961 – and the Simca – in 1962 – had the first gear turned synchronized.

In some small and medium cars disc brakes was soon offered as an option.

With the large ones, the Simcas earned a much more powerful engine that evidenced the Brazilian creativity and the capacity to increment and develop products of imported technology, as well as the Aero-Willys had its displacement and power output increased.

The Aero had been completely restyled and the Simca, in 1967, had been so deeply changed that its nameplate was changed – it was called Esplanada now.

Resulting from the crisis experienced by the automotive industry, the government opened a special line of credit for popular cars: very Spartan versions deprived even of the basic and essential for minimum comfort or even safety.

Genuinely national sports cars had been launched. Among them, in 1964, the Brasinca 4200 GT; in 1966, the FNM Onça and the GT Malzoni; in 1967, the Puma GT, together with the Democrata, a car that was to be launched by a Brazilian company – IBAP (Indústria Brasileira de Automóveis Presidente) – that made many people to invest in a project that failed.

Sporty versions also had been introduced by automakers here installed: the Simca Rallye, in 1962; the Renault 1093 and the FNM Timb in 1965. Vemag, by its turn, had entered in the upper segment with the DKW-Vemag Fissore.

ANOTHER OPINION

Generally speaking, the progressive industrialization of Brazil after Wordl War II had been very well conducted, to the point of installing a vigorous automotive industry under guidance of the Auto Industry Executive Group (Geia) and that would be reinforced with the arriving of Japanese brand Honda, with Toyota increasing capacity through a new plant in Indaiatuba (SP). Three French giants, Renault, Peugeot and Citroën also settled in the country, the last two under the PSA Peugeot Citroën group umbrella, currently the eighth largest auto manufacturer in the world behind Honda, Nissan, Daimler-Chrysler, Volkswagen, Ford, Toyota and General Motors, this the world leader (but seriously threatened by Toyota). Renault lies ranked 10th, behind South Korea's Hyundai-Kia. All these newcomers have arrived here in second half of the 1990s. In Brazil, Fiat, number one in 2005, 2006 and certainly in 2007, com 25%-plus market share, is 12th in the world behind Suzuki. In 2006, Brazilian production topped 2,600,000 vehicles with over1,9 million sold domestically. Some makes also disappeared in this process, but this is quite normal. Vemag ended being absorbed by Volkswagen, Willys-Overland by Ford, and Simca by Chrysler, all in 1967. This last one left Brazil when purchased by VW in 1981.

September/2007

TECHNICALLY CORRECT

To the wide variety of automobile models produced in Brazil two exclusively Brazilian characteristics interpose. One should be highlighted: the ethanol car. The other, all the criticism: we do not have diesel cars. The ethanol car was introduced in 1979, the result on an understanding between the Brazilian government and the auto industry in face of the creation of the National Program for Ethanol (Proálcool) in November of 1976. During the following decade production concentrated in alternate-fuel vehicles, which reached over 90% of the domestic market in the late 1980s. Currently the ethanol-only car practically disappeared, its place being taken by gasoline-ethanol flexible-fuel one as of 2003. National total ethanol production has reached 16 billion liters in 2006, 2 billion of wich were being exported and 8 billion used to fuel the fleet of over 2,2 million flex-fuel vehicles produced and circa 2 million ethanol-only burning car. As for not existing diesel cars in Brazil, it is a shame. It is due to a government mandated dated from 1976 on grounds that there was interest in making the diesel fleet larger, seeking to control expenditures in importing diesel fuel. A wrong measure that makes Brazil an "island surrounded by diesel on all sides" – it suffices to cross the any border to see diesel car freely running, many of these made in Brazil. Meanwhile, in the European Union diesel cars already represent more than half of new car registrations. Everybody in the world may own a diesel car, therefore being respected according to what is determined by Art. 27 Item 1 of the Universal Declaration of the Human Rights, of which Brazil is signatory: *Everyone has the right to freely participate in the cultural life of the community, to enjoy the arts and to share in scientific advancement and its benefits.*

September/2007

0
20
40
60
80
100
120

From left to right and from fore to background: blue, green, golden, brown and gray. The Renault Willys lineup with French Renault Dauphine-derived models and Volkswagen of Brazil with the Sedan 1200, derived from the German homonymous, were the options for small automobiles in the first phase of the national auto industry.

Small cars

(1959 to 1967)

Volkswagen Sedan 1200 and Renault Dauphine and Gordini

To give access to the world of the automobile or, sometimes, to that of a brand new car, was the noblest mission small cars fulfilled when purchased new.

When bought used, they certainly were part of the approach path for the new car, or represented then the ingress to the privileged world of Man and his individual, synonymous of freedom, transport mean.

The first national cars to fulfill these noble missions were the Volkswagen Sedan 1200, which at that time was popularly called Volks, and the Renault Dau-

phine, manufactured by Willys-Overland of Brazil. They were launched in 1959, although the VW had been stumbling in Brazil since 1950 on importation régime and assembled some time later.

In 1961, the VW would be produced with a slightly larger rear window, synchronized first gear and turn indicator blinkers replacing the semaphores with semi-spherical ends that lit orange and were housed in the central columns – right and left – between the side windows – front and rear – and locked horizontally when activated; they were nicknamed "bananinhas" (small bananas).

In 1962, the Renault line expanded. The Dauphine underwent a technical-mechanical improvement process, from then on marketed under Gordini nameplate.

The Dauphine was repositioned as base model without the Gordini's advancements and remained in production until 1966.

After the first evolutions, the VW Sedan and the Willys-made Renaults became the landmark of the first phase of the Brazilian small car.

Limitations, both had many, but even so they fulfilled with honor – in a time the first car was not an impossible dream any more, although still very difficult – the noble mission of giving Man wheels.

They also started to exert the function of the second car in a household, i.e., they have spread the use of the automobile by women.

Noble missions for restricted yet mission-accomplisher automobiles.

In spite of disputing the same market segment and adopting a few similar solutions, the proposal, presentation and strategy of each were quite different.

To notice any parenthood between the two, only by paying a lot of attention or through a rigorous "DNA examination". Czech Ferdinand Porsche was the "father" of the Volkswagen, an automobile he designed by order of Nazi dictator Adolf Hitler.

Later, when he was jailed in France on charge of collaborating with the Nazi régime, he was forced to help in the development of the "popular Renault", the Renault 4 CV, the antecessor of the Dauphine.

From left to right: brown, green, blue and gray. Both the Renaults and the Volkswagen had roundish lines. The Renault engine compartment formed a volume of its own, while the Volks' was integrated to cabin.

There were eye-clear differences in product, advertising, development and especially in the "personality" in each of these little cars:

- It begins with the manufacturer. Volkswagen produced the Volks, a car whose design and development only and exclusively belonged to itself, while the Gordini was a Renault produced here under Renault license by Willys-Overland do Brasil (WOB). Its development depended more on France than WOB.
- The Gordini advertising highlighted performance, while the Volks' was practicality. Willys entered races with the Gordini and advertised the results, yet VW advertised that the Volks was the best car to the races – except that it was to just watch it.
- The Volks had two doors, whereas the Gordini had four.
- The VW used air cooling and the Willys used water cooling.
- The VW engine displacement was 41% higher than the Renault's (1,192 cm^3 *versus* 845 cm^3).
- The VW carried the fame of being indestructible; the small Renaults were deemed extremely delicate.

But there were similarities:

- Both had rear engine and drive.
- Both the Volks and the Gordini were discrete performers, quite more suitable for city use than on road: they reasonably accelerated up to 80 km/h and sustained cruising speeds at around 100 km/h on level roads. As for slopes, not very rarely speed was not above 60 km/h.
- Roadholding was not privileged, they were extremely oversteering – the rear hanging out in bends – for, besides being rear-engined cars, both had swing axle rear suspension.
- Luggage room was minimum, short of desirable, although it was larger in the Gordini.
- They were easy to drive.
- Their fuel economy was high.
- Room was just reasonable for four occupants and, as to keep this concept, rear seat passengers ought to have an elastic concept of what reasonable is about.

The cars evolved and included new versions and models, in a very different way:

- For the Volks, in 1961, first gear – it already had a four-speed gearbox – was made synchronized, while the Gordini evolved in 1962 in relation to the Dauphine in earning one speed – instead of three, it now had four, although first continued "hard", i.e., non-synchronized.
- In 1962, the Gordini could count on 40 hp SAE gross (equivalent to 32 hp net), therefore almost 25% more powerful than the Dauphine (32 hp gross, 26,5 hp net), while the Volks engine was improved in 1967 only, when displacement was raised from 1,192 cm^3 to 1,285 cm^3 and horsepower went up from 30 hp to 38 hp net (from 36 hp to 46 hp SAE gross).
- The Gordini evolved and changed in order to conquer the consumer, while the Volks did not change, in that according to advertising it did not change,

it evolved. In order to stress the changes, the nomenclature of the Gordini earned Roman numerals, like II in 1966, III in 1967 and in 1968, IV – the II was importantly improved at rear suspension by having been fitted with radius rods, and alternator; the III, front disc brakes and the IV, just the final, phasing-out version. Yet the Volks had front disc brakes for its most powerful version, the Fuscão (1500), in 1971, and alternator in 1984.

- In 1965 both were added a version with extremely Spartan finishing that lasted until 1966. If they normally were basic and little equipped, these versions deprived owners of the even minimum dispensable. Produced under the popular car theme, the VW was called Pé-de-Boi (Ox-footed, a Brazilian expression that means laborious worker) and the Willys', Teimoso (stubborn).
- In 1964 and 1965 a spicy version of the Gordini, called 1093, was produced; Volks also tried something sporty for its sedan in 1964, when it offered the sun roof as optional.

The market

In terms of market, the Volks was voracious. It occupied its own space, it eat up the competitor's and yet "bit" pieces of other segments, although technically its profile was not that absolutely sovereign.

Competed with the Volks, in the same market segment, the Dauphine and the Gordini. The Dauphine was launched in 1959 and remained in the market until 1966, although as of 1962 it became just a more affordable option of the Gordini that, in practice, was its evolution.

Without "surgical" precision, but, as a matter of fact, the small rear-window Volks competed with the Dauphine and its successor Gordini.

In relation to the Dauphine – with one more speed in the gearbox and more power – the Volks added performance, that the Gordini would beat.

The Volks' own market segment was that of the "popular" cars as its own "Volkswagen" nameplate suggested, which in literal translation means people's car and, in a freer one, popular car.

The car that, very probably, was the first step to Man to purchase "his own wheels" also should grant a winner image to its owner. The conquest should not go unnoticed and, forcefully, should be linked to success.

In spite of the automobile being associated to many things, undoubtedly in this market segment the most expected qualities of a car were practicality and dependability, exactly the attributes that weighed in favor of the Volks.

Even the Volks engine having a displacement close to 50% higher than the Gordini's (1,200 vs. 850 cm^3), it was less powerful (36 hp vs. 40 hp SAE gross).

The Volks was also heavier, therefore its power-to-weight ratio did not favor it and, as a consequece, performance was inferior to that of the Gordini.

The same ratios – hp/liter (specific power output) and power-to-weight – that in a first analysis were unfavorable to the Volks, indicated that it was more sturdy and reliable.

In spite of the Volks having two doors and the Gordini four, the doors of that one were larger than the Gordini's and, taking the competitor as reference, could be considered good.

The missing rear doors in the Volks made rear seat access quite more difficult.

However, they were large enough for good front seat access and worked well, especially when compared to the Gordini's.

The Volkswagen suspension was not efficient in roadholding terms, and the same could be said about the Gordini, which had similar rear axle geometry. Yet the Volks' was extremely robust and quite more adequate to the Brazilian ground than the Gordini's, which was very fragile.

Small windshields and proportionally long hoods marked the look of these little cars. On the road, performance and roadholding left much to desire. Room was scarce and comfort, limited. Even so, both fulfilled well their tasks as popular cars, within the standards of the period. These were some in common points in these automobiles.

The Volks' gearbox was efficient and easy to use, well superior to the Gordini's, which even did not have a synchronized first gear.

The engine, even less powerful, met urban traffic situations well and, once again, beat the competitor in reliability and dependability.

For the speeds both could attain, the brakes were sufficient. For being light automobiles, they did not suffer brake fading when descending long hills.

As they were lighter and smaller than most cars around here, steering in both cars was infinitely lighter and maneuverability was incredibly better. In a direct comparison between the two, the rack and pinion steering of the Renault was well superior to the Volk's worm and sector.

Yet room for driver and front seat passenger was superior to the Volks', while at rear, the absence of the floor central tunnel helped the Gordini in compensating less elbow room.

The trunk (front) of the Volks was smaller, however there was an extra luggage zone right behind the rear seat that balanced luggage capacity with that of the Gordini, besides enabling an extra resource as of 1964: by folding the seat back over the seat cushion, a ample luggage zone for bigger volumes could be obtained – since there were no rear seat passengers.

In almost all aspects the Volks was more practical than the Gordini.

In quality and internal finishing look, they also matched. Those were items that did not compromise and were absolutely in accordance with the purposes of the little cars.

Driving the Volks in town was pleasant. The engine had a good torque and revved up quickly, it was well-mated to the gearbox, but sports driving left do desire when compared to the Gordini, whose engine revved higher and reacted more promptly.

In the late 1950s and early 1960s, the rear engine with rear-wheel drive solution was quite usual in small-size cars. Therefore, in spite of not being the more classic one, it was not surprising that both Renault and VW had chosen this layout. As a consequence, the Volks and the Gordini had some similar handling characteristics (they oversteered, i.e., the rear went wild in bends) and space distribution.

The market found different paths for the Volks and the Renaults, that fell into completely opposed vicious circles. While it was ever easier to resale the Volks, an automobile considered durable, the "fragile" Gordini was bought by people who could not afford anything more valued, whereas its devaluation was severe.

Additionally to the Gordini, its more direct competitor, the Volks also bit some of the DKW-Vemag market, a larger (medium-size) car whose main virtue was also practicality.

For being smaller and easier to drive, the Volks ended taking some market – as a household car – from the DKW-Vemag, an automobile with quite heterodox solutions, even if compared to the Volks.

The performance of both was adequate to urban traffic and their dimensions made life easy when maneuvering and parking. They were light to be driven, did not require great experience, neither extra skills – except for the habitual task of engaging first gear in the Gordini with the car moving.

At the wheel, the Gordini was nimble and offerd more pleasure, while the Volks was more practical and dependable.

ANOTHER OPINION

There has always been a strong rivalry between Volkswagen and Renault and between their owners as well. Specially after the "40 hp of emotion" Gordini was introduced, which left the 1200 Volks way behind in any situation. Even the DKW was quite pressed in front a well pushed Gordini. The secret of the Renault was nothing but one: low weight, just 750 kg. When driving one, it was surprising to find how good for any car is to be light in the scale, which seemingly runs effortlessly. If the low, 845-cm^3 engine displacement is considered, it becomes ever more evident the expertise of Renault designers. The cars of the lineup counted on the undeniable advantage of having four doors (which normally is weight increasing) and even featured inside door latch inhibitors, a way of making safer taking children in the rear seat and neutralizing the two-door competitor's word on alleged more safety for this reason. Besides the Renaults were far more quieter onboard than the VW due to the water-cooled engine. Air-cooled engines do not benefit the thermoacoustic effect of water jackets and, additionally, the Volks's turbine for cooling air always produced the characteristic noise.

The Volks sold more and was more robust, but its performance was inferior to the Gordini's.

TECHNICALLY CORRECT

Air cooling undoubtedly provides "peace of mind" to owner, for the system is virtually foolproof. The only trouble a Fusca owner could face in this area was the dynamo belt rupture, but it was easily replaceable (inclusive, a new belt was part of the equipment supplied with the vehicle). But not everything are flowers with air cooling. Combustion chamber temperatures are far higher, with forces lower compression ratio.

As a result, fuel thermal efficiency suffers, resulting in less power output. It is quite more difficult to direct air than liquid and, more importantly, heat transfer from engine to cooling medium is slower with air than with water. Besides, to drive the air turbine is necessary certain power, in the order of 5 hp, which logically is subtracted from that available to power the car. But these factors were ignored by Volkswagen advertisement, which said "air does not boil". Many remember that after a high-speed run the warning green light for oil pressure went on blinking when the engine was idling, and indication that oil pressure was near zero.

The owner's manual said it was normal, there was no need for worrying. The cause of the low pressure was the high oil temperature, close to 130° C. In other words, the air does not boil but the engine – any engine – may overheat.

PRICE TABLE OF SMALL CARS[1]

	Model	1957	1958	1959	1960	1961	1962	1963	1964	1965	1966	1967	1968
Willys Renault	Dauphine					545	675	1,055	2,298	3,848	4,550		
	Gordini							1,140	2,510	4,198			
	Gordini II										5,242		
	Gordini III											6,066	
	Gordini IV												
	1093								2,663	4586	5,427		
	Teimoso										3,000		
VW Sedan	Sedan					580	725	1,226	2,418	4,230,8	5,192	6,164	
	Sedan w/ Sunroof										5,393		
	Pé-de-Boi										4,148		

In 1961, a Volkswagen Sedan had a suggested retail price 6% higher than a Dauphine's. In 1963, with the coming of the Gordini, the difference climbed to 16%. Even in relation to the Gordini, the Sedan was 7.5% more expensive. In the following years, the Gordini and the Sedan suggested retail price practically matched.

The Renault popular version, the Teimoso, was much cheaper than the Volks Pé-de-Boi, whereas the sporting version, the Renault 1093, cost 10% over the regular one.

PRODUCTION TABLE OF SMALL CARS[2]

Make	Model Year	1957	1958	1959	1960	1961	1962	1963	1964	1965	1966	Until 1967	1967	1968	Até 1968
Renault	Dauphine			528	7,491	5,294	7,197	2,926	430	21			23,887		23,887
	Gordini					2	4,585	7,908	10,185	6,591	7,417	**3,553**	40,241	811	41,052
	1093							367	336	18			721		721
	Teimoso									6,296	2,521	**150**	8,967		8,967
	Total Willys	0	0	528	7,491	5,296	11,782	11,201	10,951	12,926	9,938	**3,703**	73,816	811	74,627
Volkswagen	Sedan 1200			8,445	17,059	31,025	38,430	42,362	51,755	59,966	77,624		326,666		326,666
	Sedan 1300											**91,821**	91,821	123,069	214,890
	Total Volkswagen	0	0	8,445	17,059	31,025	38,430	42,362	51,755	59,966	77,624	**91,821**	418,487	123,069	541556
Small	**Total**	**0**	**0**	**8,973**	**24,550**	**36,321**	**50,212**	**53,563**	**62,706**	**72,892**	**87,562**	**95,524**	**492,303**	**123,880**	**616,183**

The first Renault model launched by Willys, in 1969, was the Dauphine, which would be phased-out in 1965. In 1962 the Gordini would come, more sophisticated, and it would the captain car in sales. The line was added by a sporting model – the 1093 – produced between 1963 and 1965, and by a popular, basic one – the Teimoso (stubborn) –, built from 1965 to 1967. The Gordini lived to 1968. Total sales in 1960 was equivalent to 44% of the VW Sedan's, i.e., 30.5% of the small car segment. In 1966, the last year of the VW Sedan 1200, this one sold nearly eight-fold its competitor from Willys. In 1967, with the introduction of the VW Sedan 1300, small car production rose 9%, while production of the Renaults dropped 37%. In early 1968, the VW Sedan would become the only available automobile in the category.

1. Prices informed in thousands of Brazilian cruzeiros by *Quatro Rodas* magazine, January issue of each year.
2. Data according to documents supplied by Anfavea.

VW Sedan 1200

(1959 to 1966)

When the Brazilian auto industry was still in its first steps, Volkswagen, installed for just 16 months at new São Bernardo do Campo plant, in the Greater São Paulo region, started the production of the Brazilian Volkswagen Sedan 1200, which immediately became very mutch known, as Volks!

Before the Volks, many automobiles were successfull in Brazil and, after it, many others would also be.

However, they would not anticipate or repeat the success experienced by the VW Sedan, a phenomenon that at international level can be only compared to the Ford model T.

I gained market share in all segments, bursting more direct competitors!

In 1967, the Sedan 1200 would be replaced by the Sedan 1300, yet the more modern look, earned in 1961, would not suffer major changes. There were several evolutions, however this basic design has always been preserved.

The technique and the results

The rear engine and driven wheels only stopped being uncommon after the success of the Volks.

The success of the car was such that its solutions started being reproduced. Even in the USA, where the orthodox formula of water-cooled engine up front was unquestionable, General Motors' Chevrolet division tried for its more compact model, the Corvair, the Volks' recipe: air-cooled, horizontally-opposed engine placed aft of the rear axle.

The Volks engine was not powerful, yet it was pleasant and sufficient for city driving. Air-cooling eliminated many components subject to failure, however it did not allow better efficiency in fuel economy and performance. Some mechanical noises were more audible. Water exchanges heat more efficiently and is good sound deadener.

The roundish lines rendered it several nicknames. It was a two-volume that enabled a reasonable space usage. The non-integrated fenders and the running boards denounced that its design was prior to World War II.

A very few followers of the Volks' recipes achieved success, since they were somewhat limited and, perhaps, what made they to work fine in the Volks was the fact that it was a limited car, born to be popular.

The choice of the engine in boxer layout (horizontally-opposed four-cylinder in this case) came from the need of dispersing heat. In air-cooled engines this design allows to externally circulate in a more homogeneous way, besides minimizing heat transmission from one cylinder to another.

Air-cooling, even in a boxer engine, is undoubtedly less efficient than water's in an inline arrangement, since this one is well-dimensioned, what in no way happened at the time.

"Air" engines used to produce more noise, as water helps to isolate the mechanical clashing from engine work, besides producing a lower specific power output, for a lot of energy is wasted under the form of heat due to the lesser cooling capacity. However, as trade-off, they present less cooling system problems, i.e., even being short of the same capacity, the system was more dependable.

The boxer layout usually demands engines with cylinder bore very much larger than piston stroke, that is, oversquare. In practice, the easiness for revving up without transmitting any harshness originated there. As for shaking in idle speed, it was above average.

The engine placed aft of the rear axle was not granted the best solution concerning space distribution and even less in what refers to roadholding. Yet relatively to the conventional layout of front engine/rear-wheel drive, it dispensed the driveshaft that absorbs space and power, which by itself was too precious in a small car, besides the driveshaft being responsible for failure and maintenance. Comparing to front-wheel drive, it also dispensed the necessary universal joints for combining wheel steering and driving, a true source of problems in view of the technology of the time.

The rear engine over the driving wheels also proportioned superior traction in slippery paving.

The Volks's suspension was independent of all four wheels and torsion springs were used, an assembly of leaves up front and bars at the rear. The advantages, relatively to coil springs or an assembly of flexing leaves, consist in a simpler way of attachment system and not requiring towers or anchorage points that take up space or result in added weight to the car. As trade-off, the compromise between driveability and comfort is mode difficult. In a car with excessive mass concentration at rear as the Volks', at least 65%, the mission of combine roadholding and smoothness ended being even more complicated.

In spite of torsion bars being not more resistant than traditional springs, there are also advantages in maintenance: since its attachment was very simple, there were not many rubber, mounts and other complicating items that could cause problems.

The suspension of the Volks was extremely efficient on uneven pavements that, together with superior traction conferred by the rear engine with well-distributed torque, made the Volks a winner. Worse were the conditions, the better the Volks did the job.

The chassis was platform-type, almost exclusive. In spite of not resulting in great adjectives in weight and torsion, it was responsible for low repair costs in accidents.

The distribution of room for luggage, with a front trunk and a space right after the rear seat that could be only accessed through the passenger doors, was interesting enough, in spite of the total, 277-liters added volume was not one of the biggest.

Finishing was always in rustic materials, yet long-lasting and easy to maintain.

In brief, all the Volks' solutions were more efficient for maintenance and practicality in use than in absolute performance or even comfort terms.

In case of a frontal collision, the fuel tank and the rest of the car seemed to be protected by the spare tire up front. Space distribution in the trunk did not allow putting a large volume there. Behind the rear seat there was an empty area that greatly increased volumetric capacity reserved to luggage, since it was distributed in small volumes.

As they were well-executed, the little car ended fulfilling with honor the task of giving wheels to its owner, without leaving him stranded.

Temper

The Volks was the more logical and uncomplicated option of accessing individual transport, for at a lesser value, only the collective one.

Not having to take a bus or a tram, the collectives of the time, was a relief. To go by itself, without depending on schedules or others, conferred a wonderful sensation of comfort, speed and freedom. As its name suggested, it was popular. The Volks could be seen much more than a "best-employee".

Daily, urban driving

Access for driver and front seat passenger did not require any special movement. It was straightforward.

The first start in the morning with a cold engine was easy, as well as its working was uniform already at the first moments of the day.

The gearbox did not present any engaging difficulty, the minimum turning diameter was reasonable and the steering, for the standards then, light.

Short distances were easily covered. To start from a traffic light, and having to slow down soon after, seemed to be the little car's specialty.

Daily tasks, like go shopping in a supermarket, or go to the office, were accomplished with honor.

The Volks was easy to drive, easy to put small packages in, easy to maneuver, easy to repair, easy...

As distances increased and speed rose, the Volks started showing its limitations that, however, excluded the fear of not arriving.

Driving position, with askew feet to the right; the slowness and the excessive engine noise caused certain tiresomeness. Yet, no other car could provide anything much better.

The doors of the Sedan worked well and did not require any kind of care or a more delicate movement. Opening angle was good, making easy access, to sit and exiting of front passengers. The windows were conveniently sized and in driver's door there was a map pocket.

As well as the quarter windows, the swiveling windows, introduced in 1964, helped air circulation. Both made easy stealing the car and could become a source of noise, but it was better than nothing. The opening rear windows were replaced by cabin air outlets in the rear columns in 1974, when air vents in the dashboard would help the quarter windows job.

The lack of any cabin venting was sensed. The only resources in rainy days were the quarter windows and, as the 1964, the swiveling rear windows.

At the rear seat, besides lacking adequate room – vertical, transversal and longitudinal, i.e., in all directions – for medium-sized people, it caused certain clear, claustrophobia sensation.

The 6-volt electrical system was not brilliant: the starter motor worked lazily, headlights were not powerful enough and the windshield wiper, very bad, not only for the electrical side but also for the mechanical one, responsible for wiping.

Visibility was not brilliant either. From the driver's seat, in any direction, no extremity of the car could be spotted.

In spite of these deficiencies, the Volks – the world over – was market leader, a phenomenon. After all, the technology of the period was not capable of conferring a more appropriate car to average needs for the same cost.

For urban use these were unpleasing limitations, although not compromising ones. In all, the car as a whole was satisfying and, within the standards of the time and if compared to larger cars, could be considered an economic car as far as fuel consumption was concerned.

The rear window of the Sedan changed size several times before it was produced in Brazil. Here its format has always been the same, but it grew larger in 1961. Since then, no more changes were applied to it. Through the grille beneath it, air for the engine was conducted.

On the roads

The Volks had undeniable merits for the Brazilian conditions of the 1960s:

- It faced any road, being able to go through ways where they did not exist. Of course, logically, it was no off-road vehicle.
- It covered long distances without mechanical hazards, and Brazil as continental-size country.
- Service, additionally to the one implemented by the manufacturer, fell into "public domain". No matter what happened and wherever it was, the Volks would not feel "orphan".

Nonetheless, the Volks was very limited and, by free choice, it would hardly be the option for those who frequently traveled. However, it was the mostly seen automobile, roads included.

It was the most common fleet car, as well the most economically feasible to be used as work tool.

Long trips for work were not usual at the time, as well as to work in a city 100 kilometers from home, for example, was also uncommon. Yet when on any of these events, the 1200 Sedan was the most used tool.

Also, for sure, who could afford the "luxury" of having a car in the garage, could not deprive the family of a good motoring on the weekend.

The small 1200 Sedan, both for room inside and power output, suffered to cover distances when loaded.

Its design was different and not even the manufacturer dared to advertise it as attractive, but step by step it conquered admirers that began to consider it as charming. Extremely charming.

Some hills that were "won" at speeds close to 60 km/h, with an empty car, turned into "winners" when the car had more weight on board. They made the route look longer, especially to rear seat occupants that on many occasions was "overcrowded" with three passengers. An annoyance, but the Volks was tough and, for such, rarely spared.

The ride with the family was a privilege, even without much comfort.

By the way, the same lack of comfort was usual at the leisure cities that, however, offered attractions for leisure capable of breaking the apathy of the week routine.

No matter the destination, beach or country, the 1200 did well in transport within the country.

Easy for parking and brilliant for short distances were not its only attributes in these occasions. With it, it was possible to adventuring in rides to difficult-access sites, a versatility that could make a difference.

The wheels did not have windows for the cooling of the brakes. At the hubcaps there was one of the few identification of the make in the model.

On the way home, the Volks being dirty from sand or mud, cleaning was quite easy. Besides all finishing being washable, they were also easily removable, seats included. At that time to wash the car at home was quite usual, and turned in leisure when, with nothing else to do, hose bath and beer were added to it.

Regardless of being a work or leisure tool, the Volks did not ensure comfort and quietness, roadholding, performance etc., but it accomplished its mission with versatility and for a low, matchless cost.

Experience with the 1200 Sedan

In 1967 the VW 1200 was replaced, in our market, by the VW 1300, the same but improved car an, especially, more powerful.

In 1968 the 1200 was replaced home by the 1300, therefore after seven years old I began to loose contact with the Volks 1200.

Even without full lucidity, I keep in memory some specific details of my first experiences with it.

Very vaguely I recall my parents saying that our Volks (1961, I suppose) did not have the turn indicating semaphores (called "bananinhas", small bananas in Brazil) that frightened my sister. I clearly remember that, since then, when walking in the streets I searched for "bananinhas"-equipped Volks. However, they soon became rare, for they were replaced either by conventional blinkers, or by a light at the "B" (central) column where it was nestled before.

I remember that the Volks of a lady friend of my mother had an under-dash plastic, tube-like reservoir and a speedometer needle wider than ours'. The tube served to spray water in the windshield.

Over the front fenders, not integrated to rest of the body of the car, turn indicators (blinkers) were installed, in 1961. In this same year, the taillight assembly, with the upper lens in amber color (for the turn indicator) replaced the single color one that served for tail and brake light. Before them, the turn indicators were the "bananinhas") – semaphores at the central columns that deployed horizontally.

My mother's and my aunt's Volks, after serving our homes, went on to serve the company (and for long years).

When I was 12, therefore in 1973, I managed to "pilot" the 1965 Volks that belonged to my aunt in the garage of the apartment building I lived.

In this Volks there was a detail common to "playboy" VWs: the gearshift was shortened – the remaining of it was just a little stub, whose actuation required stretching the arm – with the aim of reduce movement and increase shifting quickness. Besides this detail, experience demonstrates the longevity these small cars had, even when used as work tool.

The straightforward dashboard indicated by instruments instant speed, the kilometers ran and fuel volume only. Apart from that, there were warning lights for oil pressure and battery recharging system, besides those for monitoring turn indicator and headlight high-beam use. The pedals were offset to right; the steering wheel was correctly sized – with the symbol of São Bernardo do Campo city on center – and the gearshift, quite long, rested near to the knee. It would become shorter in the 1980s, but not as short as those sold as accessory at the time.

In adult age, i.e., after obtaining the driver's license, I had the opportunity to drive the VW 1200, then known as Fuscas, in 1988 only, when I started working with antique cars.

One of the first discoveries I made at its wheel is that Tietê and Pinheiro riverside avenues – two of the main São Paulo city expressways – were not absolutely level. The car's speed varied: in some stretches it began to fall, recovering it others, randomly (these were upward and downward invisible to naked eye slopes).

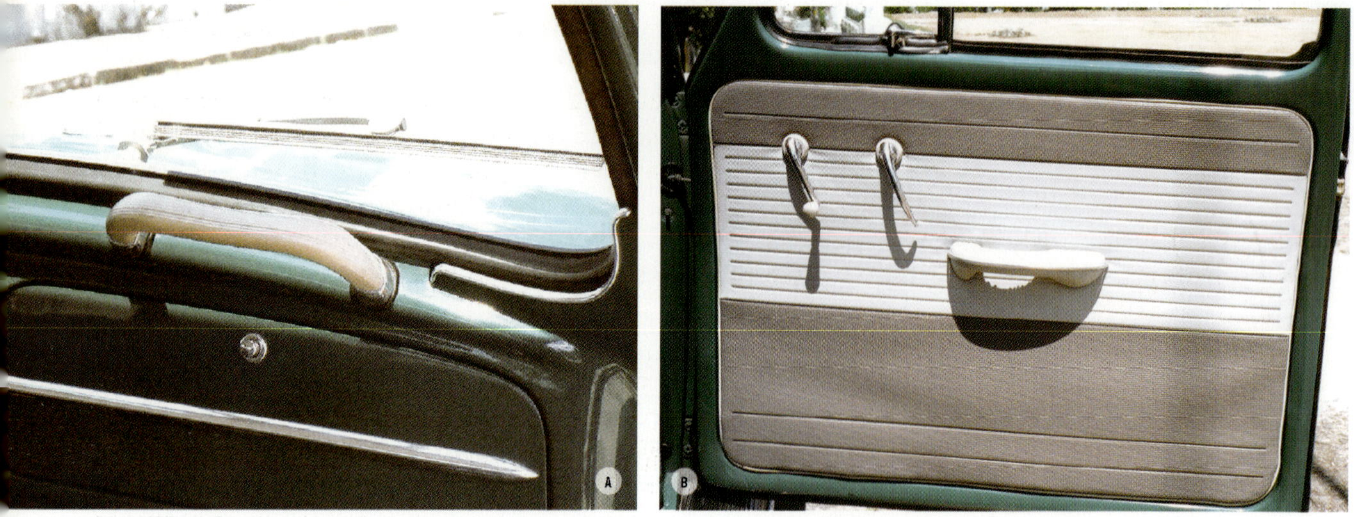

A) Up to then nobody was concerned about safety belts. Therefore, the handle above the glove box was a very important aid. Always grabbed following some fright, they soon became known by a dirty expression, often said on these occasions, whose short for, very well known, is "pqp" (sort of "God damn"). B) The finishing of the Fusca was extremely straightforward. Materials used were rustic and easy-care, yet quality has never been discarded.

Later, in 2000 already, I bought a restored 1200 Sedan in excellent condition. In daily commuting I noticed it still had an adequate performance for slow, stop and go traffic of the large cities. It did not show any lack of power to move from standstill and its acceleration through gears was sufficient.

The standard of smoothness and precision of gear engaging was not obsolete yet and the working uniformity of the engine, although long outdated – since the replacement of the carburetor by electronic fuel injection – was still impressive.

Suspension seemed to be magnificent, after all paving had improved. If at its time the car already went over potholes without demonstrating "pain", now it seemed to ignore them almost completely.

Yet on longer runs, more common with the suburban life a city like São Paulo of the 2000s obliged, the lack of intimacy with higher speeds was more noted.

After driving several days using the Sedan I did not feel any extra wear, neither physical – like backache – nor emotional – originated from tension caused for fearing being stranded.

The Volks demonstrated that the phenomenon was not without reason.

ANOTHER OPINION

It is no exaggeration to say that the VW Sedan, that began to show here in 1950, first imported, soon after assembled by the Brasmotor company and, during some time, simultaneously, by this one and by Volkswagen of Brazil, this founded 1953, was the car that effectively put the Brazilians on wheels. Besides called on abbreviation by its own name – Volks, for "Volkswagen' is difficult to pronounce even today – it did not take long to appear, in Rio de Janeiro, then the capital of the Republic and where the country's most cultural manifestation emanated from, the Fusca nickname (to become Fuca in Southern Brazil). The name Fusca caught on so strongly that the factory officially adopted it in 1983, very late, but it did. The Volks, or Fusca, brought in its bulk a character that was one of the reasons for its success: German technology, war machine and air cooling. The German technology was already part of the Brazilians life even for the simplest things like Solingen steel knifes or shoes in German chrome leather. War machine because, even when information could not by far compare to today's, the qualities of the Volkswagen utilities used in the battlefields of a bloody war ended a little over five years only where already known; and air cooling, for the notorious immunity of these utilities to North Africa's scalding heat. For this reason the Volks, even being an absolutely strange car in its shape, quickly turned from acceptable to highly desirable – even in the early years, with its small 1,100-cm^3, 25-hp engine that in 1954 changed into the 30-hp 1200 that would remain untouched until 1966.

TECHNICALLY CORRECT

The torsion bars used for elastic medium in the Volks' suspension can also be credited for the success of the little car. In those early 1950s the idea about springs was that they were fragile elements, that easily ruptured in the countless potholes that always marked the paving of Brazilian streets and roads – when there was any paving, for dirt roads dominated even in most developed South-Eastern and Southern regions. When the consumer learned that the Volks had torsion bars, it was like they were the dreamed protection against the annoying and costly spring failure. In fact, it is pure myth, for any kind of spring may collapse, but the fact is that in the people's minds torsion bars did not. What was also highlighted in the carefully factory-prepared advertising was the four-wheel independent suspension, seldom seen. If, by one side, this constituted an enormous advantage, especially on rough terrain like ours, the mechanical solutions to reach it were inadmissible from the standpoint of cornering behavior. The superposed trailing links up front, besides limiting wheel steering angle and resulting in too large a minimum turning diameter – 11 meters – for the car size, lead to camber change proportionally to body roll, besides inducing shimmy, the rhythmic tramp after a front wheel hitting a bump. This shortcoming, or characteristic, was attenuated in 1963 only with the adoption of a factory-installed steering damper. At rear, the swing axle solution charged a high price for its bad conception by the known and usual oversteer that caught surprised drivers even in normal driving. A flipped-over Volks was a relatively common scene.

TECHNICAL INFORMATION OF VOLKSWAGEN SEDAN 1200

VEHICLE	VOLKSWAGEN SEDAN 1200	1959 and 1960	1961 to 1966	Pé-de-boi 1965/66
Type	2-door sedan, 5 passengers, rear engine and drive	*	*	*
Chassis and body				
Type	Separated platform-type chassi and body; steel	*	*	*
Engine				
Type	Horizontally-opposed 4-cylinder, block and cylinder heads in light alloy, air cooled. Overhead valves (OHV)	*	*	*
Mixture formation	28 mm single bbl carburator	*	*	*
Bore and stroke (mm)	77 x 64	*	*	*
Displacement (cm^3)	1,192	*	*	*
Compression ratio	6,6:1	*	*	*
Maximum power (SAE)	36 hp at 3,700 rpm or 30 hp (DIN) at 3,400 rpm	*	*	*
Maximum torque (SAE)	7.7 m.kgf at 2,000 rpm	*	*	*
Transmission				
Type	4-speed manual transaxle, non-synchonized first	*	1st synchr	1st synchr
Brakes				
Type	Single hydraulic circuit, no powerbrake	*	*	*
Front	Drum	*	*	*
Rear	Drum	*	*	*
Suspension				
Front	Independent, superposed trailing arms and torsion leafs	*	*	*
Rear	Independent, swing axles and torsion bars	*	*	*
Steering				
Type	Worm and sector	*	*	*
Dimensions and capacities				
Wheelbase	2,400	*	*	*
Lenght (mm)	4,026	*	*	*
Width (mm)	1,540	*	*	*
Height (mm)	1,500	*	*	*
Ground clearance (mm)	152	*	*	*
Fuel tank (liter)	40	*	*	*
Curb weight (kg)	740	*	*	680
Wheels and tyres				
Type	Steel wheels and cross-ply tyres	*	*	*
Tyre size	5.60-15	*	*	*

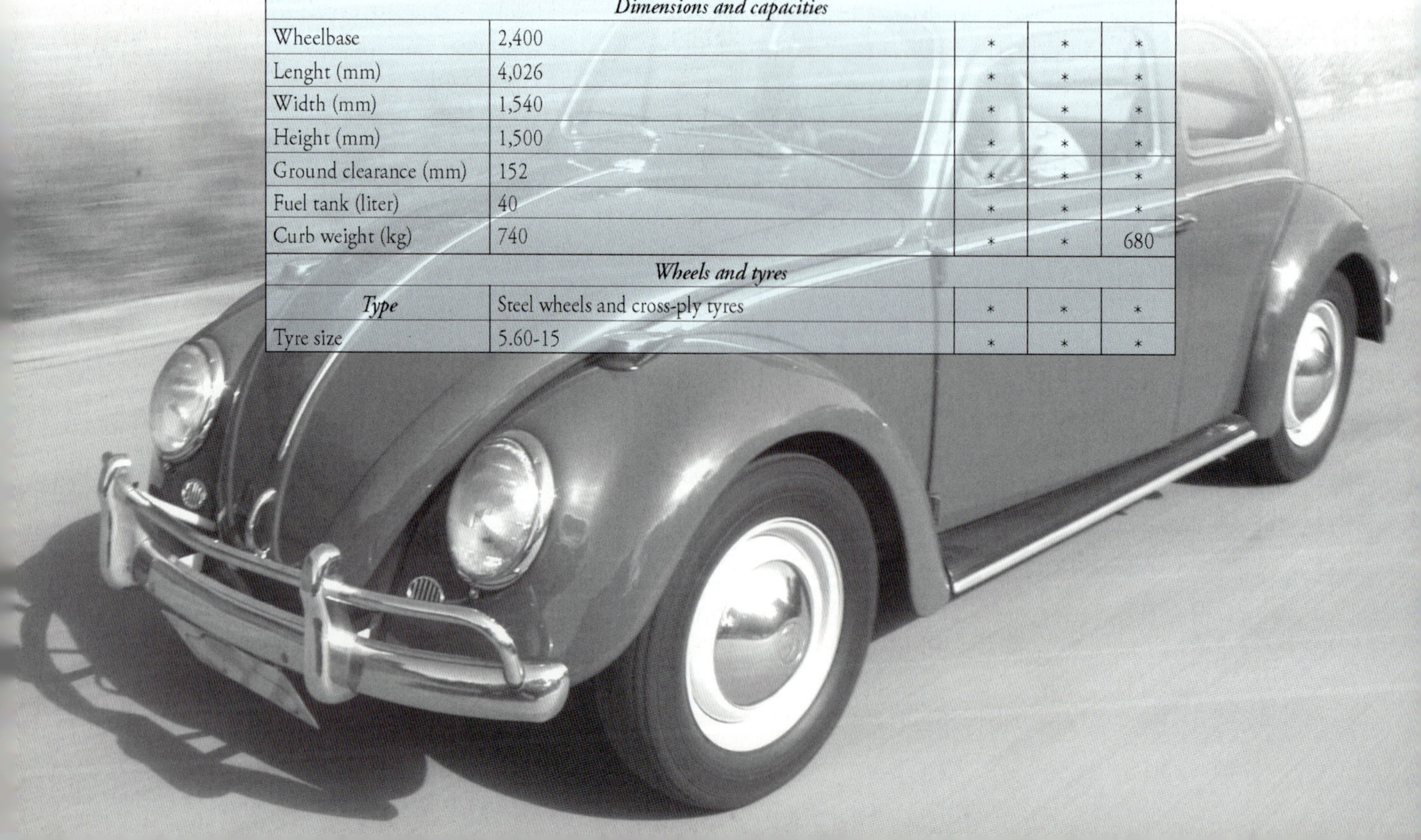

Amor ao primeiro quilômetro

Ela sentou pela primeira vez no Volkswagen, deu partida e enfrentou corajosamente o tráfego. Ràpidamente, foi-se familiarizando com o automóvel: sentiu a obediência da direção. Surpreendeu-se com a maciez do câmbio. Admirou a excelente visibilidade e a ação instantânea e suave dos freios. Fêz a mais fácil baliza de sua vida, numa vaga em que nunca teria sonhado estacionar com qualquer outro carro. Então ela compreendeu por que suas amigas viviam disputando com os maridos o direito de ficar com o Volkswagen. O VW é um carro sólido e valente. É também macio, confortável e fácil de dirigir e manobrar. É a solução do bom senso em automóvel.
Peça uma demonstração ao seu Revendedor Autorizado Volkswagen.

VOLKSWAGEN DO BRASIL S.A. – S. Bernardo do Campo – S.P. o bom senso em automóvel

From left to right: on asphalt gray Dauphine and golden 1093; highlighted: blue Gordini III and brown Teimoso.

Willys Renault

Dauphine, Gordini, Gordini II, Gordini III, Gordini IV, Teimoso and 1093 (1959 to 1968)

To replace the Renault 4 CV (quatre chevaux, four horsepower in French, a fiscal power output for fiscal purposes), popularly known in Brazil as Renault Rabo Quente (Hot Buttock Renault), the most affordable car of the Renault lineup, was born in France, in 1956, the Dauphine. With the same nameplate Willys would start producing it in Brazil as of 1959, to divide the market with the devastating Volkswagen Sedan, as it so happened there.

In 1958, the French model was handled over to Amedée Gordini, a famous automobile tuner who had already been responsible for several successful racing cars. At that occasion, the Dauphine went through many improvements as to be marketed under Renault Dauphine Gordini nameplate, a more sophisticated and evolved Dauphine version.

In Brazil this same model was christened just Gordini, and produced in parallel with the Dauphine as of 1962.

The reputation of weak and the strength of the competitor forced the Gordini to undergo frequent changes and improvements. However, the little Renault did not change that much.

Dauphine (1959 to 1966); Gordini (1962 to 1965); Gordini II (1966); Gordini III (1967); and Gordini IV (1968), as well as the sports variant, the 1093 (1964 and1965) and the popular version Teimoso (1965 and 1966), were the names attributed to the models that made the history of this Renault in Brazil.

The French Renault Dauphine line was produced here, under license, by Willys-Overland of Brazil. There were over there similar models: the simpler was the Dauphine, the regular was the Dauphine Gordini and the sporty, the Dauphine 1093. In Brasil, the equivalent models kept the same nomenclature, however the simpler maintained the name Dauphine. They were known here as Renault-Willys.

Technical solutions and their practical effects

Unitary chassis and body; inline four-cylinder engine displacing 845 cm^3 only and high-revving, with maximum horsepower at 5,200 rpm – which was high enough at the time – water-cooled and rear-mounted; curb weight 750 kg only; very slow steering (24:1 steering ratio), i.e, many steering wheel turns for little actual wheel turning; four-speed gearbox and independent suspension front and rear on coil springs and swing axle at rear, were the main solutions adopted for the small Renault, that is, in its base they all followed the modern, post-war European trend for economy cars: rear-mounted powertrain and unitary construction.

In spite of the simple look and the little ambitious proposal, the cars of the Renault Willys line were bearers of many functional and intelligent solutions integrated in styling manner. The headlights embedded in the front hood was one that drew attention.

What was to influence and characterize the behavior of the Gordini was the low weight, a consequence of its small dimensions, unitary construction and engine and transmission combined at the rear.

The light assembly allowed a small and hi-revving engine, without much torque and it did not require much powerful brakes or even a very sophisticated suspension to run and stop well.

The weight concentration at rear caused such a definte oversteering effect that the air cushion system fitted to the Gordini (and Dauphine) officially called "Aerostable" became popular known as "Aerocapotable" (something like "Aero-turn over") – an allusion to how easily the little car could have wheels pointing to the sky.

The rear was the shortest section of these little cars. The curved glass and the high roof reinforced the sensation.

In the Gordini and the Volks as well, each rear half-axle oscillated in a pendulum-like motion according to effort, in a way that the wheels hardly would stay parallel to the vertical plane. The characteristic was quite detrimental to road-holding, besides causing uneven tire wear above normal.

The Gordini II would feature a new system for rear wheel longitudinal location by radius rods that, if not perfectly solved the swing axle layout deficiency, at least it was capable of reducing oversteer somewhat by keeping more constant rear wheel toe-in. This solution was also responsible for turning the Willys' small car more dependable, since the original French half-shaft pivoting caused several

The good engine torque and the somewhat tall second surprised in some situations. In specific conditions, the Dauphine could be faster than the Gordini.

A small pocket in the dashboard, at left of the driver, clearly showed concern with the use of space. Flat floor, without the central tunnel, was a resource that enabled better seating, but it did not allow transporting objects in the front passenger foot, wich could be convenient and useful.

31 hp gross at 5,000 rpm, produced by the Ventoux engine, original of the Dauphine, were not that impressive, yet elasticity was incredible. Displacing only 845 cm³, maximum torque, 7,7 mkgf, occurred at 2,200 rpm. It had plenty of power at very low engine speeds already, even being capable of reaching high revs (at the time, 5,000 rpm was astonishing!). Hence the three-speed only gearbox.

failures. It was the weakest point of the fragile Dauphine and Gordini and one of main guilt form their delicate fame.

Engine was an inline four of common conception at the time, with in-block camshaft and overhead valves (OHV). The crankshaft turned on three main bearings. Overhead camshaft was an unusual sophistication in cars of its category, as well as five main bearings for the crankshaft that certainly would result in a more balanced and reliable assembly, with less vibration.

The air intakes for the engine harmonized with the body, to the point of becoming an adornment.

The engine was located rearmost and longitudinally, where also laid, ahead of it, the radiator. Fresh air was admitted by the sides and by the underside of the car, reaching the radiator through an ingenious solution.

In normal conditions, even under hard use, there was no overheating, but the air deflectors were subject to deformation by shaking. In this case the water temperature climbed to above normal and the coolant (water) went boiling (steaming).

In spite of not bearing a sophisticated conception, the engine was good in obtaining power,

According to advertising, there were 40 hp of emotion. Net horsepower, the one that really matters, was around 32 hp. It does not seem much, but displacing 845 cm³ and with the resources of the time, it was. It was enough for a performance superior to that of the VW Sedan 1200, which displaced 41% more than its own.

did not cause annoying vibration nor was responsible for the little car's fragile fame.

As far as powertrain (engine-transmission) is concerned, sports driving could be definitely considered amusing.

The engine revved up quickly and gear staging did no present valleys. Gear changing was quick in spite of certain gate imprecision.

For urban use and the admitted speeds, the small size of the car was responsible for nimbleness – the Gordini would fit in any space – and the low weight, for quick stopping.

The difficulties, when driving it fast, were for roadholding and the low capacity the car had to go over certain types of waved paving.

As for inside room, it was quite reasonable for a car so small-sized, which meant efficient space usage.

The spare wheel, located under the trunk, which was up front, was accessed through an opening with a lid behind the bumper. Luggage room was very good for a rear-engine small car.

The spare wheel laid in a dedicated location, under the trunk. This location allowed a good space use for luggage, good access, it seemed to protect in the event of a crash and was well adapted and explored by the car's design.

The floor was absolutely flat, there being not a central tunnel to inadequately advance over the rear passengers' legs space.

However, it lacked for front seat occupants, where the driver was at constant risk of having his right foot – when on the gas pedal – stepped over by his escort's left foot.

The lack of a tunnel also made difficult transporting small objects, those that usually are carried on the front passenger foot. If something was placed there, after some bends it would be nestled at the driver's feet.

Willys increasingly introduced changes in its models. Some generated new denominations. The Gordini III, in practice, was the last stage of evolution of the little car (the IV did not innovate), in that disc brakes were added to the recipe. Driveability positively impressed, although roadholding left to desire.

Two men over 80 kg weight in the front seats would constantly touch shoulders; if over 1.80 meters tall, their feet would interfere each other. Evidently, at the rear seat it was even more complicated.

Even a sleeker and shorter person, to engage reverse the driver had to move the right leg to the left. Yet for engaging third or top gears it was necessary to ask for excuse to the escort. It may sound weird, but an admissible annoyance for a car of its category.

The styling of the Gordini pleased, it was nice. In spite of being a classic three-box, its forms were roundish and, evidently for its reduced dimensions, there were no large parts. They were all minute.

The front hood opened opposed to movement, what prevented it to open with wind. The latch system was very dependable. With time, this direction of opening, which was considered safer, began being questioned: in case of a frontal crash, the hood tended to penetrate in the cabin.

Seen from the side, one noticed two very small doors, narrow and proportionally high respectful to length; front fender little extended and rear minute, everything roundish, additionally to the windows that raised from well above the shoulder line of the car and had little height.

Frontally, one can note the well-designed trunk lid that hosted the headlights. It opened from bumper level and inverted to the car's motion sense and, proportionally, it was long respectful to width. The large size feeling about the trunk lid was enhanced by the small windshield.

The rounded rear window was the biggest glass of the car. Yet the engine hood was somewhat short. The rear seemed even smaller than it really was.

Regardless of where the car was watched from, there were no edges anywhere.

Access to engine compartment was easy and the closing system was very good. At the time it was usual that other cars had bad lock working.

Good-looking and with well-distributed spaces, design was one of the happiest aspects of the car.

Temper

In spite of born with the purpose of being an affordable car that, above all, it should serve – with minimum acceptable conditions of comfort and speed – the top mission of conferring individual transport to mankind, the Gordini did the job with elegance.

It was an automobile to be driven merrily and very appealing when observed.

Fragility interfered in its purpose, but it price the consumer felt obliged to pay in order to have access to a higher satisfaction at the wheel.

The Gordini was nimble and plesant; maybe its better definition was youngish.

Willys had to prove that its Renaults were reliable. With this purpose in mind it took the car to the Interlagos circuit – currently José Carlos Pace International Speedway, in Interlagos district, São Paulo City – where it set various records. Nothing could put its delicate fame down, but on the other hand the youngish image was ever more fed.

Daily use

To be able to count on the Gordini for the urban life routine was more than just count on an individual transport mean.

The first engine start in the morning was easy and after less then one minute working it was ready to go, since some normal care were respected until working temperature was attained.

To enter and to exit was an easy exercise for driver and escort, although a wider bill shoe – or a foot one size larger – obliged certain maneuvering.

The tiny doors did not provide the best access for all. To have rear doors was better than nothing for rear seat passengers, but it ended stealing important space that could be used for larger doors, that would make easier life of front seat occupants. To check if all doors were duly locked was an extra task.

Door latch system was crude and to open or close them it was important to apply a little tenderness.

Front windows glasses were conventional, i.e., crank-operated and vertically descending. The system worked alright and was trouble-free.

Since the windows were narrow, to put the arm out to signalize change of direction, slowing down or even to adjust the outside mirror, required certain gymnastics. Curiously the outside mirror was not regulated, indicating lights (blinkers) either. Therefore, to signalize with the arm stretched out was a must; more than recommended, it was mandatory under the traffic code.

To extend the arm outside the car required certain "contortionism". The front windows were small! At the time, to signal a direction change intent or braking, by law, should be done with the arm.

The rear windows slid horizontally and the locks, with the trembling, turned into a source of noise.

The rear windows were sliding, avoiding more complex mechanisms for opening or closing them. This way there were cost, weight and maintenance gains, but the trade-off was noise, poor sealing and less convenience.

The rear door locks were hard to use by passengers, which was not a problem at all, since the concept of the time said that they should only be operated with the car at a stop, in order to avoid theft or with the purpose of cancelling the action of the internal handles if a child sat in the rear seat.

A break-in – someone opening the door to steal the occupied car – was very unlikely.

It was an annoyance to handle the four door but it was highly compensated by the easiness to access the rear seat, however the preference of the Brazilians for two-door car began to fade when electrical devices for door locks and window lifters spread.

Short distances were nimbly covered. To find a spot to park was easy and to place small volume inside the car was a simple task, since there were rear doors.

Ride was soft, but the wheel travel was insufficient for large potholes. Seats held the body in a reasonable way only and there was lack of room for medium-sized men.

By the way, room was always a problem. For example: medium-size feet became large for the clearance between pedals, a discomfort aggravated by the steering shaft too close to the clutch pedal that turned together with the steering wheel.

The pedals enabled sports maneuvers like the "punta-tacco" (toe-and-heel), a resource widely used for downshifting. The gearshift, displaced to ahead of seats, favored wider seat cushions, very welcome in car lacking elbow room.

Once settled to the lack of room, which was usual in an economic car of its time, the driver would have to live with the annoying first speed engaging, an extremely repetitive action in urban driving, whose frequency tends to increase proportionally to jammed traffic. Therefore, the more stressing the situation outside, the more bothersome first speed would be.

At average urban speeds, where there were no traffic jams, the behavior of the Gordini was nearly perfect.

In the large avenues, where speeds close to 80 km/h could be attained, the Gordini still had some breath, although engine became noisier than desirable.

The Gordini's high-revving engine ended demanding more gear changing and, in spite of the smooth clutch and the uncompromising gear shifting, both could be more precise and smooth. In all, one ended feeling more tired at the end of the journey.

Considering the standards of the time, all these annoyances were within the context of a popular car. There were technological limitations that obliged the manufacturer to opt for this or that discomfort.

The Gordini was no exception to the rule.

These same technological limitations were responsible for headlights, windshield wipers, turn indicator switch and several more items, not always efficient. The same can be said about cabin aeration, which was only possible by opening windows, quarter window included.

Controls next to the steering wheel and easy-reading panel were some Gordini "pluses". Not all cars had pedal set that enabled sports driving or easy-reaching gearshift. The Gordini did.

Straightforward and easy-reading, the Gordini's instrument panel had a good-sized speedometer, odometer and water temperature and fuel gauges. There were the usual oil pressure and battery charging system warning lights.

In 1966, with the Gordini II, the round taillights were replaced by these, rectangular ones, located a little higher. The new disc brakes, besides braking itself, also counted on more powerful and better displayed – higher, above the – not hidden any more by – upper bumper reinforcements.

Steering was light at the cost of some slowness, which did not match much to other controls of the car, although it represented additional comfort.

As expected, the Gordini was nice for daily driving in large cities. In the Gordini II there were improvements both in dependability and dribeability.

Traveling with a Gordini

To go down Serra do Mar (Sea Hill) en route to the São Paulo state coast was the most common program of the motorized São Paulo resident.

Two possible routes were possible to descend from the 800-meter altitude São Paulo capital to sea level: the Anchieta Road (Via Anchieta) or the Sea Way (Caminho do Mar), at the time called "Old Road" (Estrada Velha).

Among the coastal beach cities to visit, Santos, 80 km distant, was the most common, but going a little farther, such as Praia Grande, 100 km, was also usual.

Traffic was intense, no matter the choosen route and the descent was made through a tortuous design and quite steep.

To go by the Old Road was an option to escape from the Anchieta Road's usually jammed traffic, however the Sea Way almost always was crowded. The road – single lane and two-way – mixed asphalt-paving with cobblestone sections.

Since the Sea Hill is the dampest place in São Paulo state, wet, slippery road was the usual condition the driver would have to face to get to the beach. Especially on the Old Road and the cobblestone sections that when wet were really slippery, the Gordini did not do bad. The narrow tires and low weight made it safer than many larger automobiles in this condition.

Brakes were hard-used and even those of the models until the Gordini II, still drums, for disc brakes would come with the following model only, did not fade, thanks to the little car's low weight.

Wheels with ventilation windows for cooling the brakes existed only in more sophisticated models. They were absent in the Dauphine and the Teimoso. They probably increased by much the cost of production.

Model diversification was an attempt to penetrate in a wider market band. The Dauphine was a simple model, with a finishing equivalent to that of the Gordini, but less powerful and with one gear less. The Teimoso had the mechanics similar to the Gordini, but its accessories' level was very low. The 1093 presented a look somewhat more sophisticated and the extra "horses" of its engine provided the *status* of a sporty car.

In the other parts of the road, the Gordini, when carrying a family and luggage it could put in the car, usually struggled to keep up with the faster ones. To cruise at 100 km/h was usual to faster cars, while the Gordini managed to sustain speed close to 80 km/h and that dropped to 60 km/h uphill.

Going back to the hilly section, the windshield wipers did not help much and there was no venting system to help avoiding glass fogging.

During the weekend at the beach, the Gordini displayed qualities. It was easy to park and, since those days, it was hard to find parking spots in leisure cities on weekends; it covered small commuting, from one beach to another, with superiority, besides fitted with washable finishing materials that did not demand special care.

The most common discomfort was the very high temperatures its courvin-upholstered seats and hard plastic steering wheel reached after a long period parked under the action of the – desirable, on weekends – sun rays. To wear a bathing suit and sit directly on the seat was an act to be tolerated by a fakir only.

If in the way down the hill descent imposed difficulties, on the way back to the capital, even if by the Anchieta Road, which could be classified as less bad than the Old Road, the Gordini carried a few passengers more – "ghosts".

The ghost of excessive clutch wear-out, if the car was too loaded, especially on days of very slow traffic.

With traffic flowing somewhat better, the Gordini driver had to practice patience only and deal with the discomfort of going uphill in lower gears and at speeds that hardly exceeded 40 km/h.

Evidently, roads were not the "beach" of the Gordini, although with a little calmness it could cover small distances.

By the way, the leisure concept of the medium class considered a certain discomfort to enjoy something out of routine. Certainly the beach apartment also required that some people slept in the living room, others in the double deck bed and so forth.

So, the Gordini was absolutely fit in this context.

Other versions

Willys developed two versions over the base Renault Gordini.

One with the sports theme – the Renault 1093 – and the other with even more popular proposal than the conventional one – the Renault Teimoso.

Sporting –Renault 1093

In 1964 the Renault was launched, sold in red color only and in 1965 it would be offered in golden color solely.

The color was part of the décor that, additionally to badges, was the only external identification of the sports model Inside, a mechanical revolution counter of the brand Jaeger, a griffe in precision instruments and located in the small

The Renault-Willys might be little dependable, but it was very pleasing at the wheel.

pocket in the dashboard at far left, provided the sporty touch. Rev counter was an instrument fitted in sports cars only. Next to it, in center, a quite pretentious speedometer, with 30 to 30 km/h readings up to 180 km/h and capable of "telling" large and exaggerated lies.

The differences in mechanics were in suspension, whose fixation would equip all the lineup as of the Gordini II in 1965; in the gearbox, with a shorter fourth

The 1093 dashboard was responsible for an important differentiation that helped to give the sporty *status* to the little car. In the dashboard there was Jaeger rev counter, a griffe in metering instruments. The yellow warning zone started at 5,500 rpm and the red line was 6,000 rpm. In the steering column, left side, there is a stalk for parking lights, headlights and high/low beam switch, and horn, all in an unique lever. The turn indicator lay at the opposite side. The 1093 of the photo is equipped with a sports F-1-branded steering wheel, but originally it came out of the factory with the conventional one, identical to the other models'.

speed (gear ratio 1.07:1 instead of 1.03:1) and in the engine that – in spite of many believing the "1093" was related to displacement in cubic centimeters – displaced the same 845 cm^3, but more powerful thanks to a hotter cam, to the 2-bbl carburetor, as well as special intake and exhaust manifolds, additionally to a higher compression ratio, 9.2:1 (Gordini, 8:1) that required the higher octane gasoline of the time, tinted blue.

In absolute numbers, the 1093 power output was 53 hp SAE (42 hp net), i.e., 31% more than the Gordini's – a significant difference.

There were several after-market equipment and accessories to improve look and performance of any Gordini, nevertheless the aura of the 1093 was differentiated, thanks to the model being entered in racing, what made out of this Renault the favorite when it came to be equipped.

A few things identified the 1093. The exclusive body colors, golden or red, and the 1093 emblem were the most evident ones. At rear it was possible to note the twin exhaust tips and the "sports" note it emitted. The aluminum, larger-capacity and finned oil sump, under the engine, was a highly-coveted accessory for this sporty model.

For those who did not settle for less, there were kits (cylinder liners, pistons and piston ring assemblies, for the cylinder liners were removable from block) that could raise displacement up to 998 cm^3 (63 mm cylinder diameter), but the most common was the 904 cm^3 kit (60 mm diameter); larger capacity oil pan in finned aluminum for improved cooling; valve cover also in finned aluminum;

A) Finned aluminum valve cover was a sophistication that did not come from the factory, but it was a quite common accessory to the Renaults, which always maintained an sporting appeal. The 1093, with the two-barrel carburetor, higher compression ratio and bigger duration camshaft, was inviting to step on the gas pedal. In the owner's manual there was an alert to the driver to not go fast while not being used to such a fast car's reaction. B) The rear location of the fuel tank enabled a sizeable trunk up front, although it spoiled weight distribution. Its lining was a carpet made from coconut fiber.

Wheels were identical to the Gordini's. They counted on air windows, a plus.

there was the option of several camshafts for higher revs and power, as well as special intake manifolds and exhaust headers for power increase.

The owners of these cars used to remove the side sections of the bumpers aiming a sportier look to the 1093. It was also usual to use the center adornment of the Willys Interlagos hubcap, in form of a butterfly nut for wheel central attachment, in lieu of the series' chromed bolt to hold the hubcap in place, and the replacement of steering wheel for a smaller diameter one, almost obligatory items.

In spite of some improvement of the 1093 efficiency in relation to the Gordini, performance was not sporty as expected,

The upper reinforcement of the bumper, made after the rest of the car, covered part of the parking light. It was usual dealers making holes in the body for attaching their own emblems. The consumer, in general, was loyal to the brand and the dealer.

by engine roar and the easiness it overcame the Volks and other Gordini was enough to make the driver happy.

There was a sensible difference between them.

But the car temper was sporty. It challenged the driver to try to get most of it in acceleration and speed it could attain, around 140 km/k.

Popular – Teimoso

If there was one thing the Gordini did not excel for was a great variety of comfort or even safety equipment and accessories.

The Gordini was an economy car, whose buyer-public was very interested in accessing an affordable car and much more than that. Therefore, when in 1965 the government established a special line of credit for popular cars – to be created and homologated by the automakers – Willys felt compelled to "depilate" the Gordini that already ran almost plain naked.

With no roof lining; no seat side upholstery; no upholstery over Duratex panels (medium density fiberboard from wood) as door lining; no sun visors or even pas-

Fenders and front hood were lengthy, especially when compared to other sections of the car. The very short windshield reinforced the impression of largeness of the front section. In the Teimoso there was no trim in the windshield sealing rubber or even a wiper on passenger side. The lower central section of the front bumper was also removed.

A) The many contours of the Renault Willys did not combine with ample, total and unrestricted lack of adornments: the brown color, of a weird tone; the single-blade bumper, with two apparent joints and painted "dull silver"; the rod of the engine hood latch cut by half and absence of side taillights did produce an harmonious look of the rear, although the multi-function light over the license plate (parking light, brake light and license light) was interesting. B-C) From the rest of the Renaults it maintained the rear grille, destined to letting air out and the hole to turn the engine with the wheel removing tool, very useful for services at the shop. The mechanics were exactly alike the Gordini's. There were no linings at all!

senger-side windshield wiper; absolutely no chrome work; no limiter for engine hood opening, which did not have a lock either and was smaller than the original, not even turn indicator lights; just one central-mounted light unit both to illuminate the license plate and perform as tail and brake light; without...

Meet the Teimoso ("stubborn"), a car that upon leaving the dealership obligatorily started to be equipped; after all it is unimaginable to use under the sun a car that for not having any inside lining had a cabin temperature similar to sauna. Or every time it came to change lanes the driver had do gymnastics for passing his arm through the minute window, had to be extremely cautious for traffic and so on.

The success of the Teimoso, as well as other popular's, was compromised, more than anything, by the need of *status*.

To purchase a popular and then equipping it could even turn economically unfeasible, however the Brazilian was willing to own an automobile that could

The interior of the Teimoso was as poor as its external look suggested. There was absolutely no lining, neither in the roof, nor in the doors, or even at the sides of the seats, that looked like beach chairs. The instrument panel had speedometer and odometer only. Fuel and water temperature gauges were replaced by warning lights. There were no pockets in the dashboard and the glove box had no lid. The gas pedal was replaced by a tiny wheel.

show some similarity. He wanted to look youngish, sporty or sophisticated, not a mere employee.

Mechanically, the Teimoso was superior to the Dauphine – that was still an option – but the absence of any finishing and the poor image jeopardized it.

It did not last long.

The Gordini and I

The Gordini was phased-out in 1968, therefore I was seven years old.

Every now an then there was a second car at home — my mother´s. And it always had been a Volks.

I slightly remember of my father showing up one day with a Gordini home, a car that was very appealing to me.

In spite of my enthusiasm, my father said what I already had heard about it "It is not worth a cent."

Even among children there were jokes about the little car and playful nicknames for it. The most popular was "Leite Glória", a new brand of powdered milk to be mixed with water, whose advertisement at the time highlighted that it mixed without using a mixer due to its exceptional solubility, the first of a kind. The car would undo by itself...

Different from most automobiles, these Renaults did not have a front grille. Historically, Renault was one of the last automakers to adopt a front radiator, going against a trend firstly used by its main competitor, Peugeot. Maybe this justifies the know-how in designing front hoods without this element.

But there were others, such as orchestra – "Each stop a concert" –, the word 'concert' (with a 's') means "to fix" in Portuguese. And there were others that used dirty words, which obviously were my favorites.

Therefore, I only came to have real contact with the little car in 2000, when I purchased a 1093. Later, in 2001, I bought a Teimoso. Both restored made me

No turn indicator; no chrome work; no bumper reinforcements; no hubcaps and no ventilation windows for cooling the brakes. From any angle, even a small part of the Teimoso could be seen, it was possible to note several "no".

The radiator laid ahead of engine (placed at the rear), in an interesting position that required engineering solutions. The side air intakes was one of them. Gracefully integrated in body it was beyond creativity.

feel the pain and the pleasure of owning a Gordini.

The 1093, much more useable than the Teimoso – with no accessories, just as it left the factory – was the one I used most, as my car for daily commuting.

In special, this 1965 golden 1093 was fitted with a 904-cm³ kit, finned, aluminum oil pan and valve cover, a sports steering wheel, Interlagos hubcap ornament and some self-indulgence.

I had doubts about the car's ability to keep up with traffic and I confess I was surprised that the 1093 not only did it, as it also reveled to be quite nimble.

It is obvious that it was necessary to make full use of everything the engine had to offer, what I did with pleasure. After all, the high revving engine and the sporty tone, together with the quick changing gearbox, are inviting to sports driving.

It is obvious, the 1093 departed at full steam, while the others just moved off.

On the expressways, in fewer traffic hours, the maximum and controlled speed by photo radars was 90 km/h. The Renault easily sustained it, although when traffic flow caused speed to drop to some 60 km/h then climbing to 90 km/h, in this moment it was left behind, taking long to recover to the other cars' speed.

As every driver that always choose the same routes, I took chances in some minor stretches to speed above the limit.

I believe the little car ended attaining something around 130 km/h top speed, after circa 3 km in a straight.

The pavement undulations (technically absurd they exist, no matter if in 2000 or even in the 1960s) caused certain instability, both to the car's on the road and the driver in his seat.

In high-speed bends the rocking rear transmitted a sensation of low safety, even for a driver like me, used to drive cars whose roadholding standards laid in the 1960s.

At the end of each day I felt rewarded for riding in a car that did not turn the act of coming and going in something monotonous, although I could feel somewhat more tired, both in my body and in my mind.

The noise level, the "tricky" engaging of first "hard" gear, the number of gear changing infinitely greater than usual for other cars, the lack of room and things like that have lead to certain stress on driving the little car in the turn of the century.

Forty five years after phasing-out, the 1093 had to do its best to keep up with much more modern automobiles.

In a hill, where I did not demand everything out of its first speed, I noticed a VW Kombi passenger van to grow larger in my mirror. I pushed to the floor. It was in vain, the Kombi, with its 58 hp, left behind my 42-hp 1093.

The Kombi, which did not go through an evolving process that kept it up with its segment (passenger van), in 1965 had the same engine as 2000's, only less evolved and displacing: 1,200 cm³ and 30 hp, *versus* 1,600 cm³ and 58 hp. Its engine, which had been adequate for the 1960s, when traffic accelerated and

A) Although a little pretentious, the speedometer scale in the Dauphine started from 10 and ended at 130 kilometers per hour. B) In the Gordini they were a little more sophisticated – or in the Teimoso, that used the same powertrain – went up to 150. C) As for the 1093, the presumption was flagrant: besides going up to 180, it increased in 30s – a resource already used by super machines of the time, as in the Ferraris – that induced to the thinking that the needle movement going up was so quick that it was the only to follow it. In the Teimoso instrument cluster water temperature and fuel gauges were replaced by warning lights.

stopped less, had to grow, as the 1093 would also have grown if it remained in production.

Certainly the rhythm of life was calmer and the usually covered distances in large cities such as São Paulo, smaller.

Everything we believe that demanded comfort and performance could be more than satisfying with the small sporty, which has not lost by anything its temper and continues to incite its driver to pilot it and to challenge other cars, although with no chance of winning, except if the other car is as aged as.

Yet the Teimoso, which I used it in medium temperature days only, demonstrated driveability and temper close to the 1093's.

Possessing all the same 1093 limitations, such as the room for the driver's feet (probably the sole of the shoes have increased in these years, causing certain confusion between feet and pedals) and enhancing others: the lack of space added to the askew driving position in an inferior seat; lack of acoustic insulation amplifying noise; lack of thermal insulation; lack of turn indicators that obligated to signalize all the time with the arm that barely went through the window; lack of... Tiresomeness at the end of the day was even greater, although the driving pleasure proportioned by a similar mechanics was almost the same.

ANOTHER OPINION

As a design, the small Renaults were exuberant, a product of the known French ingeniousness. The problem was Willys-Overland, which produced them under Renault license, having not applied to them the necessary "tropicalization", such as certain suspension and structure reinforcements. Their design were the perfect synthesis of styling and function, in total accordance with the concept of the car. The absent front grille due to the rear engine and the side air intakes before the real wheel arches are examples.

The solution of the spare wheel horizontally laid under the trunk floor and accessed by a dedicated lid was simply brilliant. Their performance, especially that of the Gordini and even more the 1093's, were the show of their times, besides being very economical, something that would be very valued today. But they had roadholding problems as much as the Volks in view of the swing axle rear suspension – more to a certain point, for the front suspension by superposed triangular arms was far better, from the standpoint of dynamic behavior, than the German rival's. A very interesting detail in these cars was the engine air intake inside the trunk, obviously up front. The advantage was to completely eliminate breathing noise and to proportionate a cleaner engine intake air, relieving work from the air cleaner. But there a bunch of stranded cars when some object, like a shopping bag, unintentionally blocked the intake.

TECHNICALLY CORRECT

Since the engine of the lineup was water-cooled, there ought to be a radiator. It was indeed a bright idea to place it immediately before the engine, skipping from making use of long piping for outbound and inbound water, associated to the bigger difficulty in filling the system for it is necessary to purge air by the highest point (current Porsche 911's technicians know exactly what it is like). Air was conducted to radiator by already cited air intakes and also by a small "air hunter' deflector under the vehicle before the rear axle. The exit of all this air was through a grille at the end panel at the rear of the body which gave a distinct air to the car and, again, form and function combined with each other. The small engine to which the factory gave the name Ventoux, in a homage to the mount in the south of France were there is a famous hillclimb race, gathered the state-of-art of the time such as overhead valves in an aluminum head and removable cylinder liners, but its sin was the fact of having three main bearings only. The 845-cm³ displacement resulted from small, 58-mm diameter cylinders and very long, 80-mm piston stroke. This rendered good torque in the lower rpm range and as consequence, good power output in low rpm as well, what made possible fitting the Dauphine with a three-speed only gearbox. It was one of the more elastic engines of its time, regardless of displacement. Out of this entry model to the Interlagos sports car, going through the 1093 version, the whole family was powered by the 845-cm³ engine.

TECHNICAL INFORMATION OF RENAULT

VEHICLE	Gordini 1961 to 1964	Gordini II (1966)	Gordini III (1967)	Gordini IV (1968)	1093 (1964 to 65)	Dauphine (1959 to 66)
Type	4-door sedan, 5 passengers, rear engine and drive	*	*	*	*	*
	Chassis and body					
Type	Unitary construction, steel	*	*	*	*	*
	Engine					
Type	Inline 4-cylinder, cast iron block and aluminum cylinder head, water cooled. Overhead valves (OHV)	*	*	*	*	*
Mixture formation	32 mm single bbl carburetor	*	*	*	2-bbl 30/34	28mm
Bore and stroke (mm)	58 x 80	*	*	*	*	*
Displacement (cm³)	845	*	*	*	*	*
Compression ratio	8.0:1	*	*	*	9,2:1	7,75:1
Maximum power (SAE)	40 hp at 5,000 rpm	*	*	*	53cv	31cv
Maximum torque (SAE)	6.6 m.kgf at 3,300 rpm	*	*	*	6,8 at 4000	7,7 at 2200
	Transmission					
Type	4-speed manual transaxle, non-synchronized first	*	*	*	*	3-speed and reverse
	Brakes					
Type	Single hydraulic circuit, no powerbrake	*	*	*	*	*
Front	Drum	*	Disc Opt	Disc	Disc	*
Rear	Drum	*	*	*	*	*
	Suspension					
Front	Independent, superposed arms, coil springs	*	*	*	*	*
Rear	Independent, swing axles and coil springs	*	*	*	*	*
	Steering					
Type	Rack and pinion	*	*	*	*	*
	Dimensions and capacities					
Wheelbase	2,270	*	*	*	*	*
Lenght (mm)	3,985	*	*	*	*	*
Width (mm)	1,520	*	*	*	*	*
Height (mm)	1,440	*	*	*	*	*
Ground clearance (mm)	150	*	*	*	*	*
Fuel tank (liter)	32	*	*	*	*	*
Curb weight (kg)	750	*	766	766	766	725
	Wheels and tyres					
Type	Steel wheels and cross-ply tyres	*	*	*	*	*
Tyre size	145-380	*	*	*	*	*

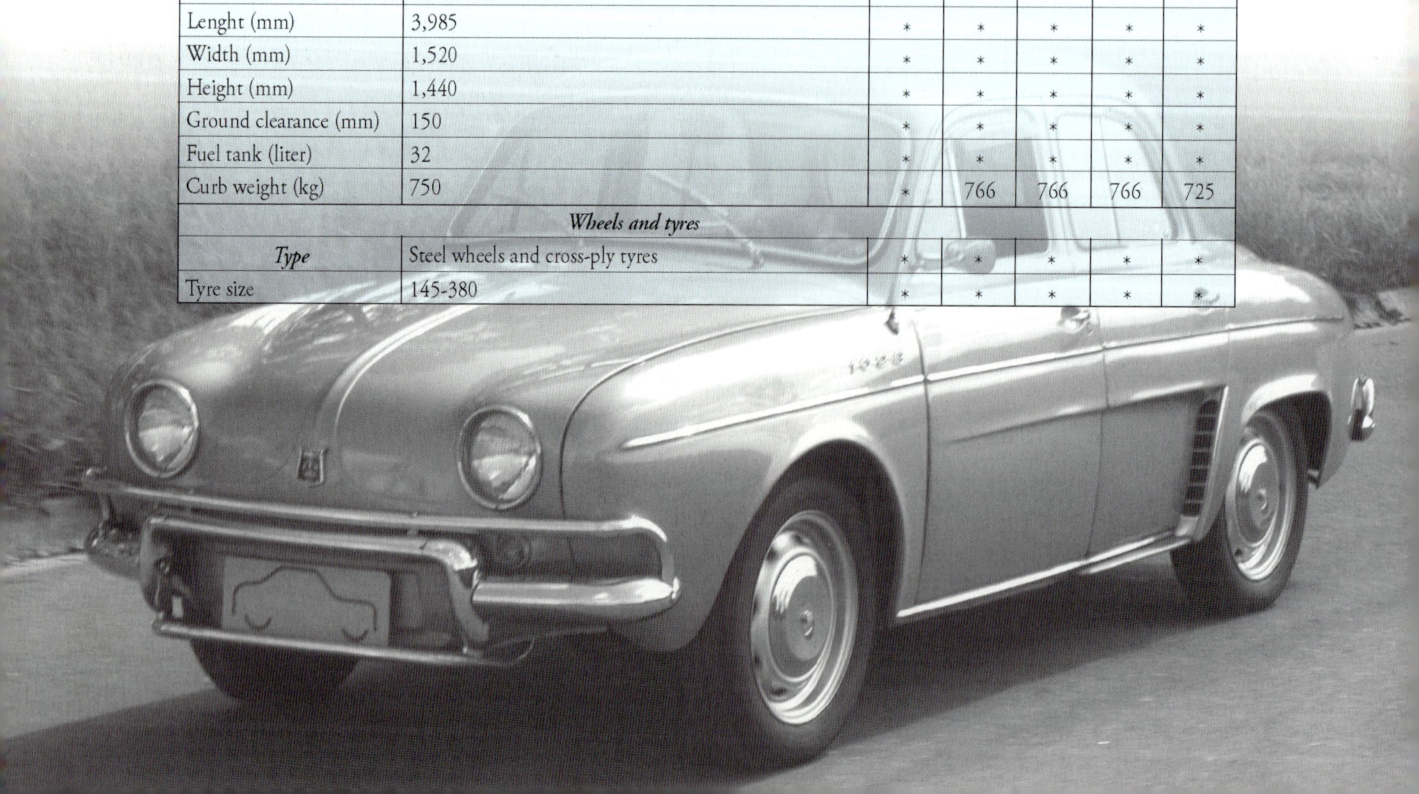

UM CARRO ESTÁVEL COM A POTÊNCIA QUE V. EXIGE
QUANDO V. ENGATA A PRIMEIRA, DE SAÍDA V. SENTE A PODEROSA ARRANCADA DO RENAULT DAUPHINE. COM A SEGUNDA, V. DESLANCHA FÀCILMENTE ATÉ 75 KM. EM TERCEIRA, ASSIM QUE V. TOCA O ACELERADOR, O RENAULT DAUPHINE DESENVOLVE VELOCIDADE, ALCANÇANDO MAIS DE 100 KM POR HORA. E QUANDO V. EXIGE POTÊNCIA NAS SUBIDAS — OU VELOCIDADE NAS ESTRADAS — O RENAULT DAUPHINE CORRESPONDE: SEU MOTOR DISPÕE DE FÔRÇA. E É EXTREMAMENTE ECONÔMICO: FAZ, EM MÉDIA, 16,7 KM COM APENAS 1 LITRO DE GASOLINA. MOTOR SIMPLES E SILENCIOSO: 4 CILINDROS — VÁLVULAS NO CABEÇOTE — 31 H.P. FORTE, ROBUSTO, RESISTENTE. ALTO ÍNDICE DE NACIONALIZAÇÃO E COMPLETA ASSISTÊNCIA TÉCNICA — A MESMA FACILIDADE DE PEÇAS DE TODOS OS VEÍCULOS DA LINHA "JEEP".
— o carro gostoso de dirigir
RENAULT Dauphine
WILLYS
UM PRODUTO DA WILLYS-OVERLAND DO BRASIL S.A. — FABRICANTE DOS VEÍCULOS DA LINHA "JEEP" E DO AERO-WILLYS - SÃO BERNARDO DO CAMPO - ESTADO DE SÃO PAULO
AEROSTABLE

Esta é uma das razões por que colocamos freio a disco no Gordini III.

Esta é outra.

Na hora da chuva, quando sua espôsa vai levar as crianças à escola, você fica preocupado? Se ela estiver de Gordini III, fique tranqüilo. Mesmo que ela dirija há pouco tempo. O Gordini III é facílimo de manobrar. Tem estabilidade. Corre na hora de correr. E quando é preciso parar pára, porque tem freio a disco.*

O freio a disco do Gordini III nunca patina, por mais molhado que esteja. Reduz a distância de freagem. E resiste ao superaquecimento, mesmo com uso frequente. Mesmo com chuva. Mesmo em alta velocidade.

* (opcional)

GORDINI III RENAULT 67

Produto da Willys-Overland
Fabricante de veículos
de alta qualidade.

40
60
100
120
140
160
km/h
VDO
CURTAS

Medium-size automobiles and station wagons

DKW-Vemag range: DKW sedan (1958 and 1959) and Belcar (1960 to 1967); Universal station wagon (1956 to 1959) and Vemaguet (1960 to 1967); and Fissore (1964 to 1967)

The first automobile produced in Brazil was a DKW-Vemag. It was the station wagon version of the little car, called Universal in Germany, and it had entered history as the trail blazer of the pioneers, in November 19, 1956.

Among all the automobiles of the first national harvest, those of the DKW-Vemag lineup held alone the position among the small (Volkswagen Sedan 1200 and Renault Dauphine/Gordini) and the large (Aero-Willys, FNM (Alfa Romeo) 2000 JK and the Simca lineup). Therefore, they were the medium-size cars.

Not so limited in performance and interior roominess as the small, not so limited foi daily commuting in city like the large, they presented three basic variations of proposal – all for the family – over the same mechanical basis: a four-door sedan (that would later be christened Belcar); a two-door station wagon (that, also later would be called Vemaguet) and a third version, as of 1963, more luxurious – the Fissore.

From left to right and from fore to background: 1967 blue Vemaguet; 1963 gray Caiçara; 1965 white Fissore and 1967 dark blue Belcar. The DKW were born with the recipe and finishing of a popular car. In Brazil they filled alone the medium-size segment, without failing to offer some combinations that satisfied several tastes. The Caiçara, made from 1963 to 1965, did not show any luxury. The one in the photos has no hubcaps, that instead of chromed was painted in dull black. It was a series item.

For its greater sophistication, the Fissore was looking for a superior *status*: it was an automobile to be classified as medium-large.

Very probably, who could afford to own two cars in the household, would prefer a large and a small one, however who could afford an unique car to serve the family and had a somewhat more elastic budget – enough to run away from the barriers that forced to choose a small car – would choose a medium-size car. Since all médium-size options belonged to the DKW-Vemag lineup, the choice limited was to a four-door sedan and to the versatility of a household station wagon.

Yet the segment filled by the Fissore, that of the medium-large automobiles, could only be considered the niche formed by whom could afford to, but did not need a large car, however wanted to own one with a higher degree of representation.

The market

In a certain way, the DKW-Vemag lineup did not have direct competitors, but it clearly had, in an indirect way, to conquer the consumers of the economical VW Sedan 1200 and Renault Gordini as to expend some more and be able to enjoy superior comfort and power output. It also had to demonstrate to be a more intelligent and economical option than the large one of the Simca and Aero-Willys lines.

Once the market of the time was depurated, within some limits it was possible to detect that the main competitors of the DKW-Vemag were the Volks, as a more economical option, and the Aero-Willys, as more sophisticated. As for the DKW-Vemag they were much more practical, functional and dependable sort of car than pompous or sports, as the Simcas and the Gordini, respectively.

Therefore, in spite of being in a comfortable position, as the sole option, they had to compete with almost all the other national cars, facing with much proximity the Volks' voracity.

Relatively to the Volks, they lost in:

- Initial purchase price;
- Maintenance cost;
- Easy driving in town, especially because they were bigger and more difficult in maneuvering;
- Fuel consumption – they were less economical;
- Controls – brakes and steering were heavier, as well as the clutch was less progressive and engine torque distribution, less uniform.

Many of its atypical solutions – some of them would spread and others would absolutely be abandoned – made them somewhat more difficult to drive and slightly complicated maintenance – what definitely did not happen with the Volks.

However, when compared to the Volks, the DKW-Vemag were superior in:

- Comfort – extremely roomier, either for passengers or luggage, an advantaged enhanced at the Vemaguet;

- Performance – besides far better in this aspect, the DKW-Vemag had an excellent roadholding, opposite to the Volks;

Yet when compared to the Aero-Willys, the evident disavantages were:

- Sumptuosness – they were much less pompous;
- Comfort – less roomy and far more noisy, the DKW-Vemag, in spite of seating six and having a station wagon version with a good luggage capacity, could not compare to the roomy Aero;
- On road performance – the Willys had no roadholding and brakes to face the DKW-Vemag in a sweeping road section when driving fast; however, with a two and half times higher engine displacement, in average roads and driven in family mode, it could sustain higher cruising speeds.

The Fissore's chassis and the mechanical platform were the same as the rest of the DKW-Vemag line, yet it had a much more updated body. All 1967 models would have the grille and headlights inspired on theirs. The good-sized windshield should inhibit the use of the cap, an inelegant outfit for a driver.

The loss in items concerning comfort and performance was evident when comparing to a car of the Aero's size, as well as its gains in what refers to cost and practicability were flagrant:

- Fuel economy was sensible;
- Maintenance well less costly;
- Lighter controls and practicability in urban driving, non-discussable;
- The DKW's roadholding, as wells as the engine vocation for higher rpm, made sports driving possible and pleasuring; in the Aero, it was almost impracticable.

Until here, all is obvious: the DKW-Vemag were less economical and practical than the Volks, as well as less comfortable and fast than the Aero. Nevertheless, had better fuel economy and were more practical than the Aero, as well as more comfortable and fast than the Volks.

Therefore, what could make them more or less attractive was its capacity to balance its virtues and limitations.

In the road they were tough, capable of sustaining speeds close to the larger cars' of the time. Depending on the situation, they could be faster and more dependable than some larger automobiles. In a challenge with other cars of the make, the Fissore would be under serious risk of "eating smoke".

After some observing, it also becomes obvious that:

- The ratio between external dimensions and inside room was extremely favorable to the DKW-Vemag. Maneuverability was more to a small car's and its roominess, to a large's;
- Controls' weight were closer to the Volk's than to the Aero's ;
- Purchase and maintenance costs, as well as fuel economy were practically in the same level as a small car's;
- In spite of performance was a small car's, roadholding enabled good average speeds in trips, not too short of the Aero's .

In brief, the ratio was favorable to the DKW-Vemag, although not always they could please as a small car or fully replace a large one.

ANOTHER OPINION

Vemag tried to leap farther than its legs allowed when it planned the Fissore model and failed. The car demanded heavy investment in stamping tools that could never be amortized. The big problem with the Fissore was too much weight for the engine. It could never work. To make matters worse, the first Lubrimat systems (automatic oil metering system) had insufficient oil flow and a succession of total engine failures followed. Also, the fact that the model was launched in a time of deep economic recession and when the company was already severely, financially troubled. Besides the fact that the model was a two-door sedan, not very adequate for the segment it aimed to.

TECHNICALLY CORRECT

A characteristic of the DKW-Vemag was the separated, chassis and body construction, which was found in the Volkswagen Sedan and Karmann Ghia only. After the DKW, all the automobiles that followed but the Ford Galaxie would feature unitary construction, also known as monocoque, and that is present until today. Only medium-size and large pick-ups follow the tradition of separated chassis and body.

In a time the technique of automobile construction was well short of current standards, a car having a chassis was in advantage in terms of robustness, especially in the hard conditions of our ground. It was not by chance that the DKW-Vemag and the VW Beetle were claimed the more robust car in the market.

The VW used a different chassis concept, basically a platform reinforced by a central tunnel, where up front the front axle assembly was bolted to and at rear, on a bifurcation, the transaxle-engine assembly. Yet the DKW adopted the box-profiled beam chassis with an X-shaped central reinforcement.

Contrary to the VW, whose floor was the chassis itself, the DKW body had its own "floor". There was not even a tunnel on it, a factor that proportioned ample internal room fore and aft.

Another constructive detail on the DKW-Vemag, and exactly at the chassis, was that it reached the rear axle only.

From that point on there was no support whatsoever, in a way that the rear section of the body was self-supporting. Maybe the Auto Union engineers did not think about it, but the fact is that this solution conferred a highly crushable zone in the event of a rear collision, thus absorbing the impact energy. Currently, the whole auto industry incessantly searches this protection to occupants.

PRICE TABLE OF MEDIUM-SIZE AUTOMOBILES AND STATION WAGONS[1]

	Model	1957	1958	1959	1960	1961	1962	1963	1964	1965	1966	1967	1968
DKW - Vemag	Sedan Four-door					733	989.7						
	Belcar							1,883	3,662	5,980.3	7,628	9,414	
	Station Wagon					698							
	Vemaguet					698	949.7	1,763	3,436	5,632.7	7,628	9,414	
	Caiçara							1,548	2,994				
	Pracinha										4,000		
	Fissore									8,333.7	9,675	11,940	

In 1961, a DKW Sedan four-door was priced 34% over a Dauphine, the most affordable national car of all, and 26% more than a VW Sedan, the most popular of all. In relation to the large cars, the Aero-Willys and the Simca Chambord, its price was 20% and 36% lower, respectively. In 1966 and 1967, its last years of production, the price of a brand-new model was already almost 50% higher than a Gordini's or a VW Sedan's, the least costly cars of the time. As for the Aero-Willys, it remained between 15% and 20% of it.

PRODUCTION TABLE OF MEDIUM-SIZE AUTOMOBILES AND STATION WAGONS[2]

Make	Model / Year	1957	1958	1959	1960	1961	1962	1963	1964	1965	1966	1967	Total
DKW - Vemag	Belcar		2,189	1,773	3,097	4,642	7,123	7,541	6,291	5,519	6,980	6,007	**51,162**
	Fissore								624	857	631	377	**2,489**
	Vemaguet	1,166	1,642	2,524	4,446	4,695	7,806	6,267	4,975	3,847	5,392	5,009	**47,769**
	Caiçara							260	814	99			**1,173**
	Pracinha									4,938	1,812		**6,750**
	Peruas Total	1,166	1,642	2,524	4,446	4,695	7,806	6,527	5,789	8,884	7,204	5,009	**55,692**
Medium	**Total**	**1,166**	**3,831**	**4,297**	**7,543**	**9,337**	**14,929**	**14,068**	**12,704**	**15,260**	**14,815**	**11,393**	**109,343**

The first ever automobile produced in Brazil, and officially accepted as such, was a DKW-Vemag, station wagon version, in 1956. It was the embryo of the whole industry and of the DKW-Vemag lineup that filled the medium-car segment between 1957 and 1967, when it was discontinued for good. The volume produced, year by year, showed certain stability, but Vemag was bought by Volkswagen in mid-1966. The little orthodox solutions of the car, that included a two-stroke engine, limited its development and Volkswagen, instead of keeping it in production, decided for ending it in favor of vehicles of the brand that would adopt its traditional solutions.

1. Prices informed in thousands of Brazilian cruzeiros by *Quatro Rodas* magazine, January issue of each year.
2. Data according to documents supplied by Anfavea.

DKW-Vemag line

(1956 to 1967) Sedan, Belcar since 1960; Perua Universal, Vemaguet as of 1960 and Fissore.

Contemporary of the first movements of the Brazilian auto industry, the automobiles of the DKW-Vemag lineup were launched and filled the enormous marketing gap that existed between the small and large cars in late 1950s and early 1960s.

Evidently, the model range offered by the national industry – as a whole – was very small, as also small was the market, which could be considered as satisfied. There were automobile options enough to its basic needs.

Applied technique and practical result

As in the 1980s the recipes for designing automobiles became homogenizing, exactly the opposed to what happened fifty years before.

The search for a popular car – low costing and good in service – during the 1930s departed from several different recipes. Just like Porsche's Volkswagen, the DKW also went through its own way.

Besides offering sedan and station wagon bodies, and more than one finishing option, during the years they were produced the DKWs evolved in mechanics, accessories and styling.

Taking into account that the engine is to an automobile as the heart is to man – both in physical and poetical meanings – it would suffice for the DKW the use of a two-stroke engine to let it be seen as "different".

The two-stroke engine, besides its own solutions and singular characteristics, especially regarding torque and power output distribution, ended making necessary a series of parallel solutions in the little car's powertrain.

But additionally to the "different" engine and the necessary apparatus for its civilized use, the DKW adopted almost singular characteristics for chassis construction, suspension and mechanical elements layout.

Engine

When in use, the major differences between two and four-stroke engines are:

1. In the first, characteristically, torque and power output appear in higher engine revolutions. In low rpm they usually are apathetic, absolutely with no power, while in high ones they are brilliant, hence being widely used for motorcycles and outboard engines.
2. In the four-stroke engines lubrication is made by an independent system, in a dedicated circuit. Oil consumption only happens basically by leak or bad working. Resulting from plays and wearing out. Yet in the two-strokers oil id mixed to fuel and will "burn" together with it. There is no oil change, oil is added when refueling. At the time, "conventional" engines needed to change oil at 2,500 km intervals on the average, while the DKW used one liter of oil for each 40 liters of fuel, i.e., one liter each time the nearly empty tank was replenished.

Many of the DKW solutions were singular. The one that drew more attention was the two-stroke engine with three breaker points and three ignition coils, additionally to the cooling system by thermo-siphon that dispensed a water pump and had the radiator installed aft of the engine and high. Torque came in at a narrow engine speed band, what imposed a different driving. No, there were no tricks, as some taxi-line chats suggested, but there were particularities. In the photo, at right, the Lubrimat's oil reservoir.

The Fissore, since it began being produced, and the rest of the line as of 1965, counted on the Lubrimat, that automatically metered oil to gasoline. It was not necessary to open the hood to note the difference the equipment did. Excess smoke at the exhaust pipe denounced its inexistence.

3. In the two-stroke engine the oil burning generated a bluish and smelly smoke emitted by the exhaust, similar to that indicating the "life end" of a four-stroke engine.
4. The dimensioning of the exhaust system is crucial in the two-stroke engine, quite more than in the four's, and the exhaust tone usually is – an the DKW it was in fact – high. In decelerating or in engine braking condition it was like several and successive blows similar to popcorn popping in a pan were occurring.
5. Engine braking effect, by the way, is insignificant in a two-stroke engine, that is, engine braking action on the wheel is almost none. When lifting off there is almost no speed reduction, resulting in more brake demand than in those with conventional engines.
6. Two-stroke engines usually have a small number of cylinders, for its construction is quite more complicated and expensive when the number of cylinders increases, hence the DKW having three cylinders only.
7. The possibility of achieving more power output per swept volume, the so called specific power output, is greater with two stroke engines, as well as its simplicity of its working incurs in low production (they are cheaper) and maintenance costs, for having a lesser number of moving parts.

For all these differences, the manufacturer Vemag developed a series of accessories for making more trivial the coliving with the two-stroke engine.

Equipments and accessories to improve two-stroke engine use:

1. Free-wheeling, which could be set on and off through a lever under the dashboard, actuated in wheel-engine relation. It enabled the driving wheels, the front one in the case of the DKW, to connect to engine if it was in fact pulling the car, resulting in more speed or acceleration than those created by inertia or gravity, on down hills. The manifesting of engine braking effect was eliminated, as it happens with the wheel-pedal relation in bicycles. Its main purposes were improving fuel economy and, in extreme cases, to avoid that an unexpected engine seizing the therefore the front wheel's, put occupant safety in risk.

A) Materials and lack of precision in assembling the cars, common denominator in all cars of those years, demanded a break-in period, when some additional care should be observed. B) To avoid mistakes when refueling, Lubrimat-equipped cars had a warning sticker at the rear window, next to the refueling filler.

2. Lubrimat – in order to reduce the amount of oil used by the engine and exhaust smoke, a device called Lubrimat was incorporated in 1965, consisting of a small piston pump belt-driven from an additional pulley to fan shaft's. The system included a dedicated reservoir for the lubricating oil, which no longer had to be added to gasoline when refueling. Besides putting an end to this inconvenience, the Lubrimat avoided mistakes in the proportion of oil and gasoline. The more oil was added, besides excess smoke there was the risk of spark plug fouling and acceleration of the carbonizing process and, less of it, engine's faster wearing or even seizing.

But it as not in the propulsion section only the DKWs adopted differentiated solutions.

Chassis, suspension and layout

1. The structure of the DKW was not unitary construction. Less sophisticated, it used an independent structure that aggregated mechanics and supported the body. To increase resistance of the chassis rails (longitudinal beams) that formed the chassis, there was an X-shaped reinforcement, hence the expression "Chassis with an Ex', used by the automaker for advertising. In fact, the structure was robust and low-costing, although it contributed to making the car heavier.
2. Front suspension was independent and, like the rear one consisting of a rigid axle, had a transversely mounted semi-elliptical leaf spring assembly, as at the rear. Besides performing well, it was the cheapest and more robust solution to be adopted. Up front, the spring assembly also played the role of upper control arm (wishbone), again an efficient simplification.
3. Engine and transmission were longitudinally installed at front. The transverse solution had been tested by DKW (in Europe) on the two-cylinder models, however the shifter was costly and worked badly. The front pow-

ertrain would become absolute in the next decades, proving to be the best solution in space use and cost for small and medium-size automobiles. At the DKW time, the system of universal joints next to the driving wheels, responsible for the combination of steering, drive, body roll and suspension travel, was highly subject to failure, demanding constant maintenance and repairs.

To front-wheel drive were attributed the two main virtues of the car – roadholding and roominess. Technically analyzed, the roadholding of a front-wheel drive vehicle is not that superior. However, the good cornering behavior of the

A) When wrongly closed, as in the photo, the engine hood seemed misaligned. The oval frontal grille and just a pair of circular headlights were the elements that marked the look of the DKWs until 1966. B-C) In the Caiçara, the bumpers consisted of a single blade and dull paint, not chromed. The lines of the station wagon were simple and unpretentious.

automobile with this layout is easier to be administrated by the ordinary driver, but perhaps the high appraise of the DKW's roadholding was more a result of comparison to the Volks and the Gordini – "one worse than the other" – than its own merits'.

As for roominess, its excellence was undeniable and, rightly so, the superiority came from the powertrain layout.

There were several other solutions aiming simplicity and lesser construction and repairing costs.

According to the philosophy that less components used for a job, lesser would be the chances of failure, the DKW dispensed the water pump. Liquid circulation was assured by thermo-siphon, much more simple and primary: since cold water is heavier, it naturally flows down, while hot water flows up.

The radiator laid behind the engine, differently to what conventionally occurs, i.e., close to front grille, as to make easy the flow of the liquid due to radiator height in relation to engine.

The fan, that normally pulls air to the radiator, pushed it and was driven by a shaft that was positioned over the engine and that was driven by the generator belt. As a joke, the system was nicknamed SOHF (short for single overhead fan shaft), in a parody for SOHC (single overhead camshaft), the solution used in most of the modern foreign engines in a period the most common here was the cam-in-block design.

DKW and the name of the manufacturer, Vemag, formed the designation used in all models here produced. The emblem, with a styled "V", inspired in the Cadillac logo, and the pride of being Brazilian, embellished the banner of the brand.

The fuel pump, instead of the usual mechanical actuation, was pneumatic, actuated by pressure and vacuum created in the third cylinder (the foremost) carter, resulting from the piston's alternate motion.

These systems worked well, but when they were higlly demanded, they had limitations that became evident, as with the GT Malzoni sports car, that had all the DKW underpinnings. In this car, the cooling circuit included a water pump, since the radiator was lower in height due to the lower hood line, as well in the racing versions they were forced to adopt an electric fuel pump as to provide higher fuel flow for the tuned-up engine, always stressed to its maximum.

Another very uncommon solution linked to engine was the ignition system. Instead of one set of breaker points, coil, condenser and a distributor that, respectively, would break the primary current and take the charge of distributing the secondary (high tension) current to the spark plugs, the DKW had one breaker and one coil for each of the three cylinders. This solution made adjustment difficult and more time-consuming, demanding certain intimacy and expertise for a good ignition adjustment that, however, after well done, would sustain for a long time if breaker points lubrication precautions were taken, which demanded a special grease (Bosch FT1V4).

There were unjustifiable eccentricities that did not bother, but required driver adaptation to them:

- The shift pattern was inverted in relation to the conventional "H", i.e., odd speeds (first and third) were at bottom, while the even ones, on top. Not better neither worse than conventional, but if the driver regularly drove another car, some concentration was needed to avoid mistakes. When shifting from third to second gear, for instance, it corresponded to downshifting from fourth to first in most cars, as well as all movements that in other cars would

The easy-reading speedometer; the odometer; the fuel gauge, which had to be precise, for from its readout the driver knew how much oil should be added to gasoline, and water temperature gauge, also dependable, where the instruments in a cluster. The "3=6" emblem was an allusion to the superior efficiency of the DKW engine.
It suggested that the three two-stroke cylinders were equivalent to a four-stroke six.

be for downshifting, in the DKW it would mean shifting up, from third to fourth and vice-versa.

• The turn indicator stalk was right-hand operated.

• Until 1963, front door opening was inverted, backwards. For being more prone to open in case of an accident and also because in this situation it did not represent a restraint to body ejection, they were nicknamed "suicide doors".

Besides, they could entail certain constrain to ladies wearing a skirt or dress that, upon entering the car, would not have the protection normal opening door provide (hence another nickname for the little car, "Deixavê", Portuguese for "let me see". It is worth explaining that "vê" in this case origins from German alphabet W letter and so pronounced in German. In Brazil, instead of calling the car as DKW, people used to say DKV in plain Portuguese pronunciation).

• A very interesting equipment, optional as of 1964, automatically actuated the clutch, suppressing the clutch pedal, the Saxomat.

In 1964, the doors opened the conventional way. The former ones rendered the "Deixa vê" (let me see) and "Suicidas" (suicide) nicknames for, respectively, they did not provided protection for a woman wearing a skirt when she was entering or leaving the car and, in case of a frontal crash, were more subject to opening suddenly open, without preventing the body to be thrown out, in a time no one wore seatbelts.

• The two-stroke engine was more "tricky". The "absence" of torque in low revs required frequent gear changing, after all the car practically did not respond to gas pedal but in higher rpm ranges.

- The lack of power at low revs forced the two first speeds to be very short. Since the gearbox had four speeds only, there was a "valley" between second and third, in order to provide better performance, after leaving inertia behind, in higher speeds. This aspect of the two-stroke engines is quite similar to the turbocharged ones, which also require the two first speeds to be quite short.
- It is not hard to imagine that in indoor garages the smoke really bothered. It would be impossible to live with that in apartment building when more than one DKW was cold-started. This was an unlikely situation at the time, however the habit of warming the engine up, to let it work for one or two minutes before moving. This was an equally usual procedure with other cars, which also emitted toxic, exhaust gases in large amounts, however well more "co-living with" for brief moments in a garage than amid a dense oil smoke. There was also a regular habit among DKW-Vemag users: to spin the engine before shutdown with the foot "floored" in the gas pedal until it came to a full stop. This was a polemic, smoke-producing technique from unburned fuel and oil, as to keep the engine lubed. The worst of all is that the procedure was factory-recommended for a certain time, but cancelled later.

In spite of all peculiarities, the DKW-Vemag, considering the period, was apt to achieve the difficult task of offering large-car roominess with economy and versatility of a small one.

Even after restyled in 1967, when it had the headlights integrated to a new, chromed grille, the Belcar continued an unpretentious touring car.

A) Space usage was very good. For seating up to four people, it did demand sacrifices, but since the households were bigger, and made more program in common – besides less people had cars – it could seat six. The trunk surprised for the good volume available. B) The two-stroke engine, with little braking effect, required better brake cooling, inasmuch the wheel of the DKWs always had windows for brake cooling. C) Lighting at night, with four headlights, was a welcome change. D) The dashboard was good and the controls, decent.

Character

For its technical solutions, heterodox is the adjective that was mostly attributed to the DKW.

Among them, the most attention-drawing is the use of a two-stroke engine, of a well different working than the four-stroke normally used. It does without the camshaft, the multi-lobed, or eccentric-full shaft, since there are no intake and exhaust valves.

If there were no eccentrics in the engine, they were at its solutions for sure.

Preceded by a loud and characteristic noise – easy to be recognized even before the eyes spotted its exotic and rounded shape – the DKW let a curtain of blue smoke when the engine was not fully warmed up.

Exhaust smoke and noise were typical of two-stroke engines, as well as its design was from the first years after World War II. Originated from a German design of the late 1930s, therefore from a time Germany was not going through its best days – the war had already started.

If the look of a standing still DKW was already exotic, in motion – eccentric.

With little orthodox format, the DKW was designed to meet, and it did, the most ordinary needs of the most ordinary drivers, therefore it was above all a versatile automobile, with a domestic temper.

Daily, urban driving

The first start of the day, with a cold engine, was not difficult. The smoke cloud was the only annoyance.

Driving the car, it was nimble when starting from traffic lights and its controls were not heavy to the point of causing discomfort.

Driving position was quite reasonable and visibility would become compromised when maneuvering, when some extremities of the car could not be spotted.

Doors and glasses opened and closed satisfactorily and access to rear seat, in the case of the four-door sedans – especially after the enlarging of rear door opening in 1961 – was excellent; yet in the station wagons, the two doors required one gymnastic more.

A) Access to front seats was good, while to the rear ones was not agreeing to the family-use purpose, although it was within quite decent standards, for the time. Luggage compartment was excellent. B) The folding, split rear seat enabled various space arrangements. The split tailgate that gave access to luggage compartment did not provide a 100% convenient use, but it did not produce noise with shaking nor presented closing problems.

The trunk, even the sedan's , was roomy and accessing it did not require to "dive in" – it was easy and practical.

Due to the front-wheel drive, minimum turning diameter was not brilliant, for at the time the universal joints imposed serious restrictions.

Riding was smooth and comfort was diminished by constant gear changing and intense exhaust noise only. The engine was also very noisy in breathing.

The suspension handled well potholes and pavement unevenness that could be bothering respectful of traction – the DKW had difficulties on the wet, for the wheels easily lose traction. In those years, when cobblestone paving was commonplace, if they were wet they became extremely slippery, it was bad for

The DKW-Vemags were correctly dimensioned, combining well – both in size and performance – city and road use. As years went by, the car earned some refinement, but it had never succeed in hiding its major vocation, that of a popular car. The rear windows of the station wagon, for instance, were horizontally sliding.

heavy and powerful automobiles, as well as for the front-wheel drive ones like the DKW.

Maintenance was free from oil changes, a common obligation in other cars that, especially due to quality of the motor oils and the materials, had to change oil at 2,500 km intervals.

The only cabin ventilation by air circulation was through the windows, that were four in the sedan, additionally by the quarter windows that – in spite of banned by the auto industry for turning into a source of wind noise as cars got older – were absolute at the time, there existing no other way to promote air circulation in cold or rainy days. Since these were not efficient resources, in case of rain the glasses of the car evidently fogged, another common characteristic to all its country-mate and contemporary cars.

On the road

The bench seat that in city reasonably played its role, in trips was inefficient as for body lateral restraint. In more sweeping sections, to force the left foot against floor was the only safe resource, however not always it proved enough, to grab the steering wheel – not at all adviced.

The drone of the engine transmitted certain monotony and was tiring with time. "It awakened sleep".

In a high-grade road hill the right gear could be lacking for the little car to go at an adequate speed, while going down by the same section the brakes would certainly – gradually – fade.

Present in the foremost part of the engine hood, the emblem identified the origin in all the cars of the brand.

As for climbing, the DKW would not loose in performance for any other small car, being sufficiently powered to go with the first Simcas and having a roadholding good enough to beat the Aero-Willys.

In the descents, the little engine braking effect greatly overburdened the brakes, which could, besides compromising the pace of the trip, affect safety to a great extent.

The dependability of the DKW's mechanical ensemble enabled long trips, with littke risks or frights, as well as, in spite of some mechanical peculiarities the demanded specific knowledge, service for DKWs was not difficult to find.

The smooth ride and room were adequate. Both were in a higher level than offered by smaller size cars.

In straight roads, after gaining momentum the DKWs had a great facility in sustaining high cruising speeds, running close to its top speed, something between 120 km/h and 130 km/h.

The only ghosts that frightened on the way, if its top performance was required, were overheating and fuel pump failure.

In general, the DKW fulfilled with honor the task of taking the family for motoring on weekends or for a longer trip.

Its finishing was simple and practical, what made cleaning easy.

The same plastic materials that bothered quite a lot when the car was left on the sun, were efficient when it came to clean the trash of a weekend in the beach or country, including the bits of eaten cookies.

TAXI

The DKW served as taxi for a long time. Even after phase-out, the DKW went on as the most used car for taxi service or, as customarily said, to serve at "the square", an old expression in Brazil from the time taxis were mostly found parked in squares waiting for clients.

The preference for the DKW was a consequence of its approval by the professionals that had in the car their only work tool.

The DKW was dependable, did not absent from work for failing or malfunction and was economical in fuel or repair costs.

More fundamental than these virtues was the fact of being a four-door automobile and offer plenty of room for passengers and luggage.

In São Paulo city it took long to be replaced, for the Chevrolet Opala and the Ford Corcel (four-door first) were launched in late 1968 only and the VW four-door sedan, in 1969. As it always happened, new cars were seen with distrust by taxi drivers, who did not go that easily for them.

Of those, the VW was the only one that was trusted by the category for reliability and low maintenance cost, yet room for passengers was little and for luggage, insufficient.

The Chevrolet Opala was a larger size car, too big for "the square".

The Corcel seemed better sized for the job, but it the beginning its quality was questioned. The first units presented problems that became rooted not in the automobiles, but in the memory of the class.

Therefore, the DKW kept being the most common taxi car and the last units that were in use in São Paulo city were as taxi.

The DKW and I

As with all cars of the first stage of the Brazilian industry, I could not, as a driver, have any contact with the DKW when it was still produced.

When it was discontinued in 1967 I was just six years old. At this time my co-living with the DKW was restricted to child-passenger, both in my uncle's (who

"The best car in the world", according to my cousin, older than me – he should be around eight when his father had a DKW. It was unlikely, but understandable in view of the passion. The rear of the Vemaguet station wagon, until 1966, was this one. In 1967 it would earn a new, split bumper and larger taillights.

owned one until 1970) or whenever I took a taxi (until circa 1972, when replacement parts became scarce and the DKW left the job.

My cousin son of my DKW uncle was one year older and we were neighbors – we lived at the same building. There was no weekend we were not together, with my family or his, and some tasks of the week we accomplished together.

My uncle was the typical driver of the 1960s: he loved his car and enjoyed the freedom of traveling – or at least just motoring – on weekends, therefore I ended developing certain intimacy with the DKW.

I recall a certain occasion we were descending the 8 km in the Anchieta road hilly section and my uncle was complaining that the car had lost brakes. He was not an expert driver (and I knew it already) and his statement worried me a lot, but nothing happened. By the way, I do not remember being stranded even once with the DKW due to mechanical failure.

I remember the worry we all had for my uncle's drowsiness when driving. Perhaps the fatigue caused by the monotonous symphony from the car's exhaust had something to do with it.

I also remember my cousin, when we went to school, highlighting the virtue the car had over the Volks: four windows. My aunt would be at the wheel and he beside her, in the front seat, next to the passenger door. The other four children, I among them, fought over the windows in the rear seat and he always insisted that we should not fight, after all if it was a Volks, we would not have windows that could be opened.

Another quote that also reminds me of the DKW, was also from this cousin: "The DKW is the best car in the world."

I did not know if it was the Rolls-Royce or the Mercedes-Benz the "best car in the world" when the DKW got into the dispute. I could not believe in my cousin, who insisted and affirmed that my uncle told him that.

On consulting my uncle, he did confirm it, although with one further explanation: "The best car in the world is our car, the one that takes us for rides and is the one we like most." To me it is the top expression of the relationship of the average man of the 1960s with his car, not by chance a DKW.

After my 18 years I drove DKWs again in the early 2000s only, a Fissore and a Vemaguet purchased in the same occasion.

I could then confirm: the DKW had its own solutions and had to be driven in a singular way, yet it fulfilled its role of a versatile automobile.

THE FISSORE

Less renowned than Pininfarina, for example, but even so well considered, Fissore was the name of a Italian studio for car body design, responsible for the DKW-Vemag Fissore.

The Fissore arrived to fill a very specific market niche. It was supposed to be a "prestige DKW", that is, to become a share in between the medium-sized and the large cars.

The DKW was a car of mere 1,000 cm³ – born from a design of the late 1930s, in a troubled and warring Germany – whose purpose was to be a popular car for the family. Therefore, to occupy a segment of higher prestige in Brazil of the mid-1960s...

All the sedan's underpinnings would be assigned the task of transporting a larger size vehicle, plusher ant, therefore, heavier. On the other hand, it should perform better.

The dimensioning of the DKW for a car the sedan and the station wagon were – to meet the requirements of these car's owners – varied between the sufficient and the critical.

Its acceleration and power to sustain good average speeds were decent, yet its brakes could not deal with the car's weight without developing brake fade.

The engineering of Vemag, with the launching of the Fissore, had to "unfold in one thousand" as to achieve the "miracle". Of this "miracle" some fruits became surpluses to be later adopted by the rest of the line.

A) The dashboard was elegant. Years later, in 1974, the Passat was launched, with the instrument cluster design apparently inspired on it (VW acquired Vemag in 1966). B) Finishing with splined material and a radio with the car's brand name on it were signs of sophistication.

The lines of the Fissore were "light-years" ahead of any national car. To compare them with the other DKW's was not even possible. The high shoulder line and the wide glass area, besides modern, provided a great sensation of well-being to passengers. Different from all other DKW-Vemag, its main virtue was the beauty.

The Lubrimat – that would integrate the whole lineup in 1965, with the launch of the Rio series, commemorative of the 400th anniversary of the city; the disc brakes up front, that were fitted to the racing GT Malzonis (1966); and the more powerful engine that would integrate the DKW Belcar S (1967) were part of the effort to adequate its performance to the category it would belong to.

All these improvements, additionally to shorter gearbox speeds (third and fourth), resulted in an automobile that went in very similar way with the less pretentious models of the lineup.

Even very limited, the Fissore pleased those who liked the DKW's singular solutions and did not care about a superior performance.

Manufacturing care could be seen in all details, but even so it was hard to sell a DKW for the price of a larger car. There were its suggested retail price surpassed that of the Simca Chambord and Aero-Willys. Its details would be used in other cars, launched many years later. The VW SP2, the car of the make with the highest *status* in the 1970s, used the Fissore door latches.

Its biggest merit – exactly the opposite of other models of the brand – was on its lines, extremely advanced, of avant-garde and good taste.

Besides its own limitations, Vemag was not duly equipped to produce this model. Besides the limited production, it had a high final cost. Its price has made it a direct competitor of Simca and Aero-Willys, automobiles of much superior size than its own.

ANOTHER OPINION

No other car in the history of automobile in Brazil, after Word War II, was target for so many myths as the DKW-Vemag. They were about everything, from driving techniques to mechanical tips. How to negotiate a bend? With full acceleration only, many said, so the front driving wheel would pull the car to the inside. False: as traction force increases, side cornering force the tire is capable of generating diminishes. In all normal use spectrum, the DKW could be driven as any other car. In the field of "tips", when the engine tended to overheat, people used to put a piece of flaming match between the radiator cap rubber seal and the cap seat – but the system pressurization was gone and the water that boiled at 120° C only under pressure now did it at 100° C. Another classic one was high-octane gasoline "burning" the engine, never to be used, a great nonsense, since it would benefit the engine.

Therefore, the DKW was a car like any other, nothing justified so many myths about it. I just had a two-stroke engine and the gearbox featured a free-wheeling mechanism that could be put in operation or not, it depended on the driver only. Many cars of the 1930s and 1940s also had free-wheeling, although associated to the transmission fitted with an overdrive. The mechanics of the DKW was not more or less complicated than other cars'. On the contrary, its engine was singularly simple. The adjustment of ignition took longer to be done because there were three independent systems, not because it was difficult to do.

TECHNICALLY CORRECT

For being a two-stroker with lubrication by adding oil to gasoline, until the metering pump Lubrimat came into scene in 1964, it was necessary some attention by the owner in this matter. The recommended proportion by the factory was 1 liter of motor oil for 40 of gasoline. It was pouring the oil first, then gasoline. Nothing else was needed. But since fuel capacity was 45 liters, the driver should wait the tank go almost dry as to be replenished with 40 liters of fuel and 1 liter of motor oil, totaling 41 liters. This was a nuisance. Because of this, many had the habit of stopping to refuel whenever the fuel gauge dropped below half a tank, pouring ½ liter of oil and 20 of gasoline. It helped to buy motor oil canned a quart of a gallon, or 0.946 liters, quite usual in the 1960s. Therefore, the 1:40 proportion was obtained with just 38 liters of gasoline. By the way, this proportion issue was always polemic. There were always those that recommended "to reinforce" engine lubrication by lowering the proportion to 1:35 or even 1:30, usually claiming the personal experience of driving thousands of kilometers with the engine without any problem. Also nonsense, for what the factory recommended was more than sufficient, not forgetting that more oil meant more engine carbonizing. There were also many discussions on what of oil to use. Vemag always recommended two-stroke oil or motor oils for four-stroke engines with the highest API service, MS/DG then (gasoline engine, heavy duty use/diesel), SAE 40 grade. Period. People start punching each other on this is an exaggeration, but that it lead to much discussion, no doubt about it.

TECHNICAL INFORMATION OF DKW-VEMAG

VEHICLE	DKW Sedan and Belcar 1958 to 1966	Belcar S (1967)	Perua Vemag (1958 a 67)	Perua Vemaguet S (1967)	Fissore
Type	4-door sedan, 6 passengers, front engine and drive	*	2-door SW	2-door SW	2-door SW
Chassis and body					
Type	Separated chassis with "X" members; steel	*	*	*	*
Engine					
Type	Inline 3-cylinder, cast iron block and aluminum cylinder head, water cooled; two-stroke.	*	*	*	*
Mixture formation	40 mm single bbl carburetor	*	*	*	*
Bore and stroke (mm)	74 x 76	*	*	*	*
Displacement (cm^3)	981cm^3	*	*	*	*
Compression ratio	7.25:1	8:1	*	8:1	8:1
Maximum power (SAE)	50 hp at 4,500 rpm	60	*	60	60
Maximum torque (SAE)	8.5 m.kgf at 2,250 rpm	9.5/2,500	*	9.5/2,500	9.5/2,500
Transmission					
Type	4-speed manual transaxle, non-synchronized first until 1961	*	*	*	*
Brakes					
Type	Single hydraulic circuit, no powerbrake	*	*	*	*
Front	Drum	*	*	*	Disc
Rear	Drum	*	*	*	*
Suspension					
Front	Independent, lower A-arm and transverse leaf spring	*	*	*	*
Rear	Rigid axle, transverse leaf spring	*	*	*	*
Steering					
Type	Rack and pinion	*	*	*	*
Dimensions and capacities					
Wheelbase (mm)	2,450	*	*	*	*
Lenght (mm)	4,480	*	*	*	*
Width (mm)	1,690	*	*	*	*
Height (mm)	1,480	*	*	*	*
Ground clearance (mm)	170	*	*	*	*
Fuel tank (liter)	45	*	*	*	*
Curb weight (kg)	940	*	975	975	975
Wheels and tyres					
Type	Steel wheels and cross-ply tyres	*	*	*	*
Tyre size	5.60-15	*	*	*	*

GÔSTO NÃO SE DISCUTE
(MAS, PELA LÓGICA, VOCÊ PREFERE UM DKW-VEMAG)

Há quem goste de um carro sem nem saber porquê. Outros têm razões para gostar (donos de DKW-VEMAG, por exemplo). E você, que ainda vai comprar ou trocar seu carro?

Uma coisa é certa: você não se decidirá por impulso ou capricho. Nem por uma questão de gôsto superficial. Você vai estudar, analisar, comparar, para fazer a melhor escolha.

Estudando, analisando e, principalmente, comparando, você verá que o DKW-VEMAG leva a melhor. Nêle, você notará o perfeito equilíbrio entre confôrto e economia. Entre sobriedade de linhas e impecável acabamento. Verificará a qualidade mecânica DKW-VEMAG, agora com Lubrimat.

Faça a comparação e concluirá que nenhum outro carro lhe dá tanto pelo seu dinheiro

CONVERSE COM SEU REVENDEDOR **DKW-VEMAG**

SOLICITE A RELAÇÃO COMPLETA DOS REVENDEDORES DKW-VEMAG AO "DEPTO" DE PROPAGANDA · CAIXA POSTAL 8232 · S. PAULO

Ao passar de um carro menor para um Belcar

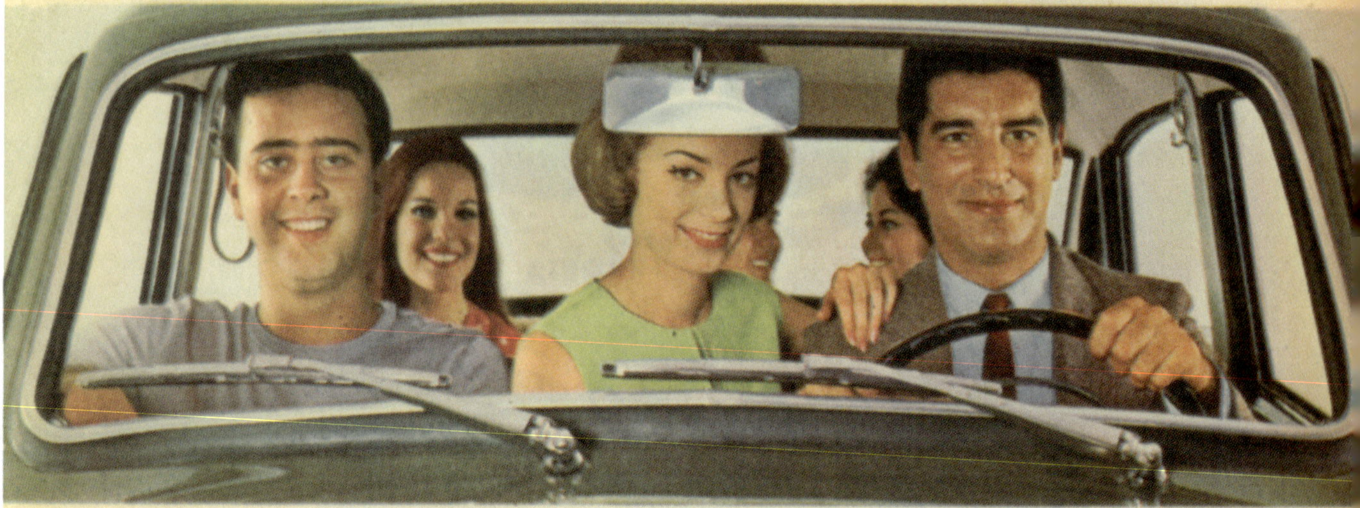

não é só você quem sente mais estabilidade e melhor desempenho

Ninguém melhor do que você, porém, sentirá a superioridade mecânica do Belcar. Os 50 H.P. num arranque impetuoso, o deslanche, a melhor estabilidade dentre os carros nacionais, a exclusiva tração dianteira e a sólida suspensão à prova de buracos. Tôdas as características, enfim, que fazem do Belcar o carro que dá menos oficina e mais satisfação. Custando apenas um preço médio, pois é compacto. Vá a um Revendedor Vemag e passe para um Belcar. Porque, além de tudo você terá o confôrto de um automóvel. Com quatro portas. E, desculpe lembrar, com espaço para 6 pessoas. . .

DKW-VEMAG

80 100 120 140 160 180
HORA
OLEO
RESERVA

From left to right and from fore to background: 1967 red "Alfa Romeo" FNM 2000; 1967 blue Aero Willys 2600; blue Simca Chambord Três Andorinhas; 1965 greenish Simca Jangada Tufão & 1968 golden "Alfa Romeo" FNM 2000 Timb. Models Aero-Willys 2600, FNM 2000 and Simca Chambord were the chief-cars of their lineups. Other more luxurious or sporting versions, like the FNM 2000 Timb, or yet with simpler finishing or station wagon body, like the Simca Jangada, made the option range of large-size national cars.

Large cars

(1959 to 1967)

Aero-Willys, FNM 2000 JK and Simca

In1959, therefore at the dawn of the Brazilian auto industry, the Simca Chambord was launched – its first product for large size segment.

From left to right: 1965 greenish Simca Jangada Tufão; 1962 blue Simca Chambord Três Andorinhas. The Simca lineup was the one that offered the widest range of models, with more engine options, finishing and decor. Even for body, there was variation: besides the traditional sedan, the Jangada station wagon. As for evolution, it was the one that announced more changes for its cars. To each of them, a new name for the line. The Três Andorinhas, in 1961, was the first. Later, in 1964, came the Tufão one, with new engines and details, like the redesigned front grille.

In the future, a wide model range based on the same automobile, in addition to the Chambord, would form the Simca family. Together, they offered options both in engines and finishing. They had gone on a rich road, as for technical evolution, styling or finishing throughout the years they remained in production.

In 1960, Fábrica Nacional de Motores (FNM) started producing the Alfa Romeo 2000 berlina (Italian for sedan) under license of Alfa Romeo of Italy, named FNM 2000 JK here. Unlike the Simca, it did not suffer significant changes and just one sports version – the Timb – was added to the line until 1969, when the model evolved to the FNM 2150.

The Alfa Romeo-FNM line was the one that did fewer changes to its model. Changing the name in 1964, from FNM 2000 JK to FNM 2000, was not caused by any technical event, but politic: with the military régime, the initials of president of Republic Juscelino Kubitschek, now politically canceled, were suppressed.

The Aero-Willys, also launched in 1960, was the third and last large car of the pioneering phase launched, immediately turning into the category's biggest sales success. A deep restyling occurred in 1963 and thereon slight changes occurred. As for mechanics, except for simultaneously increasing horsepower and adding one speed to the gearbox in 1964, there were little changes. In 1966, a plush version, the Itamaraty, would be the only model added.

The biggest discrepancies in relation to what was happening abroad were exactly in this market segment.

The Brazilian Simca, of French-American origin (drafted in the US for the French market), was designed in the early 1950s. Its sales performance in the Old Continent had been far from brilliant and it disembarked in Brazil, its production was close to discontinuing in the mother company.

It was immediately welcome, yet with some quality control problems and other inherent to the design which had given certain discredit for image of the car.

The level of development applied to the Brazilian Simca had taken it to a level of advancement never experienced by the French Simca, which it originated from. The lineup became bigger and developed with the firm goal of getting rid of the stigma of being fragile and slow, but the poor quality control always let flaws and even after achieving in making the car suitable in performance, it resulted in producing a little dependable product.

The Simca range consisted of classy and comfortable automobiles, featuring excellent brakes and roadholding and – depending on the model, especially the model-year – it could be faster ou slower, varying from very slow to very quick.

The Aero-Willys were also from the US and were also designed in the early 1950s. They were not commercial success either.

They were not elegant or sumptuous – especially the first models – as the Simcas, nevertheless they were roomy inside and, although they were not top on dynamic capacities such as accelerating, braking, sustain high speeds and road-holding, they were dependable and easy servicing.

At front, traces of designs aimed for the same market could be noted. The embedded headlights in an extension of the fenders and auxiliary lamps in the grille were some of them. The larger windshield of the Aero-Willys is a result of the 1963 restyling. The sizes of the cars were about the same, but the FNM seemed to be a little lower and narrower. The look reflected the more sportive accent of the FNM, the Simca's pomp and the Willys' non-pretension.

Close relatives of the Jeep Universal, a vehicle born for military duties, they brought in their lineage inherent qualities that made the lineup the first of large size Brazilian cars – whose maintenance and driving were within an average standard, coherent with the local resources – that could be used without worry regarding breakdowns and stranding. The Aero made the large national car feasible.

The JK was a derived Italian designed with the American market in view. The Alfa Romeo 1900, a direct ancestor of the Alfa Romeo 2000 (JK twin), had also a design dated from the early 1950s. The Alfa 2000, in fact, was an improved and restyled edition aiming to conquer that market. Like the other two, it failed.

The Alfa Romeo badge stick to the center of the front grille would assure sumptuousness to the automobile that, evidently, exhibited high technical sophistication.

The limited production and the sports vocation were aimed to a very special niche: that of luxury sports sedans.

In spite of not presenting the problems of the Simca, it had in the electrical system its Achilles heels. Worse than the problems was the incompetence of the technicians of the time in solving them, due to the more sophisticated mechanics.

It was less roomy than the Aero and the Simca, however it seated up to six and had a good luggage space.

In spite of little significant for the market in terms of volume and share, the JK ended influencing it by a large extent on technical evolution and for being, among the pioneers, the most sophisticated and fast.

Besides all of them having originated from automobiles designed in the early 1950s, having some American "accent" and not being successful at their own markets (the Simca, in practice, was not produced any more for selling locally and the Aero had been long discontinued), they had to obey certain common precepts.

Prerequisites for a luxury sedan (1960s):

- *The had to sit six occupants and all their luggage* – even being extremely roomy, the Simca fell short of the Aero in this. Even the JK met this requisite, only without brio. It was the smallest of the three.
- *It should be comfortable, i.e., smooth and quiet* – the Simca's suspension and engine were capable of providing smoothness and quietness far superior to the Aero's. The JK followed another standard, it was sportive, and more than quietness it was after a pleasant tone, as well as its suspension was firm. It was not harsh nor noisy, but did not pursue the standards of a luxury automobile.
- *High cruising speeds, above the average then, should be sustained with comfort and safety* – the JK was the only one to feature a mechanical character capable of offering the right performance and roadholding, for the Simca lacked engine punch for the first models; a little better for model Tufão Super (1964 through 1966); and no lack at all for the Emi-Sul (second half of 1966 only). As for the Aero, until 1964, when gearbox and engine improved, everything was missing: roadholding, brakes and even engine behavior at high speeds had always been a problem.

At the rear section of the three there were many elements in common. The shape of the trunk lid with rounded edges and crimps; the chromed bumpers were massive and the taillights laid vertically and embedded in the fenders formed a bulge until meeting the rear window – a style resource that by convention was called fishtail. Also, until the 1962 model-year the rearmost column was slim. In the 1963 restyling it was enlarged though. A parallel development would occur within Simca, that for the 1964 Tufão line would repeat this trend in roof design.

- *The automobile should be sized as to show a superior status* – the external dimensions by themselves, imposed respect to the three, but the Simca exhibited more impressive adornments and design; the JK, although less ornamented than the Simca, had also many trim and chrome work, rounded shape and exaggerated taillights, besides the aura of bearing the mechanical sophistication of an Alfa Romeo; as for the Aero-Willys, it was the simplest of the three, and even after 1964, when its design underwent deep changes that ensured quite more pomp, continued to be the more discreet one.
- *Internal finishing should be made in a way to assure a welcoming and sophisticated environment* – Simca and JK, with absolutely different recipes, involved passengers in a differentiated environment, while the first Aeros revealed more practical and functional, with the refinements that would come in 1964 only.

The solutions of each

Headlights were embedded in the upper corner of the front fenders, that conserved the cylindrical shape – at their highest point – until meeting the windshield; the taillights were vertically laid, following a triangular shape and were embedded in the fenders also, these continuing to meet the rear window with this format; they were three-box, six-seat sedans; gearshift was column-mounted; engines were longitudinally-installed and driving was through the rear wheels; engine displacement remained between 2,000 and 2,600 cm^3; front suspensions were independent on coil springs; rear axle was rigid; drum brakes; and the structure, unitary construction. In spite of all these characteristics being common, the solutions, as a whole, were quite distinct:

- The JK's gearbox had five speeds, all synchronized; as for the Simca, it always had a three-speed and first was not "hard" anymore as of 1962 only, while the Aero adopted the same solution as the Simca's until 1962, when the gearbox was replaced by a four-speed, all synchronized.
- The JK's engine was a 2,000-cm^3 four-cylinder, with cast iron cylinder head and hemispherical combustion chambers, in addition to the double overhead camshaft; the Simca went for a 2,400-cm^3 V8, although there were 2,300 and 2,500-cm^3 versions, with in-block camshaft and valves, although, again, there had been in the last months of production the option of the Emi-Sul engine, with an aluminum, overhead valves cylinder head with hemispherical combustion chambers; and the Aero was fitted with a 2,600-cm^3 inline six with in-block exhaust valves and overhead intake ones.
- The JK's suspension was by superposed unequal triangular arms; Simca's, by McPherson system and the Aero's, by an upper triangular arm and a single lower one.
- Springs of the JK's rear suspension were coil, while the Simca's and Aero's were semi-elliptical.
- The JK's brake drums were made in aluminum and finned (for better cooling); the Simca had two brake cylinders per wheel (normally there is one); and the Aero was 100% conventional.

The JK had already radial-ply tires. The Aero's and the Simca's were normal (cross-ply).

In terms of performance...

When launched, the JK was the only national car capable of providing performance and safety for traveling at cruising speeds close to 130 km/h.

This was the main virtue that highlighted it from other cars made here.

The Simca, in spite of featuring good roadholding and brakes, was not able to go over 120 km/h in a straight and level road. Therefore, in good road, to sustain speeds next to 100 km/h was all what to expect from it.

Besides the same can be said about the Aero in terms of speed, in everything else pertaining to dynamics, to the running of the automobile, the Aero would loose the comparison to the Simca. Brakes were much worse; it fell short in roadholding; it had slow steering and controls; it was heavier to drive and less soft.

Until 1963, the Aero and the Simca were similar automobiles in performance (acceleration and top speed), for with three speeds the Willys was penalized in the same conditions as its competitor's.

In 1964, with four speeds, the Willys started easily doing better than the rival in medium-speed hills, which it had to overcome at some 50 km/h and now – more effortlessly – could do it at 70 km/h; Simca had significantly improved engine power output with the Tufão series.

The JK's five synchronized speeds provided ability to go up through twisty roads in an incomparably superior way to the other two, which had three speeds only and first was not synchronized.

For city use, in spite of demanding certain steering and all other controls effort, the synchronized first as one plus convenience, as the superior acceleration was a blessing.

The controls of the Aero were not lighter than the JK's and the Simca required certain, additional care, such as leaving the garage with engine already pre-warmed up.

As for price, restrict production or performance, the JK was, in fact, a better option to the imports than its country-mates.

The American sedans were more powerful and comfortable than the JK, but were incapable of providing a sports driving.

When the Simca evolved in 1964 to the Tufão line, in spite of still continuing slower than the JK, it had less tedious acceleration and speeds to its occupants, as well as the synchronized first, as of 1962, that reduced the driving drama in urban circuits.

In 1964, with four synchronized speeds and a more powerful engine, the Aero 2600 had left slowness aside.

Therefore, as of 1964, Brazil was producing large automobiles other than the JK that, at least, "had power to start from standstill". However, the JK continued dynamically sovereign.

In 1966, Simca launches the Emi-Sul. With this engine, its cars offered higher acceleration and top speed than the FNM 2000, although it remained matchless in cruising speed.

Therefore, the JK was no longer the only national automobile option capable of seating a family and providing traveling at decent speeds.

In 1967 the Esplanada would come, an evolver Emi-Sul Simca, and the Itamaraty 3000, the Aero-Willys' plush version with a 3,000 cm^3 engine.

In spite of lacking a sports character, inherent to the Willys lineup, the Itamaraty was capable of taking roads at speeds very coherent with the traffic of those times, at around 100 km/h.

Yet in 1967 the Ford Galaxie 500 would be launched.

Of the same American standards of then, the Galaxie definitely surmounted the JK, the Simca or the Aero in prestige, although it owed much to the two first in sports driving.

Practicality and habitability

If the Willys was the less advisable for who enjoyed fast driving, as a trade-off it offered advantages both in the aesthetical side and concerning use: practicality, maintenance and dependability.

It was the more roomy, both for passengers and luggage, although the extra room was not its best attractiveness, since this was also one of the Simca's virtues, a car that with a smooth ride, quieter and more welcoming.

However, if there was ever a difference in favor of the Willys in relation to competitors, it was robustness and mechanical dependability. On the extreme end of what happened with the Simca, it was at the level of the best imports of those times, while the Alfa Romeo was just too sophisticated for the level of service available then.

Maybe this is the Aero-Willys' happiest angle. When it was redesigned for the first time, in 1963, the flaps over the headlights resulted too long, which rendered it a dirty nickname, "whore nails". After the size was trimmed off, they harmoniously integrated to front style. Performance and driveability were virtues an Aero should not be chosen for, but it was the more practical, the easier to be used, in daily life.

The only one to present a station wagon body was the Simca. The version originated from a large car made all sense, in being a car for the household. Simca did not forget the look, but performance below the desirable in the sedan worsened even more because of the extra weight. When fully loaded, the engine showed its lack of power.

Styling and prestige

Of the models launched in its first series, the Simca was by far the more pompous. Rightly sized, with many contours and loaded with chrome work, it could prompt a well greater visibility to its owner. Inside, the color matching, as well the design of instruments and accessories, also drew attention.

The JK, in spite of smaller dimensions, had its own style, a rich look and the heart-shaped grille that identified it as an Alfa Romeo, a symbol of *status*. The instrument cluster and other controls were of a sports griffe.

The lines of the first Aero were quite straightforward and unpretentious, as was its interior. With the 1963 restyling, the Aero shortened the distance that separated it from the Simca in relation to sumptuousness, although the Simca models, or even the FNM, remained much more attractive.

In 1963, the Aero interior was redesigned and new materials were applied in its production. From then on, the internal ambiance had greater sophistication, closing the gap to the Simca.

Evolutions, models and naming

Of the Simcas:

Chambord, the most common; Rallye, the sports version; Alvorada and Profissional, the more basic; and Jangada, the station wagon, were some Simca models. Aquillon, the engine that powered the first Simca; Aquillon Super, a more powerful version of the first; Tufão (Typhoon), second version (1964); Tufão Super, more powerful; Emi-Sul, with overhead valves and hemispherical combustion chambers (1966) were some of the powerplants. Três Andorinhas (Three swallows), as of 1962; 3-Sincros, second half of 1962 through 1964; Tufão, 1964 through 1966; and Emi-Sul, second half of 1966, were the names given to the series.

The Rallye was Simca's sports model. Two 2-bbl carburetors instead of one, also 2-bbl, ensured better performance. All details suggested production care and suggested that it was fast.

Of the Aero-Willys:

The Aero-Willys, when restyled in 1963, was called Aero-Willys 2600. More powerful, it would be retouched in 1964, when it earned the four-speed gearbox. The plush version called Itamaraty was launched in 1966 and in the following year a 3,000-cm^3 engine was fitted to it.

Of the Alfa Romeos:

The FNM 2000 lost the JK suffix to be called just FNM 2000 in 1964 because of the military régime that seized political rights and homages to the former president. The sports version, supposed to be named Jango, ended being called Timb (short for Turismo Internacional Modelo Brasileiro) when launched in 1966.

Proposals

The Simca was sophisticated, far from being a mere transport mean.

The Aero was a touring car and it was easy roomy, simple to drive and easy to maintain.

The Alfa Romeo was a car aimed to sportiveness.

In common was the fact of being automobiles capable of seating six people with relative comfort.

Yet it competed with the Aero, maybe even more than the Simca's or the Alfa Romeo's, the models of the DKW-Vemag lineup and the Chevrolet Veraneio utility.

Coming from an inferior category, the DKW embodied virtues quite similar to the Willy's, despite being a quite smaller-size automobile and, except for cost or a more spirited and suitableness for city driving, there would be no excuse to buying it in detriment of the Aero.

With quite a heterodox proposal, having its own segment, a niche, the Chevrolet Veraneio also was able to carry a family with comfort, offering performance and convenience although it was not a touring car.

Conclusion

It was hard to establish a comparison. Each represented a specific concept and had their own place in the same market segment.

The JK was the sporting car, good for high speeds, but its maintenance was complicated and its handling heavy for driving in the city.

The Simca was very refined and the most comfortable, but it lacked the most important of attributes: dependability.

Before restyling, the Aero-Willys showed quite roundish lines and small glass area – actually smaller than the Simca's ou JK's. Its performance was unpretentious and followed aerodynamic concepts. It was the simpler, the less charming and the one with the worse driveability, yet it was clearly the most suitable for our conditions.

The Aero was not as powerful as the JK, nor as refined as the Simca, it just did its come-and-go mission with honor, offering comfort to up to six passengers.

ANOTHER OPINION

Before the Ford Galaxie and the Dodge Dart, the Brazilian market had to settle with one of these three to carry four or five people with relative comfort. In a way or another, each did its job well, depending on the user profile. The Aero-Willys served well who wanted to use the services of a private driver, while the FNM 2000 JK was crafted to be driven by the owner; a driver was unimaginable. The Simca was in "twilight zone", would fit in one or another. It was an interesting moment of history, for large, foreign cars, whose importation was barred, went steadily giving room to the ones made here. It was a change in scenario that seemed definite, but early in the following decade importation would be allowed again. In the Brazilian scenario the small Volkswagen sedan and Dauphine and Gordini dominated, in addition to the not-so-small DKW-Vemag.

TECHNICALLY CORRECT

The three had a rigid rear axle, but only the FNM 2000 JK had coil spring on it. Unlike what most people think, the coil spring is not softer than other types, for example, the semi-elliptical assembly. They do not present friction between leaves and are capable of accumulating more energy in relation to their own weight. For being fitted with coils springs, the FNM 2000 JK's axle location was achieved by a lower radius arm on each side and a reaction triangle that linked the top of the differential housing to the structure, a good solution. In the Aero-Willys and the Simca, rear axle location exclusively counted on the semi-elliptical leaf springs between each axle side and the structure, a primitive solution called Hotchkiss suspension. But where Simca really innovated was at the front suspension the world knew for the first time with the 1949 Ford Vedette. The steering knuckle forms a unit with a strut the houses the shock absorber and the assembly is linked up high to the front structure through a bearing, so it can turn to steer. In the case of the Simca the strut had a plate around it where the coil spring was mounted. At the bottom end the strut is linked to the structure via a control arm, while the anti-roll bar longitudinally locates the wheel. It is not by chance that it is one of the most widely used suspension today, if not the most, and it is applicable either to small, low-cost cars or sophisticated ones, like BMW and Porsche. The Aero-Willys and the FNM 2000 JK that the conventional independent front suspension of the time, the superposed arms kind.

Some angles of the FNM 2000, when seen separately, pleased more than when done as a whole. The layout of the "Sporting Heart" was that of a true shield.

PRICE TABLE OF LARGE CARS[1]

	Model	1957	1958	1959	1960	1961	1962	1963	1964	1965	1966	1967	1968
FNM	2000 JK					1,000	1,848	2,450*	5,423*	9,060.6	10,980	15,280	
	Timb											18,280	
Simca	Chambord					1,153	1,360	2,025	4,175	7,865	9,300	12,192	
	Alvorada								3,495				
	Profissional										6,050		
	Rally							2,325	4,975	8,190			
	Rally Special									9,330	11,040		
	Jangada							2,150		7,585	9,560	12,995	
	Jangada Std								4,175				
	Jangada Luxe								4,350				
	Esplanada											14,700	
	Esplanada 6sp											15,600	
Aero-Willys	Aero Willys					895							
	Plastic Upholstery						1,187						
	Hide Upholstery						1,515						
	Aero Willys 2006 mod 1145							1,988					
	Aero Willys 2600 mod 1146							2,078					
	Aero Willys Standard								4,107				
	Aero Willys Luxe								4,174				
	Aero Willys 3-speed									7,754			
	Aero Willys 4-speed									7,510	9,235	11,612	

In 1961, the pomp of the Simca Chambord assured its success, even if its price was 30% higher than an Aero-Willys': in 1963, with the restyling of the Aero, the difference dropped to less than 20%. The mechanical dependability of the Simca cars, step by step went on making difficult its sales performance and, in 1966, the suggested retail price of an Aero-Willys was nearly equal a Chambord's. The FNM 2000, produced by a state-owned company, and a political price. In 1963 and 1964, a two-year old sample reached a value higher than a brand-new vehicle sold by the automaker (which could be purchased at the suggested retail price through some political influence only). On the average, for the price of a large car two small ones could be bought.

PRODUCTION TABLE OF LARGE CARS[2]

Make	Model / Year	1957	1958	1959	1960	1961	1962	1963	1964	1965	1966	1967	Until 1967	1968	Total
Willys	Aero-Willys				6,124	7,747	9,508	14,541	15,056	14,095	11,109	8,603	**86,783**	7,462	94,245
Simca	Chambord			1,217	3,570	5,641	6120	7,042	9,034	5,647	4,367	272	**42,910**		42,910
	Rally						449	592	1,213	1,141	597		**3,992**		3,992
	Alvorada							378					**378**		378
	Jangada						215	1,450	652	220	135	33	**2,705**		2,705
	Total Simca	0	0	1,217	3,570	5,641	6,784	9,462	10,899	7,008	5,099	305	**49,985**		49,985
FNM	2000				414	454	378	258	161	388	474	714	**3,241**	1,115	4,356
Large	**Total**	0	0	2,434	13,678	19,483	23,454	33,723	37,015	28,499	21,781	9,927	**189,994**	8,577	198,571

In the beginning there was even a certain strength balance between the Aero-Willys and the automobiles of the Simca lineup. The Aero-Willys used the well little sophisticated, although low-cost and dependable mechanics originated from the Jeep. The advantage was forwarded to the consumer who could, for a lower price, buy a car less costly and more dependable than a Simca. With more sophisticated and less dependable models, the automaker of French origin offered a greater range of versions and optional equipment, as to enchant the public. In 1965, even after evolving considerably, the Simca range sold something around 50% that of the Aero-Willys'. The FNM 2000, from 1957 to 1967, had a market share inferior to 2% to the large-size cars'. In 1968, following privatization, production raised sharply, however far from a considerable volume. The FNM was representative for its technical qualities, but the physical volume it occupied in the market was insignificant.

1. Prices informed in thousands of Brazilian cruzeiros by *Quatro Rodas* magazine, January issue of each year.
2. Data according to documents supplied by Anfavea.

FNM 2000 (1960 to 1968) and JK (until 1964)

Between 1960 and 1968, the short period it was produced, the FNM 2000, at first with the suffix JK, did not undergo any modifications that changed in a significant way co-living or using the model.

As for comparing and deciding upon buying it, the scenario kept changing. Many other cars evolved and new models were offered to the market. However, neither among the new ones nor among the evolutions there was one automobile that could be considered its direct competitor, for the JK, since the beginning, could satisfy a specific niche only.

Fábrica Nacional de Motores, its maker, was a state company with small production capacity that suffered with the political winds blowing from Brasília, the city inaugurated by Juscelino Kubitschek (JK) in April 21, 1960. Besides being the celebration date for local martyr Tiradentes, hanged the Portuguese for insurgence against the Crown in the colonial period, it was the year the FNM 2000 JK was officially launched.

The small production volume indicated a restrict public, willing to pay quite more for an automobile with exclusive characteristics that demanded an almost specialized driving style.

The sophisticated mechanics and the differentiated finishing asked for a highly skilled labor that ended up not being trained in Brazil after all and, maybe for that

In spite of designed with the purpose of hitting the American market, its lines denounced the Italian origin. The Alfa Romeo shield was prominent, among several styling appendices. The low roof enhanced the sports vocation. The FNM 2000 was the most sophisticated including its mechanic.

reason, the JK had never represented – in fact – a volume (physical) as meaningful as the importance of its presence in the Brazilian market.

In the early JK (the car) years, the other large cars made in Brazil were the Simca and the Aero-Willys. In 1967 there was the new Simca Esplanada and the then advanced Ford Galaxie. In late 1969 the Chrysler Explanada, by now not Simca anymore, would be replaced by the Dodge Dart, a more up-to-date automobile.

The JK – at that time it had already lost the initials our former president – still could not be considered obsolete, but to keep the concept in the same level, something in terms of evolution should be done.

In 1969, with production already under Alfa Romeo control, the FNM 2150 was launched and sent the old 2000 into retirement.

Description and results of the applied technique

The mechanical layout was commonplace: front engine and rear-wheel drive.

Suspension also followed the traditional solution: independent up front and rigid axle at rear.

The brake system, drum on four wheels, was commonplace also, as well as the unitary construction of the body was widely used for European cars after Word War II.

The steering box, by worm and sector, was absolute.

In spite of the orthodox solutions, none of them was built in the usual way or employed ordinary materials, beginning with the four-cylinder engine that, like most European sports cars', was a cast aluminum, double overhead camshaft and hemispherical combustion chamber design with sodium-cooled exhaust valves.

The Alfa Romeo engine, with four cylinders, 1,975 cm^3 and double overhead camshaft in the aluminum cylinder head, with hemispherical combustion chambers and sodium-cooled exhaust valves, was the perfect alibi for a sporting car.
Externally, there were no differences between the 2000 engine and the Timb's, which was identified by the number 200 instead of 210. In the pictures, the Timb's is not showing the painted cylinder head, but it was black, like the "regular". The carburetor, downdraft 2-bbl progressive opening, was also the same, like the red car's, yet the Timb came with reserved room for fitting two sidedraft 2-bbl carburetors, sold at the dealers. Without air filter in the photo, they are in evidence.

The rear window was quite curved, involved by a thick, gleaming trim; the double, wrapping bumper, with bumper overriders, was all chromed and quite voluminous; the frame of the taillights was also chromed, as well as the rear badges. Frames of remaining glasses and the license plate's, as well as trim and hubcaps, were chromed or made in inox steel. Brightness was not missing in its decor.

Gearbox was a full-synchromesh five-speed unit, in a time most cars, even in world level, were three-speed. The gearbox case was made of aluminum and, above all, clutch actuation was already hydraulic, what made it possible to fit the car with a hefty pressure plate-disc set.

The rear axle, even of the rigid type, a system far less sophisticated than an independent suspension, then extremely rare even on most sophisticated automobiles, was coil spring sprung, a far more efficient design that then widely used semi-elliptical leaf spring assembly's.

The wheel windows were assigned the task of taking air to the brake drums, which were externally covered in finned aluminum. The hubcap matched with the design and the radial-ply tires Pirelli Cinturato 175 R400 made a great difference. At the time all other national cars had cross-ply tires, much less suited for speed.

Yet front suspension was independent by coil springs, like in almost all cars from the 1940s onwards. However, it had the most efficient design of them all: unequal wishbones (A-arms) as in racing cars and the best sports car only.

The large-diameter brake drums had a big swept area. They were made of aluminum and were finned, for better cooling, just like the drums of racing cars before disc brakes came into scene as of the second half of the 1950s.

Compromise with sportiveness included radial-ply tires, an absolute novelty in Brazil, where just cross-ply ones existed.

A tall-geared steering, calculated to result in a quick action rather than light, was also chosen.

Its five-speed gearbox served as a reference for the whole world. It was really top: precise engaging and the right gear ratios, resulting in a superb feature.

To make best use of the gearbox's qualities (better say, vice-versa), the engine responded uniformly, with excellent elasticity. Its pleasant tone made rpm changes even more pleasant, inciting fast driving.

Roadholding was the best in business, by a great extent resulting from the radial-ply tires and the JK could sustain high speeds, above 120 km/h without compromising safety.

Yet the brakes were not as efficient as their specification suggested, although they were far better than average and did not fade even under hard use.

The JK was sports car and also a family sedan.

The combination of proposals almost antagonistic – especially for a four-cylinder – ended affecting both performance, when compared to a grand-touring, and comfort, when compared to a family sedan.

However, at the wheel – in spite of absolute performance was by no means impressive (in world terms, since it was definitely above the Brazilian standards) – the spirited driving was not only possible, but also very pleasuring, especially because controls' precision was absolute.

Without any doubt, the JK's technical reading is enthusiastic and it shows that an automobile with the best of the technique applied to the most sophisticated sports and racing cars could only feature a sports behavior, although being a sedan for normal use, it was too heavy for an absolutely convincing performance.

Interior room was sufficient, in spite of being below the standards of the time. The solution adopted then in cars for household use, the bench-type front seat, only deprived the driver from lateral support in curves, since the sophistication of a reclining seat back was offered.

This front seat layout forced the gearshift to be column-mounted, which however did not affect precision and agility in the JK's case.

A) Independent of bench or individual seats – like the Timb's – all FNM had a reclining seat back. The system, with a hatchet in each end, used to fail in the 2000, after all two hatchets sometimes had to support the supporting weight of three people, while in the Timb there were two hatchets per occupant. As for lateral support in bends, the bench type was terrible. The one from the Timb was very bad. Gear engaging, even when actuated by the column-mounted gearshift, was precise. B) Doors were heavy and its latches were prone to bad working. Yet upholstery denote care.

The sports environment inside the car was assured by the instrument cluster that included a horizontal-scale speedometer, trip counter, regular, circular rev counter, oil pressure gauge, besides what any other cars were fitted with: odometer, water temperature gauge and fuel gauge.

The headlight high/low beam switch was also stalked in the steering column, what made driving well easier. There was a control for headlight flashing by means of a button right at the center of the steering wheel. In those days the headlight beam switch was operated with the left foot and headlights did not flash.

There also were auxiliary fog lamps in addition to the main headlights.

The windshield wipers had two speeds and cabin ventilation included two air vents on dashboard ends, as well as those aimed to the windshield.

There was an electric fan that, like the fog lamps, was not efficient at all. The lines of the JK did not find many admirers throughout the world, but enclosed

A) What drew more attention in the FNM 2000 frontal section was the engine hood dome that departed from the Alfa Romeo shield. In the Timb, in order to provide a more sporty and updated look, it was suppressed. At the front grille, inside the same circle, there were two lenses: the lower, in amber color, was for the fog lamps, very little efficient, and the transparent upper one, for the turn indicator. b) At rear, one of the many small details was the exhaust pipe tip that went through the bumper. With shaking, it invariably became a source of noise. C) Trunk was spacious. In spite of inconvenient, the under-floor spare wheel allowed good distribution.

by the Alfa Romeo aura, whose badge was proudly shown in the front grille, were also responsible for the prestige of the car. After all, there were plenty of chromed parts, lights and contours to ensure the pomp of an exponent in Brazilian land.

As a touring car, the JK embodied all faults of a sports car, except lack of room.

Temper

The absolute performance itself would not be able to provide what the Alfa Romeo vein assured it in excess – sports driving.

Definitely, the JK was an automobile with sports temper.

FNM's emblem was an abstraction of the Alfa Romeo original. The main symbol of the Italian brand, its shield, is known as sportive heart. Our FNM, by its temper, could exhibit it without any shame.

Urban, daily driving

The JK worked uniformly, even with engine cold, before reaching the ideal temperature.

Acceleration from stop lights was more than enough, as well as the engaging of the first synchronized gear was quite reasonable.

In spite of not having a soft nor a very quiet ride, the JK did not happen to punish the occupants, after all it was far from being harsh or noisy.

Even being feasible for daily commuting in a large city, undoubtedly the JK was not the best solution for this kind of use.

The JK was an attention, technique and effort demanding car for driving it. No action was meaningless.

Reverse engaging required a special technique: move the shifting lever to halfway in the second or fourth gear channel and then engage it, in order to avoid gear clashing and the unpleasant noise there of. This was caused by the faulty clutch decoupling most samples had.

The clutch pedal required effort to be pressed and since the clutch was strong, a certain sensitiveness was needed to obtain progressiveness when moving from standstill.

The gearbox, in spite of precision and smoothness, clearly demonstrated to like precise and delicate operation, improperly reacting to rude action.

The brakes also required pedal effort.

The gas pedal had not a convenient position and in spite of making fast driving easy, caused discomfort with time. By the way, the floor-pivoting pedals were not convenient either.

Steering was heavy and required skill and muscles. The needed power to steer with a standstill car was higher than an average man's and insisting to continue invariably caused damage to the steering box

Another bothering detail was the front vertical visibility. When stopping at any signal placed slightly higher than usual, reading became impossible, especially at traffic lights.

The doors were heavy to open and hard to keep that way when uphill; the side windows were small and the elevators did not work well.

The trunk was roomy, but as it happens with all large cars, day-to-day use was inconvenient.

For all what was said, the FNM was not ideal for the daily use of an average driver, although not unfeasible.

Yet the driver ever willing to drive, the FNM 2000 was always ready to demonstrate its virtues and to respond with precision the action it required.

On the road

In the early 1960s there was one option only for people who wanted to travel in a fast and safe car: the JK.

To face it, there were a few imports only.

Those of American origin were efficient in good roads, but these did not exist here. In more tortuous roads they were too slow, although competent in comfort.

Even among the Europeans, a few were apt to face the JK in a direct comparison. Automobiles like the Mercedes-Benz family sedans, for example, were not nimble in our roads that demanded constant speed varying. In spite of not too

It was on the road that the Alfa Romeo's mechanics made difference: a good engine; five speeds, in a time four were already a plus; running on radial-ply tires and with the suspension tuned for high speeds, besides brakes with cooling, were the guarantee of much superiority, especially when compared to other national cars.

Tuning for sporty use punished somewhat passenger comfort: its suspension was slightly harder than other luxury sedans'. It was also a little smaller than its competitors and the low roof took off part of the room feeling. Engine tone was pleasant, but the car was not quiet. After a long trip, the driver could feel somewhat tired, a result of heavy controls and poor body support provided by the seats.

rarely safely attaining top speed higher than the JK's, they accelerated, braked and recovered speed with more difficulty.

Without any doubt, for the standards and conditions of the time, the JK presented itself as a grand routier, a road master, since the driver was willing to meet all the requirements the model imposed.

The JK's main virtue was "sincerity". It communicated the driver its limits and warned what attitude to be taken. It "refused" to overtake with the wrong gear, for instance.

The five speeds were a resource to be explored.

Despite that on the road clutch and brake are less frequently used and the steering wheel weight decreasing with speed, at the end of trip the driver would feel tired.

The pleasing engine tone, after hours, really caused certain stress (no one knew what it was about then), as well as gas pedal location – that made the right leg to remain in a inconvenient position – caused muscular discomfort, that could be felt even after the trip.

They who traveled much could only opt for another sedan if "driving obligation" represented a heavy burden.

For those who did not travel much and were used to double-lane highways, the services of the JK could be dispensed.

For these roads, American and European sedans were as competent as and more comfortable than it.

The FNM 2000 and I

Of the most important models in private automotive history, some Alfa Romeos outstand, yet those of the FNM 2000 and FNM 2150 deserve a special place.

The car models I have a more remote remembering are the Volkswagen Sedan 1200 and the JK, respectively my mother's and my father's cars in the first half of the1960s, therefore from my first years of life (I was born in 1961).

The FNM 2000 had the most complete instrument cluster ever among all national cars. As well as the other controls, they were proper of the best European sports cars. Any child would de fascinated! A good driver would get the best out of it!

The JK fascinated me much more than the Volks. Larger and full of instruments, to ride in a JK gave many a magical moment.

The two speedometers (one was not a speedometer, but the rev counter), by itself, already led my imagination to voyages far more distant than the wheels of the car could do.

The true speedometer displayed speed through a horizontal scale where a magic red slipped. When I grew up I understood it working, simple enough by the way, in spite of many adults having childish fantasies about it.

My father sold his last JK probably in 1968 and, from then on, he always referred to the model in a missing mood.

Even when produced, the JK was a car hardly seen on the streets and even my alert eyes seldom spotted one.

In 1974 the Alfa Romeo 2300 was introduced and again we had a car of the brand home, a direct descendant of the JK.

Years went by, I grew up (I received the driver license) and the fascination for the car, a ghost that in fact could not be seen even in the junkyards, only increased.

In the late 1980s, the Brazilian antique car movement expanded.

It vertically expanded, for static auto exhibits earned volume and importance for the preservation of cars already worshiped was increasing, as well as the traditional.

It expanded horizontally, for automobiles that were being forgotten began to be preserved. Dynamic exhibitions of antique cars – in form of racing or even second-category rallies – were novelty and became frequent. In these rallies, automobiles from the 1960s and early 1970s, i.e., those that only then were granted the *status* of antiques, were the majority.

National cars no longer were treated as "trash", although still despised, and started to be admitted in spaces.

I then started to participate in antique car movements, especially those speed-related.

The second more antique car I bought was a 1967 FNM 2000.

After years without seeing one, two blocks away from my office I met the one that would be my future FNM 2000. It was in good condition and for sale.

With this car I took part in all kind of antique car events, several times.

I also used it for trips and daily use.

I have restored it more than once.

As time went by, I used many tune-up recipes.

Briefly, my understanding about this car kept growing, including reading material. With few automobiles I reached such a degree of intimacy and I have many picaresque stories about it.

I have entered in many races, with wins rightly scored. I have taken part in several rallies, where arriving first was missed by little. In hillclimbs too, for successive years we held the record for Brazilian cars.

In circuit racing

There were much participation with enthusiastic disputes and, not rarely, class wins.

However, at least once an overall win fell to my hands, after disputing with automobiles of very superior category in expected performance. Of all, this is the one that better illustrates the potential of a JK.

It was a race restricted to cars conserving certain degree of originality – that were not uncharacterized and maintained "civilian" use characteristics.

Few modifications were allowed.

Different categories would gather in a same grid.

Together with my 1967 FNM 2000, a 1963, 1,600-cm^3 Porsche 356; a 1970, 5,700-cm^3 Chevrolet Impala and a 1972 FNM 2150 would fight for the checkered flag. Also in this grid many other cars were positioned, ranging from a 1974 Mini Morris (a super compact) to a 1958 Oldsmobile Ninety-Eight (over two tons heavy).

My JK had some FNM 2150 parts fitted.

The engine was a 1969 2150's. In this model-year compression ratio was 8.25:1 – like the European's – instead of 7:1 of all Brazilian-made Alfa Romeos. Additionally to this model's bigger displacement and higher compression ratio, the cylinder head was cut 2 millimeters (to further increase the compression ratio) and the carburetor was recalibrated.

The brakes were from the 2150 also, with discs up front.

The other FNM in the grid had Alfa 2300's engine, brakes and suspension, as well as the Porsche had front disc brakes too.

In spite of the modifications, the fact is that the cars were suitable for daily use only and regained the vigor lost throughout the years. After twenty years, for sure there was in these cars – that had no spare parts available any more – plays and frictions.

The only modification that resulted in real gain in performance in relation to the original models when new was that at the tires.

The JKs rolled out from the assembly line with radial-ply tires, the Cinturato Pirelli CF67 175-400. The "400" referred to wheel diameter in millimeters (400). A very few automobiles had tire size with rim diameter in millimeters (in Brazil, the JK and the Renault Dauphine/Gordini/1093 were the only ones) and the tire for JK was hard to find even when the car was produced. In the 1980s and 1990s they were definitely phased-out, therefore to be able to use a JK it was necessary to go 15-in. wheels and use the tires accordingly.

In the mid-1980s, low-profile tires started to be manufactured here. The 195/60-15 were the more appropriate for the FNM, because combined with the Alfa Romeo

2300 differential it resulted in the same engine speed to vehicle speed relation. The same top speed would be attained at the same engine revolutions.

Another option of tire was to use the 14-in. wheel, but for this purpose the whole set of brakes and suspension from the 2300 had to be also used, the solution adopted by the FNM 2150 that disputed first place against mine.

I do not remember the starting order, which was done by chance, however I recall well my expectations: I thought the Porsche would be invincible and that the FNM 2150 would fight for second with me.

Right at first lap, upon braking for Bend no. 3 of the old (and the original) Interlagos circuit, I was surprised to overtake the Porsche.

In entering the Curva do Sol (Sun Bend), a long right, high-speed bend – that in the case with the JK could be made flat-out (no lifting off) – my JK misfired, cutting the engine for moments. I immediately lifted-off and gave way to the 2150, which had overtaken the Porsche also.

After this, the car worked perfectly until the next right bend – Laranja's (Orange's).

I was worried and thought about retiring, but at the Subida dos Boxes (Pit Hill) I overtook the 2150 again, crossing the finish line first.

When contouring the Sun bend, again the car misfired and when crossing the finish line, I was first again.

In Interlagos, at the Ferradura (horseshoe) bend of the old circuit, with my 1967 FNM 2000. Behind me, the 1972 FNM 2150, runner-up in the race. Our first races are meaningful. Those we win, unforgettable. In spite of the car presenting a failure that spoiled performance, victory came. The antique Alfa Romeos had always been excellent partners in motor racing.

At this point I was already aware that the car's engine misfired on right-handers, however it was faster in other sections of the circuit.

In the Sun, the FNM overtook me and the Porsche got closer, but my car had more breath elsewhere, including at Pit Hill, where it was impossible to bar me from overtaking.

I started to be more relaxed, for in spite of losing first place at the Sun bend, in all laps, I had recovered the lead before the finish line.

In the last lap, after being overtaken by the FNM 2150, I noticed that in my tail it was not the Porsche, but the Impala – 5,700-cm³ displacement and, therefore, theoretically, much faster than me at the Hill.

I did my best on the inside of circuit, but right-handers were fatal. That big American sedan, supposedly unsuitable for low speed bends as Interlagos' insiders, succeeded in keeping up with me.

I entered the Junção (Junction) bend that leads to Pit Hill with the Impala very close, however with more momentum. I expected the engine "to speak out louder", but I did not bother to look back. I went to overtake the FNM 2150 and a back-marker Mercedes-Bens 230 S. Only after that I checked the mirror.

To my surprise, the Chevrolet was way behind: the JK's five-speed gearbox had provided an enormous advantage over the Impala's three-speed automatic and, even displacing less then half, the FNM could be superior.

Amazing! How could a four-cylinder national car of the 1960s/1970s and seating up to six passengers to overcome a Porsche (a sports car) and an American V8 of the 1970s? By the way, runner-up was another FNM, with the Impala in third and the Porsche in fourth place. Yes, the Brazilian Alfa Romeo was fantastic.

In 1990, soon after inauguration of the new circuit design – much more short-radiused and slower than the former, therefore less favorable to heavy and long wheelbase cars like the FNM – I took part in another race.

I knew beforehand that the JK's potential was not the same, however I again started hoping for a good result.

In addition to mine, two JKs – much more souped-up – were in the grid, more permissive respectful of originality than before and even in this circuit design that demanded more braking and good speed recover after bends (an there high weight is a very negative factor) and finished first and second.

The problem of engine cutting in right bends had been cured already (the pick-up tube – responsible for "sucking" fuel from the tank was to blame), but in this race the clutch was slipping.

The state of São Paulo has always been a great "exporter" of used cars, especially the larger and more luxurious ones. Rio Grande do Sul state, on its hand, always imported this kind of vehicle. While the people from São Paulo counted on just one speedway in the 1970s, those from Rio Grande do Sul had two. "Noves fora" ("Casting out nines" in Portuguese), cars such as the FNMs went on the streets and the racetracks of the South for quite a longer period than in São Paulo. In 1999, in a classic car race, I had the chance to feel how good it is to drive a FNM Timb in Tarumã (Rio Grande do Sul). As always, this Alfa Romeo's behavior in circuit was impeccable, but what marked me most were the cheering fans.

I had nothing left except the satisfaction of setting best lap and watching two other FNMs (both 2150, '69 and '70 model-year) to win the race, a demonstration that the JK defied the logic that indicated that its layout was unsuitable for this kind of circuit. Best lap in the 7,960-km long original circuit, even with the engine cutting, was 4min09s and in the new, 4,309-km one, 2min31s.

To drive the JK in the racetrack was a fascinating experience, that numbers and results, even those of a win, can not express.

The engine-gearbox unit works with precision. In no point of the circuit the engine "gets fooled" – without pulling power – as if it needed a gear that does not exist.

Gear changing is a pleasure. The gearshift, even steering column-located, allows total precision of movement and synchronization is just perfect, including on downshifts, in spite of the sports concept saying it should be floor-mounted.

The brakes work well and even in the "post-1990" circuit design, very demanding in braking, there is no fading.

On bends, the car shows an almost neutral behavior, although past the limit is the rear that breaks out (oversteer).

Steering is too low for track driving, besides too heavy. In spite of this, driving is precise.

At the end of a race lasting not more than one hour, arms, as well as legs, are tired. Arms, from turning the steering wheel and legs, from trying to restrain the body in the bench seat. Without a seatbelt it would be absolutely impossible to drive. The driver would end up in the front passenger zone in the first bend.

At the wheel of a 1968 Timb, the sporting version of the FNM 2000 – produced between 1966 and 1968 – had individual front seats and floor-mounted gearshift, a higher compression engine (8.25:1) and room for fitting quadruple carburetion (dealer

Before the race in Tarumã, the cars are exhibited in Porto Alegre (RS). A 1967 2000 and a 1968 Timb, side by side, full of stickers, drew much attention. A beautiful picture.

installed), green-tinted rear window and smooth engine hood, besides other minor changes – I also took part in races in Interlagos ("post-1990") and in Tarumã (RS).

The mechanical differences from this Timb to the FNM 2000 were restricted to engine. It kept the original FNM 2000 crankshaft (the same as Timb's) but piston came from the Alfa Romeo 2300. As a result, displacement raised from original 1,975 cm^3 to 2,142 cm^3 (the 2150, with a different recipe, displaced 2,132 cm^3), carburetion was quadruple and it had hotter camshafts fitted.

In these two races I entered with it, the grids were quite heterogeneous, consisting of far better performing cars and many inferior to the Timb.

What I could experience at the wheel were sensations quite similar to the ones I had with the less spirited version.

The individual seat restrained the body far better than the JK's bench, but only this would loose the comparison with the Timb: the floorshift allowed a slightly better handling and the engine, more powerful, performed a little better.

In the practice session, the Timb lapped better in 2min30s in Interlagos, therefore 1 second quicker than the 2000. However, on the average of all laps, it was far quicker.

In Tarumã, it defeated several highly-modified DKWs (of the carretera class, with fully-modified bodies) and lost by very small margin (it won some races) the faster Italian Alfa Romeo gtv's – a grand-touring –, proving its qualities in more than one circuit design.

In hillclims

Annually organized in São Paulo, the Jaraguá Peak hillclimb is open to antique automobiles that start one at a time, against the clock.

The steeply route is 4,380 meters long, through a really tortuous road that take to Jaraguá Peak, in the São Paulo city surroundings.

A

B

A) The Pico do Jaraguá hillclimb, in the outskirts of São Paulo City, is the oldest antique car racing event in the state of São Paulo. The JK has not a very adequate profile for it: a family sedan for six has a long wheelbase and it is heavy. In this race the JK surprised: while the rules called for cars produced until 1974, the record for sedans was mine: first, on a 1967 FNM 2000 and years later on the Timb. In the first photo, a 1974 Alfa Romeo GTV 2000, between the 1968 Timb and the 1967 FNM 2000, high on top of the peak. B) The moment of race start.

In this hillclimb the JK's high weight is a burden. Even with all the engine elasticity and the excellent gearbox staging, when nearing the end of the route bends and grade get harder, second became too short and third too tall.

Interlagos, 2004 – Through the Alfa Romeos I met many people and won many friends. At the track (in motorsport) I managed to mix the word rivalry with colleagueship, companionship and friendship. Starting from pole position (the grid was determined by chance), the friend of the photo (FNM 2150) took the lead, with in second with the Timb. I held the position until the Lago bend, where I spun. There were much and many faster cars and the spinning anticipated the loss of position only.

Until 2002, no other family sedan, even imported, did the elapsed times I registered at the wheel of the FNMs.

In rallies

The same speedometer that fascinated me when I was a child and thrilled me by fulfilling in red almost the whole scale (180 km/h), at the old main straight in Interlagos used to display more than 160 km/h, showing precision, as well as the other meters when in second-category (average speed, not sheer speed) rallies. In this kind of competition we must verify its reading that only looses in importance to the odometer.

A good rev counter may help and the JK's proved to be excellent when in one rally the speedometer stopped working.

Besides its good instruments, the JK was always able to accomplish the assigned average speeds. When it came to overtaking, its acceleration always met the driver's intentions; when there were many bends, it did not lack roadholding.

In brief, the JK was apt to win rallies.

Even when the speedometer was gone (it was first and only time, although it could not be in the worst moment) the "second speedometer" (the rev counter) did the job my child imagination imputed to it. If the odometer did not fail after a few kilometers, I certainly could not have won this competition, but I would be quite nearer the front rather than back runners (as I eventually was).

In exhibitions

The same FNMs that won races were also awarded prizes in concourses d'elegance and could only have won and were prized for having undergone long restoring processes, and they were even completely disassembled.

The disassembling/assembling fuzz, together with regular maintenance, revealed the construction details that resulted in virtues and faults of this Alfa Romeo.

Structure was in fact reinforced. It was not supposed to have torsion in hard use or fatigue with the passing years.

The FNM was the king of the road. When I was a kid, as a child escort of my father, I dreamed about driving one. Later, in the pre-adolescence, I started imagining how cool to drive this Alfa should be. Time went by and the FNMs seemed ever away from my life. The wish was fulfilled in 1988 only, when I bought the 1967 red FNM 2000. I only learned about the Timb after becoming an antique car enthusiast. I have been driving these cars for years and my enchantment is ever increasing!

In suspension: springs, arms, fixing points and all components were robust and clearly dimensioned for high performance that, however, did not adjusting resources.

The engine, additionally to the aluminum cylinder head and the sodium-filled exhaust valves, did not save in materials for connecting rods, pistons and especially the forged steel crankshaft.

Crankshaft and flywheel were heavy in order to provide the necessary low-end torque to push a six-passenger sedan, whereas the cylinder head lodged large-diameter valves for good high-speed breathing.

This combination enabled easily sustaining high speeds, for after the engine gained momentum, it could easily keep high revs. This contributed to the JK being a road master.

Now, this same combination was responsible for engine harshness it came to overcoming its own inertia, that once overcame counted on combustion chamber design quite suited for high engine revs.

The brake drums were mammoth, hence the need of using 400-mm – or 15.74-in. – wheels, as mammoth was brake pedal effort.

The body was well built, however the locks not always worked fine and the steel blanks used, as well as the lack of anticorrosion treatment, were one of the responsible for the almost total extinction of the model.

Heavy structure; heavy suspension, heavy rear axle; heavy brakes and heavy powertrain, therefore very heavy a car for a four-cylinder.

Heavy at the scale and heavy to drive.

Torsion-free structure; sophisticated and over-dimensioned suspension; big brakes with finned drums; noble materials; sports design of engine guts, therefore an automobile made for speed.

ANOTHER OPINION

In Brazil of its time, the JK was 10 years ahead of competition. It was an import, and of the good ones, except that it was made in Brazil. There were those that tried to scorn its image by saying it was an old design, that did not succeed and because of this it had come to here. But regardless of the clear campaign against the JK, it is a fact that it was an exceptional automobile in 1960 and in the following years. If we mentioned a current car brand that corresponds to the spirit of the JK, just one: BMW. They who had the chance to drive it when brand new is over 60 years old now, but it remains indelible in memory a collection of sensations that would never repeat in Brazilian industry, with the exception of the Chevrolet Omega, built from 1992 to 1998. Both JK and Omega were conceived for the European environment of sweeping roads and long highway stretches where people usually travel at high speeds, especially on the unlimited-speed German *Autobahnen*. The two cars were created for those who know what an automobile is about and enjoy the pleasure of driving. The JK was attractive inside out, from engine to finned aluminum brake drums, going through the five-speed gearbox, in a time four seemed to be the limit.

TECHNICALLY CORRECT

Looking at the engine, for those that like automobiles, was like looking at a piece of art. One could feel the smell of a racing car in the air, with the double valve covers, one for each camshaft, and the spark plug right on the middle of them. It was a 2-liter, 115 hp gross/95 hp net at 5,400 rpm, but that would easily zoom to 6,000 rpm, that was always in the right rpm band thanks to the Italian-style gear staging, i.e., exact.

There are two things that the Italians always do with utmost precision: gear staging and gas and braked pedal arrangement for easy, no-contortionism, simultaneous operation of both with the right foot – the *punta-tacco*. It is evident that this touch from Italy was in the JK. Even the column-mounted gearshift, in a first glance strange in a car of this lineage, was not any problem even when going at the limit. In fact, in the several endurance races it participated, this has never been an obstruction. Another meaningful fact of the JK introduction was the radial-ply tire that made the cross-ply ones belong to the Jurassic period. The higher rigidity of the tread, due to the belt (hence Cinturato, belted in Italian, the name adopted by Pirelli) at the tire periphery, produced certain harshness on uneven pavement, such as the usual cobblestone of the time. Many people criticized the harshness, even attributing it to the car, but for the purists it was nothing but a detail.

TECHNICAL INFORMATION OF FNM 2000

VEHICLE	FNM 2000 1960 to 1968	Timb 1966 to 1968
Type	4-door sedan, 6 passengers, front engine and rear drive	*
	Chassis and body	
Type	Unitary, steel	*
	Engine	
Type	Inline 4-cylinder, cast iron block and aluminum cylinder head, water cooled. Double overhead camshaft (DOHC)	*
Mixture formation	1 double-bbl 30/34 staged carburetor	*
Bore and stroke (mm)	84,5 x 88	*
Displacement (cm^3)	1,975	*
Compression ratio	7:1	8.25:1
Maximum power (SAE)	108 hp at 5,700 rpm or 95 cv (DIN) at 5,700 rpm	122hp (SAE) at 5,700rpm ou 105hp (DIN) at 5,700rpm
Maximum torque (SAE)	15.9 m.kgf at 3,200 rpm	19,3 m.kgf a 3.900 rpm (SAE)
	Transmission	
Type	5-speed manual, synchronized, and reverse	*
	Brakes	
Type	Single hydraulic circuit, no powerbrake	*
Front	Drum, finned aluminum	*
Rear	Drum, finned aluminum	*
	Suspension	
Front	Independent, unequal upper and lower triangles, coil springs	*
Rear	Rigid axle, coil springs	*
	Steering	
Type	Worm and sector	*
	Dimensions and capacities	
Wheelbase (mm)	2,720	*
Lenght (mm)	4,710	*
Width (mm)	1,700	*
Height (mm)	1,452	*
Ground clearance (mm)	170	*
Fuel tank (liter)	60	*
Curb weight (kg)	1,360	*
	Wheels and tyres	
Type	Steel wheels and radial tyres	*
Tyre size	175-400	*

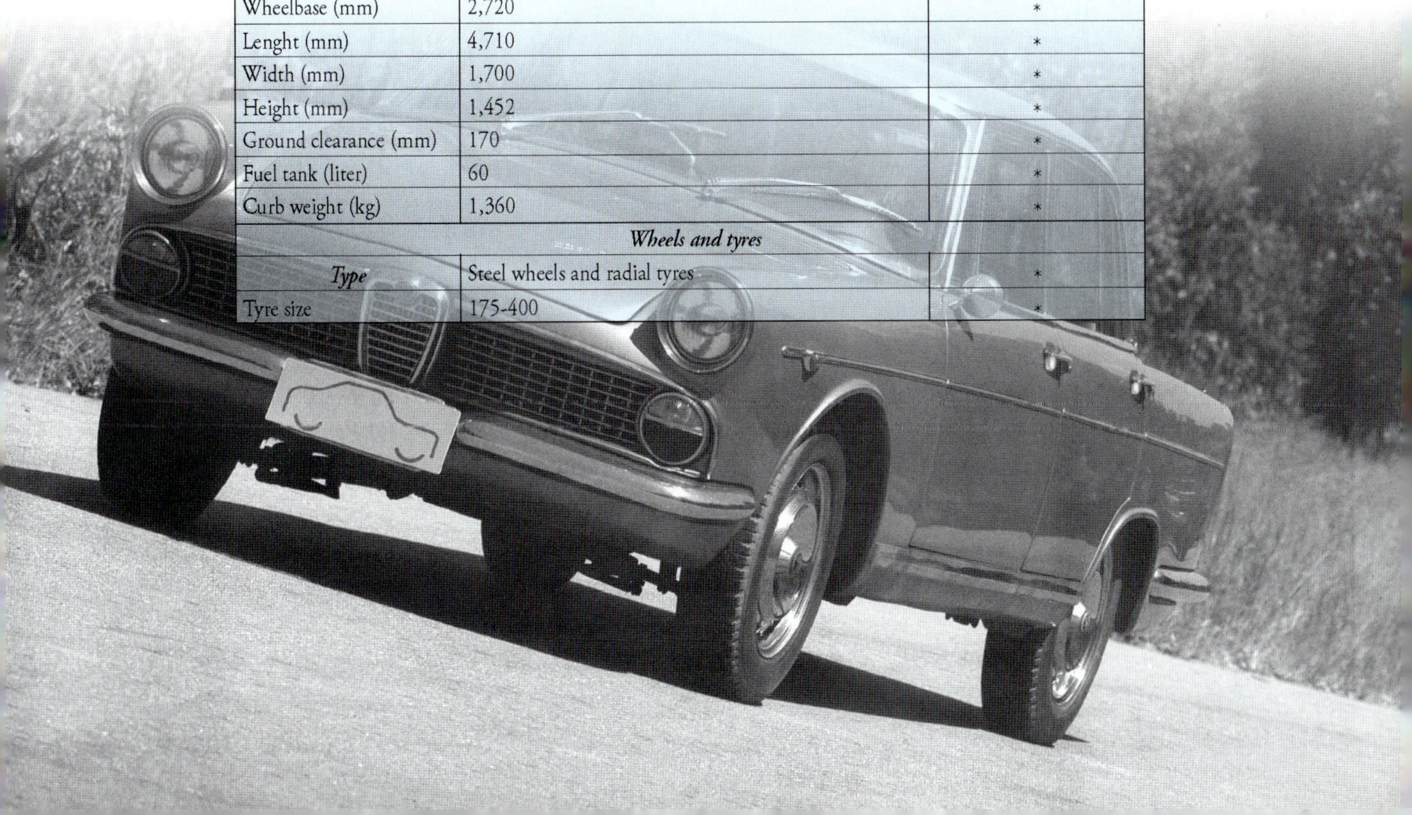

CATEGORIA
TRADIÇÃO
FNM-2000

modêlo JK

Categoria... a de um carro que é fabricado com precisão, arte e orgulho profissional... que oferece o confôrto do carro grande... a economia do carro compacto e a perfeição mecânica do carro esporte. Tradição... de um carro que resume a experiência internacional da Alfa-Romeo... um carro fabricado e montado dentro dos mais exigentes padrões. Realmente, o FNM-2000, modêlo JK é um carro à parte, uma jóia na mecânica e na apresentação - o máximo que v. pode desejar quando pensa em automóvel. Afinal, o FNM-2000 é um Alfa-Romeo, líder mundial na fabricação de carros de classe.

■ Motor com duplo eixo de comando de válvulas no cabeçote - Potência de 95 c.v. (SAE 122 H.P.) - 100 km com 10,5 litros de gasolina - 160 km/h de velocidade - Tambores de freio de alumínio com aletas de resfriamento e revestidos internamente com ferro fundido - Suspensão por molas helicoidais.

Um produto da

FÁBRICA NACIONAL DE MOTORES S.A.

— sempre a melhor qualidade em veículos para o Brasil!

Aero-Willys 2600 (1960 to 1967) and Itamaraty (1966 and 1967)

The Aero-Willys was the third and last of the large national automobiles to be launched in the pioneering phase of our industry and also the one with greatest commercial success. Before it the automobiles of the Simca range and the "Alfa Romeo" FNM 2000 JK were launched.

The Aero was neither the best looking, nor the fastest not even the most sophisticated, however it was the most practical and better suited to that moment.

Willys-Overland do Brasil was purchased by the Brazilian Ford in 1967, yet the Aero's production was extended until 1972. In 1973 the factory replaced it with the Ford Maverick.

In spite of having its life extended by the hands of Ford, the Aero, as of 1968, began gradually to lose representation *status* in the market, for its competitors belonged to a younger, with more potential, generation.

The early youth of the new competitors still guaranteed a loyal public for the car, already mature enough and free from the inherent faults of recently launched automobiles. At that time, the first years of production were seen with a lot of distrust by the consumer, after all the models used to suffer from some chronic problems, besides always being launched in less sophisticated versions.

The Aero-Willys line, among the pioneers, was the last to be launched. In the beginning it faced the Simca in equal terms, but it soon turned more adequate to the taste of the Brazilians. It has reigned with large car status until 1967, when more advanced models were introduced. It remained in the market until 1972 with no great strength, repositioned via lower prices for the medium-large segment dispute.

The Aero-Willys, therefore, has lived its best and more significant days in the first phase of our industry, when it had as direct competitors, among the large sedans, the fragile Simca and the JK, a car of public and production very restrict.

Indirectly it had its market "bitten" by smaller-sized DKW-Vemag automobiles and by the Chevrolet Veraneio, a mixed use station wagon, derived from the brand's work vehicles.

The model introduced in 1960 integrally preserved the lines and solutions of the American Aero Ace, launched in the early 1950s, which did not know any commercial success and, therefore, was short-lived, until 1955 only.

In 1962, the Z-shaped side trim that divided the car in two "inexact halves" of colors, what was conventionally called "skirt and blouse", was replaced by a straight one at full side, leaving the vehicle with a more elegant look.

Following World War II, some automakers bet that the United States would buy more rational cars, less exaggeratedly sized and more efficient. It was not what happened! They wanted larger and more powerful automobiles. The Aero did not work out and Willys bet in the Brazilian market. In spite of being well dimensioned for our market, the lines of the first Aero-Willys seemed too unpretentious to offer large car prestige.

In 1963, a total restyling, a job 100% made in Brazil, according to Willys, since the design was absolutely identical to the one made for the 1955 Ace – never launched in the US – gave the definite basic form that has lead to the car's success until its last days.

The first national car to undergo complete restyling process was the Aero-Willys, in 1963. The new design was very modern indeed, especially for featuring a quite larger glass area and straighter lines. Some excesses were commited: flaps over the headlights, too long; leaning rearwards taillights and too much trim, did not please. In 1864 model-year they would be corrected, redone or removed.

In 1964 the design underwent some retouches and the gearbox was four-speed, all-synchronized now. Up to then it was three-speed, with a "hard" first gear. Engine power output was raised also. Therefore, from then on, the Aero definitely consolidated its success. It was the first large-size national car to conquer confidence of the consumer.

The Aero's technical development went on parallel with its most direct competitor, the Simca, for even keeping the three-speed gearbox, earned the synchronized first gear in 1962.

There was a restyling and the adoption of more powerful engine in 1964 with the Tufão (Typhoon) line, and later, in mid-1966, a new restyling and the Emi-Sul were to be introduced. This engine – yet at the end of that year – would power its substitute, the Esplanada.

Adopted solutions and practical results

The name Aero was a reference to the unitary construction, the same kind used for the World War II aircraft. It was also allusive to the nearly streamlined design of the model.

The unitary construction spread in Europe soon after the conflict. At that time, in the US, the automobiles, more than ever, were exaggeratedly sized with maximum compromise with comfort. The technology in the search of more mechanical sophistication and efficiency was relegated to a second plan and, therefore, the American cars continued to be built with separate chassis and body. Aerodynamics also did not draw consumer attention, whose eyes were more aimed to lines that looked somewhat like rockets than to those that meant efficiency.

In spite of the American origin, the Aero had a unitary-construction body, but is dimensions were not exaggerated at all and neither its lines were thrilling.

Even if the different technique for the chassis, the practicality of its design and the car's size did not assume any compromise with wasting, the Aero was equipped with a quite rudimentary powertrain and suspension system, which did not do any good for a superior dynamic behavior but, however, were extremely robust components for household use. As for fast driving, better not even to think of it.

The engine, brought from the Jeep, was brilliant at low revs and free from problems of bad working, since one did not try to sustain high speeds. In fact, to be used – later, in the 1970s – in the Ford Maverick, it had to undergo several changes and even so it did not work out. Valve location stayed in middle of the way, between the new and the old – exhaust valves were in block and intake valves in head, as in the more modern engines. As modern does not accept "half", the engine maintained behavior that of the old ones, i.e., no vocation for high revs and poor mileage in a trade-off for excellent working in idle speed or in low engine revolutions.

Since the engine is the heart of the automobile and defines by itself vocation, the Aero, to be coherent, should have a docile engine in low engine revolutions that could even ignore high ones.

Suspension "almost" in nothing suffered with the bad care from the very bad paving then, but it would be far from desirable in a race.

The brakes were also capable of accomplishing the ordinary tasks, without causing fright or panic, but, as the rest of the car, they were not adequate for high speed and hard use. In these conditions they would certainly loose efficiency, beside not ensuring a balanced path.

A) The same engine as the Jeep's, which proved to be efficient for hard work, was incapable of sustaining the same concept when powering a touring car, even if for that purpose it counted on one more carburetor. It was an inline six and its layout contemplated in-block exhaust valves, a solution surpassed for long that privileged low engine speed working, but severely limited higher ones. B) Dashboard design up to 1962 was very straightforward. In 1963, with wood fittings, it would earn more grace and sophistication. In 1964 its design would change again, improving readout quality. To release the reverse gate with the four-speed gearbox, a little button at the far end of the gearshift had to be pushed.

Front suspension was independent and used coil springs, as in almost all post-war cars. Rear's was also the usual rigid axle with leaf springs.

The gearbox column shift, until 1963, was a three-speed, so common a system that it as conventionally called universal.

When a four-speed gearbox was fitted (the first ever 100% design of a gearbox in Brazil), there a was button at the end of the handle that, when pushed, released the lock for unintended reverse engaging and enabled doing it. It was not top in precision, but it did not compromise either and was adequate for the whole system. The gears were extremely short, in that as of 30 km/h the car could go in fourth with good response for lively acceleration. Again, it was coherent with a car that was not compromised with speed. The clutch did not slip and the pedal effort, if far from being light, was not that heavy.

Usually nomenclature contemplates first make and then model. Whenever there is a numerical reference, this lies at the end normally. In the case of the Aero-Willys this order was not respected.

Steering was very slow (many turns were required for little actual steering), for it was not power-assisted. This way, it was not so heavy at low speeds or too sensitive when going fast. Evidently, it privileged again everyday use, not fast driving.

The 13,5-meter minimum turning radius pointed that the car was not suitable for maneuvers, however it was acceptable considering its size. The system by worm and sector was absolute then and in heavy cars (like the Aero) remained that way for a long time.

Urban driving

As with all large cars, the Aero's daily urban commuting in a big city could be the best thing. In the case of the Willys, always taking its size (4,80 meters overall length) into consideration, it was not the worst.

High seating in relation to other cars resulted in a very pleasant sensation of looking at the occupants of other cars from a higher level. Visibility was also privileged and certainly no one would be claustrophobic or feel oppressed in traffic aboard an Aero.

The toughness of the suspension and the car's as a whole transmitted to the driver a feeling of strength and power.

In a utility, the action of entering the vehicle requires first to go up, then sit; in a passenger car, on the contrary, it is necessary to squat first and in the Aero – a very tall car – it sufficed to sit. Its seats were ideally located in height for doing it. In short runs comfort in entering and exiting makes a difference, as well the excellent door operation, somewhat rustic that seemed not to require gentleness, also pleased.

The starting from traffic lights was reasonable, nothing outstanding, but it was not slow either.

Yet clutch, gearshift, brakes and steering controls were heavy or imprecise for driving in the city, causing certain exhaustion to driver after a day of "stop and go'.

The engine always worked fine and provided good performance in expressways where the speed limit was 80 km/h.

In household living situations like going to the supermarket, the trunk had good capacity. Evidently it was very lengthy and required certain "diving in" to retrieve the goods purchased. Opening and closing the lid was easy, although as in any large car, it demanded more effort and a more ample action. Literally, by Physics, it meant more work.

A) Even updated in 1964, the lines of the Aero-Willys reminded that of the mid-1950s. B) The taillight, in spite of discreet, remained vertically mounted, integrating the rear fender design. C) Trunk had an excellent space, yet the spare wheel spoiled a better distribution. To accommodate bags and goods it was not too practical, but it was big enough for the luggage of the whole family.

On the road

Without the least compromise to driving pleasure, the Aero could deliver great satisfaction in taking the family to the road with comfort and mechanical dependability.

Going out from São Paulo (SP) to a first visit to Iguaçu Falls (state of Paraná) was a common motoring those days and, for sure, the Aero was one of the favorite models for this route.

The first lodging city was Curitiba (PR), where at evening there were some restaurant options to enjoy.

This initial 400 kilometers stretch was ran on the BR-116, Régis Bittencourt road, whose nickname excuses any other reference: "Death Road". Single lane, twisty sections, very bad paving, meteorological conditions not always favoring visibility or the best traction and, especially, heavy vehicles traffic far superior to road capacity.

To be able to take this route with the family was already victory and, since there was no hurry, the Aero could accomplish it with no fright, except those inherent to luck.

Evidently, the Aero's speed had to be well lower on the wet. Its traction and braking were extremely affected, therefore caution and reduced speed were absolutely obligatory elements then.

Regardless of road surface conditions, patience on overtaking. Not that the Aero accelerated poorly respectful to the speeds of the trucks attained then, but it was advisable to abuse on the car's roadholding, braking included. To wait the right time to overtake and then do it, avoiding surprises and emergency maneuvers – as good habits determine – made more sense than ever.

On an empty stretch, the Aero was easy to drive. Its controls responded to the action of an average driver with the necessary response and precision.

Cruising speed of 100 km/h could be achieved since momentum was not lost. Going uphill amid curves, the speedometer indicated something around 60 km/h.

Shortly before reaching Curitiba, the road became straighter and flatter and, just to relieve stress, it was possible to run a few kilometers "biting" 120 km/h, a speed that could be considered high for the time and for the car. It was more than enough to overtake small cars.

From Curitiba to Iguaçu Falls it was a shade above 600 km in single-lane roads and highly bumped paving.

Suspension ended winning the struggle with the asphalt and passengers could count on the extra comfort for being sit on cushions far from floor and, therefore, with a good angle for the legs, besides the seat backs being high enough for a good back support.

The driver, after 600 km in a car whose controls were not that smooth and whose roadholding required extra attention, certainly would be tired.

In the US, Willys had no more market to go, changing hands several times. It came with "body and soul" to Brazil, where it sustained its brands and invested in product until 1967, when it was acquired by Ford.

In Iguaçu Falls, the region's touring booklet was accomplished in three days, including a visit to the falls at the Brazilian side; the visit at the Argentine side of the falls which could not be done by car; and the Paraguayan side, with no water falls, yet with shopping and casinos.

The Aero's comfort and the visibility, once again, helped to compose pleasant moments.

The way home could be done by the North of Paraná, passing by Londrina. The region was a very rich agricultural one, however it offered little in touring terms. For this, it was not uncommon to do it in one day. In this route the roads were well more straights, although the Castello Branco was yet to be built.

To take the same route outbound was an option also. A stop in Vila Velha (Old Village), in Paraná or in the Caverna do Diabo (Devil's Cavern) yet in São Paulo, could be a plus.

The trip concluded, the pleasure of having crossed new borders. Pleasure at the wheel, almost none. The Aero was an authentic touring vehicle.

The Aero-Willys and I

Little contact I had with the Aero, either as a passenger in the years it was produced or as a driver, when years after I got my driver's license I became an antique car aficionado.

When I was a kid, in the Aero-Willys years, my father's family who lived in São Paulo was well-divided in terms of cars: an uncle drove a Volks; another one, DKW's; the third, Aero's; and my father, JK's. Another uncle of mine drove a Rural or a Veraneiro, in Rio Grande do Sul.

I remember very little motoring on the Aero with my uncle, for in 1968 he traded the Willys for a Ford LTD automatic. He had a problem with his left knee and an automatic transmission was not only recommendable, as it would represent part of the cure.

At this time the Volks's uncle improved his garage – in lieu of the Volks, an Aero "underpants blue".

Two things that fascinated me in automobile, I had them in the Aero: a beautiful dashboard with two circular meters, one of them the speedometer that, in the case of the Willys, the scale read 160 km/h; the other was the height I was sit in, that enabled me to peep inside other cars, so that in some cases on the road I could even read their speedometers.

A) Latches and handles worked fine and had a rustic design. Upholstery was done in synthetic material of very plastic look, yet resistant. B) Rear seat passengers found sufficient room, besides counting on magazine pockets and ashtray, in a time smoking was not politically incorrect.

In fact, my experience with the Aero has always been minute, however I got to know other models of the Willys family that shared with it some common parts. From 14 to 25 years old I usually went to a farm where the service vehicle was 1963 long wheelbase Jeep. It was a long Jeep with two sideways rows of benches in the rear section, a very rare model nicknamed Bernardão, maybe a popular homage to the city of São Bernardo do Campo, where it was produced.

Visual identity was not a brand concern, yet the Aero's frontal grille maintained the same design as the Rural's. It rendered some lightness to the whole. The Aero-Willys had never attracted my preference as an automobile. The more I discovered the car's characteristics, the less I felt enthusiastic about it. In a way, the more I understood its purpose and reflected about Brazil in that moment, the more it won my respect.

Cross-ply tires, so common they were, used to be called conventional. The design of the hubcap was a straightforward one and harmoniously integrated to that of the wheel. The ten well-sized windows were assigned the mission of taking fresh air to brakes.

The engine of the Jeep was the same as the Aero's and demonstrated aptitude for work and little breath for traveling.

In 1988 I bought a 1967 Willys Itamaraty. The Itamaraty was a plusher version of the Aero and had the same underpinnings, except for the engine enlarged to 3,000 cm^3, and the same body except for décor finesses. The Executivo model was the Itamaraty limousine and, in spite of peculiarities inherent to the model, I learned quite a lot about the Aero.

As for the direct Aero competitors, the Simca and the JK, I had a greater intimacy.

All these experiences, peripherals to the Aero, made me to respect it quite a lot, for I began to understand that it was the first option of a large national car really capable of "putting Brazilians on wheels", thanks to its simplicity and dependability.

The unattractive driveability did not trigger my interest in buying one, at least until 2002. I am aware that I am not a regular automobile consumer: if I was one and had the necessary resources (and age) in the 1960s, this would have been my car.

ANOTHER OPINION

The Aero-Willys was unique. But not in the good sense, as the initial affirming may seem. Excluding the unitary construction, it was the quintessence of the old. It did not go very far in its country of origin, but as a function of our atypical market and of the dampened demand, it even achieved some notoriety and even commercial success. It was awful to drive, it served more the purpose of carrying people with some comfort and slowly than efficiently and with a good dynamic behavior that mark good designs, even those contemporary ones. It was said at the time, as a joke, that even the best driver became a bad driver at the wheel of an Aero-Willys. Brake and clutch pedals pads were strangely circular, and the pedal rods went through floor. Even when honking by pressing the horn ring, a semi-circle pointing down, was weird, one had to move the torso a little bit to achieve it. It was a "large car" at its time; today it would be nothing but a medium-size sedan. The fact of being "large" has helped its sales in Fusca, Dauphine/Gordini and DKW-Vemag times.

As of 1963, the pedal pads were no longer circular, but pedals continued to sprout from floor.

TECHNICALLY CORRECT

The Aero-Willys has always been an automobile one can call basic. Not for equipment and comfort and convenience items, but for its constitution. It was a car launched in 1960 but it might as well suggest that "suddenly it's 1950": it moved backwards.

The inline six-cylinder engine, which at a first glance would be a plus, revealed it self not. It put out 90 hp gross only (some 70 hp net), one of the lowest specific output around, 34/27 hp/liter gross/net.

It really could not do much with its "F" head – intake valves overhead only, for exhaust's were in the block.

It does not help to let in a great amount of air-fuel mixture, exhaust gases must go out easily, untrapped also. Later on, when the four-speed gearbox was introduced, a very little improvement for first was turned too tall and fourth, as direct drive as the previous gearbox, was maintained.

When driving it one noticed that gear ratios became too close, numerically speaking, for the engine characteristics, a true "close-ratio" gearbox.

TECHNICAL INFORMATION OF AERO-WILLYS

VEHICLE	Aero-Willys 1961	1962	1963	1964	1965 and 1966	1967 to 1972
Type	4-door sedan, 6 passengers, front engine and rear drive	*	*	*	*	*
	Chassis and body					
Type	Unitary, steel	*	*	*	*	*
	Engine					
Type	Inline 6-cylinder, cast iron block and cylinder head, water cooled. Overhead intake valves and in-block exhaust valves (F-Head)	*	*	*	*	*
Mixture formation	Single bbl carburetor	2	2	2	2	2
Bore and stroke (mm)	79,37 x 88,90	*	*	*	*	*
Displacement (cm^3)	2,638	*	*	*	*	*
Compression ratio	7.6:1	*	*	*	8:1	8:1
Maximum power (SAE)	90 hp at 4,000 rpm	110 to 4,400	110 to 4,400	110 to 4,400	110 to 4,400	110 to 4,400
Maximum torque (SAE)	18.8 m.kgf at 2,000 rpm	19.4	19.4	19.4	19.4	19.4
	Transmission					
Type	3-speed manual, non-synchronized first and reverse	*	*	4 forwd speeds syncho	4 forwd speeds syncho	4 forwd speeds syncho
	Brakes					
Type	Single hydraulic circuit, no powerbrake	*	*	*	*	*
Front	Drum	*	*	*	*	*
Rear	Drum	*	*	*	*	*
	Suspension					
Front	Independent, single upper arm and lower A-arm, coil srings	*	*	*	*	*
Rear	Rigid axle, semi-elliptical longitudinal leaf springs	*	*	*	*	*
	Steering					
Type	Worm and sector	*	*	*	*	*
	Dimensions and capacities					
Wheelbase (mm)	2,738	*	*	*	*	*
Lenght (mm)	4,700	*	*	*	*	*
Width (mm)	1,828	*	*	*	*	*
Height (mm)	1,593	*	*	*	*	*
Ground clearance (mm)	170	*	*	*	*	*
Fuel tank (liter)	72	*	*	*	*	*
Curb weight (kg)	1,410	1,446	1,446	1,446	1,446	1,446
	Wheels and tyres					
Type	Steel wheels and cross-ply tyres	*	*	*	*	*
Tyres size	6.45-15	*	*	* *	*	6.45-15

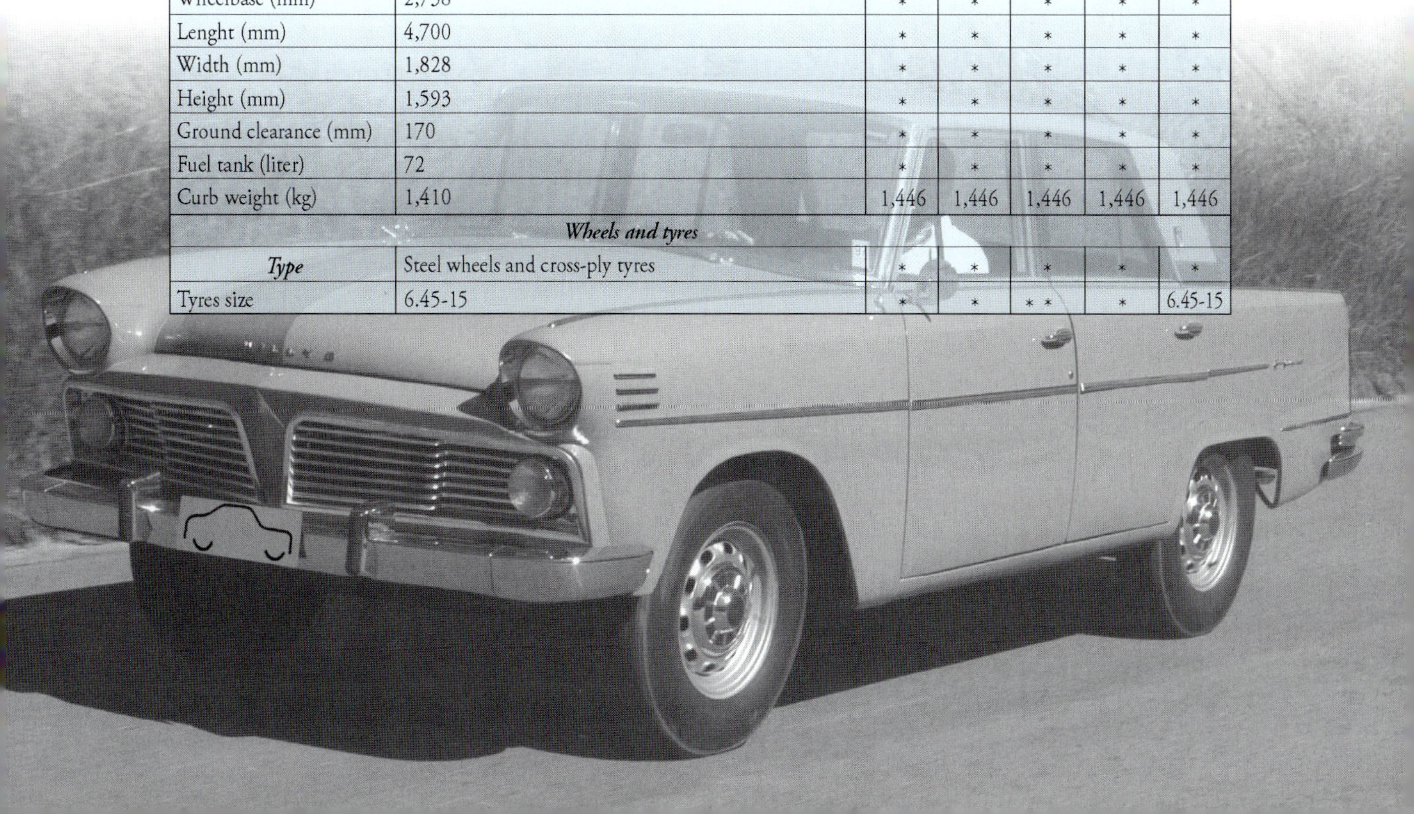

Não é atoa que dizemos que o Aero-Willys é o carro dos homens bem sucedidos.

Quando dizemos que o Aero-Willys é o carro dos homens bem sucedidos, estamos apenas repetindo uma verdade corriqueira.

Se não, responda: qual o carro dos seus amigos que estão progredindo na vida?

Qual é o carro que, quase sempre, ostenta as chapas douradas dos Tribunais de Justiça, dos Ministérios, das Assembléias Legislativas, das Secretarias de Estado, Prefeituras, etc.?

Qual é o carro grande, fabricado no Brasil, que você mais vê nas ruas?

Não precisa responder o óbvio.

A razão dessa preferência é simples. O Aero-Willys além de bonito, luxuoso e sóbrio, é resistente. Muito resistente. Inspira total confiança. Você sempre pode contar com êle. Pessoas que alcançam sucesso na vida são dinâmicas e ativas e não podem perder tempo em oficinas.

A propósito: qual é mesmo o carro que você vai comprar?

Aero Willys 67 — Produto da Willys-Overland – Fabricante de veículos de alta qualidade.

Simca

Series: First (1959 a 1962); Três Andorinhas (1962 to 1964);
Tufão (1964 a 1966) and Emi-Sul Series (1966 e 1967),
models: Chambord; Présidence; Rally; Alvorada; Profissional and Jangada

The first automobiles put in the market by Simca of Brazil probably were imported, but immediately, through obscure ways, were considered locally-made. Introduced in 1959, the Simca Chambord is the first model of a large, luxury car officially produced in Brazil.

Many charges were filled for irregularities in the Simca "national" production, so in the following year it possibly began assembling in Brazil its cars of the European, Vedette line, but with parts brought from the mother company. The cars remained identical to the French models.

In 1962, when there were no more doubts about the local production, they were named Três Andorinhas (Three Swallows). At that time, the Simca lineup presented three versions with distinct finishing e motorization: the Chambord, which was the basic one with the basic engine, a single 2-bbl carburetor; with a second carburetor that assured superior performance, the Rally was the sporting version, and the Présidence, the model of more prestige and representation. In the middle of the year the Três Andorinhas line was prized with a welcome improvement in the gearbox, where the three speeds were now all synchronized. Such evolution received the name 3 Sincros to the model range. In 1963 it was time of the station wagon version, called Jangada, that shared the same engine with the Chambord and had its own finishing.

The Chambord was the best-seller of the Simca lineup. Its design was US Ford's, but it was retouched by Simca in France. There were many details, adornments and color matching. The Três Andorinhas line was the first to earn some "Brazil" touch.

The Tufão line, successor of the Três Andorinhas one, counted on powerful and dependable engines. The design underwent retouches, featuring some more modern lines. The extra "horses" were welcome. The Jangada Tufão station wagon would end being not faster than a Três Andorinhas sedan. The added mass by the body represented a very big burden for a still insufficient engine.

Yet the base Chambord was a luxurious vehicle at its time, what enabled Simca to launch a "naked" version for the model, the Alvorada, which was planned for services like taxi.

In 1964 came the Tufão (Typhoon) line to replace the Três Andorinhas one by the same models, except the "nacked". Which would be replaced by the "depilated" Profissional (Professional). The Tufão line improved on quality, power output and structure over its antecessors.

Much more powerful, in 1966 the line Emi-Sul was launched, dividing room with the Tufão's in Simca's option range, with the same models.

The first Simcas were slow, lousily adapted to our conditions and short of dependable. The Três Andorinhas line was real evolution in relation to the pioneers, as for performance, finishing or dependability, while the Tufão line represented more a decisive evolution. As for the Emi-Sul, although fitted with a more powerful engine and several times superior in operation to the Tufão, suffered from reliability problems that would resuscitate the recently-asleep "ghosts" that circled the cars from the Simca range. "Frightening" that had recently put in bed with the "Tufão's lullaby".

Used technique and practical result

The design was born at the US Ford and the car would be aimed to that market. At the time, Ford bet that soon after the war, the local consumption trend would fall in smaller sized cars and with engines quite more modest than what was on the pipeline, as in fact would happen as of 1950. With this in mind, it was the way this was dimensioned, that has never been built in the US and ended being so by Ford of France. At that time, American cars guaranteed *status* at Paris streets and, looking for this market, Ford set for producing a "mini American car" in France.

Ford France and the factory were bought by Simca, which has put a half American styling for the automobile, now without the Ford nameplate and called Simca Vedette. Success did not come. Simca's solution, as to make the investment feasible, was send the car and its tooling down to Brazil.

The history of the Brazilian Simca denounces its technical solutions and puts in evidence its practical results. The Simca was an automobile rationally sized and weighted for a large car and was powered by an engine short of its needs.

The Simca mixed some very advanced concepts for the time with quite outdated others, like the engine, the heart of an automobile, was.

Among the advanced ones are standing out the unitary body construction – more sophisticated than separate chassis and body, more common then – and the McPherson front suspension, another advancement respectful of what went on in the world. Together, these features were responsible for the healthy structure and a relatively low vehicle weight.

Although the rear suspension was by semi-elliptical leaf springs and rigid axle, alike most American cars from the time, its work in tune with the body and the front suspension was very good. The weight do deal with was lesser.

The brakes, even by drums all around, were efficient, for they had a large swept area and a system with two brake cylinders per wheel up front (patented under Twimplex name), besides counting on, once again, with the roadholding provided by a good front suspension a less exaggerated weight.

The steering system, by worm and sector, was absolute at the time. For not featuring any power assist, steering was heavy, but less than its competitors'.

The three-speed only gearbox was insufficient to make a car of its size and power more briskly.

On models up to 1962, first gear engagement was difficult for it was not synchronized, causing certain inconvenience in city driving.

What was less pleasing in the whole car was the engine, a V8 displacing 2,300 cm^3 only that would be enlarged to 2,500 cm^3, but ever insufficient for a sedan

It was a small-displacement V8, 2,351 cm^3 and 84 hp gross. At an "archaic" conception, with side valves, it was brought to Brazil under the "Aquillon" name. In 1962, in the Três Andorinhas (Three Swallows), with 2,414 cm^3 displacement, it would put out 90 hp gross. In 1963 horsepower would increase by 5 hp and, in 1964, the Tufão (Typhoon) would achieve 100 hp. Externally, small details identified the Três Andorinhas and Tufão engines. The oil cooler, featured for the Tufão only, was one of them.

The Simca interior was not deceiving. The upholstery looked good and the design was refined. As in the outside, it was full of small adornments. Even with rubber mats, the Utilitário version, the simplest of the Jangada, did not compromise trim and frames.

of its size. Its design included side, in-block valves – an outdated solution – that would be replaced for the Simca line 1966 model-year, with the launching of the Emi-Sul engine, a lot more powerful but as little dependable as and so a gas guzzler as its antecessor.

The car's layout was always the same: front engine and rear-wheel drive.

The design of the body favored an excellent relation between inside room and size of the car (4,75 meters overall length). Like many automobiles from the early 1950s, body height was reasonable (1,45 meters) and the legs of the occupants laid in an angle well close to vertical.

Internally, the Simca followed the pattern. Front seat was bench type, enabling the seating of driver and two passengers, totaling six passengers rear seat included. At the time it was the classic, after all families were greater and gathered to go out, besides lifts being commonplace in a time a very few owned a car.

Except in the Alvorada and later in the Profissional, seat upholstery denoted quality and extra care with fabric design combinations.

To aid the driver, the dashboard featured a nice instrument cluster, with more meters than usual then. It had a clock and trip counter, besides the almost compulsory speedometer, odometer, and meters for water temperature and fuel. Yet, there were warning lights for fuel reserve, headlights or parking lights on and to alert that choke was in use, more the conventional for high beams, battery charging circuit and oil pressure.

Even announced with overconfidence, the Simcas did not deceive in performance. Brilliance came through the Emi-Sul line, yet the pretension was ever present. The speedometer scale exaggerated and grew beyond the engine "horses": until 1964 it was 160 km/h; with the Tufão, it was extended to 180 and with the Emi-Sul, 200. As for other parts, the instruments did not change and conserved the same design. The Jangada Utilitário, as well as the Alvorada and the Profissional, the more basic sedans of the family, did not feature direction controls for dynamic and forced cabin ventilation, inexistent resources in these models.

The main controls – parking and headlights, turn indicator, two-speed windshield wiper and horn – were stalked at the steering column, indicating a trend of the 1970s that would become a rule in the next decade. However, the location was not that practical, making impossible quick and automatic action for the driver's hands.

Other controls like cabin vent, both forced and ram, instrument light dim, choke and trip counter reset were well positioned.

As said above and adding to conventional, there was a switch for horn tone – city or road –, besides a parking light of the kind found in many European cars (one side only, that of flowing-by traffic, remained lit). The turn indicator featured automatic return to off by an electric timer instead of the traditional mechanical system. These were equipments that brought charm and comfort, but were responsible also for more maintenance.

Gear changing followed the pattern of the time that, as a rule, had the gearshift column-mounted. The pedal set, already of the hanged type was universally used today, was convenient and well-located.

A) Any innovation deserved a new badge, to be integrated to bodywork as a decoration motif. Even the lock had a cover. The Chambord Três Andorinhas, as well as its predecessor's, was a two-tone job. B) The chromed hubcaps covered the whole wheel, recalling the wire wheels with wingnut central locking, typical of racing cars of the 1950s. C) Its "fishtail" was the more pronounced among the national cars and its taillights the most exaggerated ones. D) In all, the look of the Simca promised a great car.

The car's ride was soft and quiet. Noises started to bother at speeds near 100 km/h, when the engine seemed to be delivering all it had to deliver.

Much more than for the inviting interior, the Simca impressed for its external look.

An American car retouched by French taste, in a time France still kept a certain finesse for automobile design, resulted in an extremely pompous car.

Temper

The translation of the national Simca regarding technique, results, its use or even its temper, goes, more than with any other automobile, through its history.

Created in the USA, where it was considered inadequate for the local market, it was "deported" to France, where it did worked out. The solution was to send it to south of the equator, with no changes at all in relation to the model made in the Old Continent. It looked like it would be a success, after all it did not lack pomp and the Brazilian had always been a good-humored and tolerant people. But, in the case of the Simca, the good humor brought many jokes, of which it became the victim.

To say that the temper of the Simca was that of the "Bello Antonio" – character of an Italian movie of the time that attracted all the women, but at the "H" hour failed – as one of the jokes attributed to it, would be, in all, unfair. Now, to say that the Simca was top in performance would be inappropriate. A hypocrisy!

The Simca was a car with family temper that did not deprive the driver of a more pleasant driving and, thanks to its look, it won respect. Nevertheless, it could leave any user stranded, without any warning.

Soon after landing in Brazil, the Simca became "orphan" of the mother company's attention, that only decided to demonstrate any interest when it effectively launched the Três Andorinhas series. Since then, the car went leaving the "Bello Antonio" behind, however it could never enjoy with plenty its conquering temper again.

Daily, urban driving

The styling at the "Jangada" badge show attention to details. Many, enchanted with such attention, were deceived by the mediocre performance or, even worse by having to push the car when it refused to go "on its own wheels".

The first start in the morning was easy. When cold, before reaching the ideal temperature, the engine of the Simca did not have the necessary power to overcome a more inclined ramp. However, once warmed up, it provided an adequate performance for dealing with the traffic of the time, but not to a car of its category. By the way, the engine of the Simca was at the bare limit, therefore only in ideal conditions it was minimally capable of accomplishing its obligations. This is an undeniable truth for the first Simcas, appliable to the Tufão series, but improper for the much more powerful Emi-Sul.

In any situation the Simcas were quite comfortable. The large glass area and the decor, welcoming and carefully made, added to the smooth and quiet ride. The ambiance was pleasant! With no power steering and slow to accelerate, the driver was the only among passengers that could have some stress in urban circuits.

The working of the engine was always smooth and quiet, as smooth were all controls, except steering. It was not heavier than the competitors' that did not feature power steering, on the contrary. Any car of its size requires many muscles and technique to be driven in city, when all actions applied at the steering wheel are transmitted to the wheels through mechanical means only.

The Simca's controls were very soft and well dimensioned, providing a good relation between effort and quickness, always taking the far from modest dimensions of the large car into consideration.

Before it had the first gear synchronized, the task of engaging first with the car running demanded technique and some patience. Slow and heavy traffic is tiresome by itself. The slower it is, more tiring and on many occasions it was necessary to engage first.

Once first was engaged, to move the car a certain attention to the clutch was necessary. Although it featured a progressive coupling and was not heavy at all, it was delicate and dimensioned below needs.

Already in motion, acceleration was weak and, until the car was released from inertia, the riding was lazy. In constant stop-and-go of large cities' traffic, the performance of the Simca seemed not to be ideal. Yet on expressways it did reasonably well, easily sustaining speeds near 80 km/h.

If the Simca performance was not convincing and its size and weight were exaggerated, the same could not be said about its comfort and functionality.

The ride was soft and quiet. The potholes of the very bad paving then went unnoticed and the Simca's seating were very good. The high seating of the occupants and the large glass area assured an excellent sensation. Inside room was more than enough.

Doors permitted easy access to interior, besides working ideally: they were not heavy and opened and closed gently, as well as latches and handles did a good job.

Trunk was spacious, but as in any large car, inadequate for daily shopping.

On the road

The Simca did not brilliantly accelerated nor recovered speed – except for the Emi-Sul series – but it was capable of sustaining good speed (something around 90 km/h for the first models and 110 for the Tufão), always riding smoothly. Roadholding was very good and the brakes were precise, however – although less than mostly contemporaries – they were prone to fading under hard use.

The "ghost" of overheating "frightened". In the first models it was a confirmed "passenger"; with the Tufão line it was occasionally present; and with the Emi-Sul it would show up in extreme conditions only.

Yet the "ghost" of fuel pump overheating never left the Simca in peace. Going uphill the Anchieta road between Santos (São Paulo state coast) and São Paulo

On the road, the most important was to loose not momentum. The Simca had a good roadholding and brakes. Inside room satisfied and the trunk had the best distribution of all, thanks to spare wheel location. In the station wagon, it was even better! Internally, frames and trim combined with upholstery, in synthetic materials, a pleasant ambiance. At the front fender was mounted the mirror, which could not be reached and adjusted from the driver's seat. In mid-1962, when first gear became synchronized, a badge that represented the "3 sincros" was attached at the side. Later on it would be replaced by "Tufão".

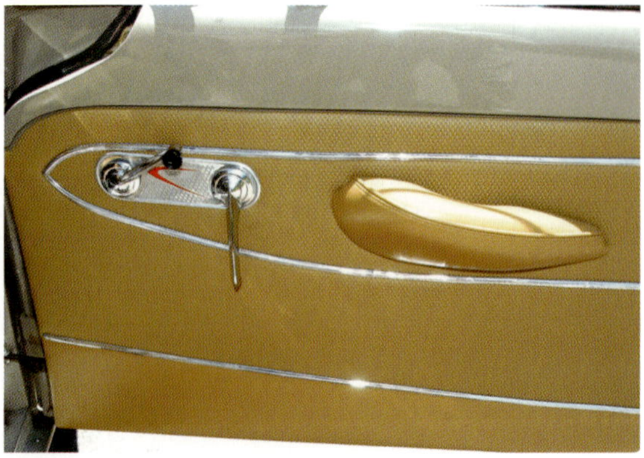

city (the state capital), there was a faucet where a great number of cars on the road made a stop to cool it and put more water in the radiator. Among the many that stopped there – of many brands, origins and countries – most Simcas traveling could be found.

In roads with less traffic and with not too steep a profile, the Simca revealed its virtues. Tranquility was a sensation resulting from the smooth it rode with and the safety transmitted by its roadholding and braking. Therefore, for a longer trip or in a not so stressing road, the Simca would be an excellent equipment, if it was not for the "damn ghost" of low mechanical dependability who bought one defied and, not rarely, was winner.

At the center of the front grille of the Tufão line there was a shield with two symbols of the brand: a swallow and the "S" letter. The grille was different before and the emblem, a styled "V", almost flat, laid in the hood.

To travel between São Paulo city and the former State of Guanabara (1960-1975), Rio de Janeiro city, was very usual.

The Dutra road, that links the two largest Brazilian cities, always presented conditions very diverse in traffic, topography or paving.

At the time, going out of São Paulo to know the "Wonderful City" was an excellent program for family during a "super holiday", those that added one or two working days to Saturday and Sunday. Heavy vehicle traffic – buses and trucks – was intense and speed recovering frequently required.

A household head that had a Simca could seat wife and three sons – children and teenagers –, besides all the luggage. In this condition, the performance of the Simca was compromised and momentum should not be wasted.

In sections with lesser traffic, the Simca overtook smaller cars and sustained good average speed. In the more full ones, it suffered a little, but even so it would not be overtaken by a Volkswagen or a Gordini. Yet a DKW might follow it.

The first Simcas had a small fuel tank, 55 liters, very little for a car with low fuel economy. Taking average mileage of 4 km/l into consideration, two fuel stop would be necessary. As of the Tufão series, the tank was enlarged to 85 liters, which enabled just one stop for refueling. To check water and oil, besides stretching the body and have a snack were the minimum care to take at least once during the route.

Leaving hush aside, the Simca was always comfortable and safe.

To go motoring in so charming a car was a reason for pride and conferred a special aura to the program.

The Simcas and I

Since when I was a kid, the cars of the Simca lineup have always fascinated me. I was enchanted, something like hypnotized, each time I spotted one, but since then I already heard that "this car is not worth a penny".

Then a Simca with the spare wheel over the bumper (Continental kit, featured for the Présidence model) went by, I asked myself in a low tone: *"Is this one not worth a penny either?"*

The same reasoning I did each time I saw a different model. How could so an imposing car be not worth anything?

Among my parent's friends and uncles, no one owned a Simca. I am afraid to say – after all it may be fantasy –, but I remember in one sole opportunity my father coming up with a Simca, I car I recognized by the brand, but not for the model.

This may have occurred in 1965 or 1966, therefore when I was very small, but I remember.

I recall returning from Guarujá to São Paulo one night and laying in my mother's lap, my father was driving. I think I remember my father saying that the car did not perform according to what he expected for a large car (at the time my father had a FNM 2000, or maybe a JK).

If this trip really happened, probably this Simca could have been lent for a "test-drive" (a term that did not exist then) and was not approved.

In 1967, therefore I was six years old only, the Simca was replaced by the Esplanada, what justifies my short contact with the car when it was still produced.

Since then, everything I heard about the Simca were the jokes.

When I started to be interested in antique cars, one of the first automobiles I bought was an Esplanada GTX, the last of the Simca descendants. I confess that I got surprised with its good performance, its brakes and roadholding, as well as its smoothness and comfort.

Later I purchased a 1962 Três Andorinhas. It had almost all the GTX's predicates, but it was frighteningly slow for whom expected a performance close to that of a GTX.

From the experience with the GTX I already knew that the fuel pump was to be replaced by an electric one, but I took long to do it. It was a mistake. The only thing that left me stranded at a street was the fuel pump.

Since the car had over 100,000 km on the clock and some dents here and there, I did a light restoration on it. With almost 40 years old, the Chambord, surprisingly, was not too rusted.

I overhauled the engine with big hope that its performance would improved. Once again I was surprised, for it was in a good shape with this mileage and its performance did not improve much.

A symbol of the make and other of Brazil, integrated in harmony. The name "SIMCA do BRASIL", with bigger emphasis than usual for the country name, was the frontal badge of the Simca Emi-Sul, a car that was proud of is engine developed in the Southern Hemisphere.

Adjustments, fixing and other adjustment. Its performance improved a little, but nothing that made a speeder out of the Simca, but it did improve a lot. A Três Andorinhas Simca with a perfectly tuned engine achieves the minimum performance necessary to keep up with traffic.

The first, non-synchronized gear, to be engaged with the car going, requires a technique called doublé-clutching – depress the clutch pedal, disengage second (or third), release clutch pedal, a burst of acceleration, depress the clutch pedal again and engage first. It seems more difficult than it really is.

For the rest, the car is pleasure only. Among the many antique cars I am used to drive, the Simca is the one that draws more attention, at least during the 1980s and 1990s.

Cheerful reactions were majority, but some of them had some joking. No matter what, it will awake thoughts that the Simca would be the photography, in automobile format, of a promising Brazil. Its showed a certain pomp, but did not have the strength to go ahead, nor the seriousness to be dependable, during the second half of the 20th century.

Another Simca I purchased was a 1965 Jangada Tufão station wagon, a kind of automobile that turned out rare. Its finishing was more Spartan, after all it was the utility version, simpler than the luxury's, that followed the Chambord's pattern.

More powerful the Três Andorinhas', the Tufão engine shows breath, but it is choked by the station wagon's higher weight.

As the condition of the Jangada was not brilliant to use it, a meticulous restoring started to be made. Meticulous and hard, for the construction of its rear section is complicated and requires hours and more hours of body shop work to be redone.

One of the parts that traditionally present fatigue in Simcas is the central column, especially in the Jangada. This Tufão was not exception to the rule.

Another thing I found out with her was that in spite of the foldable rear seat, making an excellent room for cargo, in this condition the driver's seat must adjusted so much towards the front that only a midget could drive the car without complaining about lack of room.

In special, about the Jangada I have in my memory that in my childhood, much probably from eight to ten years old, a neighbor owned one. Since the playground and the garage of the apartment building I lived mixed up, I remember that I liked very much the step that existed between the rear hatch and bumper. I could comfortably sit there.

The Simca station wagon featured the sedan's faults and qualities. Its development also followed in parallel. The taillights, which were the same, and side trim, that recalled those of the car, would also changed upon the arrival of the Tufão line.

Another remembrance is the Jangadas working as ambulances for the recently-inaugurated Israeli Hospital Albert Einstein. I was probably 12 years old and did not figure out how could a Simca be used in such a high responsibility service. Well, this hospital is an institution that proved to be serious enough and its actions would always deserve all credit, so...

ANOTHER OPINION

The Simca Chambord undoubtedly had a charm: the engine was a V8. It was something that only existed in the large American cars, something that denoted power. The brand was even relatively known in Brazil, where there were Simca 8 – clone of the Fiat 1100, produced under license of the Italian brand – and Aronde. V8 engine not in an American car was also known here, in the Ford Vedette, a product of Ford France that soon after would be absorbed by Simca in France. For this reason, there was a certain enthusiasm when it was announced that Simca would come to Brazil and that model would be powered by a V8. But deception did not take long to happen, the power output of 84 hp (gross) was insufficient for the expected performance.

TECHNICALLY CORRECT

If there as a factory that really committed to increase power output of the engines, it was Simca, pressed by need, of course. The company achieved rapid improvement of the engine, that ended putting out 112 hp – 33% over the original – without significant displacement increase, that from 2,351 cm³ went up to 2,505 cm³ (just 6,5% more), a huge feat. But there was something missing. Because of this, all the merit once again for having set for a radical solution, that of extensively modify the engine through new cylinder heads with hemispherical combustion chambers, that reached nothing short of 140 hp. The engine went

from outdated to advanced during the night. The aluminum cylinder heads had the valves in an angle, in a similar architecture to that of Chrysler's anthological Hemi engine of the time and that until today thrills thousands of owners of the new 300 C model. However, in relation to the early 84 hp power has climbed 67%, overstressing the crankshaft that, even worse, ran on three main bearings only. There were many engine failures, which would affect Simca's image for good. Not even when the company was in Chrysler's hands in 1967 it could do anything about it.

TECHNICAL INFORMATION OF SIMCA CHAMBORD

VEHICLE	Chambord 1959 to 1960	1961 1962	1963 1964	Tufão 1964 to 66	Emi-Sul 1966	Rally, Rally Tufão and Emi-Sul
Type	4-door sedan, 6 passengers, front engine and rear drive	*	*	*	*	*
			Chassis and body			
Type	Unitary, steel	*	*	*	*	*
			Engine			
Type	V8, cast iron block and aluminum cylinder heads, water cooled Side valves	*	*	*	Overhead valves	Same as Présidence
Mixture formation	1 double-bbl 32 mm carburetor	*	*	*	2xbbl 40	Same as Présidence
Bore and stroke (mm)	66,065 x 85,725	*	*	Stroke 88.03	Stroke 88.03	Same as Présidence
Displacement (cm³)	2,351	2,414	2,414	2414	2,414	Same as Présidence
Compression ratio	7.69:1	7.69:1	7.69:1	8:1	8:1	Same as Présidence
Maximum power (SAE)	84 hp at 4,800 rpm	90 hp	95 hp	100 hp	130 hp	Same as Présidence
Maximum torque (SAE)	15.5 m.kgf a 2,750 rpm	*	*	16.5	21.0 at 3,300	Same as Présidence
			Transmission			
Type	3-speed manual, non-synchronized first and reverse	*	3-speed synchro	3-speed synchro	3-speed synchro	3-speed synchro
			Brakes			
Type	Single hydraulic circuit, no powerbrake	*	*	*	*	*
Front	Drum	*	*	*	*	*
Rear	Drum	*	*	*	*	*
			Suspension			
Front	Independent, McPherson, coil springs	*	*	*	*	*
Rear	Rigid axle, semi-elliptical longitudinal leaf springs	*	*	*	*	*
			Steering			
Type	Worm and sector	*	*	*	*	*
			Dimensions e capacities			
Wheelbase (mm)	2,690	*	*	*	*	*
Lenght (mm)	4,720	*	*	*	*	*
Width (mm)	1,770	*	*	*	*	*
Height (mm)	1,450	*	*	*	*	*
Ground clearance (mm)	170	*	*	*	*	*
Fuel tank (liter)	55	*	*	85	65	55 and 85
Curb weight (kg)	1,215	*	* (Jangada 1,386)	1,290 (Jangada 1,365)	1,290	1,306 and 1,312
			Wheels and tyres			
Type	Steel wheels and cross-ply tyres	*	*	*	*	*
Tyre size	165-380	*	*	* *	*	*

NOVO CONCEITO DE LUXO E BELEZA NA MODERNA PAISAGEM BRASILEIRA

Combinando harmoniosamente sua aristocrática beleza com a superlativa perfeição de tôdas as suas partes mecânicas, o Simca Chambord provou – nas cidades e estradas do Brasil – que nenhum outro carro para 6 passageiros o supera em desempenho, confôrto, facilidade de manêjo, resistência e economia. Veja-o ainda hoje no Agente Autorizado Simca da sua cidade!

Sedan 4 portas. Estrutura super-compacta à prova de ruídos e vibrações. Possante motor "Aquilon" V-8. Suspensão "Stabimatic". Vidros e janelas panorâmicos. Espaçoso porta-malas.

SIMCA DO BRASIL

SIMCA CHAMBORD

– o carro de classe fabricado no Brasil!

From left to right and from fore to background: 1967 red Willys Itamaraty; 1967 silver Mercedes-Benz 230 S; !960 blue Buick Electra 225 Dynaflow; 1965 black Simca Tufão Présidence; 1967 black Willys Itamaraty Executivo; 1963 blue Chevrolet Bel Air. Among the Brazilian solutions, the Willys Itamaraty and the Simca Présidence, coming from Europe, a Mercedes-Benz S Class, symbol of prestige anywhere in the world, and a Buick Electra made in USA, a car for *status* even in the land of Uncle Sam. In the background: Itamaraty Executivo, the only limousine ever made by a big automaker in Brazil, and the Chevrolet Bel Air, although a medium-size car for the American standards, here, deservedly, it offered more *status* than the representatives of the brand.

Prestige and representation cars

(1958 to 1967)

Imports from USA; Imports from Europe; National: Simca Présidence and Willys Itamaraty

Before the establishment of the Brazilian auto industry, Brazil evidently "already ran on wheels", it just happened that there was not the option for a car "Made in Brazil", nor a favorable scenario to car buying.

Right at the beginning, the Brazilian industry launched big cars, however they all resulted of designs from mid-1950s that had not achieved much success in their countries of origin, hence the room left for imports. They were the only options for those who wanted, in fact, an updated and sophisticated automobile.

For having an imported car, high taxes had to be paid and, unlike the national one, it did count on incentives for commercialization. Even so, some of them landed here.

The rear volumes kept traces of the 1950s. Quite in an American fashion, all of them pursued the "fishtail" style. The Buick's, designed for the 1960 model-year, was the most pronounced one. The curved rear window was integrated to the Willys and Simca designs until 1963 and 1964, respectively, when they were restyled. In the Simca, the "Continental Kit" that reserved a place at rear for the spare wheel, drew attention.

Those coming from the United States, even when considered popular over there, down here seemed like big cars, they were objects of desire.

Some models also came from Europe. A few and always luxury cars, and very expensive. They were automobiles that featured the highest degree of luxury and refinement, rendering the biggest degree of representation to their owners.

When talking about sports cars, those from the Old Continent, for their greater sophistication, were the favorites.

As for the touring family cars, the Americans, with richness in finishing and in accessories, besides the wide range of choice, were the logical choice.

Another aspect that differentiated the Americans from the Europeans was price, far lower for the first ones.

The Brazilian auto industry revealed prodigious in developing its products, introducing modifications and improvements. The evolution of the "first harvest" was sensible and the models brought in experienced a stage of evolution never reached in the countries they came from, as well as sophistication, or more elegant versions, did not take long to appear.

Simca, in 1960, introduced the Présidence, a plusher version of the Chambord (of 1959). It had the same décor and luxury of the homonymous French version, which it descended from. In 1964, the Simca lineup was named Tufão (Typhoon) and the Présidence was then called Simca Tufão Présidence. Very much evolved in relation to the original, it was an authentic option for a prestige car, although it remained condemned by the fragility common to Brazilian Simcas. In 1966, the Emi-Sul line replaced the Tufão, with considerable improvement in performance.

In 1966, Willys-Overland introduced the Itamaraty, a version much more sophisticated than the Aero-Willys 2600 – a car that, in spite of being dependable, did not offer sufficient luxury to be considered an authentic representation vehicle.

In 1967, the Itamaraty began to count on a 3,000-cm^3 engine instead of 2,600-cm^3. So equipped, the performance significantly improved and, even without other qualities or the slightest intention to be fast, to drive it was much more pleasant. Yet in 1967, a limousine version was produced (25 units only). That year, Ford absorbed Willys and introduced the Ford Galaxie, an automobile considerably more modern and efficient than those of the Aero-Willys line. Therefore, the Itamaraty's *status* as automobile of representation was short-lived.

Fábrica Nacional de Motores (FNM) took a different way. Instead of a more sophisticated model in comfort accessories, it presented in 1966 a model with a more sporting accent – the Timb (short for Turismo Internacional Modelo Brasileiro). Simca had already made the same in 1962 when it presented the Rally (in 1964 it was called Rally Tufão).

Comparing the Simca Présidence and the Willys Itamaraty will result in very similar conclusions as to those about the more basic models of the brands, the Chambord and the Aero-Willys 2600.

Yet the imports presented a vast selection of choices. Undoubtedly superior options could be found, but for quite higher prices.

Vocation, by origin of each of them

When the subject was luxury or family car, several American models competed, besides doing it with a few European models, especially the Mercedes-Benz sedans, and with national top-of-line versions from Simca and from Willys, the Présidence and the Itamaraty, respectively.

Most models imported from America were larger, richer in comfort accessories such as power windows, air-conditioning, power steering and automatic transmission. Their engines were higher-displacing, had a minimum of six cylinders, when not V8, were softer and had a larger range of options than the Europeans', besides being easier to fix.

The models brought from the US were larger, with plenty of trim, badges, curves and chrome work integrated to body. The Europeans were far more discreet, although design took into account the American taste. Inside, the same observation: the Americans were loaded with all kinds of little ornaments and many convenience accessories, while those from the Old Continent were concerned with quality of materials, using leather and wood. For the mechanics: size, power and ride smoothness for the Americans, and efficiency, sophistication and driveability for the Europeans.

The Europeans adopted richer technological formulae and chose nobler materials for producing their luxury cars. They were well dimensioned and efficient – better roadholding, more fuel-efficient, better brakes, were more suitable for sustained high speeds and were better sized for Brazil's roads and parking spaces.

In relation to the national ones, both Europeans and Americans were quite more modern and sophisticated. Survival of national models, indeed, depended on super protection from the government, through very high importation tariffs.

The national car also counted on a trump: a patriotic feeling resulting from driving a national car, a different *status* from that of the imports, that ensured more pomp and transmitted an image of power and richness.

Solutions, applied technique and results achieved

In the "Made in USA" that existed here

American cars, by large, were conservative in manufacturing and made use of few complex solutions. Results were not rated for efficiency, but in final values.

Engines usually were "big", i.e., large displacement (large swept volume), while the technical recipe was, almost always, more straightforward.

As a result, a lot of final power output (lot of horsepower, hp), yet specific power output – horsepower per liter, which indicates efficiency – was quite low.

But torque (absolute power) was abundant from the lowest engine speed, when wear and tear are very low. This dispensed nobler materials and, as a rule, enabled low production and maintenance costs, besides long engine life, yet to the detriment of a lower fuel economy.

Roominess, smoothness and quietness were top in these cars. The pursuing for comfort was restless, even to the detriment of roadholding. The Chevrolet was much smaller, less sophisticated and powerful than the Buick, but it was much larger, more equipped and faster than the national Willys and Simcas.

At the wheel, such engines did not require much gear changing for driving, which tended to be smooth, as idle speed also was.

Since they had plenty of power, comfort equipment that absorbed it did not affect performance of the cars to a large extent, which seemed not to feel the "stealing" from the automatic transmission, hydraulic power steering and air-conditioning, items almost invariably present. Even the elaborated exhaust systems that consumed many horsepower to favor an almost absolute silence, could not spoil the immediate response from steeping on the gas pedal.

The engine was the heart of these automobiles – by the way, the engine is the heart of all automobiles – and the remaining of the vehicle respected and enjoyed its limitations and virtues, respectively.

For its power output, the engine required compatible materials and mechanisms. Only the much reinforced and heavy parts, or the ones made in noble materials (light and resistant), as well as a small number of parts subject to stress or pivoting mechanisms very well elaborated, would be prompt to do the combined work without failures.

Since the big American cars were produced in very large series, they clearly adopted the simpler and cheaper recipe, i.e., reinforced parts with the addition of many rustic material and mechanisms.

They had separated chassis and body (instead of unitary construction); front engine with rear-wheel drive; independent front suspension on coil spring and rear suspension by rigid axle on longitudinal semi-elliptical leaf springs; drum brakes all around; with servo; steering by worm and sector with recirculating balls, power-assisted; three-speed-only gearbox, either manual or automatic. Engines were inline sixes displacing approximately 4,000 cm^3 or V8s displacing over 4,500 cm^3, which could go beyond 7,000 cm^3, always with the camshaft in block and overhead valves (OHV).

Invariably, the most powerful versions were the V8 powered ones and the especially more powerful customarily made use of the same recipe: four-barrel carburetors by means of quadrijet carburetors instead of single or double-barrel carburetion, commonly known as bijet, as well as high compression ratio, which required high-octane gasoline, which was tinted blue in Brazil.

As dealing with weight was not a problem at all for their engines, the cars had oversize dimensions and also did not spare space: to offer it to the occupants, an enormous body sufficed. There was room to spare for everything and for everybody.

Automobiles with non-integrated chassis and body are always heavier and less suitable for light units than those with unitary construction. Nevertheless, their construction is a lot cheaper and more than one body is possible. Front engines with front-wheel drive do not provide better space usage, although it is the classic layout and the case of large automobiles. Technically, they constitute the best solution (besides the fact that space distribution does not matter much). The adoption of leaf springs for the rear suspension and the rigid axle do not entail high performances, but in heavy automobiles they are rewarding for the lesser maintenance need.

With the technology of the time, efficient disc brakes for powerful and heavy automobiles were rare, while drum brakes, since counting on power brakes, even if not as powerful as the disc's, could require little brake pedal effort and would loose to disc brakes only under hard use. Besides, the kind of tires used, always cross-ply, privileged smoothness, being little efficient regarding balance during braking or any other situation, as well as the suspension. The engines with a very high torque and the extremely soft suspensions, together with the tires that favored comfort to the detriment of roadholding, did not require more than three speeds for the transmission, and the manual versions could not always be faster or to feature better vehicle driveability than the automatic ones.

Steering systems by worm and sector were absolute until the 1980s for large automobiles and, in the case of most American cars, had exaggerated hydraulic assistance and high gearing (fewer steering wheel turns for much wheel steering), therefore they were light and quick – excellent in maneuvering to the point of making unnoticed the car's dimensions and weight, however they were the worst imaginable and even dangerous for high speeds.

And the engines were very strong, quiet and low-maintenance, although little efficient in fuel economy.

It was all in the name of comfort. The long wheelbase enabled an extremely soft ride and excellent driveability in long, wide and straight road, scarcely existent in Brazil in the 1960s.

Added to quietness and smoothness were the comfort equipment (air-conditioning, power windows and seats etc.).

Even more, size and richness conferred safety sensation and respect attitude towards the occupants.

All emphasis given to comfort could only result in automobiles extremely comfortable, pleasant to be appreciated both at the wheel – since the sports driving was deleted from the menu – and as mere passengers.

The ones we imported from Europe

European continent countries still suffered some trauma of the war economy they were twice subjected in the first half of the 20th century.

The mentality of the people that lived with the general lack of resources made out of the search for efficiency and its related results a religion.

Their automobiles reflected these aspects, but the largest consumer market for luxury automobiles was the American one, which did not settle for "misery".

Therefore, the luxury European automobile from the mid-1950s to halfway the next decade was, in spite of some undersizing, a mixture of efficiency with the right to some excesses.

Their engines had no big displacement when compared to Americans', however as time went by and with the war years way behind, they increased in cubic centimeters. Final power output did not reach, neither would not, on the average, that of the American cars, but the automobiles were customarily lighter and aided by superior transmission systems.

An European car, even luxurious, could be powered by an engine of six cylinders maximum and displacing not more than 2,500 cm^3, not for some exception that confirmed the rule, in that it could near 4,000 cm^3.

For the engine, noble materials like cast aluminum – instead of cast iron – were used in the construction. Aluminum was usual for the cylinder head, when not for the block also.

Instead of the camshaft remain in the block with overhead valves (OHV), it was always in the cylinder head (SOHC, single overhead camshaft) and, many times, it was doubled (DOHC, double overhead camhshaft).

The conquering of the American market demanded concessions, yet the European car did not loose focus in efficiency and functionality. The bodies were designed with better space usage possible in mind, as well as in the mechanics the key-word was performance. The paid price for the sophistication found in a European luxurious automobile was well above the power, size and equipments of an American "big car".

Since they were more efficient, they worked in higher speeds and, for such, they needed gearboxes with at least four speeds, one more than in most American cars. If they could not be considered economical, for they should power luxury automobiles at high speeds, when compared to American cars they were in fact.

In order to reduce the weight they had to transport and provide better road-holding and driveability, their construction were always unitary. Classical solution of front engine and rear-wheel drive was customarily used, and showed as the most efficient for large automobiles.

Invariably, front suspension was independent as the American cars' were, and the rear one always designed with coil springs and, in many cases, it was independent. In the American cars it was always by rigid axle and almost always with semi-elliptical leaf springs.

Some European cars were fitted with disc brakes and radial-ply tires, yet it was usual to be imported with cross-ply tires and drum brakes.

By the way, for a long time, independently of where they were brought from, the cars came without tires. In their place, "wooden tires", that would be changed upon disembarking by national tires, because importation of tires was not allowed.

In the car's interiors, not very rarely, uholstery was made in leather and there were fittings in prime wood in several panels, a solution that differentiated them from the American cars, where the ample fitting of synthetic material was the rule.

The body was far better designed respectful of space usage, as well as better were almost all results in efficiency obtained by a good European sedan when compared to an American. Yet the absolute results were discussable and met different tastes.

Among the relative results, the amount paid for an American automobile was infinitely more inviting than the expended for one of the Old Continent. One could get a lot more for the same amount of money.

The Itamaraty was launched in 1966, the year the Présidence was discontinued. Respectively originated from the Aero-Willys and the Simca Chambord, they embodied the virtues and faults of less sophisticated versions. The recipes for making them more sumptuous and fast followed different concepts: Willys went for the practical and Simca, the pleasant.

The ones made in Brazil

Our first large automobiles were the result of automobiles designed by the mother companies in the early 1950s, and they very little evolved when compared to cars from abroad, both from Europe and the US form the early 1960s. During World War II the car barely evolved and, in the period immediately following the conflict, new designs still derived from those before the war, therefore, they embodied an absolute outdated technology. It was in the mid-1950s that true evolutions took place and the technological level really leaped ahead.

The Simca Présidence had a V8 of American origin from the early 1930s. This engine had side valves, a system abandoned long ago. The Willys engine derived from the civilian Jeep launched after the war, with overhead intake valves and side exhaust valves, a mid-term of dubious efficiency.

Therefore, both engines bore an old architecture and displacing around 2,500 cm^3. They were obsolete even when compared to Americans, who did not care for cutting-edge technology and had engine displacement close to the European's. Evidently, they could not provide reasonable performance or fuel economy comparable to the imports'.

In all other aspects, the mechanics remained quite alike the Americans', with quite similar solutions, except for the structure, which was unitary. Dimensions were close to that of the European cars. These top-of-line versions adopted a décor rich in adornments and chrome work, typical of the American cars', and inside they blended the americanized synthetic with prime wood and leather.

The Simca Présidence and the Willys Itamaraty were not exclusive designs, born to be prestige cars. The found formula to make compatible consumption reality with the national production of prestige and representation cars had lead to an upgrade of models of the large-car segment. Despite they could not, as a whole, be comparable in efficiency or in final result with the imports, the fact is that Brazilian conditions were not alike the western world powers'. The scenario in Brazil demanded rustic and practical automobiles, as the locally-made were.

Performance

The American imports were faster than the European ones in accelerating from standstill and recovering speed, but these had, in general, higher top speed and more facility to sustain it.

Where there was room, be in urban ways or in highways, the Americans were matchless; yet in narrow roads or in a tiny town street the Europeans were nimbler.

In a country like Brazil where even those tiny streets were rare, the Europeans earned prestige for performance, although they could not fly-off beside an American car without being left way behind, but really way behind.

Yet the national samples, even less powerful, were capable of adequate speeds to the Brazilian streets and roads.

Practicality and habitability

There was one real advantage for the Brazilian cars, this was practicality. They counted on easy service and, at that time, even those that came from the First World needed it.

Another advantage of the national cars was size. In spite of not being as plush as the imports, they seemed more prepared to survive in the Brazilian "urban jungle".

The European cars suffered from maintenance, for there was neither skilled technicians to attend their sophistication, or available replacement parts. The Americans, with quite a simpler and spread mechanics, were much more at ease in this context, yet the cars' exaggerated dimensions did not fit the national reality.

Styling and prestige

Any luxury import guaranteed prestige and differentiated styling.

The Americans – with a richer look – ensured pomp, suggested power and were in fact imposing, while the Europeans were more discrete, yet gave maximum prestige and representation.

The national cars, for their side, satisfied both in styling and in prestige those that intensively lived a promising Brazilian moment.

Conclusion

These were three different proposals that, in common, ensured *status* and comfortable transport.

Cars imported from America and Europe and national top-of –line guaranteed excellent choices for any lifestyle.

Besides, the range of options was vast and, to be honest, not every American car was alike, as well as the Europeans also exhibited many differences. Also different were the Simca Présidence and the Willys Itamaraty.

One of the best feelings in life was to own a prestigious and sprendid car in such a time when to own any car was already a privilege.

ANOTHER OPINION

The first years of motorization in Brazil in post-World War II were not easy ones, they could even be called strange. There was luxury and simplicity in coexistence, to the point of Silveira Sampaio, a medicine doctor and presenter of a talk-show – the first in Brazil, on TV Tupi – customarily referred to Brazil as "Cadillac Country", with his own and unique sarcastic style by saying in French, "*Au pays des Cadillacs*". It was too high an opulence for a country still underdeveloped and whose foreign exchange reserves were rapidly draining due to the massive importing fine automobiles like the Cadillac and austere ones like small ones, namely the British Austin, Morris, Ford Anglia and Hillmann and the French Renault, Peugeot and Citroën. An incoherence in itself. This was this scenario that triggered the determination, first of the Vargas administration, than Juscelino Kubitschek's, to implant the auto industry here. The idea was to prevent Brazil from being an agricultural economy only. Who could afford to, set for buying the best in both sides of the Atlantic. Who could not, settled for more affordable European cars. But importation had its days numbered and it was more difficult to buy a car each day. It all began to change when Volkswagen began assembling Sedans and Kombi in a warehouse at Ipiranga district in São Paulo city and when local production of DKW in 1956 and Volkswagen, Renault (Dauphine), Simca and Aero-Willys in 1959/60 began.

TECHNICALLY CORRECT

In spite of the contrast between luxury and simplicity, what were seen in the cars of this period were great and interesting mechanical solutions in many occasions. Like the automatic transmissions, something that at the time was very intriguing for most people. It was intriguing and frightening, in case service was necessary, for there were no skilled technicians with full understanding of the systems. As the saying goes "in land of blind he who can see is the king", a car mechanic called Irineu, from Rio de Janeiro, dedicatedly serviced automatic transmissions and soon became known as "Irineu Hidramático", such was his popularity in the auto world. 'Hidramático' is the converted in Portuguese spelling for Hydramatic, the trademark for the General Motors' transmission used in Cadillac, Oldsmobile and Pontiac. Buick and Chevrolet, from the same corporation, had the Dynaflow and Powerglide systems, respectively. It was also during this period that the world got rid of the valves-in-block engine layout, which had moved to the cylinder head. The Simca came with this antiquity in valve location, to be solved by the introduction of the Emi-Sul engine in 1964. The six-cylinder Aero-Willys engine also had the valves block-mounted, while the intake ones laid in the cylinder head, and this way it remained until the end. Even when it "moved" to the Ford Maverick, in 1973.

PRICE TABLE OF PRESTIGE AND REPRESENTATION CARS[1]

	Model	1957	1958	1959	1960	1961	1962	1963	1964	1965	1966	1967	1968
Simca	Présidence						1,675	2,445	4,775	9,520	11,260		
Willys	Aero Itamaraty										11,460		
	Itamaraty											13,947	
Importados	Chevrolet Impala 3-year used					1,500	2,100	3,500	8,500		10,000 to 30,000	10,000 to 35,000	
	Buick 3-year used					1,400	2,900	3,500	6,700		10,000 to 30,000	10,000 to 35,000	

The price list of the Simca Présidence suggested a price approximately 20% higher than a base Chambord's, which used the same unitary-construction body and mechanical platform. The Willys Itamaraty was introduced in 1966 at an equivalent price to the Présidence in its last year of production. The American, three-year old imported Chevrolets were quite more expensive and prices varied considerably. After used, some simpler models were more valued than sophisticated ones for not being fitted with equipment that required specialized maintenance.

PRODUCTION TABLE OF PRESTIGE AND REPRESENTATION CARS[2]

Make	Model / Year →	1957	1958	1959	1960	1961	1962	1963	1964	1965	1966	1967	Until 1967	1968	Total
Willys	Itamaraty									648	5,701	4,837	**11,186**	3,197	14,383
	Itamaraty Executivo										2	21	**23**		23
	Total									648	5,703	4,858	**11,209**	3,197	14,406
Simca	Présidence				63	173	120	103	189	128	72		**848**		848
Prestige	**Total**	0	0	0	63	173	120	103	189	776	5,775	4,858	**12,057**	3,197	15,254

Simca Présidence and Willys Itamaraty did not face each other. The first was phased-out in the same year the other started being produced. The Itamaraty happened to add sales to the Aero-Willys. In its first year of life, almost seven-fold more units were put in market than the Présidence's in seven years. The Executive model had a limousine-type body.

1. Prices informed in thousands of Brazilian cruzeiros by *Quatro Rodas* magazine, January issue of each year.
2. Data according to documents supplied by Anfavea.

(USA)

Buick Electra 225 Dynaflow (1960) and Chevrolet Belair (1963)

Buick is a division of General Motors, a brand of intermediate *status* between Chevrolet (more simple) and Cadillac (more sophisticated) in the American market.

As of the early days of the Brazilian auto industry, in the early 1960s, any imported new car was very rare and above all a symbol of *status*. At that time, some cars were still imported and any Chevrolet would assure immediate prestige. However, here as well as up there the representation level of a Buick was superior and Cadillac's, even higher.

The 1960 Buick Electra 225 belongs to a segment that is very close to the top of a luxury pyramid, among the cars that arrived here by then.

The Electra represents a school, but it was not equal to any other model. Not every American car was alike. Not all General Motors products were equal. Not every Buick was equal.

Any American car, even after over five years in use, had qualities and would be considered a prestige car. General Motors owned many of the favorite makes: a Chevrolet was enough, but a Buick rendered a superior *status*, although it could not be compared to a Cadillac. In the Bel Air, the grille-embedded headlights denounced the three years less in relation to the Electra. Yes, here "size matters!"

A) The sedans were almost absolute majority, although some station wagons had been imported. The resale value of the simpler cars, as a rule, was higher than the more sophisticated ones'. An automobile with a six-cylinder engine, manual transmission and without power steering meant a lesser potential of maintenance costs. B) The nearly plain windshield did not take access space for the driver. In this station wagon, a third row of seats allowed the seating of two more short passengers.

Final result and the technique

The Buick Electra 225 was exaggeratedly dimensioned, but really exaggerated.

Large and richly equipped, this Buick counted on a V8 engine and a four-barrel carburetor, like the best American big cars. It was a V8 of intermediate/high power output, taking the "Yankee" standards of the time.

The Buick's engine cooling system, contrary to that of some imports and even some locally-made cars then, was dimensioned to stand the tropical climate and, in its case, the "overheating ghost" did not play around.

The automatic Dynaflow transmission, that helped to make Buick models best sellers in the United States, had two forward speed options only: "D" (drive, for normal driving) and "L" (for more pulling power). There was no automatic shifting between them (but it could be hand-operated while in motion) and Drive serve both attaining top speed and launching the car from stopped.

Low should be user in extreme conditions only (launch from stop on hills or to get engine braking). The torque converter, a complex hydraulic mechanism used in practically all automatic transmissions, took care to automatically adjust torque multiplication to traffic needs and conditions. It was a good match to the smooth running engine.

The drive gear ratio provided by the sole epicicloidal gear set was naturally direct drive (1:1), therefore the transmission was somewhat short, capable of providing traction from launching to top speed, evidently not too high. Everything added, it did not seem the ideal combination for high speeds. As a matter of fact, the car was far from provoking in this sense. What it really did was to invite easy motoring and with all comfort.

Headlights and parking lights no longer integrated the fender extensions, yet the fishtail and an upper lip up front composed the Buick look.

Suspension was soft and long-travel, making potholes to pass by unnoticed. The soft, high 82-profile cross-ply tires also contributed to this.

The steering wheel was large in diameter, as in the cars of the time. The steering box had a sufficient high-ratio as not to demand too many turns in order to obtain a good amount of wheel steering, but the hydraulic assistance was overdue. In all, steering was very light and the car managed to have a minimum turning radius surprisingly smaller than its bulk suggested, thus helping city driving. At speed the steering wheel was too sensitive to any unwanted turning, however response was slow and would compromise safety if action was ample and quick only.

In the beginning, when driving the Buick in Brazil, one faced some inconvenience regarding the car's size, but in everything else the car was truly pleasant.

It was full of "toys", besides those more evident. There were electric controls for seats, window glasses and antenna; in the valved push-button radio, the buttons formed the Buick name; the speedometer display was seen through its scale reflected by a mirror with manually adjustable angle, as to avoid reflexes; there was a turning knob to select the speed a warning chime should play as to warn the driver that it was attained, among other amusement.

As in almost all automobiles of its time, the front seat was of the bench type and the gear selection lever was at the steering column. Gear positions P-N-D-L-R was not the one to be adopted later as to be the conventional one, P-R-N-D-L.

Reaching the total size of the vehicle, the windshield design was called "boat", because of the enormous, panoramic format.

Wrapped around towards the rear, it stole precious door opening when accessing the front seat. In spite of the size of the car as a whole and that of the doors – that would not always find room to completely open and forced a certain contortionism for entering the car – the knee tended to hit the prolonging lower windshield frame.

In the Electra, nothing was short of. Its look did not hide that under its hood laid a mammoth engine and that it had been made to offer luxury and comfort.

On the outside, many contours and chrome work; huge bumpers; a large frontal grille; integral hubcaps and everything else that could be added to. The same thing happened with the interior, where colors, materials, drawings, upholstery materials and an enormous number of adjustments and knobs rendered an extremely rich environment.

On the inside, the Buick was also exaggerated: it was colorful; it had an enormous dashboard, but with a few gauges; seats were adjusted and the windows, that performed an articulated up and down movement, were electrically-actuated; the radio could be pre-selected for five stations and its antenna obeyed the touch of a button; pedals were really big and the windshield wrapped around to the lateral space of the car.

Daily, urban driving

In spite of the Brazilian cities not having neither streets nor parking spots reasonably dimensioned for a large car like this one, it did not demand major efforts when running and did not seem to be so big. Obviously, there was a physical limitation that many times ruled: besides the car being too large to park – to find a vacant parking space –, when going through narrow streets it was usual to pass over a bus or a truck. In such situation, sometimes it was necessary to pull over to allow the vehicles to pass over each other.

At the very rare commercial facilities that had provision for customer and/or employee parking, there was enough space for the car to maneuver and park. This also happened in apartment buildings, in a time that even those condominiums that lodged wealthy residents that could own an import, not always had a garage and even rarer were those with a garage and apartment-assigned parking spaces.

The owner of one of these cars, probably had also had a second, smaller vehicle for daily use.

The driveability of the Buick in urban circuits was pleasant, for hydraulic power steering and the brakes, power-assisted as well, reduced to a minimum any driving effort. The power of the engine made it easy the task of start moving from traffic lights.

Shopped goods could easily be placed in the trunk that, as with most large cars, presented a major inconvenience to open and close its immense lid, as well as dipping into and reorganizing the volumes when it came to take them out.

Buick was a General Motors division aimed to luxury cars. The other divisions were: Cadillac, Chevrolet, Oldsmobile and Pontiac, all them focused in cars of greater: prestige; market penetration; boldness and simplicity, respectively.

Yet on weekends, motoring on pre-established routes and to places with easy parking, to take out the well-seated family, with no crowding and very smoothly, was a pleasure to raise envy to the simple mortals that drove their "ordinary" cars.

A-B) Here size is everything, especially if added to quantity: many trim, many chrome work, many contours, many... Space distribution was not brilliant, yet it was not short of: the trunk had a sizeable volume for a lot of luggage. D) Together with the main name, Electra, number 225, referring to overall length in inches (equivalent to 5,74 meters), and Dinaflow, its automatic transmission's trade and prestige mark. C) The wheels had full-size hubcaps and cross-ply tires fitted to them.

On the road

There was a kind of road which it was created for: the American interstates – very wide, straight and flat, with enforced maximum speed and free from hazards. In these it was absolute, but unfortunately there were a few of these similar in Brazil and, with this specific profile, never.

In our narrow roads, with badly-designed curves, in very bad conditions and with drivers above the law (ever inadequate, by the way), this big car was not suitable for them in any way, but, undoubtedly, it had a performance superior to that of almost all national cars. No one could contour a curve faster or to brake later than a Simca, nevertheless it had power to be a lot faster in approaching curves and much more power to recover speed.

As one does not drive in the roads like in the circuits, the import very well accomplished the fate of touring cars – to cover distances with full comfort. In case the driver looked for a faster driving, except for rare exceptions of some models, the option should be automobiles from Europe or to go after real grand-touring or sports cars instead.

Temper

The car should be an extension of home: comfortable and safe. However, more than a home, the car could be shown as a symbol of wealth, success and promotion.

The automobile shall be an extension of the home. This was the axiom of the American cars.

Since the wealthy Brazilians had houses quite different from the American medium class', the axiom was a little unfocused.

Here, much more than at its country of origin, an Electra 225 was a show-off and rendered a special *status* to its owner.

But, as it was over there, the big cars were aimed to household leisure. They were family cars.

The 1960 Buick Electra 225 incorporated all the recipes common to American "big cars". It included everything that addressed the message of a rich look in sophisticated and comfortable environment. It also transmitted solidity, i.e., it conferred a sensation of safety. In brief, it represented what should be the extension of the typical American home – comfortable and safe.

American family tourism cars and I

The pioneering phase of the Brazilian auto industry coincides with the first years of my life and my early automotive memories.

I remember that my parents found it funny that I knew automobiles, either by brand name or model, as well as type.

Any very old car (up to 1940) was called a jalopy (with no depreciative intention), as well as any pick-up truck was a *caminhonete* (or "small truck", as it was named in São Paulo) and so on.

National cars, I knew them all, when not by model, by brand – I knew it was a Simca, but not the model, for example.

The most ordinary American cars were those of the 1950s, which I just called "old car", regardless of model. The ones from the 1960s were scarce and I only knew the Impala, whose taillights – three small, circular on each side – fascinated

When I was a kid, the Impala was one of the few imports I recognized by the model. Besides being one of the more imported, the three little taillights and the jumping animal drew attention. With all that size, it was for sure a car for the wealthiest.

me. The badge with the jumping deer was attractive also. Judging by size alone I already figured out that the (Chevrolet) Impala was a car for the rich.

Unfortunately, my father's friends and my uncles used national cars only and, with few exceptions, European ones.

I only came to co-live with the Americans of the 1960s when, at late 1980s, my brother bought a 1960 Chevrolet Impala. It was a model fitted with a high-displacement V8, four-barrel carburetor and automatic transmission.

It accelerated quicker than any national car produced up to that period and it was not that big when compared to a Ford Galaxie, the largest automobile produced in Brazil so far (from 1967 to 1983).

My brother had the car for a short time, unfortunately. It has left an emptiness among us and in following years it valued considerably.

This automobile served as exchange currency in trading for a Buick Electra 225. Larger and better equipped, this Buick also counted on V8 power and 4-bbl carburetion, but it accelerated less than the Impala that, I believe, should have an engine of over 6,000 cm^3.

When driving the Buick for the first time, I found some inconveniences related to its big size. I found it very strange to have difficulties, after all I am used to drive cars quite different from one another.

Being familiar with it, I had fun with its many "toys". After some time I was at ease with its size, as well as with the unconventional shift pattern that in the first drives requires some attention when maneuvering.

As for the "boat" windshield, wrapped around towards the cabin, I never got use to it, and because of that many dirt words were said because of the hematomas in my knees.

In Brazil, the areas of parking spaces are not suitable for cars of the size of a Buick. Its enormous doors rarely find room for a good opening angle. For someone of my size, weighting over 90 kilograms, entering or leaving the car demands certain contortionism. To make matters worse, the wrap-around windshield takes up a precious space. Difficulties to enter and exit is one of the last things one expects from a car of this size.

The Buick looked alike many other, contemporary American cars. When, in 2002, I bought a 1966 Chevrolet Corvair Monza, an American that is the major exception to the best techniques worth until then, I managed to confirm that the Buick was one of the more similar-looking ones, for there were some "more different".

The Corvair is literally the exception and the confirmation of the rule; it was used as a (negative) example for the thesis leading for the elaboration of the fundaments of the American consumer rights.

In the early 1960s Ford was still very much know for the image of Ford model T (launched in 1908), an affordable and very tough car, whose fame enabled the brand to harvest excellent reputation as a popular car automaker. In this market segment the Ford Falcon was sovereign and General Motors had to try a much heterodox recipe to fight it.

To power an automobile by an air-cooled boxer engine installed at the rear, opposed itself to all standards. It was a concept clearly inspired in the Volkswagen, whose success in the highly disputed North American market was impressive.

The Corvair replicated the Volks' basic layout and the air-cooling solution, but the car was dimensioned for the taste of the American, with a quite larger and roomier body, as well as a six-cylinder engine.

The Volks was in fact a phenomenon, however its solutions did not favor a great potential for size and power output optimization – in spite of Porsche having built some

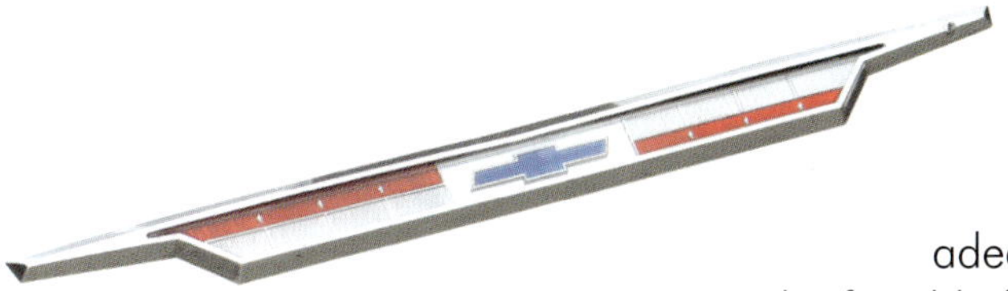

At the emblem, the Chevrolet "bowtie", one of the greatest automotive symbols and the 20th century's. Chevrolet was the brand that more contributed to General Motors to become, and for a long time, the largest company in the world.

of the most wanted sports cars in the world by making use of them. Engineering and the necessary materials to adequate such improvements over the Volks format would not be feasible for producing an adequately-priced popular car.

The Corvair, among other characteristics, was oversteering (the rear hangs out), as well as the Volks or even the Porsche. This behavior requires certain skill in high-speed driving, something – for the American market then – admissible in a sports car and acceptable in a small popular and low-powered car like the Volks, however, inadmissible in a car supposed to be "the extension of the home ".

In spite of the differentiated recipe, certainly the Chevrolet division was after a car to serve the ordinary American user, to meet his needs.

The reflex of the American consumer reaction was a "monster" lawsuit, with reverse results, that General Motors filled against the author of a published book that claimed the Corvair as dangerous and inadequate: Ralph Nader and his *Unsafe at any speed*, 1965.

This lawsuit inspired the American Consumer Protection Code and, later on, the consumer protection codes the world over.

The Chevrolet Corvairs were GM's compact models for the American market. They compromised known techniques to almost all American cars, such as front, water-cooled engines, but did not to regarding comfort, even if in detriment of roadholding. Used as an example of the carelessness of the American auto industry with safety in the book "Unsafe at any speed", it became the target of a polemic that would trigger the first consumer protection code in the world. It is worth remembering that the car should an extension of home, safe, above all.

In Brazil, a country that loved the Volks, the Chevolet Corvair – or just its engine – achieved some success. As with almost any import, it was technically more evolved than the local products and considered a prestige car.

Its 2,300-cm^3 engine was adapted to the Volks and Karmann Ghia. With this mechanics, theses cars successfully took part in races and rashes (clandestine races on open roads).

The Democrata, a genuinely national automobile that Ibap (Indústria Brasileira de Automóveis Presidente) promised to produce and conquered a roaster of enthusiasts, was clearly inspired in the Corvair. In the times I went out with the Corvair, it did not seem so "dangerous" to me and, even not being as American as the Buick, it was smooth and comfortable as all cars from there were. By the way, the book said that American cars, in the name of cost reduction and sales needs, neglected quality and safety. It accused the automakers and their products even those with the pedigree of a Buick Electra; however, the used example was the Chevrolet Corvair.

ANOTHER OPINION

The Buick Electra 225 reflects a time of plenty and trivial gasoline prices across the United States. At that time, size was a must, which was not a problem at all in a country customized for truly huge cars. It is not by chance that until present the USA are the country of the limousines, the limos, as they like to call them. It was really a large car, "225" was the overall length in inches, corresponding to 5.71 meters. Wheelbase was not nothing short of 3.12 m, and neither the weigh, from 2,080 kg to 2,120 kg. It did provide *status*, different from the Mercedes, but it did.

TECHNICALLY CORRECT

The V8 engine displaced 401 cubic inches (6.5 liters) and power output was 325 hp at 4,400 rpm, with 61.7 m.kgf of torque. SAE gross numbers, at it was usual in the USA then. As an estimate for today's net figures, it would something around 230 hp and 45 m.kgf of torque (30% less), considerable number even so. Compression ratio was too high for the Brazilian gasoline then, 10.25:1. Even premium gasoline was sufficient, obligating to retard ignition advance to avoid detonation and, as consequence, to loose a lot of power. Who could find a way to, used to add some aviation gasoline per tankful, which made the 225 perform as foreseen by the factory.

TECHNICAL INFORMATION OF BUICK ELECTRA 225

VEHICLE	Buick Electra 225
Type	4-door sedan with front engine and rear drive
	Chassis and body
Type	Separated construction; steel
	Engine
Type	V8, cast iron block and cylinder heads, water cooled. Overhead valves (OHV)
Mixture formation	4-bbl carburetor
Bore and stroke (mm)	106.4 x 92.5
Displacement (cm^3)	6,572
Compression ratio	10.25:1
Maximum power (SAE)	325 hp at 4,400 rpm
Maximum torque (SAE)	61.7 m.kgf at 2,800 rpm
	Transmission
Type	2-speed automatic amd reverse
	Brakes
Type	Single hydraulic circuit with powerbrake
Front	Drum
Rear	Drum
	Suspension
Front	Independent, single upper arm and lower A-arm, coil springs
Rear	Rigid axle, longitudinal semi-elliptical springs
	Steering
Type	Worm and sector with recirculating balls, power-assisted
	Dimensions and capacities
Wheelbase (mm)	3,208
Lenght (mm)	5,738
Width (mm)	2,032
Height (mm)	1,397
Ground clearance (mm)	180
Fuel tank (liter)	76
Curb weight (kg)	2,110
	Wheels and tyres
Type	Steel wheels and cross-ply tyres
Tyre size	8,00-15

NOW—*more than ever*—

When better automobiles are built

Every window of every Buick is SAFETY PLATE Glass

Buick will build them

Have your headlights aimed twice a year — AIM TO LIVE

See TALES OF WELLS FARGO, starring Dale Robertson, on NBC-TV and THE PATRICE MUNSEL SHOW, starring Patrice Munsel, on ABC-TV

The unique OPEL —the imported car made by General Motors in Germany – can now be ordered in Sedan and Caravan Wagon models through authorized Buick dealers.

GM 1908 · 1958

THE AIR BORN B-58 BUICK

Buick Division of General Motors

(Europe)

Mercedes-Benz 230S

(1967)

In Germany, late 19th century, in regions considered distant – since there were no automobiles yet – Daimler and Benz separately worked for transforming the dream of a car come true. There was practically a rush for its invention and both Gottlieb Daimler and Karl Benz were among the leaders. Both had started in that century to produce and sell their inventions in "industrial scale" – according that period.

In 1926, the companies Daimler – founded by Daimler – and Benz – founded by Benz – merged: it was the birth of Daimler-Benz, which would manufacture Mercedes-Benz automobiles (Mercedes was a Daimler brand since 1903), a nameplate of world prestige that from then on earned an even greater importance.

The three-pointed star – originated from Daimler – that means sky, sea and land – started as its top identity, stick to the radiator grille, which outlined the frontal positioning of the part, a peculiar characteristic of its cars that would become the pattern in almost all cars – all automakers – to come.

When the national industry was creeping through its first steps, in the second half of the 1950s, Mercedes-Benz produced, as always, high-luxury cars, appreciated all over the world and focused at the American market.

The factory's "S" range was destined to luxury cars, with vocation for motoring, i.e., not for sport. Models produced between 1958 and 1967 adopted the

In the 1950s, Germany still resented the effect of "housing" and loosing two major wars, which had occurred in the first half of that century. The Mercedes-Benz automobiles had always enjoyed high prestige and even before the 1960s started, they had recovered the lost time by incorporating new technologies – many of them born during the war, originated from the warfare industry, especially the aeronautical one – and began to introduce automobiles with a less austere look, with "less fear to being happy". The Mercedes with the "little fishtail" are the result of this moment and were produced from 1959 to 1967.

same body for the sedan model, which became known as "the one with a little fish tail", for displaying this typically-American ornament that conflicted with the sober Germanic style.

Of the available engines, the most powerful one was the Mercedes-Benz 230 S' ("230" refers to 2,300 cm^3). Besides it, the car could be equipped with the "190", the "220" and with the diesel versions.

In Brazil, as everywhere else in the world, a Mercedes-Benz imposed respect and those of the "S" lineup were the more diffused during the first phase of our industry.

The technique and final result

The Mercedes-Benz 230 S was larger than any car produced in Brazil until 1967, when the Ford Galaxie started being produced. However, its dimensions do not draw attention when compared to the large Brazilian cars of the time. Its decor did not dispense chrome work and ornaments so necessary to shine in "Uncle Sam land", however their number was much smaller than the American cars' then. What drew more attention, and it showed it by itself, was the chromed front grille, with the stuck three-pointed star on top of it.

In the dawn of the history of the automobile, Daimler and Benz shared the market. The first always produced more sophisticated cars, while the other believed in the popularization of this transport mean. The Mercedes brand was used by the Daimler representative at the Austro-Hungarian Empire, He used to implement some modifications on the originals, being one the first to adopt the radiator up front. With the merger of Daimler and Benz, Daimler-Benz adopted the Mercedes-Benz brand. The visual identity rested on the three-pointed star (sky, land and sea) stick with haughtiness on top of the protection grille for the radiator.

The outside look transmitted a feeling of solidity that was ratified right at the moment of handling the doors: the latch had a precise operation, as well as the sound of opening and closing the doors did not leave any doubts about how serious it was.

The size of the seats and the firmness they supported the weight of a body also did not allow any questioning about its robustness, as well as the upholstery – in leather, fabric or in MBTex (the trademark of the synthetic material used by Mercedes) – seemed to be (and it was) extremely resistant and lasting.

A) Mercedes-Benz automobiles invariably send the sensation of solidness. To open and close a door is enough to know that all mechanisms are precise and long-lasting. The upholstery in Mbtex, the maker's trademark, was extremely durable and had an aspect close to leather, yet touch was absolutely synthetic. B) The dashboard used prime wood. Gauges and warning lights laid in a sole module. Speed was indicated by a sharp column that ascended together with speedometer vertical scale, changing color according to speed: yellow, up to 40 km/h; red-striped yellow, up to 60 and from then on, red.

The dashboard was made in prime wood (walnut root), a touch of class common to the cars of the brand. Meters for fuel level, water temperature, oil pressure and the speedometer had a ascending scale and were set in an unique cluster, rectangular-shaped and vertical. In this same cluster, quite compact, there were also the trip and totalizing odometers, as well as several warning lights.

A sharp stripe, whose end indicated speed in the speedometer scale, went up and changed color according to speed, a detail that permitted some relaxing in a very Germanic environment.

The seat involved well the body, even when it was a bench. Once seated at the wheel, again solidity and precision were promptly noted, no matter the control handled. The pedal set was well arranged and dimensioned. The accelerator pedal permitted the right sensitiveness for modulating acceleration; the same thing happened with the clutch pedal, hydraulically-actuated and very progressive in operation; the brakes could be power-assisted, which eased pedal effort enough and, in 1967 only, shifted to discs. Steering was quite heavy, however power steering was optional (it was not a widely used equipment as in American cars) and gear changing, with steering column shift, was precise in engaging. The mechanism, however, demanded certain maintenance or inevitably play would build up and spoil gear changing.

Engine was a 2,300-cm³ six-cylinder with overhead camshaft fed by two staged 2-bbl carburetors. Fuel economy was better than American big engines' and it could attain sustained high speeds on the road, yet it suffered to take the car out of standstill. Since the Mercedes cars aimed the world market, they did not overheat, even in a tropical climate country.

Turn indicator stalk, windshield wiper switch, headlight switch, parking brake operation and other controls, all of them, the smallest they were, were supposed to transmit precision and robustness when used.

The car's dimensions resulted in a very roomy interior, even when compared to American automobiles, the same with trunk volume, very well laid out. At front there could be two individual seats or a bench and, in this case, in some models, there was – retractable and embedded in the center of the seatback – an armrest for the driver, very useful in long journeys.

The engine, a six-cylinder 2,300-cm³, with aluminum cylinder head and the camshaft on top of it, was smooth-running and suitable for trips, where it prompted sustaining high speeds and reasonable fuel consumption. Fuel feed was realized by a pair of progressive 2-bbl carburetors that worked well but hard to adjust. It was an engine that worked well in high revolutions and, therefore, it demanded the two first speeds were low enough – for a convincing launch of the heavy and large car – and the two last ones tall – to enable a high maximum speed, an important feature for any luxury automobile to survive in the German market, where there is no speed limit on the highways. Four speeds were insufficient to avoid a certain emptiness in acceleration resulting from the excessive engine rpm drop, especially when shifting from second to third.

Having always the high speeds these highways allow in mind, roadholding had to be quite reasonable and the brakes, efficient, as it happened with the Mercedes. As for that country's short and narrow roads – where high speeds were not allowed under law, there was enforcement and, above all, heavy traffic – the Mercedes was not nimble at all, but offered comfort anyhow.

In spite of the weight and the touring car vocation, the Mercedes-Benz S Class could be tuned for all kinds of racing. The independent rear suspension enabled good performance in several kinds of paving. In the picture, when passing by São Paulo, a sample that happened to be participating in an antique car event of the 1990s, the "London-Mexico Rally".

The front suspension was independent by coil springs and the rear one also by coil springs and semi-trailing arm. Wheels were fitted with cross-ply tires, 13-inch rim diameter and very high profiled (82), so high that added to the minute – for the pattern of the time – wheel rim, the diameter of the complete wheel remained with the usual. It was an assembly that suggested good roadholding for fast driving, yet it provided comfort and good driveability at any speed. Suspension was firm, it was not soft, but it did produce any harshness, as well as noise level was quite distant from the American cars'. Nevertheless, the engine sound was pleasant and did not end causing discomfort.

A

B

C

D

A) Some deluxe European cars, designed in the late 1950s with the goal of conquering the American market, were very interesting to be closely seen. All corners were carefully elaborated. The Mercedes 230 S was not exaggeratedly large, not too small at all. Space distribution was perfectly realized. B-D) The rear lighting group had several subdivisions, but one module alone gathered all functions, as well as the main headlights, with high and low beams, shared an unique bloc with the auxiliary fog lamps and the turn indicator blinkers. C) Wheel diameter was 13-inch and the cross-ply tires very high-profiled, yet roadholdiing was very good.

The front section of the S Class drew attention, besides the radiator grille's, by the peculiar headlight shape that in an sole group had main headlamp and the auxiliary fog light. Seen from the side, the cabin air outlets could be noticed embedded at the rearmost columns. And from behind, the wide taillights, laying horizontally under the fish tail, were the most standing out detail. In all, the car imposed respect.

Daily urban driving

The Mercedes did not suffer from the uneven paving often found in our streets: it did not seem to wear out or presented noises when going over bumps and undulations, nor made its occupants to copy the relief with up and down jerking.

The engine did not overheat in anyway, even in the most jammed traffic, which was a plus in comfort. Yet, in a counter-effect, it suffered from the car's weight when starting to move.

As the reaction to the gas pedal movement was slow, gear changing were also, besides being often required. Steering was heavy when without hydraulic assist and was inadequate for driving in city. Brakes, on their side, were burdened by weight.

The S Classes were not nimble nor pleasant to drive in heavy traffic, but, even so, at the end of the day the car's comfort counterbalanced matters. Good seats did not permit the body to arrive exhausted after a torment of hours in the already-chaotic traffic then.

Obviously, it was easier to find a spot to park a smaller-size car, however the Mercedes was wisely sized and, when equipped with the optional power steering, easy to maneuver. The small minimum turning diameter – 10.8 meters, less than the Volks' 11 meters – enabled it to maneuver in proportionally small spots.

Since it was a representation car, it was quite uncommon to meet one of them on way to a supermarket, although its trunk size was advantageous enough and – always taking the Mercedes' exaggerated dimensions into account – it was not among the worse to use.

On the road

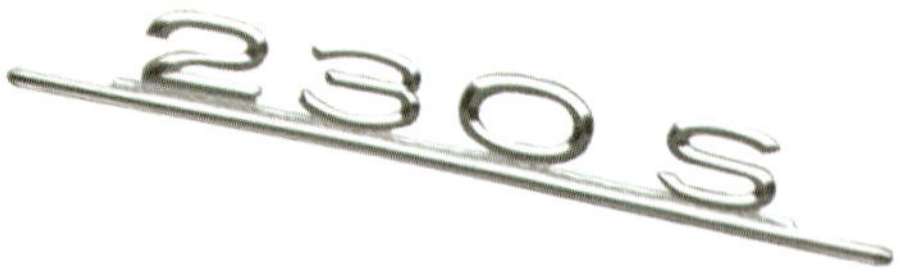

The "230" number was allusive to engine displacement, 2,300 cm³, and the "S", to the S bodies, the ones with the highest prestige.

Mercedes-Benz automobiles were never focused in just one market and were born under several influences.

Evidently, the German "accent" was strong, after all its cradle and its main market were there; then "it tried to speak English", for the United States were the largest consuming market of large luxury cars in the world; then importance was given to the rest of Europe and, finally, what remained of the world, where it should be the car of diplomatic corps and wealthy people's in general.

It did not matter where or how, if the extreme desert heat or the freezing cold of Nordic countries; in the best American asphalt or in pot holes of an African country; in the narrow roads that cross the Andes or in the German highways, its cars should be absolute.

But and for this reason, it had best vocation for very well built highways as to go at high speed; then it went pretty well at medium speeds, as enforced at the excellent American highways; once again it went superbly in sweeping and narrow roads like the ones that crossed several European countries and, finally, it went through with merit roads like ours, not always paved.

In the mid-1960s, it was possible to go on long journeys throughout Brazil on a Mercedes-Benz, even not counting on service outside São Paulo or Rio de Janeiro. For such, people counted on the dependability of their cars.

A) Space distribution was excellent and the spare wheel location, impeccable. In American cars, it was usual for them to bear false air intakes that worked as ornament only. The Europeans looked for integrating functional details in a way to compose the design. B) The cabin air outlets earned an inox steel frame in this model.

The 230 S was no exception to the rule. Even not possessing all the necessary nimbleness in roads like ours, it did not do bad and provided comfort all the time.

Besides low in number, our roads were poorly designed, poorly built, poorly maintained and with roadside assistance at all. A very few were two-lane but even so, and also because of it, to travel aboard a S Class made all the difference. The safety it transmitted was, together with comfort, the difference that justified why to pay so much more to go on a Mercedes than do it on other cars.

The Mercedes-Benz 230 S and I

In 1968, my father traded his FNM (Alfa Romeo) 2000 JK for a 1963 Mercedes-Benz 220 S, black with white leather inside. I loved the JK, but a Mercedes-Benz, "the best car in the world" according to some of my little buddies, was not a trade-in that could lead to any deception.

In a direct comparison to the JK, the Mercedes lost in: the horn that did not work without the key in; the lesser number of "little chromed buttons" in dashboard; the lack of a second speedometer (rev counter) and a very ordinary design for the gas pedal. However at the end there was a tie for there having a "child seat" (an entirely wrong use for the rear-seat armrest); the speedometer that changed colors; a radio that searched stations by itself and more room for the child's bed (another abusively wrong use, that of the parcel shelf).

My father complained much of the performance of this Mercedes, a model of car that contrasted with some of his personal profile. It had expensive service, which demanded skilled labor and some care in use, three things that bothered him. Yet, since he traveled constantly and the car was also a work tool, solidity, dependability and comfort compensated it.

His speech suggested that the Mercedes would be traded for a JK, however, amid businesses, the 220 S ended up being replaced by a 1965 230 S in 1970.

The 230 S was dark blue with interior in red MBTex. The front seat had an armrest and, for the rest, it was practically identical to the 220 S.

It was in this car that we had our first long trips with the family. Once we went to visit the new capital, Brasília, and in another one, Foz do Iguaçu. Despite the car did not count on roadside service, it went flawlessly all the way.

I also remember several, minor trips, some of them with the car crowded with friends. I still could not distinguish the comfort of a Cadillac in relation to a Kombi van, traveling was all that mattered.

It was in this Mercedes that, as a passenger, I had my first car accident. My father was traveling to Rio Grande do Sul, his homeland, with three nephews and I, when at the BR-116 ("Death Road"), under rain, we fell into a bank. I only remember the car "jerking" quite a lot, for as I was sleeping, I saw nothing. The accident delayed our trip, that proceeded with the car quite smashed, although with no mechanical damage. After the delay, we headed to Santa Maria (RS) by a route where there were unpaved roads. The Mercedes, quite loaded, lost the exhaust pipe, a short of new occurrence in my stories as Mercedes child-passenger or even JK's.

In the early 1990s I purchased a silver 1967 Mercedes-Benz 230 S with wine red inside. Differently from the car that belonged to my father, it had individual seats up front, disc brakes and power steering.

When driving it, I knew my father was right: it was, in fact, slow in city traffic. I recalled that once it struggled to engage reverse. I realized that maintenance was in fact expensive and demanded skill.

On the other hand, I have traveled with comfort and I sustained good average speeds, even for the 2000s, with this S Class, a car that for many years suffered a certain marginalization by appreciators of the brand who deemed its lines too American. Today, in the early 2000s, it draws a lot of attention and show all the charm and power of a Mercedes-Benz.

It blazes a moment. It is the very best we found in representation cars.

No doubt my wife made the right choice: the 230 S was the "bride car". Already in the first moment I knew that command belonged to me when it came to drive the old Mercedes. If I am not mistaken, the first party my parents took me to and brought me home late in evening was in a model like this one. I went home sleeping, kneed over the floor with my body leaning on the rear seat cushion. It was 1968 or 1969. Almost forty years later…

ANOTHER OPINION

The Mercedes-Benz always had an all-special aura of prestige. They were already born with this character, since the company was founded in 1926. It's quality was not only visible as sensed in every detail. To own one really gave (and still gives) high *status*. The three-pointed star really made a difference. Maybe for faithfully believing in this was that the manufacturer did not achieve the expected success with the small A Class, made in Juiz de Fora (MG) from 1998 to 2005. The Brazilian appreciated and appreciates Mercedes-Benz cars, but sized as he is used to, not a small and tall car. Not even the power of the star was enough to assure its permanence in the market. Sales in seven years reached what was expected to be yearly: 70,000 units.

TECHNICALLY CORRECT

A fact that deserves praise for the Mercedes-Benz medium and large cars, always front engine and rear-wheel drive (a rear engine solution was tried in the 1930s, but the idea did not go forward) was the independent suspension even at the rear, when most cars of this layout, until some time ago, had rear rigid axles. Especially the Americans, that even in models recently re-launched like the Mustang keep the heavy and inadequate component at the rear. But the Mercedes' rear independent suspension, until 1962, was the ill-fated swing axle, used even in the famous 300 SL "Gull Wing" sports car, produced from 1954 to 1957.

The look of the Mercedes-Benz sedans with the wheels "closed", when seen from rear, was pathetic. Fortunately the factory woke up and fitted semi-trailing arms for the 1963 model-year and later came the more efficient multilink, as it is currently so in all rear-wheel drive models of the brand.

TECHNICAL INFORMATION OF MERCEDES-BENZ 230S

VEHICLE	Mercedes Benz 230S (1967)
Type	4-door sedan, 6 passengers, front engine and rear drive
	Body and chassis
Type	Unitary, steel
	Engine
Type	Inline six, block in cast iron and cylinder in aluminum, water cooled. Overhead camshaft (SOHC)
Mixture formation	2 double-bbl 35/40 mm staged caburetors
Bore and stroke (mm)	82 x 72.8
Displacement (cm^3)	2,306
Compression ratio	9:1
Maximum power (SAE)	135 hp at 5,600 rpm
Maximum torque (SAE)	N/A
	Transmission
Type	4-speed manual, synchronized, and reverse
	Brakes
Type	Double hydraulic circuit with powerbrake
Front	Drum (disc optional)
Rear	Drum
	Suspension
Front	Independent, superposed A-arms, coil springs
Rear	Independent, semi-trailing arms and coil springs
	Steering
Type	Worm and sector with recirculating balls
	Dimensions and capacites
Wheelbase (mm)	2,750
Lenght (mm)	4,875
Width (mm)	1,795
Height (mm)	1,500
Ground clearance (mm)	200
Fuel tank (liter)	65
Curb weight (kg)	1,350
	Wheels and tyres
Type	Steel wheels and radial tyres
Tyre size	185-330

Tradition
reflected
in
progress
Our tradition is based on principles of lasting val
idity Quality in every detail true craftsmanship
and elegant styling The scrupulous application
of these principles in the design and manufac
ture of all Mercedes-Benz products is
the products performance and beauty
Benz vehicles of today are the
75 year tradition of progressive
in every sphere of car design and
MERCEDES-BENZ

The Itamaraty was, in practice, the deluxe Aero-Willys. The Aero's design was from the 1950s also, although submitted to many modifications in 1964. the Itamaraty model was introduced in 1966, the year the Présidence was phased-out and restyled for the next year. The trend was that of a quite cleaner look, without so many ornamentations. From different times, they practically did not compete against each other. The Itamaraty Executivo was an attempt to sustain the prestige of the Willys, since much more modern cars were in the pipeline.

(Brazil)

Simca Présidence (1960 to 1966) and Willys Itamaraty (1966 and 1967)

Simca, Willys and Fábrica Nacional de Motores (FNM), in the pioneering phase of our industry, were three automakers that produced large, luxury cars. Simca and Willys competed directly in some market segments, while FNM manufactured the Alfa Romeo, a sedan with sporting accent.

Basically, Simca lineup cars and those from the Aero-Willys' had a more family profile and each of them had a more refined version, for more luxury and representation, that was able to complement their lines and render more *status* to the brands.

For such, common recipes of the two factories included much more refined finishing, distinguished décor and, since from beginning in the case of Simca and as of 1967 – second year of production – with the Itamaraty, more powerful engines. These were versions aimed to a specific public, who wanted something more in comfort and performance.

Vedette was a line of large cars from the French Simca in the mid-1950s and, although its design had roots in the United States, the versions made by Simca

The Présidence, identical to the French model namesake, was launched in t960, but it existed there since the mid-1950s. In 1964 it underwent some changes, yet conserving the basic concept: lot of ornaments and styling details.

A) Undoubtedly, the Présidence seemed to b especial. There was a blend of tastes and solutions that mixed the American with the French ones. The "Continental Kit", that allowed carrying a spare tire way behind, appeared first in the US. Its purpose was to allow the car to have two spare tires, or just to increase trunk volume. B) The "fishtail" was also an American trend, as well as to show many trim and badges. C) As for integrate them to design – as at the rearmost columns where the cabin air outlets were covered by a splined plate, was a "à la française" way. Over it a plaquette with the owner name was installed.

were designed in France. The Présidence was the plusher version and, produced in Brazil as of 1960, was about the same produced by the mother company, therefore a French inspiration of the 1950s under the luxury automobile theme created on a US-designed car. The Simca lineup was produced from 1959 to 1966, when it was replaced by the Esplanada model.

The Esplanada did not come to have a prestige version and it was the result of a national creation from the mid-1960s, on car of American design. At that time, sobriety reigned: cars had to be clean, without much trim and chrome, exactly the opposite what went on before, at the moment of the Simca Vedette lineup creation, where the most plush model was exactly the most full of adornments.

In 1963, when the first major Aero-Willys restyling took place at Willys – it wanted to bring more *status* to the models – the body earned new contours that, together with many trim work and other details, made the Aero-Willys a more imposing car. The first Itamaraty, launched with a 2,600-cm^3 engine in 1966, still carried traces of this school, but soon after the 1967 model-year, with 3,000-cm^3 displacement, went opposite way to confer more prestige to the Itamaraty, a top of line automobile.

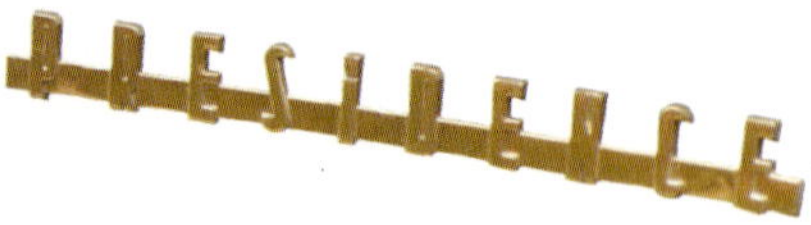

The "Présidence" denomination was brought from France. Over there, the Vedette lineup models, "twins" of our Simca, bore the name of palaces. Some of them, such as Présidence, would be kept in our equivalent versions.

A) When launched in 1966, the Itamaraty was powered by the Aero-Willys 2,600-cm^3 engine. C) At front, bumper, headlights and parking lights would also remain the same. Only the chromed grille was to change. B) At rear, the laying-down taillights, under a grille with horizontal elements, would mark the Itamaraty until the last years of production.

It followed the trends of another time, the same that had taken Simca to the Esplanada. Also coming from an American design, it had this version designed and developed in Brazil in the mid-1960s, therefore it was not contemporary to the Simca Présidence, but the Esplanada's.

The Simca lineup, while it was in production, remained with the same versions, but unlike the Aero-Willys' the line received a new nameplate at each important advancement.

In 1960, model décor was changed and all Simca models started bearing in the middle of the name the "Três Andorinhas" (Three Swallows) identification. In mid-1962, the gearbox had all the three speeds synchronized, hence a new identification: "3 Sincros". In 1964, it was time for a more powerful engine, the Tufão (Typhoon) engine and other significant changes at bodywork, included structural ones, which had lead to calling Tufão all versions. In 1966, the last change: some décor details were changed and the engine, now christened Emi-Sul. Valves not located in the engine block anymore but in the aluminum cylinder heads with hemispherical chamber layout. From the engine came the name of the lineup: "Emi-Sul".

The Emi-Sul Présidence was the true Itamaraty contemporary and although it did not have one more carburetor as in other Emi-Sul Simcas, with the new engine performance became far superior to its ancestor's (the Tufão). Yet as a plus, this Présidence exclusively had a two-speed differential, that in practice duplicated the number of gearbox speeds to six. This Présidence, the Simca Emi-Sul Présidence, had a low production and was practically the "Swan Song" of an automobile range that would evolve to the Esplanada.

The Itamaraty did not directly face the Présidence in the market, for it was produced between 1966 and 1971. As more modern cars were being launched, especially the Ford Galaxie, it stopped occupying the band of those of maximum prestige, since its attributes were no longer sufficient for, when compared, to sustain such a high *status*.

Technique and results

The Simca Présidence and the Willys Itamaraty shared the same mechanics of the other models of their lines, but engines had a power boost through different artifices: instead of using a double-barrel carburetor, equal to those of other

Simcas, the Présidence had two of them, with progressive opening (not for the Emi-Sul). As for the Itamaraty, it was basically powered by the same engine as the Aero-Willys', but with displacement increased from 2,600 to 3,000 cm³.

The Simca recipe was more sophisticated and its engine was more pleasant when accelerated, while, on the other hand, the Itamaraty's conservative formula assured a less exaggerated fuel consumption. In almost everything, as it happened with engines, the Simca sought being more pleasant and the Itamaraty, more efficient.

A

B

C

D

A) In 1967 the car would earn the definite design. The front grille, more discreet, now hosted rectangular parking lights. All decor became simpler, rendering a sophisticated look to the old body. B-C) Black dull paint was applied amid chromed stripes, both in trim work and hubcaps. D) The engine adopted the classical recipe for getting more power, being enlarged from 2,600 to 3,000 cm³. The Itamaraty had never vocation to speed, not only for its engine.

The Présidence was more refined. Engine with slight higher displacement and compression ratio and fed by two 2-bbl carburetors was no synonym of power and fuel economy was worse than many larger engines, yet it granted more performance than Itamaraty's. As for the rest, the Simca was more balanced. Details such as the fresh air intakes for the carburetors, up front, and exhaust pipes embedded in the rear bumper protectors, drew attention.

The Simca, especially after 1964, when it became Simca Tufão Présidence, had a performance capable of being pleasing in accelerating. Simca automobiles were good-mannered and balanced that, with a more "merry" engine – as the Présidence was – could even be considered fast.

The Itamaraty could sustain cruising speeds around 100 km/h, even uphill and, where fourth speed did not provide more power to sustain a reasonable speed, third did the job. Although it was not a nimble car, the performance of the Itamaraty kept it apt to show its prestige.

In what refers to bodywork, the Présidence version outlined from the other, especially by the extension between trunk and bumper, where there was vertically positioned a circular "case", with a hubcap similar to the wheels'. This "case" was suitable for carrying a spare wheel. It was a common feature in some American cars of the 1950s and it was known as "Continental kit", allusive to a Lincoln homonymous version that was created for augmenting trunk volume or for carrying a second spare wheel for traveling along the Route 66, the road that cut the USA, a country of continental dimensions larger than Brazil, linking Chicago and Los Angeles.

The Itamaraty externally differentiated from the Aero-Willys for being more sober and at the same time having a more imposing décor. Internally, it adopted

In spite of a style not hiding the designs´ age, the Itamaraty incorporated contemporary concepts, resulting in a more discreet and elegant automobile. The car's height was exaggerated, which resulted in good space usage, car easy access or exit, excellent visibility and a ground clearance that allowed it to overcome obstacles. Since it did not intend attaining high speeds, to rely on these refined characteristics was more sensible than looking for a better roadholding.

Leather and jacarandá-da-baía, a fashionable Brazilian prime wood of the time and that years later would be regulated, compose a noble mix. Refinement did not reach all accessories: handles and armrests, among other items, were common to the Aero, when not from the Willys Rural. Luxury made concessions to the practical and the functional.

a more Brazilian/European standards, where sophistication relied on leather seats and the dashboard in jacaranda-da-bahia, a prime wood that was a national symbol. Years later exploration of this wood, more than illegal, was considered politically incorrect.

In the Présidence, upholstery was in leather also, but in vibrant colors, opposite to what happened in the Willys, and the knitting between seat sprouts, door panels or even the dashboard's were deep, while the sprouts of the Itamaraty were shallow. Also in leather, there was a triple white band across the seats that drew even more attention to the model's exclusivity.

In the Présidence there were no prime wood fittings, but all details were more elaborated and they never seemed to privilege savings.

On the road

The Présidence was a more balanced automobile than the Itamaraty, it had better roadholding and brakes. The engine, with twin carburetors, provided good performance, however it resented of not having one more gearbox speed. In a hillclimb, it invariably did not have enough power in top gear and in second it did not attain sufficient speed.

The Itamaraty had no vocation for high speeds, however it was faster when going uphill, for it had one more speed, between second and top, what made it faster in this situation. The more loaded they were, the better the advantage of the Willys was, which had a better fuel economy.

When compared to imports, both lost in performance and fuel economy, however those were rare and were not part of the quotidian of our streets.

The additional power and the superior finishing the two national cars had, in relation to the remaining versions of their lines, assured quite a better traveling.

Urban daily driving

Obviously, these were not automobiles usually found performing household tasks.

In urban use, they replicated qualities and faults of the simpler versions of their lines. Plusher finishing resulted in a more pleasant environment, which was translated in comfort.

The additional engine power, especially in the case of the Simca, allowed a more pleasant driving, but did not produce miracles.

Simca and Willys did not feature power steering nor power brakes, essential for comfort in city traffic when large cars are concerned.

A) In the trunk of the Simca the spare wheel was hidden by the fender. B) The spare wheel location of the Willys took up a lot of space, yet it offered a good volume even loosing some of it.

The brazilian prestige cars and I

I recall that every and any Simca version was capable of drawing my attention. I could not identify a version by name, but the model "with the wheel at rear" was the that hypnotized me most and, by the way, not only me – a child then – but everyone, regardless of age.

The models of the Aero-Willys range were more familiar to me. I had more contact with them and less fascination, the Itamaraty was just one more Aero to me. In 1967, with the introduction of the Itamaraty limousine, a car for the president (I could not tell the

It took a long time for me to buy a Simca Présidence. It was a 1965 Tufão that needed to be restored. After a long, arduous and costly work, the car was ready. Not only for quality, but also for the importance of the model, we ended awarded, in 2006, the maximum prize an exhibitor and his national car could have: the JK Trophy.

difference between president, governor and mayor), the car earned my admiration. I was not exactly the target public for Willys that, when they launched the Itamaraty Executivo – the limousine I recognized as the Presidential Itamaraty – it exactly wanted to add prestige to its top-of-line that soon would fight against new launchings.

There was a time a very few valued the antique national car. Even the Itamaraty Executive, the only limousine made by a big automaker, with just 25 units produced, did not find buyers. In 1989, when I dealt with antique cars, I ended stuck with one of these models. I had to adopt it then. After a long restoring process the car became very amusing to drive, either as a driver or in the place of whom drives him – the rear seat.

I had contact with the Itamaraty in late 1980s only, when I purchased a 1967 Executivo that, nevertheless, I happened to use in more effective way in the early 2000s, when restoring was finished.

I also would buy a 1965 Présidence Tufão, but in late 1990s only. It went also through a long restoring process and it was ready at the same time as the Itamaraty's.

A) The instrument cluster is the same as the other Simca's .The leather-upholstered dashboard, a radio branded "Simca" and the audio fader control are the only extra equipments. The vehicle with scale until 200km/h is a Emi-Sul line. B) In the Itamaraty Executive the dashboard was similar to other Itamaraty's. The driver seat, with no adjustment at all, forced to the worse driving position I ever experienced.

When they arrived, none was in a reasonable shape and although the Itamaray was more preserved, it was far from being a good sample. The Présidence was painted in a different color from the one used at the time, it had Esplanada upholstery and door panels and, the most different of them all in relation to the original version, the engine was a four-cylinder from the Chevrolet Opala.

Any Simca, in a similar condition as a vehicle from the Aero-Willys lineup, is harder to restore, after all its mechanics, even not being of the most complicated, does not descend from the Jeep Willys', a vehicle born with the goal of being practical.

As well as in mechanics, the Simca was also harder than the Aero-Willys in bodywork and internal finishing.

Without making much ostentation, there was a model-identifying badge over the trunk lock.

If restoration of any Simca is potentially more difficult than an Aero-Willys', that of the Présidence, in comparison to the Itamaraty, is quite more, for the Présidence was the most detailed Simca ever. It did not lack any extra finishing and if there could be a chromed part or an ornament, there it was. As for the Itamaraty, it was more sober and less over-equipped, the Aero-Willys included, and the great difficulty in restoring it laid in the fact that the Executivo was larger and more difficult for body repairing.

The Présidence upholstery is much more elaborated and, for example, there is a mini-bar inside the armrest at the center of the rear seat. The seat sprouts are deep and nothing was done in a simple way, while in the Itamaraty everything is less complicated, but not to the point of being considered less elaborated.

Just twenty five Itamaraty Executivos were built and, even this was not one of the plusiet, in featured equipment such as air-conditioning for rear seat occupants, a rare option in other Itamaratys. But the privilege of who seated back was not limited to air-conditioning. There was also – besides lot of legroom, with the right of having a footrest – a cartridge-tape player and AM radio, controlled from the rear space, where the four speaker laid. A glass partition, electric quick-closing and operated from the rear seat, isolated the driver and front seat passenger, by the way an uncomfortably-located and fixed seat with no right to fore and aft adjustment at all.

By driving the Présidence in town or road, its performance positively surprised me, for I was used to drive a 1962 Três Andorinhas Chambord and the difference is enormous. Comfort is proper to pomp and the Présidence's presence is noted anywhere, not only for being an antique automobile, but for looking special.

A) "For those seated at rear, extravagance did not lack. Additionally to what eyes could see, in the rear panel there was air-conditioning and cartridge tape-player. The audio system included four speakers, all the rear section, and feet counted on foldable footrests. In case there were extra passengers,two jump seats could be folded down. B) Privacy was assured: triggered via the panel switch above the radio, a partition glass rolled up fast isolating the rear section. Who seated up front had no privilege at all.

The Itamaraty limo thrilled me for the engine torque since the first drive. The engine does not feel the weight, the brakes work well and roadholding is uncompromising, since the car is not aimed for high speeds. Driving position is very bad, but controls are not that heavy and the biggest difficult in driving the limousine is not due to its overall length – it is shorter than the average American car, like the 1960 Buick Electra – but for its proportionally enormous wheelbase in that, to drive the car, one sits well closer to the front axle that rear's. The sensation is that the whole car will go through well after the driver.

Well, logically who wants to try an Itamaraty Executivo shall not drive it, but sit and feel comfortable in the rear seat, as did the general-presidents of the Republic, contemporaries of the car. I must confess that I have done it already, however in spite of all despise to driver, the Executivo – currently – is more pleasing to be driven than to drive.

Driveability of none of the Aero-Willys lineup was worth a grade, even when compared to its contemporary country mates. The Executivo model was notable for, it could even earn a top excellence award, "punishing" its driver. Conversely, rear seat passengers enjoyed great comfort. In the Limousine, its occupants could count on many accessories and privacy

ANOTHER OPINION

Taking the old saying "No dog for the hunt, take a cat" as starting point, nothing more natural than the auto industry settled here to try to fulfill the prestige car niche, once importation was barred. Of the three large cars manufactured here then – Aero-Willys, Simca and FNM 2000 – only the last one, of Italian origin, does not fit well in this profile, due to its "hot temper", its clear sports character. For this reason, Simca and Willys-Overland went after the segment by launching the Présidence and the Itamaraty, respectively. It must be noted that "large" then is "medium" today.

All cars became larger as years went by, a market demand. Therefore, the Brazilian market earned two prestige cars, entirely made here, and up to a point they pleased their owners, yet nothing comparable to a Mercedes-Benz, for example, especially in matter of *status*. Again using a folk saying, "No one is a preacher in its own land".

TECHNICALLY CORRECT

The Simca Présidence's and Willys Itamaraty's mechanics, engine-related especially, was in a certain way dissonant with the proposal of high luxury car. The first one counted on an engine that evolved from the 2,22-liter, 60 hp Ford V8, whose crankshaft still ran is three main bearings only and lacked robustness. Besides, the known low torque resulted in poor power output in low rpm range. The second, by its side, an inline six-cylinder, was relatively robust in spite of the four main bearings, but it was not brilliant in any way. Inclusive for the unusual valve arrangement layout, with overhead intake valves and exhaust side valves, for long widely known as not a good solution. The Simca featured a clearly superior front suspension due to the McPherson system adopted (christened Stabimatic by the factory), which provided excellent steering response even with cross-ply tires, but both cars had the archaic rigid axle on semi-elliptical longitudinal leaf springs. Both were light-years behind the FNM 2000 in performance and cornering behavior.

TECHNICAL INFORMATION OF ITAMARATY

VEHICLE	Aero-Willys Itamaraty 1966	Itamaraty 1967	Itamaraty Executivo 1967
Type	4-door sedan, 6 passengers, front engine and rear drive	*	Limusine 8 people
	Body and chassis		
Type	Unitary, steel	*	*
	Engine		
Type	Inline 6-cylinder, cast iron block and cylinder head, water cooled. Overhead intake valves and in-block exhaust valves (F-Head)	*	*
Mixture formation	2 single bbl carburetors	1 2-bbl 35	68%
Bore and stroke (mm)	79.37 x 88.90	79.37 x 101.6	79.37 x 101.6
Displacement (cm^3)	2,638	3,014	3,014
Compression ratio	7.6:1	8:1	8:1
Maximum power (SAE)	110 hp at 4,400 rpm	132 at 4,400	132 at 4,400
Maximum torque (SAE)	19.4 m.kgf at 2,000	22.2	22.2
	Transmission		
Type	4-speed manual, synchronized, and reverse	*	*
	Brakes		
Type	Single hydraulic circuit, no powerbrake	*	*
Front	Drum	*	*
Rear	Drum	*	*
	Suspension		
Front	Independent, single upper arm and lower A-arm, coil srings	*	*
Rear	Rigid axle, semi-elliptical longitudinal leaf springs	*	*
	Steering		
Type	Worm and sector	*	*
	Dimensions and capacities		
Wheelbase (mm)	2,738	*	3,449
Lenght (mm)	4,700	*	*
Width (mm)	1,828	*	*
Height (mm)	1,593	*	*
Ground clearance (mm)	170	*	*
Fuel tank (liter)	72	*	*
Curb weight (kg)	1,488	1,494	1,586
	Wheels and tyres		
Type	Steel wheels and cross-ply tyres	*	*
Tyre size	6.45-15	7.35-15	7.35-15

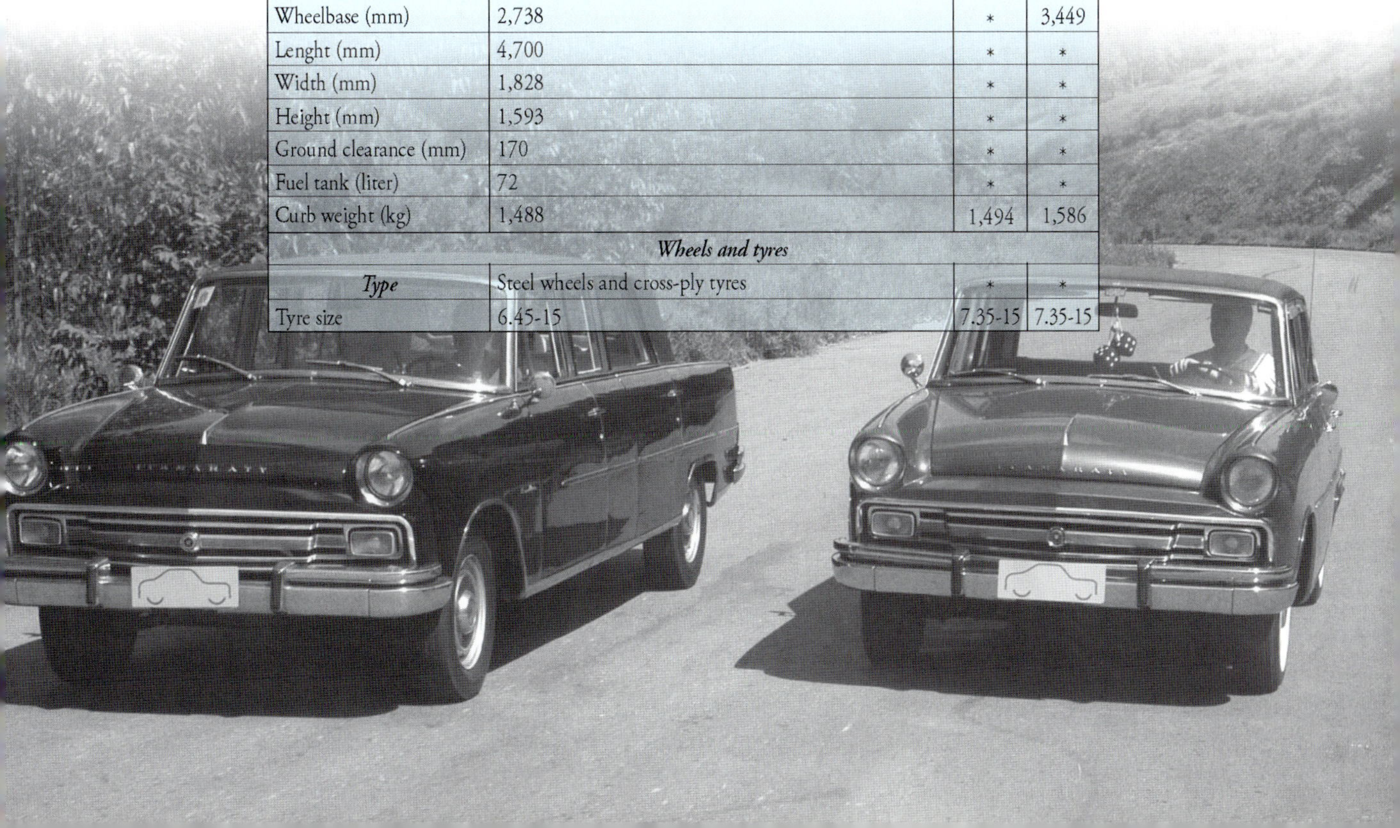

É muito difícil contentar as pessoas de bom gôsto.

São muito exigentes.

Conhecem de longe o que é bom.

Querem saber tudo sôbre o que compram. Sabem escolher.

Gostaram do Itamaraty porque êle tem luxo e confôrto, classe e apuro técnico.

O Itamaraty 67 tem um detalhe exclusivo: ar condicionado, clima a seu gôsto*.

Ainda mais: motor de 3.000 cm³, nova grade, novas maçanetas, novas calotas, novas lanternas traseiras, nôvo painel, nôvo estofamento.

Além de: tapetes de veludo, aplicações de Jacarandá legítimo no painel e nas portas, luz de leitura com foco dirigível e garantia de 20.000 km.

Tudo para contentar quem tem bom gôsto.

* opcional

ITAMARATY 67

Produto da Willys-Overland
Fabricante de veículos de
alta qualidade.

TECHNICAL INFORMATION OF PRÉSIDENCE

VEHICLE	Présidence (until 1963)	Tufão (1964 to 1966)	Emi-Sul (1966)
Type	4-door sedan, 6 passengers, front engine and rear drive	*	Limosine 8 people
Body and chassis			
Type	Unitary, steel	*	*
Engine			
Type	V8, cast iron block and aluminum cylinder heads, water cooled. Side valves	*	Overhead valves
Mixture formation	2 2-bbl 32-mm staged carburetors	*	1 2-bbl 40-mm
Bore and stroke (mm)	67.205 x 87.725	67.300x88.026	67.300x88.026
Displacement (cm^3)	2,434	2,505	2,505
Compression ratio	7.72:1	8.5:1	9.3:1
Maximum power (SAE)	105 hp at 4,800 rpm	112cv a 5.000	140cv to 5.000
Maximum torque (SAE)	16.5 m.kgf at 2,750 rpm	*	21 to 3.300
Transmission			
Type	3speed manual and reverse. Non-synchronized first until mid-1962	3 sychronized speeds	3 sychronized speeds
Brakes			
Type	Single hydraulic circuit, no powerbrake	*	*
Front	Drum	*	*
Rear	Drum	*	*
Suspension			
Front	Independent, McPherson, coils springs	*	*
Rear	Rigid axle, semi-elliptical longitudinal leaf springs	*	*
Steering			
Type	Worm and sector	*	*
Dimensions and capacites			
Wheelbase (mm)	2,690	*	*
Lenght (mm)	4,900	*	*
Width (mm)	1,770	*	*
Height (mm)	1,450	*	*
Ground clearance (mm)	170	*	*
Fuel tank (liter)	55	85	85
Curb weight (kg)	1,295	1,382	1,382
Wheels and tyres			
Type	Steel wheels and cross-ply tyres	*	*
Tyre size	165-380	*	*

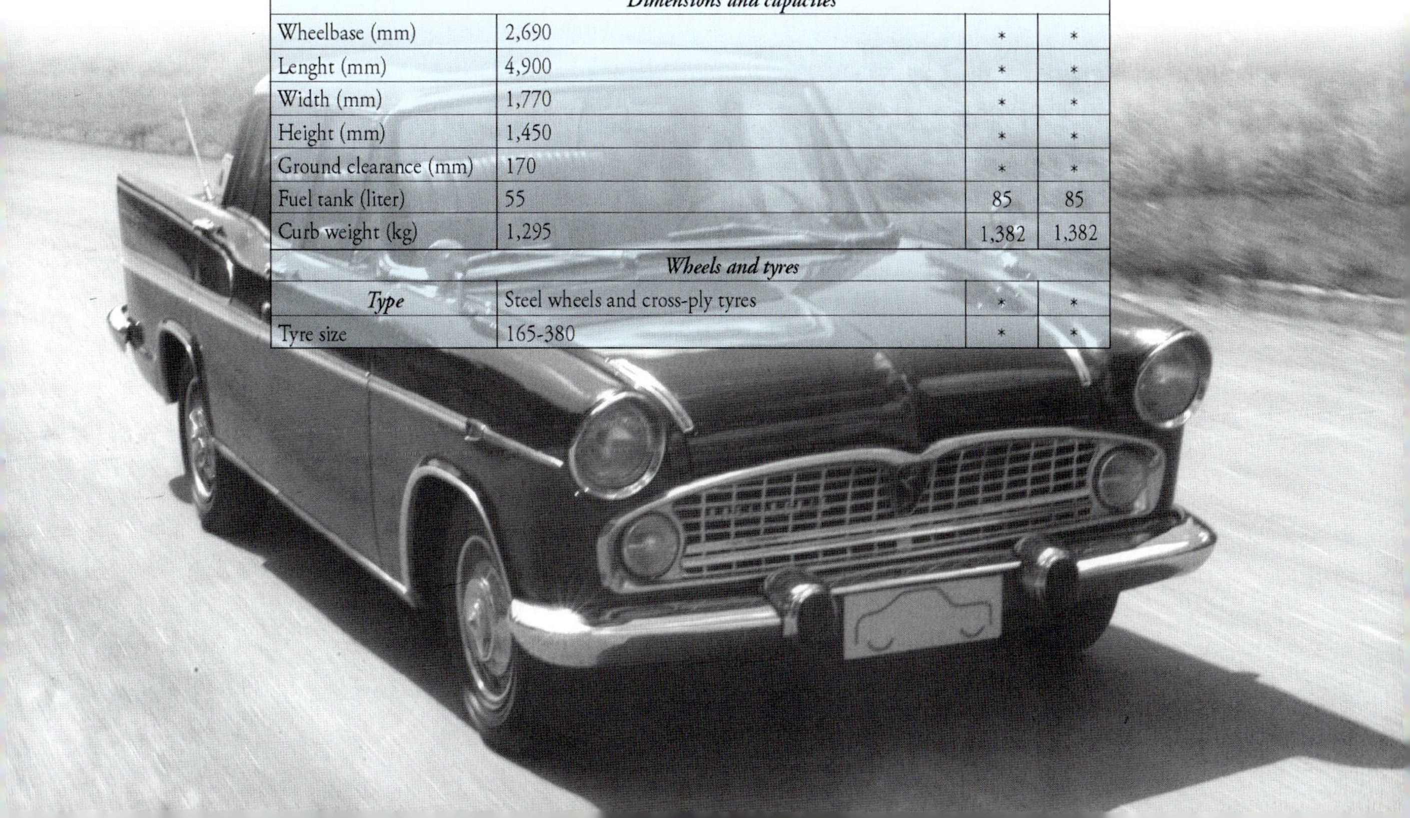

Muitas pessoas acham que êste é o carro mais bonit fabricado no Brasil.

SIMCA PRÉSIDE

Outras acham que é êste.

E muitas acham que é o Chambord.
(Talvez você prefira o Jangada.)
Entre os vários modelos Simca, existe diferenças de opinião. Mas, entre o Simca e os outros, a opinião é quase unânime. É Simca - o carro de maior categoria fabricado no Brasil. A esportividade do Rallye, a imponência do Présidence, o luxo do Chambord, a beleza do Jangada...
Em todos o confôrto Simca.

Mais espaço, mais visibilidade, mais luz, mais alegria.
Em todos, a mecânica Simca.
O poderoso motor Tufão, de 100 HP, e Tufão Super, de 112 HP, o mais poderoso dos carros nacionais. Tôdas as marchas sincronizadas.
A suspensão Stabimatic super-segura etc.. etc.
Em todos, o luxo Simca.

***Desempenho, Confôrto, Segurança* - SIMCA Tufão**

UIRAPURU

Sports cars

(1958 to 1967)

Small scale production (Brasinca; GT Malzoni/ Puma GT and Onça); Importeds (Volkswagen Karmann Ghia and Willys Interlagos)

In spite of being still at its first steps, yet in 1964 the Brazilian auto industry started to produce sports cars, i.e., automobiles whose concepts assumed bigger compromises with sensations and senses than with the basic task of providing comfort and practicality to just come and go.

The first to come was the Willys Interlagos. Introduced in three versions – Berlineta, a "mini" two-door sedan; Coupe and Convertible – it brought the proposal

From left to right and from foreground to background: 1965 white GT Malzoni branco; 1962 blue VW Karmann Ghia ; 1965 yellow Willys Interlagos Convertible; 1964 yellow Willys Interlagos Berlineta; 1970 white Alfa Romeo Giulia gt Junior 1300; 1968 red Ford Mustang GTA; 1965 blue Brasinca 4200 GT; 1967 white Uirapuru 4200 GT Convertible. In the front row, the small national sports cars and behind, the 1970 Alfa Romeo gt Junior, Italian – that repeated the lines of the Giulia GT 1600 model, produced from 1964 to 1967 –, the 1967 Ford Mustang GTA, American; and the national 1965 Brasinca 4200 GT, and the 1967 Uirapuru 4200 GT convertible. In 1965, Brasinca stopped producing automobiles and model 4200 GT started being assembled by STV under the Uirapuru nameplate.

to be the champion of the Brazilian circuits and to ratify the good performance provided by the Renault mechanics, which it used. Its lines were aggressive and suggested a superior performance.

The second would be the Karmann Ghia, in 1962, an elegant coupe of hand-crafted finishing. It was produced in a partnership between Karmann Ghia – a coachbuilder – and Volkswagen.

Built on the mechanical platform of the 1200 Sedan and marketed by the VW dealer network, the appeal of the Karmann Ghia was not its performance or its dynamic look. The coupe impressed by the harmonic look, finishing and by the assurance of image conferred to the owner – someone who in the name of beauty and of some exclusivity could expend a higher amount of money, giving up convenience and versatility.

Both the Willys and the VW were not exclusive models for the Brazilian market. The Interlagos was the Brazilian version of the Alpine A108, the French sports car that made use of Renault mechanics (the same as our yet to be launched Gordini), while the Karmann Ghia was the "twin" of the German one, also producer over there by means of a partnership between the mother companies.

The idea of launching the Alpine arose from the need the national automaker had in maintaining a winning racing team, as well as the French automaker of sports and racing cars in recognizing its model for racing. A minimum number of produced units was necessary for the car to be eligible for the Touring Car category up to 1,000 cm³.

Yet the idea of producing the Karmann Ghia was more practical and commercial, although as a sub-product – no question about it – it would associate the image of the brand to some extra sophistication. For having been the first Brazilian automobile to use fiberglass-reinforced plastic – instead of steel blanks – in building the body, the Interlagos became the school and cradle for the other national small-series sports cars launched since the first phase of our auto industry.

The first ever national sports car was the Willys Interlagos, launched in 1961, w\hen the Brazilian auto industry still crawled. Out there, in France, the car was made by Alpine – a heavy-weight name in motor racing – and used the Renault Dauphine as mechanical basis, a car produced here by Willys. In order to enter racing in the Touring category up to 1,000 cm³, Alpine needed achieve the production of 1,000 units, something the Brazilian could contribute to. Here Willys made full use of the communication power motor racing proportioned and took the model to become "invincible".

In 1964, to fight the Willys hegemony in motor racing, Vemag, the manufacturer of the DKW-Vemag, became interested in the sports car a farmer from Matão, in inland São Paulo state, called Genaro "Rino" Malzoni, had built with DKW underpinnings. The first win came in October 10, in Interlagos. Rino Malzoni made a second, slightly changed version of the car in fiberglass-reinforced plastic (the anterior had a steel body) and called it GT Malzoni, and Vemag bought three units to join the racing team. This car, whose lines suggested speed, achieved several wins in circuits in 1965 and 1966. The beauty and the success exceeded the racing boundaries and an independent company – Lumimari, then Puma Veículos e Motores

– was founded to produce it. A civilian version of the car began to be marketed with great success. In 1967, more sophisticated, it would evolve as Puma GT.

The three sports car, produced with either direct or indirect participation of the factories, were powered by engines of up to 1,200 cm^3 and, therefore, in spite of look or driveability, could not be effectively fast on the road.

In 1965, built in stamped steel, the Brasinca 4200 GT, also known and later re-christened Uirapuru, was an exception. By making use of the 4,275-cm^3 Chevrolet Brasil pick-up truck engine, the same used by the brand for its trucks – inside and outside Brazil – this sports cars definitely had a commitment to performance. It was conceived and made to demonstrate Brasinca's capability – a genuinely Brazilian producer of auto bodies – to produce a full home-designed automobile. It was and still is, until the end of the 20th century, the greatest national automotive pride.

Fábrica Nacional de Motores (FNM), by its side, shyly had put in the market the Onça, also built in a partnership with Malzoni. In the tradition of the Alfa Romeo brand, which in Italy had intensively exerted this schema, FNM handled over to the chassis to be coached by a prestigious designer. The lines of the Onça were not that original, for similarity with the Mustang was evident, however it could not be termed as a replica. After all, besides resizing, the design was interpreted through the Alfa Romeo badge. Owner of underpinnings sport-originated, the Onça matched shape to the car's behavior.

Briefly, in common the national sports cars of the first phase had the commitment of lending glamour to the art of driving and to build automobiles.

Very different between each other, they have made absurd direct comparisons.

Each one occupied own space within the restrict sports car's share of the market.

Individually, they were the "niche of the niche", yet they had to compete with quite a vast range of imported cars, both from the United States and Europe.

Close to the Brasinca's technical conceptions, there was the US-built Ford Mustang. The volume of this Ford imported to Brazil, whose price was quite competitive, was well superior to that of the produced 4200 GTs: 75 units from 1965 to 1967.

In spite of a well diverse conception, Italy's Alfa Romeo Giulia gt also participated of this niche and it had bitten a significant volume.

Who wanted a car with sporting characteristics and superior performance would have to go for cars produced abroad. It was very difficult to bring one, yet not impossible. From the US came the pony cars, automobiles like the Ford Mustang that had aggressively-designed bodies and mechanics quite similar to the brand's compact cars. The option for a V8 engine was capable of providing acceleration alike the European super machines. From Europe came medium-displacement grand-touring cars, technically quite sophisticated. Fast and with superior driveability, the Alfa Romeos were in the favorites' roster.

The first Mustangs (1964½ and 1965) featured, like the Brasinca, a six-cylinder engine, non-assisted steering and drum brakes. Evolution did not take long and soon had fitted a powerful V8, disc brakes (with booster) and hydraulic power steering, thus becoming superior to the best-made locally produced car.

The Italian Alfa, by its time, counted on technical sophistication which put in equal terms – in spite of powered by a 1,600-cm³ four-cylinder engine – with the Brazilian model displacing almost 4,300 cm³ and with the 4,700-cm³ American, regarding dynamic virtues.

For an even stricter consumer's band there were the super sports car arrived from Europe, Ferrari and Porsche and, from the USA, the Chevrolet Corvette. This was really a narrow band. It was part of the history of the automobile in Brazil as exception or reference only.

The market

The Willys Interlagos, produced between 1961 and 1966, had as its only direct competitor and only rival, both on the road and at the circuits, the GT Malzoni, in 1965 and 1966. the Puma GT, its direct descendant, was produced in 1967 only. Therefore, the Interlagos had competition when it was near phase-out only.

Willys took the lead and its team, with the Interlagos, became "invincible". Vemag went after the lost time. Genaro "Rino" Malzoni, at his farm in Matão (SP), had been building a sports car over the mechanical platform of the DKW-Vemag. After developing it on partnership, Vemag bought three samples for is racing team, which would be the leading one again. The Interlagos were phase-out in 1966, the year the GT Malzoni was launched. Therefore, in spite of the rivalry, market dispute did not exist.

Both had bodies made in fiberglass-reinforced plastic. The Interlagos had Renault Gordini underpinnings, while the GT Malzoni, that had DKW-Vemag's, had an extremely low production during the last two years the small Willys was produced. Somewhat more roomier, especially the Puma GT, they did not happen to offer convenience that justified the choice by who wanted a sports car yet comfortable, however, they could seat, even without the least comfort, taller people.

The performance of the DKW mechanics was superior to the Willys', yet the particularities that turned the DKWs into unique automobiles, both technically and in the way to drive them, were enhanced at the wheel of a sports car.

Although less fast and roomy, the Interlagos was nimbler and easier to drive.

Beauty was a common adjective of these sports cars, which exhibited coherence with their proposals in finishing also.

To own any of these cars was synonymous of prestige. The Interlagos carried along the glamour of having Alpine veins, a brand of sporting character of the highest lineage, while the DKW embodied the charm of being results of local designs of the manufacturer of genuinely Brazilian sports cars of the 20th century that would turn into the largest one – Puma.

The lack of comfort and versatility of both models equally explained – both with the DKWs and the Willys – the search for driving pleasure and beauty as being the biggest, if not the only, longing of who owned one.

The other small-size sports car in the market was the Volkswagen Karmann Ghia, which did not intend to offer fast driving. It did not stand out in the aspect of performance. It was made in pressed steel and weighted the same as the Volkswagen Sedan 1200, which it took platform and mechanics from.

The Sedan was a popular car that, did not try to or had any appeal speed-related.

The Karmann Ghia was elegant and served very well to urban tasks, in that it fell short of inside room to the best small cars of the time only. Lack of room was compensated by charm and attractiveness, preserving the concept that a sports car is the automobile that trades-off functionality for pleasure.

Who looked just for look should opt for the Karmann Ghia, however who looked for an effectively performing sports car should go to an import or a Brasinca 4200 GT, which later was called Uirapuru – the original design name.

The Brasinca made direct opposition to big-displacement sports cars imported from the USA and not directly so from medium-displacement Europeans.

In the first semester of 1964, in the USA, during the New York Auto Show, the Mustang was launched. With it, the birth of the pony car concept: sports looking cars and powerful engines, yet easy to handle as any other passenger car and capable of providing comfort, at least for up to occupants, similar to those.

It achieved instant success in North-American market. Immediately success arrived in Brazil, where it also turned out a desirable object.

The first Mustangs were powered by six-cylinder engines either 2,800 or 3,300-cm^3 and had drum brakes. The high production scale enabled new options to quick add to previous ones. The lineup range soon began to offer several engines, especially V8s with several displacements and power outputs; automatic or manual transmissions; disc brakes, power steering; fastback, hardtop and convertible body types; several finishing and decors, especially color paint schemes etc.

From Europe came medium-displacement sports cars, especially the Alfa Romeo Giulia gt. Displacing 1,600 cm^3, yet with more developed and sophisticated engines, counting on five-speed gearbox and four-wheel disc brakes, these car enjoyed *status* of winners in circuits all over the world, Brazilian ones included.

The design of the Brasinca was contemporarily conceived as the Ford's, but its birth was to happen some time later. When the Ford started counting on more powerful engines, disc brakes and all the optional items more than the Brasinca, whose handcraft production could not include them in the "menu", it is obvious that the national car became outclassed. However, it went on exhibiting the charm of being genuinely Brazilian and to embody a well more sophisticated design, with unitary construction, front mid-ship engine, low coefficient of drag and other technical sophistication that placed it in a differentiated technical level.

The Brasinca was heavy to drive and required certain extra skills to be driven at high speeds, while the Mustang was more like a passenger car, easy to drive and light in controls, in spite of not presenting a roadholding compatible with the high speeds it could attain.

On the other side, the Alfa Romeo had very distinct conception, nothing alike the Brasinca's or the Mustang's. It was, in relation to both, a light and compact car. Engine was medium-displacing and high-revving, exactly the contrary of what happened with competition, whose mechanics were American-originated. The Alfa was nimble and road holding, had four-wheel disc brakes and did not require many muscles to be driven. However, it claimed frequent gear changing as a five-speeder, and it was more sensitive, both in handling and maintenance. The Uirapuru, with plenty of torque, Chevrolet mechanics and just three speeds,

The Brasinca and Mustang designs are contemporary, yet the Mustang was launched shortly before. Elaborated under more sports concepts, the Brasinca was more sophisticated, but limitation was due to lack of resources and component available in Brazil in those years. Its engine, for instance, was from a truck. Demand did not enable heavier investment for its development. The opposite happened with the Mustang, which crowded the American roads. With many body, engine and equipment options, this Ford seduced ever more.

was much less "tricky", demanding less attention from the driver for daily driving, similarly to what happened with the American pony cars. At speed or adverse situations like slippery road, the situation inverted.

The Uirapuru and the Mustang required muscles and care for driving them, while the Alfa required cleverness and attention for itself.

ANOTHER OPINION

It was indeed a good moment of the auto industry and the national market's of cars that were different from the usual and offered pleasure to drive. Each on its own way of being and going. That is, there were sports cars almost for all tastes. "Almost" was said because the Mustang, although bearing a sporting look, was not a sports car of its own, yet it was nimbler than the average American car. Among them, the most brutal, in a good sense, surely was our Brasinca 4200 GT/Uirapuru. The more "made for drivers", undoubtedly, the Alfa Romeo Giulia gt.

Very different, they had as common denominator sporting. In the Alfa Romeo it could be found in every detail; in the Brasinca or Uirapuru, in the conception, performance and design; in the Mustang, in the performance and design; in the Interlagos and in the GT Malzoni, in the driveability and in the design; and in the Karmann Ghia, in the design. Design was the common denominator of sporting and beauty, the design's.

The Karmann Ghia can be classified as *hors-concours*, a separate chapter, for it combined unique, beautiful lines with a robust and dependable mechanics, although going fast was not its strong point due to the 30-hp-only engine. But it was the kind of plug-and-play automobile, it did not require any special care or maintenance. Its only problem, in fact, was the deceiving proneness to rust, which worsen even more in the not so pretty Karmann Ghia TC.

TECHNICALLY CORRECT

The Alfa Romeo Giulia gt, in a certain way, could be considered a dream car of the driver who appreciated virtuous automobiles. Its engine architecture, a DOHC, short for double overhead camshaft, instantly evoked motor racing. It was a marvelous engine to watch, which was aided by the two double-barrel side-draft Weber, Solex or Dellorto carburetors. It was the anti-thesis of the Brasinca/Uirapuru engine, the inline six-cylinder "sausage" Chevrolet engine, inherited from the truck of the brand, voluminous and tall that, like the Mustang, had a cast iron cylinder head. The engine of the Malzoni/Puma, a minute 981-cm^3 three-cylinder two-stroke, was a sort of "David against Goliath" in face to those with a greater displacement, with the exception of the 845-cm^3 Willys Interlagos'. Yet it was nervous and brilliant, it managed to convincingly propel the GT Malzoni/Puma GT.

PRICE TABLE OF SPORTS CARS[1]

	Model	1957	1958	1959	1960	1961	1962	1963	1964	1965	1966	1967	1968
Willys	Interlagos Berlineta							1,892		6,400	8,008		
Willys	Interlagos Coupe and Convertible							1,813					
VW	Karmann-Ghia							2,100	2,641	6,346.2	7,788	9,246	
FNM	Onça											25,000	
Puma	GT											13,500	

In spite of having very distinct proposals, the prices of the Interlagos and the Karmann Ghia were quite similar and ended being in the early years up to 70% higher than the models they shared the mechanics – Gordini and VW Sedan. Later on the difference leveled out in nearly 50%. The Puma GT, which used DKW underpinnings, was almost 50% more expensive than the Karmann Ghia, repeating the same percentage difference that was between the Vemag's sedan and the VW's. The Onça never had a significant production, serving as an illustrative reference only.

PRODUCTION TABLE OF SPORTS CARS[2]

Make	Model / Year	1957	1958	1959	1960	1961	1962	1963	1964	1965	1966	1967	Until 1967	1968	Total
Willys	Interlagos						218	138	209	149	108		**822**		822
VW	Karmann Ghia						759	1,868	2,285	1,951	2,400	3,009	**12,272**	5,000	17,272
Puma	Malzone										35		**35**		35
Puma	Puma GT											125	**125**		125
Puma	Puma Total	0	0	0	0	0	0	0	0	0	35	125	**160**	0	160
Sports Cars	**Total**	**0**	**0**	**0**	**0**	**0**	**977**	**2,006**	**2,494**	**2,100**	**2,543**	**3,134**	**13,254**	**5,000**	**18,254**

The Interlagos was built almost by hand, besides not very recommendable for daily use. The production of the Karmann-Ghia, in spite of hand-finished, was serial and its solutions enabled less discomfort, when compared to the Willys, in daily use. The Puma's construction was alike the Interlagos's, although it did not a dedicated structure – tubular. It used the DKW-Vemag Belcar chassis.

1. Prices informed in thousands of Brazilian cruzeiros by *Quatro Rodas* magazine, January issue of each year.
2. Data according to documents supplied by Anfavea.

Small scale production of genuinely national sports cars

Brasinca/Uirapuru (1965 to 1967), GT Malzoni/Puma GT(1966 / 1967) and Onça (1966)

Multinational automakers started to install in Brazil as of 1956, establishing the – so called then – automotive industrial park. It was truly an enthusiastic moment!

Formation of specialized labor, in all levels, followed immediately.

The wish of a genuinely national Brazilian automobile went latent and some designs started to concretize.

Evidently, the choice fell in cars of lesser demand, in that production did not require huge assembly lines and allowed greater creativity: less commitment on basic items related to comfort and greater freedom for styling as well as mechanical components, i.e., sports models.

The most daring of designs was that of Brasinca 4200 GT/Uirapuru, which had its own chassis and the larger displacing engine.

From fore to background: 1965 blue Brasinca 4200 GT; 1964 yellow Willys Interlagos Berlineta; 1966 white GT Malzoni; 1962 blue Volkswagen Karmann Ghia; 1965 yellow Willys Interlagos convertible; 1967 white Uirapuru 4200 GT. Both Volkswagen and Willys were in the sports car market with the Karmann Ghia and the Interlagos, respectively, yet they left room so that small companies, genuinely national, launched their products. In 1965 Brasinca started producing the 4200 GT that in 1967 would be built by STV under the Uirapuru na-meplate and, in 1966, Lumimari, which in the following year would become Puma and use this as brand name as well, would build the GT Malzoni. With some changes, it would be marketed as Puma GT in 1967. There was also a partnership between FNM and Malzoni that, in 1966, resulted in the Onça, yet with a minute production.

Brasinca / Uirapuru (1965 to 1967)

The Brasinca 4200 GT, which later on adopted the Uirapuru nameplate, the original name when on design stage, was conceived to directly face high-displacement sports cars imported from the United States and not so directly to medium-displacement European ones.

The 4200 GT featured quite advanced technical resources, especially to an almost-handcrafted entirely developed in Brazil. Just to make it clear: structure involved the cabin, what would later termed as monocoque; the body final design was adjusted in the wind tunnel and the doors had internal beams for protection in accidents, what would become mandatory in Brazil in the 1990s only. Frankly speaking, it was too much concept and low resources. From the aerodynamics studies, for instance, a low drag coefficient resulted, yet the monocoque structure made the car too wide by the frontal area, therefore making the volume of displaced air too big.

Applied technique and practical results

The Brasinca 4200 GT was designed by Rigoberto Soler, a Spaniard naturalized Brazilian that would later become well-known as automotive design professor at FEI, an university in São Bernardo do Campo (SP). The unitary construction was extremely light; the layout, well advanced by the engine location – front, between axles, mounted low to allow better aerodynamic performance and mass distribution – and rear-wheel drive. As for suspensions, the pattern was followed: independent up front, the same as the 1953 Chevrolet, and rear by rigid axle, yet using coil springs – just like in the Chevrolet Corvette – far superior than the leaf springs of most cars of American origin, Ford Mustang included. The design was studied and "approved" in the wind tunnel, resulting in a low drag coefficient; its dimensions were exaggerated for a two-seater, especially the width; its gearbox had three speeds only it was the same used in

The Chevrolet Brasil engine, equivalent to the known abroad as "GM 262 Truck Engine" – a GM displacing 262 cu. in. (4,275 cm³) – was fitted with three single-barrel, side-draft British carburetors with variable venturi. Horsepower gain was significant and hood line could be low. The chosen carburetor was the SU H4. The car in the picture is equipped with the SU HD8's, like in the XJ6 Jaguar, much larger than the original ones.

the Chevrolet pick-up truck, except for the shifting mechanism, that was adapted to floor shift – and brakes were of the drum type, also from the Chevrolet pick-up.

The engine was the inline six-cylinder, 4,275cm³ from Chevrolet which powered the commercial lineup, whose characteristics resulting from the high weight of the moving parts – crankshaft, flywheel, connecting rods and pistons – made it suitable for cargo transport: in fact, it was slow to launch from inertia – acceleration – and good when rolling. As improvement for performance, it had fitted in the factory three side-draft, variable venturi SU H4 carburetors and exhaust header and, as an option, an imported camshaft.

In spite of the light chassis, the car's overall weight was high. It's underpinnings, originating from commercial vehicles, weighted too much.

Even if its design focused on aerodynamics, the frontal area was large. It was very wide.

Its engine well aft in relation to the front axle did help roadholding, which was not brilliant.

Independently of all clever technical solutions, the components from Chevrolet automobiles of the 1950s and/or from the commercials of the brand curtailed performance.

On the other hand, even full of "truck underpinnings", the Uirapuru was truly fast. Its performance was impressive and fell within the pattern of some American V8s, with better roadholding.

In dynamic terms, it suffered from the unsuitable brakes for a truck system was fitted to it.

The whole front suspension was that of the Chevrolet cars of the 1950s that already at that time was not considered virtuous on efficiency.

Rear axle came from the Chevrolet Corvette, the super sports car that was the most prestigious of the Chevrolet brand and all America's. If it did not make a wonderful job, at least it was the best available.

The steering gear, without power steering, was also first generation Corvette's. Together with the rear suspension, they were the only imported items. The front suspension, even brought from American models, was entirely made in Brazil with local parts that existed already for the after-market.

The car was heavy to drive. In fast driving it required control effort and delicateness in moving them, quite a difficult equation to be solved by the driver. Nevertheless, a highly gratifying exercise when fully achieved, especially in view that the Brasinca attained high speeds, maybe something around 190 km/h, undoubtedly the fastest Brazilian automobile.

Temper

Cooking requires, for a good dish, good ingredients and sensitiveness in preparing it.

The recipe for a good car also requires the same qualities of ingredients and, as it happens in cooking, it will boast the personality marked by seasoning – temper.

No doubt, speaking of automobiles, the skill and the sensitiveness of the Brasinca "kitchen" proved to be efficient.

It departed from ingredients made for heavy-duty vehicles, mixed them with expertise, gave them form and design, applied advanced techniques to them and, finally, seasoned them with a lot of sportiveness.

Evidently, by using ingredients for a hamburger one cannot prepare intricate dishes, however the Uirapuru was a "sandwich" with strong personality and well-built. It counted on a pan with ingredients of American origin and, at the same time, was designed and manufactured in Brazil.

The Brasinca had a sporty temper, maybe more suitable for football – where power and speed are indispensable – rather than soccer played in Brazil – in which skill has always been the greatest of all necessary virtues.

Heavy and strong by origin, and with flexibility by creation, it got a temper of enthusiasm and sportiveness.

Urban, daily driving the Brasinca

Practical is not a right adjective for many sports cars and the 4200 GT was no exception, in spite of featuring adequate operation for daily use and easy maintenance.

The first start in the morning, still with a cold engine, was easy and its working, steady even before reaching the normal, ideal temperature for that.

Cabin access was not difficult, for, even being a low car, door opening extended to roof, a good help for this operation.

A) Nothing was just decorative, everything was functional. The low roof, like in most sports cars, could make difficult the in and out movement. Aiming to provide more comfort in this moment, there was a prolonging in the doors that advanced over the roof. At the engine hood, like in other parts, there were air outlets that helped to cut drag. However, there were side-effects: in rainy days, as the door was opened, occupants would be unprotected. Together with the good airflow, some dirt would escape from the engine compartment. B) Decorative for sure were the outside mirrors, that otherwise helped very little.

The car fulfilled without "laziness" the stop-and-go of the big cities' traffic; it was easy to sustain speed in the large avenues on it and it did not suffer nor transmitted discomfort on rough paving.

Against it, there were all the other characteristic of sports and large cars.

The classification of sports car, by itself, suggests an automobile much more committed to the act of driving than transporting.

In spite of access made easy by prolonging the doors over the roof, when it came to step out, the low seat cushion height to floor and even to ground demanded a certain effort, as well as to open the doors that, when there was not enough room to fully open them, forced to unpleasant body motions. In rainy days, the opening extension became bothersome: when opening the doors, it started to rain on the occupants.

The only room for goods was behind the rear seats. The trunk small volume at the rear was almost fully used by the spare wheel.

The acts to place goods in were not ideal, the same when it was time to take them out.

The body style did not provide good visibility to maneuvering and the heavy steering, which demanded lot of turns lock to lock, did not helped.

A) The fenders of the photographed model were widened in order to allow the use of wider wheels and tires. The original set, radial-ply like the FNM 2000's, with 400-mm diameter rim, were difficult to find at the time and "have definitely vanished" after 1973. B-C) The car's design was very up-to-date and what drew more attention the large rear window. Obsession for technique was such that even the exhaust tail pipes positioning followed wind tunnel studies.

In spite of limitations typical of two-seat automobiles, sports cars in essence, the Brasinca was not unworkable at all in traffic. Many other sports cars added to the list of inadequacies for city driving rough idle speed, tendency to overheat in slow traffic and a huge difficulty in dealing with the unevenness of paving.

Sports cars identified themselves with "sport" situations – no commitment to work. They are automobiles for pleasure, not for mere commuting. The ideal for a GT 4200 owner was to have a car for daily commuting or otherwise to exert a distinct routine, with schedules and routes of his own, different from those ordinary people who work in offices or other places customarily use.

On the road

The Uirapuru had comfortable seats; firm suspension; powerful, pleasant roar engine, thanks to the triple carburetion and to the exhaust header that produced a sound in not exaggerated volume that pleased; third and last gearbox speed reasonably tall that allowed high speeds at low engine revolutions, therefore with little noise and low vibration; a low drag coefficient, responsible for almost absent wind noise, specially with windows closed; a good wheelbase, and long wheelbases are credentials for long distances when – supposedly – there will be more stretches than curves; good accessories such as windshield wipers and

A) The seat cushions were at the same line of the structure, what characterizes it as monocoque. The seats were comfortable and the finishing followed the order of top luxury British cars: leather and prime wood. B-C) Controls were designed like in the best racing cars, with the fuse box integrating the style of the dashboard, right below the respective switches. The sporty, large-diameter steering wheel, of the Walrod brand (the original steering wheel rims did not feature chromed segments), actuated an extremely slow steering box (with many turns lock-to-lock) and even so it was heavy.

headlights; easy service and, except for the carburetion – the system included the less conventional variable venturi solution, "almost blind" for most technicians in engine service – the underpinnings of the Uirapuru was the most conventional and known of all, besides being extremely dependable. There were predicates not despicable for long trips.

The 4200 GT sustained high cruising speeds and had a hefty acceleration. Overtaking was a problem only when a balanced braking – almost impossible to accomplish – was required to get back to the original lane.

Roadholding in hilly sections was reasonable and tight radius turn only represented some difficulty, especially when braking was required.

Brasinca was a renowned manufacturer of automotive bodies. To design and manufacture a full automobile was an institutional move above all, a way to prove its competence. Hence the car had not been launched with Uirapuru nameplate. However, the stylized "B" had everything to do with a bird.

Weight and slowness of steering wheel and tension generated by the fact that the brakes were not "good companions", either for correcting an unwanted side motion or for fading, were the cons.

Luggage room was another limiting factor. Just the luggage for two for not more than a short journey could be lodged.

Between pros and cons, what weighted in favor was the fact of the 4200 GT be able to enhance a simple trip with speed.

The Uirapuru and I

In 1965, therefore I was only 4 years old then, the Brasinca 4200 GT was launched. Just 75 units were produced until 1967.

In spite of my deep interest for cars, I only noticed the model in the mid-1970s, when I began to read old car buff magazines at my school's library.

In the early 1990s, I bought samples that lacked restoring or, more appropriately, rebuilding.

One of them was a 1965 Brasinca 4200 GT that among the original specifications lost were the missing triple carburetion and the elimination of the roof prolonging for the doors.

The last produced Brasinca and, in sequence, all Uirapurus made had rectangular headlights, which replaced the circular ones from the first models. The front grille has always been the same, but this convertible, since when I bought it, has always been so. It has been modified by some owner, or perhaps STV itself, since this was one of the last sold samples. The convertible presented in the auto show also did not have front turn indicator blinkers. According to the explanation by one of the factory associates, this must have happened for 'absolute lack of time".

All the body parts of this convertible, except for the engine hood, had to be hand-made during restoration. The 4200 GT structures had a topless version in mind, but all cars were generated from closed bodies. Upon transforming them in open-body type, STV has produced just two samples. The car in the picture, one of the last 4200 GT produced (body no. 73), possibly had been bought disassembled and later transformed.

The other was a 1967 Uirapuru, probably one of the last produced and transformed into a convertible (all Uirapurus were conceived as a closed coupe, but two of them were made convertibles. The sample I purchased, almost for sure, was bought – by the first owner – not fully assembled and later on transformed into a convertible).

The cars were in such a bad shape that I had no courage to restore them before 1997.

The closed one was readied in 2000 and the convertible, which had spent years of its life as a chicken perch, in 2003.

The ample, total and unrestricted rebuilding of the rare samples has given me lots of knowledge about the car and its history.

To run it in city traffic, to travel and to participate in some racing has helped me to better understand this automobile which is, very probably, the most daring and important Brazilian design of the pioneering phase.

During rebuilding I have been able to be in contact with the main people involved in its design and production. Never an experience in rebuilding has been so rich in information and explanatory as the one lived during the dismantling and reassembling periods.

The first detail that drew attention was the chassis – the side rails were formed by a "sandwich" of steel plates with round cuts. It weighted just 200 kg and could be moved by four men during the shop operations. The design of the side rails suggested what was afterwards called a monocoque, used in racing single-seaters, that is, they surrounded the cabin up to top seat cushion level, where door openings raised from.

Restoring the closed-body model was a little less arduous, although several parts had to be redone all the mechanics rebuilt. Among the changes made by former owners, which had to be reverted, the were some quite common ones, such as eliminating the door prolonging over the roof, and eliminating the air louvers from the engine hood. These changes were usually performed by 4200 GT specialists.

The anti-impact collision reinforcement by side bars inside the doors was a design sophistication. Something so advanced that it would be seen again in Brazilian cars in the mid-1990s, when it was mandated after technical norms about occupant protection in side impacts.

Side-draft carburetors were chosen with the aim of reducing engine height and by consequence that of the hood, a requirement of commitment to streamlining.

The result was positive enough, including what refers to performance. In spite of being considered as something mysterious and hard to service by most auto mechanics of the time, in fact these carburetors were just different and even simpler than the conventional ones.

Fifteen-inch wheels and tires (215/70 R15), that maintained the original dynamic perimeter (175R400), were the option I had to take during rebuilding. Fenders had to be widened. In the 1970s, this was a widely used solution to keep the cars running, with no major changes in driving characteristics.

The engine was in fact old-fashioned and designed for heavy duty. Its crankshaft was supported by only four main bearings (six-cylinder engines – especially those that powered its contemporary American engines – had seven) and was impressively heavy.

All details were well-designed: finishing, instrument location, materials in general, electrical system etc.

During restoring, I went through a typical dilemma: to stick with the cars' usage originality or aspect. This was quite a difficult equation to solve

In both cars I decided to use wheels and tires different from original, but preserving their original overall diameter (and therefore the road speed-engine speed relation). Since the tires were wider, I had to widen the fenders. The original tires were 174-400 radials, i.e., 175 mm at cross section and made to fit 400-mm, or 15.8 in. rim diameter, the same fitted to the FNM 2000, a rare tire size and unavailable in local market as of the 1970s. Therefore, when found they were no longer serviceable due to rubber ageing. When the cars were purchased, they had 14-in. wheels and tires, quite common, but they made the car too short transmission-wise, which was not convenient, for it was more adequate for a utility.

The side-draft carburetors had also been replaced by a sole downdraft, conventional one and the exhaust header, too, the same as the truck's

Truck engine, truck recipe and truck transmission with truck final ratio could only result in driving very close to that of a truck.

With the change at the fenders, the Uirapurus were no longer eligible to win originality concourses, but in as a trade-off they could be driven like sports cars and run regularity rallies for antique cars without major trip counter and speedometer errors as long as original wheel-tire diameter were maintained.

The coupe won larger diameter triple carburetion, therefore with a higher flow than original's, whose size was very rare and not found anymore even in England, the country where SU carburetors were made.

Besides the larger carburetors, the exhaust system was refitted with a header and the camshaft (Iskenderian, American) the 4200 GT, SS version was equipped with. There was a base version with the stock Chevrolet camshaft, a heftier one with a slight sportier camshaft – the "S" – and the most powerful of all, whose camshaft was even more developed, called "SS".

In 2003, the "Carro do Brasil" exhibit – in Brasília, DF – gathered eleven of the remaining samples out of 75 produced. It has always been difficult to be spotted. Eleven units together, not even in the factory inventory.

For the convertible, I managed to find an original carburetion that had to undergo a long restoring process and worked like new afterwards. The adopted camshaft, also Iskenderian, was that of version "S" and the exhaust header was not forgotten.

On the coupe, I have restored the door prolonging, eliminated during the car's life by someone who – as almost all that really used the car for daily commuting and did not like rain water overhead at all – has spent money to make, a difficult and expensive job.

Once finished the restoring periods (in fact they never finish or are sufficiently good), the first drive with the coupe was for an exhibition in São Lourenço, at the Minas Gerais Water Circuit.

The exit from São Paulo city was via Ayrton Senna highway, a fast-traffic road. At the time (2000), cruising speed of the faster travelers was around 140 km/h, a pace the Brasinca would be able to sustain effortlessly, it was not a driveability problem from the steering system: when I bought the car it had a Ford Galaxie (1968 to 1983) power steering set and it was "undriveable". During restoration, it was replaced by a rack and pinion steering box (the original was by worm and sector with recirculating balls), that magnified the problem.

On the hill, and São Lourenço was embedded in the mountains, the problem was even more sensitive. To overcome the trip was a prize, regardless of fatigue and real risk!

During the event there was an acceleration contest from standstill to1,000 meters. The Brasinca showed what it had come to. It was the champion of the three direct confronts it was raced: it did better than a 1973 Dodge Dart, a 5,200-cm^3 V8, left behind a FNM 2000 Timb, which would break even with the Dodge, and finally if defeated a 1972 Chevrolet Camaro 5,700-cm^3 V8.

To complete its feats at the event, even if it could not be considered as "100% original", it was prized as highlight.

In 1999, at the Exposição Nacional – in São Lourenço, MG – two samples meet, soon after restoring work had finished. With mine, the blue one, I achieved to arrive by road. I met the yellow there, which came from Brasília, which was finished in the eve of loading up. The two were awarded for distinction.

The trip home, with light rain in some sections, was not easier than outbound.

The search for an original steering box was incessant. In 2002, I finally found one. The definite driveability test was done soon, in a hillclimb race.

Ran through the tortuous 4,380 m-long road that takes to Guarujá Peak – in the surroundings of São Paulo city – the competition is against the clock: start is done by a vehicle at a time with 2-minute interval and the elapsed time is registered – there is no direct confront nor overtaking.

My pretension was to break the record for national cars, which belonged to the FNM Furia, also driven by me. It was not possible, though.

In spite of the much more powerful engine and not having performance compromised by the brakes – it's an uphill run, after all – gearbox's bigger number of speeds lacked. Just three speeds restrained it from overcoming the Alfa (the Furia is an Alfa Romeo prototype from 1972) in the small-radius curves. In spite of the abundant torque does hide the lack of one more speed in the road or in town, in a hillclimb race a gearbox with at least four speeds, it did not (the Furia had five speeds).

Tight curves were never a Brasinca specialty, however its driveability did not compromise.

The car pointed well to curves with no understeer; along the curve it started to oversteer in the peculiar way of cars with mid-ship engines – it tended to turn around an imaginary axis located at the center of the car –, demanding immedi-

After crossing the finish line of the Pico do Jaraguá, SP hillclimb, the drivers, next to their cars, gather and watch other competitors negotiate the last bends of the steep and winding route. Next to a 1968 Mustang, a 1965 Brasinca displays its advanced lines. After hard work behind the wheel, I meet a friend.

ate counter-steering (to turn the steering wheel opposite to the curve) and finally blast off with "pedal to floor".

Steering movements are intense. The many necessary turns for the corrections of the route and the very big-sized steering wheel result in real hard work.

Upon crossing the finish line I already knew that my expectations were not realized. Several times I used third where I should be using a shorter speed, but not as short as second. The registered time (2:30,67s) was practically the same I had attained with a 1967 FNM 2000, worse than with a 1968 FNM 2000 Timb and much worse than 2:15,69s obtained with the 1972 Furia. The time of the 1965 Brasinca 4200 GT, even far from the record, can be considered as respectable.

Had it one more speed (the Uirapuru had a four-speed gearbox – from the Chevrolet Corvette – as an option, however a very few were fitted with this equipment) and if the tires were the same as those of the FNM I raced, the story could have been another one. They were using tires far more suitable for this hillclimb than the ones the Brasinca had – in that, originally, were fit with the same tire type.

The convertible was readied in 2003 and its inaugural drive counted on a quite common fault to Chevrolet rear axles of the 1950s – the axle end broke and the wheel fell off (almost completely) at Castello Branco highway, after 38 kilometers and at 120 km/h/. It was a light fright.

Some time later I could go by road to an exhibition in Águas de Lindóia.

The recipe for the engine, the same as the optional "S" engine, proved excellent and the car turned the heads (in a very positive way) where it went by. In Lindóia, it was crowned among the highlights, even with the widened fenders.

If the coupe arises some disagreement for its design, the convertible is unanimity: everybody likes it.

GT Malzoni

As a result of the same moment of enthusiasm and adequate human resources that of the Brasinca, in 1966 it was the time the Malzoni was launched.

The Malzoni came to life with the commitment of giving competitiveness back to team Vemag, therefore it used complete DKW underpinnings.

The differences that assured to the GT a better performance were in the body made in fiberglass-reinforced plastic, with low weight and small frontal area design, as well as for the reduced wheelbase from the original 2,450 mm to 2,220 mm. The chassis was cut 230 mm at its widest point, a little before the rear axle.

There was a close relation between Vemag and the production of the car. Differently from what happened with the Brasinca, where all details and components had to be chosen and developed, the daring of the Malzoni came from its design.

Everything that can be said about the DKW respectful of mechanical parts is applied to the Malzoni, however the sporty temper of it was exacerbated.

In a time application or even aerodynamics studies were still crawling and suspension systems were rustic, besides not being able to handle great responsibilities over to tires, the small frontal area and the low center of gravity meant almost everything. Wheelbase, shortened in relation to the DKW sedan – that has lent it the chassis and all the mechanics – enhanced the good performance in twisty circuits. Design privileged sports driving, but nothing was as important as low weight, especially for being a two-stroke-powered car, whose power came in at a narrow engine speed band only, and displaced 1,000 cm³ only.

Seating two only and very close to ground, the Malzoni was even more eccentric to be driven than the sedan.

The shifter was floor-mounted and first gear was engaged moving the lever backwards; second, straight ahead; third, parallel to first on the next channel; and fourth, straight ahead from third. All movements were thus inverted in relation to most cars: what in other cars was to shift up, in the Malzoni it was to shift down. By the way, in the column-stalked DKW-Vemag's gearshift the same inversion existed.

The engine had forced water circulation just like the vast majority of engines, but not in the DKW-Vemag, which was by thermo-siphon. For such, the GT Malzoni counted on a water pump unit coupled to the dynamo and, mechanically, this was the deepest engine modification. It was necessary because the radiator was placed lower than in the car it derived from, what made difficult a good work of the thermo-siphon. Identical solution and for the same reason had to be adopted in German model Auto Union 1000 Sp.

The engine is considered the heart of the car, nevertheless styling has a strong influence in temper and behavior of an automobile.

The first evidences concern inside room and comfort. Very different from what occurred with the DKW, entry was short of convenient, as passenger room and the minimum luggage space were also. As for design peculiarities that did not contribute at all to comfort, the windshield was very tilted, as well as the rear window (in acrylic) was curved and close to the occupant's backs. This way, solar rays invaded the cabin and "toasted" driver and escort, no matter where they came from.

In DKWs, coolant circulation was by thermo-siphon – the heated water goes up and the cooled one goes down. The GT Malzoni, for its purpose, was forced to use a conventional cooling circuit – with a water pump – with greater cooling capacity and occupying less vertical room. If thermo-siphon was used, the radiator would have to lie above the engine line, to where the water heated by the engine naturally would go, to return after being cooled.

Almost no virtue was added referring to use as a vehicle for daily commuting. However, the DKW mechanics was the same as the Belcar sedan's or even as the Vemaguet station wagon's, thus it was ready for normal use.

The GT Malzoni (1966), then the Puma GT (1967) and later on Puma automobiles on Volkswagen and Chevrolet underpinnings, were the proof that, by adding some details only, it was possible to produce good sports cars by means of a well-designed body assembled over mechanical components aimed for touring cars.

"The engine is the heart of the car, but the soul belongs to whom builds it". The GT Malzoni was born with vocation for racing and DKW underpinnings. From its first evolution came the Puma GT, in 1967. In 1968, the DKW would not be produced any more and Puma had to go for the VW mechanics, by launching the Puma VW 1500. With an inverted layout, rear engine and wheel drive, the 1500 kept the "soul" of the predecessor. In the picture, several models. The first one is a 1966 racing GT Malzoni; the second, a 1967 Puma GT; and the third, a 1975 Spartan Puma GT that has been built with the goal of keeping alive the brand at the circuits.

Technical particularities

Three were the differences that marked the sports cars with DKW mechanics from the touring cars of the brand: they were light, aerodynamic and had a shorter wheelbase. The DKW two-stroke engine, by itself, demanded an exclusive driving style, providing acceleration in medium to high engine speed only: an inadequate and undesirable characteristic in cars built for normal use, but nothing critical in a sports car.

The power-to-weight ratio was favorable.

The aerodynamics contributed to good performance in high speeds.

The short wheelbase provided greater capacity to deal with small radius curves.

And the GT Malzoni, as well as the Puma GT, looked nice. Its lines made it an object of desire.

Driving the sports car

No equation needs to be solved – until the end – to know the result: these cars did not come to the world for work but for sport.

Perhaps in the internal vision of Vemag, where motorsport was conducted with professionalism, the Malzoni had been born for work, but it was not just for this work that it could be used.

It was possible to go shopping, it was possible to face traffic and, most of all, it was possible to come and go anywhere not being stranded or bothered by faulty working.

Any trip could be made and driving pleasure would be always present. The little car performed well and valiantly sustained high speeds.

The drive, once the lack of comfort was merrily unconsidered, could be almost as pleasant as the shower or leg stretching upon arrival.

The GT Malzoni did not do good as an efficient transport mean for a person of ordinary habits and timetables, but as a source of pleasure for people who had a different day and cared to driving as a habit. Entry and exiting were little convenient, as seats and driving position would not rank among the top ten. Solar rays found free way to annoy the occupants, regardless of it from behind, the sides at front: the rear window was curved, leaning and "glued" to the seat backs; and the windshield, even not too leaning, allowed that it reached the stretched legs of driver and escort.

Roadholding was very good and the brakes (disc optional at front), sufficient. A very fews cars had front-wheel drive at the time. The Malzoni, as any DKW, made best use of this resource, but not without having to pay a price for that, as well as it would refrain from using its advantages.

The very first characteristic provided by the system was shimmy (wheel tramp) during acceleration – inevitable, even for a front-wheel drive, 1,000-cm^3 car from those years, when practically the homokinetic joints that would kill for good the problem – inexistent in today's cars – were yet to enter the stage.

The name change from Malzoni to Puma did not represent any "endless" changes. On the contrary, they were extremely alike, yet they bore some differences. The Malzoni was the result of the first ideas of "Rino" and the people from the Vemag racing team. The Puma added some more "civility". It was not just the "core", but it did not get to far away from it.

Understeer (the front plowing out) was an effect easy to live with. Considered easier to correct than oversteer, especially in front-wheel drive cars (it suffices to lift the foot of the gas pedal and steer a little more to the inside – something almost instinctive), although it was also considered as less technical and pleasure-giving (sporty).

A characteristic of two-strokers is to look "infinite", they don't seem to stop revving up. Hence the high and easily sustained top speed.

On the circuits, the Malzoni reason of being, the car showed "what it came to": it was efficient and fast.

The Puma GT was more sophisticated and civilized than the GT Malzoni, although the manufacturing of the fiberglass-reinforced body made it clear the deficiency of the handcraft process and the low resources it was made with.

Experience with the sports DKWs

The production of these sports cars was very small, however the beauty of the Puma GT, with DKW underpinnings, was not unnoticed to the eyes of the child.

If a few only were produced, fewer of them keep running. Progressively they were out of the social niches they daily frequented.

In the late 1980s I bought a GT Malzoni in good condition, recently restored and working well. The difficulty in servicing it – not that the DKW has a complicated mechanics, but it is unique – made me postpone the necessary adjustments for a good performance and a pleasant use.

It was on early 2000s only that I took the right measures for better using this old acquisition.

Even before the needed adjustments, I used the little car, including in the 1990 Jaraguá Peak hillclimb.

The hillclimb race, as its name suggests, is a racing event organized by the Auto Union DKW Club of Brazil at the Pico do Jaraguá, in the outskirts of São Paulo City. In a homage to the organizing club, more than once I had chosen the GT Malzoni to race there. My results with other cars have always positively surprised me: when I compared my elapsed times with the other competitors' in other rounds with similar cars, I was always among the best. With the GT Malzoni it has never happened. My E.T.s were always average, partially because mine is a road version, quite heavier than the racing ones, but I also know the countless times I made driving mistakes in a route so full of peculiarities.

Used to achieving good results in this competition (related more to the cars' performance than to the driver), this time I was somewhat disappointed with the car (yet to reach its best condition) and very much with myself, for not being proficient in gear changing.

The DKW engine not only should, but it must work in a narrow power band to power any automobile, and that includes the very light GT Malzoni. During the uphill run I shifted into third gear and the engine dropped by much its response. In this situation it emits a "hollow" sound denouncing lack of power. Gear engaging was imprecise – I have never achieved good shift lever precision, yet in this situation they were critical – and gear changing was never in accordance to what was previously wanted. Besides, I was never absolutely sure were the needed speed was. Since the positions are inverted, to go down from third to second it is necessary a little usual movement – that of going from fourth to first in a gearbox with a conventional gear pattern.

The registered time of 3:58,93 s was not that bad, but at the end it was very far from the best up to then obtained by other Puma GTs or GT Malzonis.

In 2002, with the car better adjusted, I entered a race at the José Carlos Pace, in Interlagos, south district of São Paulo city. I clog in the fuel did not al-

To be stranded in a start is very frustrating. I shared this experience with that of many DKW drivers. The two-stroke engine, especially the DKW's, usually promptly responds to the starting motor, however, when the spark plugs get fooled…

Vemag has always had a strong tradition in racing. The Auto Union DKW Club of Brazil kept it alive by promoting races with the cars of the time. In this one, in May of 2006, the start was Le Mans-style, i.e., first the drivers run towards the cars, them start with them. As usual, I arrived at the Malzoni in average time, but I took a while to note that the engine had started already. It has cost me first place, since I crossed the finish line in the first lap almost forty seconds behind the other Malzoni, the pole position. I finished second, seven seconds behind.

low me to go more than a few meters, therefore I could not redeem myself as a Malzoni racing driver.

Before that, in starting the light restoring of the car, I discovered a world that went around the DKW. Remaining mechanics of the time and some disciples that did not see mysteries in the two-stroke technique – on the contrary, they were intimates of it – proving that it was not complicated, it just happened that it was not conventional.

ONÇA FNM

The importance of the Alfa Romeo brand, in the history of the automobile in Brazil, goes far beyond the production figures expressed FNM (Fábrica Nacional de Motores).

In the Xerém district, a municipality of Duque de Caxias city, laid FNM headquarters, as well as Volta Redonda (RJ) was the town that hosted and lived around CSN (National Steel Company). Both were a product of the Getúlio Vargas administration under a dictatorial régime called New State, beginning in 1937 and lasting until 1945, when the president was ousted (he would return to power by voting in 1950, but committed suicide in August of 1954 amid a stormy political crisis).

These localities were part of the industrial plant (and vice-versa) that, as a whole, integrated the government's (the "boss") industrialization plan.

In the Juscelino Kubitschek administration – beginning 1956 – the Executive Group for the Automotive Industry (Geia) was created with the aim of installing the auto industry in Brazil.

FNM was integrated in this program by establishing an agreement with Italian Alfa Romeo, also a state company, with the objective of producing the Alfa Romeo berlina 2000, christened here FNM 2000 JK.

Alfa Romeo was an acknowledged brand much more for its sporting excellence than for its qualities as "population booster" for the roads. The option for the brand already demonstrated – by itself – that, besides the "go-and-come", the automobile exerted other ties within the Brazilian living.

Repeating and honoring the tradition – brought in from Italy – that the brand had in setting partnerships with carrozzieri (designers and independent car body producers), FNM has build, together with Rino Malzoni, the Onça.

FNM intended to honor the Alfa Romeo make tradition in developing partnerships with famous designers, except in an absolutely "tupininquim" (Brazilian way) format. From a partnership with Rino Malzoni the Onça was born. The monocoque structure was FNM 2000's, with a shorter wheelbase and a fiberglass-reinforced plastic body, in a recipe that repeated that of the GT Malzoni. The lines were "more than clearly" inspired in the Ford Mustang's. When Alfa Romeo from Italy learned about the initiative of its Brazilian "subsidiary", it was not that pleased and ordered that production and sales were halted.

In common with other "GTs" built under informal partnership between Malzoni and Vemag automaker, the Onça was constructed in fiberglass-reinforced plastic over the shortened platform of the FNM 2000. Also in common with the Puma GT (the GT Malzoni successor), the name of a feline.

Before launching, the Onça already caused a certain turmoil in automotive circles. It was widely known that the "Achilles Heel" of the JK in motor racing was its high weight. With the same recipe used by Rino Malzoni for the DKW, in wich weight and wheelbase reduction played a role, the Alfa Romeo underpinnings seemed invincible. In Brasília, the nation's capital the expectations for the car's debut in the circuits was such that a prototype, also using a Alfa Romeo's components, was baptized "Espingarda" (shotgun) – a weapon for shooting felines.

Onça official debut at the circuits did not happen and just a dozen units, perhaps less, of this model were produced. By originating from the JK, evidently it kept the sporting manners of the models.

Until 1973, Alfa Romeo did not allow the use of its name nor its badge in any automobile produced in Brazil. However, the world-known front grille was present and the Alfa Romeo badge could be considered illegalcopying, if it was not for Alfa Romeo agreeing with it, what transformed it in a good-taste interpretation.

The Onça design was to the Ford Mustang as well as the FNM badge was for the Alfa Romeo's. Nevertheless, in spite of the not-consenting by Ford, it could be looked as an "Brazilian/Alfa Romeo" interpretation of the Mustang. The Onça was a sports car by origin. Everything from the JK helped to compose its character and it was enhanced by a body quite more light and by the design more in tune with the temper provided by the mechanical components.

Unfortunately, the constant route changes, resulting from an industry in which the country's politics and its company decisions mixed up, did not allow the Onça to effectively meet its rationale – being at the same time the Alfa Romeo sports car and the Brazilian Mustang. However, the few units produced accomplished this mission.

Co-living with the Onça

As it had happened with the Brasinca/Uirapuru, I only learned about the model after it was phased-out.

Since a very few units were produced, I had real contact with the car at motor exhibitions only, this in 2003 already.

In spite of the intimacy I have with Alfa Romeo models – especially those made in Brazil – I had never experienced living with the Onça.

ANOTHER OPINION

It was really a golden decade, that of 1960, concerning creativity of Brazilan designers, engineers and auto mechanics. The Brasinca/Uirapuru, the GT Malzoni/Puma GT, and the Onça have marked their presence as sports cars entirely apt to start a career anywhere in the world. The Uirapuru was the most typically local-made of the three, and since it had a chassis of its own and a stamped steel body, all the merit goes to the company that had built it, Brasinca, which had made the stamping tools. These, as it is known, for the high cost involved, are normally applied to high-series production, what was not the case of this sports car. Merit for the courage, without the least doubt.

As for the GT Malzoni, a new material called fiberglass-reinforced plastic was used, which served also for the Puma GT and the Onça and that, in a pioneering way in Brazil, had been adopted for the Willys Interlagos a short time before.

Of these models, the GT Malzoni and the Puma GT only would know success that would unfold, for circumstantial reasons. The Brasinca/Uirapuru suffered the sudden and total disinterest of the factory in keeping building it, in spite of the good outlook, and the Onça, based on the FNM 2000, lacked a firm directive of its manufacturer, the state-owned Fábrica Nacional de Motores; a few units only were built, it is believed that five or six.

The 4200 GT under Brasinca or Uirapuru nameplate, closed or open body, and the DkW sports car with Malzoni or Puma name, were the more representative national sports cars of all times. Inserted amid the Willys Interlagos and the VW Karmann Ghias, they have hallmarked the most magic of all moments of Brazil's history of "automobile hall of fame".

TECHNICALLY CORRECT

The success of the GT Malzoni and the Puma GT, both DKW-Vemag-based, is due exactly to the three-cylinder two-stroke engine power famous for its performance in the circuits. They were also helped by the fact of being front-wheel drive cars, by itself and in those days capable of providing a dynamic behavior at the same time fast and safe. Besides, the mechanical base was the cheaper of the three and cost to produce them was quite low.

The Brasinca/Uirapuru had all the ingredients to reach success, it had a powerful engine as it is expected from a sports car, yet with some limitations like the three-speed gearbox, awkwardly seen by fast cars lovers. Besides, its 4.2-liter and four main bearings six-cylinder engine was too "torquey" and revved little. It was a pity that the seven-main bearing six-cylinder Chevrolet engine has arrived later, or history could have been another one.

TECHNICAL INFORMATION OF BRASINCA

VEHICLE	Brasinca 4200 GT (1964 to 1966) and Uirapuru 1967	S	SS
Type	Coupe or convertible 2-door, 2-passengers, front engine and rear drive	*	*
	Chassi and body		
Type	Unitary, steel	*	*
	Engine		
Type	Inline-6, cast iron block and cylinder head, water cooled. Overhead valves (OHV)	*	*
Mixture formation	3 side-draft, variable-venturi carburetors	*	*
Bore and stroke (mm)	92.25 x 100.06	*	*
Displacement (cm^3)	4,271	*	*
Compression ratio	7.8:1	*	*
Maximum power (SAE)	155 hp at 4,200 rpm	168cv at 5.000	180cv at 5.500
Maximum torque (SAE)	N/A	*	*
	Transmission		
Type	3-speed manual, synchronized, and reverse.	4-speed optional	4-speed optional
	Brakes		
Type	Single hydraulic circuit, no powerbrake	*	*
Front	Drum	*	*
Rear	Drum	*	*
	Suspension		
Front	Independent, upper single arm and lower A-arm, coil springs	*	*
Rear	Rigid axle, coil springs	*	*
	Steering		
Type	Worm and sector	*	*
	Dimensions and capacities		
Wheelbase (mm)	2,590	*	*
Lenght (mm)	4,350	*	*
Width (mm)	1,800	*	*
Height (mm)	1,260	*	*
Ground clearance (mm)	160	*	*
Fuel tank (liter)	70	*	*
Curb weight (kg)	1,250	*	*
	Whees and tyres		
Type	Steel wheels and radial tyres	*	*
Tyre size	175-400	*	*

TECHNICAL INFORMATION OF MALZONE

VEHICLE	GT Malzone (1966) and Puma DKW (1967)
Type	2-door coupe, 2 passengers, front engine and drive
	Chassis and body
Type	Separated chassi with "X" members; fiberglass-reinforced plastic
	Engine
Type	Inline 3-cylinder, cast iron block and aluminum cylinder head, water cooled; two-stroke.
Mixture formation	40 mm single bbl carburetor
Bore and stroke (mm)	74 x 76
Displacement (cm^3)	981 cm^3
Compression ratio	8:1
Maximum power (SAE)	60 hp at 4,500 rpm
Maximum torque (SAE)	9.5 m.kgf at 2,500 rpm
	Transmission
Type	4-speed manual, synchronized, and reverse
	Brakes
Type	Single hydraulic circuit, no powerbrake
Front	Disc
Rear	Drum
	Suspension
Front	Independent, lower A-arm and transverse leaf springs
Rear	Rigid axle, transverse leaf springs
	Steering
Type	Rack and pinion
	Dimensions and capacities (Puma GT DKW)
Wheelbase (mm)	2,220
Lenght (mm)	3,850 (3,995)
Width (mm)	1,600
Height (mm)	1,200
Ground clearance (mm)	17
Fuel tank (liter)	45
Curb weight (kg)	800 (810)
	Wheels and tyres
Type	Steel wheels and cross-ply tyres
Tyre size	5.60-15

TECHNICAL INFORMATION OF ONÇA

VEHICLE	Onça 1966 to 1968
Type	2-door, 2-passagenger, coupe or convertible, front engine and rear drive
	Chassis and body
Type	Unitary, steel floor and the remaining of the body in fiberglass-reinforced plastic
	Engine
Type	Inline-4, cast iron block and aluminum cylinder head, water cooled. Double overhead camshaft (DOHC)
Mixture formation	1 double-bbl 30/34 staged carburetor
Bore and stroke (mm)	84.5 x 88
Displacement (cm^3)	1,975
Compression ratio	8.25:1
Maximum power (SAE)	115 hp at 5,900 rpm
Maximum torque (SAE)	—
	Transmission
Type	5-speed manual, synchronized, and reverse
	Brakes
Type	Single hydraulic circuit, no powerbrake
Front	Drum, finned aluminum
Rear	Drum, finned aluminum
	Suspension
Front	Independent, upper and lower unequal-lenght A-arms, coil srpings
Rear	Rigid axle, coil springs
	Steering
Type	Worm and sector
	Dimensions and capacities
Wheelbase (mm)	2,500
Lenght (mm)	4,420
Width (mm)	1,570
Height (mm)	1,290
Ground clearance (mm)	170
Fuel tank (liter)	60
Curb weight (kg)	1,100
	Wheels and tyres
Type	Steel wheels and radial tyres
Tyre size	175-400

Êste é o único Gran Turismo fabricado no Brasil (suas linhas foram especialmente **desenhadas e o motor é Chevrolet).** É o Brasinca 4200 GT. Combina a indiscutível qualidade Chevrolet com 15 anos de experiência da Brasinca na produção de carrocerias e estruturas. Feito para quem conhece o verdadeiro prazer de dirigir, o Brasinca 4200 GT é um carro esporte veloz, luxuoso e ultraconfortável. É um puro-sangue: potente, elegante e de alta performance. Devido a tôdas essas características, é natural que o Brasinca 4200 GT sòmente seja comprado por pessoas de exigente bom gôsto. Portanto, se você tem ou pretende ter um Brasinca 4200 GT, você está de parabéns. (Não é preciso agradecer.)

BRASINCA 4200 GT

produzido pela
BRASINCA S.A.
Ferramentaria - Carrocerias - Veículos
Av. Dr. Augusto de Toledo, 105
São Caetano do Sul, SP

Willys Interlagos (1961 to 1966)

Berlineta; Cupê and Convertible

Alpine – a French sports and racing cars manufacturer – had been obtaining, in the early 1960s, an enormous success in motor racing, especially in rallies, with cars using Renault underpinnings.

The Alpine A108 took components from the Dauphine Gordini, an automobile that in Brazil was produced by Willys-Overland of Brazil (WOB), where it was marketed as Renault Gordini only. Here, the name Dauphine was removed from the model's name because it designated the simplest version of the car (Renault Dauphine).

To be eligible to enter some categories of the European calendar, a model had to attain a minimum volume of 1,000 units produced in 12 months at most. As such, the production of the A108 in Brazil could help in attaining this number.

Motor racing, within the national boundaries, interested Willys somewhat, which had already an official racing team capable of associating the image of winning team to the brand, as well as that of performance and reliability to products of the Renault lineup produced here under license.

The association of the French sports cars factory needs with the objectives of the national automaker resulted in the Willys Interlagos range, consisting of three versions: Berlineta, Coupe and Convertible, all three identical to French Alpine A108.

The Willys Interlagos was not launched with the purpose of being the best-seller of the Willys lineup. It should, through racing, enhance the name of the brand and ensure sports *status* to all Renault line. Thanks to low weight, to low center of gravity and to small frontal area, it fulfilled with honor its goal. The beauty of its lines contributed to make it an object of desire.

The Willys Interlagos was produced in three versions – Berlineta, i.e., a small two-door sedan; the coupe and the convertible. Launched in 1961, it was the first national car made in fiberglass-reinforced plastic, a material that would prove to be the ideal one for the production of small-series cars. The Berlineta enhanced the difficult to access and lack of room in relation to the coupe, what seemed impossible, yet it was the favorite for being the most beautiful. No one would buy any of the models if thinking of comfort and practicality.

The most popular of the three was the Berlineta (from Berlinetta, small sedan in Italian), i.e., the version used for racing.

The Alpine A108 was considered at first, however the name Interlagos ended up being chosen by suggestion of publicist Mauro Salles (whose advertising agency held WOB's account), and the name of the São Paulo city's speedway which was the major Brazilian motor racing arena. Popularly, all versions became known as Berlineta instead of Interlagos: Berlineta, Berlineta Coupe and Berlineta Convertible. A colloquial mistake, for Berlineta is a kind of body style, together with coupe and convertible.

With a tubular chassis wearing a fiberglass-reinforced body, the Interlagos exhibited a "out of discussion" beauty, capable of pounding on the imagination and wish of any sports car enthusiast.

Very light, just 535 kg (Berlineta; coupe and convertible, 570 kg), and fitted with the Gordini's mechanics, stock or factory-prepared, the Interlagos offered spicy driving in spite of the performance limited by the engine that in the more basic versions, the most sold, displaced 845 cm^3 with 40 hp gross output, corresponding to 32 hp net, i.e., less power than the good-mannered 1967 VW sedan's when it was upgraded to the 1300-cm^3, 38 net hp engine.

The Interlagos was an "amplification" of virtues and vices of the mechanics and solutions adopted in the Renault Gordini:

- The body that – at the same time – gave shape to the sporty temper of the engine, made it clear all the lack of an effective, better performance.
- Engine speed limit was high (6,500 rpm, in a time the VW, for instance, could not go over 4,000 rpm) and the gearbox was low geared, while vehicle weight and dimensions were minimum. Everything added resulted in a very nimble car for urban situations.
- The Gordini could be considered crowded for a family sedan, even for a small-size popular automobile. The same thing can be said about the Interlagos, which did not feature minimum room for seating an occupant over 1,80 meters tall or weighing 95 kg. Clearance between pedals, legs e steering wheel, head and roof... were bare minimum.
- Access to cabin (cockpit) was hard (very hard!), even for low height and age people. It was the minimum limit for a sports car, as well as it happened in the same proportion with the Dauphine and the Gordini.
- The engine – when subject to a sport driving – was prone to fail, and overheat, too. With use, the repeated attempts for better performance result in short life of it.

The Interlagos had also its own sporting characteristics:

- Thanks to the new design that in relation to the Gordini moved the center of gravity down, roadholding became far superior. Since wheelbase was very short (2,100 mm, *versus* the Gordini's 2,270 mm), fast driving in roads that went through hills, with small-radius turns, really turned into pleasure.
- The instrument cluster featured large-diameter speedometer and revolution counter that made it easy to drive the car at its limit.

Briefly, the Interlagos was very involving as a sports car, yet it lacked performance and comfort.

Historically, it was the first sports car produced by a large automaker, besides pioneering in the use of fiberglass-reinforced plastic for bodywork material, thus making room for almost all the country's industry of small-series sports cars. It was at Willys that this know-how began being developed in Brazil and it was from there that the first technicians that would make use of this composite material for small-scale production have appeared.

Alpine was the name of very high prestige and to associate it to Willys seemed a bright idea. To christen the national version as Interlagos was a daring attitude that would prove to be the right one later.

Temper

The sporting pre-disposition was latent. Only those interested in enjoying the pleasures of driving more than comfort would opt for using the Interlagos.

The provoking roar of the engine was common to the three versions, which with the convertible added the extra pleasure of an open car.

Undoubtedly, its temper was sporty.

Technical solutions and practical results

The tubular chassis and the fiberglass-reinforced plastic body were the resources adopted the drew more attention that anything else.

The tubular chassis was a classical solution for handcrafted sports car. Very light and semi-handcrafted built, it was used in "machines" as Ferrari and Maserati, for example.

Because it did not demand the heavy and expensive tooling for shaping metal blanks, the fiberglass-reinforced plastic was revealing itself the ideal material for automobiles not series-produced.

The central columns of the sedan-type bodies – or berlina – represented a reinforcement, therefore these were less subject to torsion than that of the

A

B

C

A) All Interlagos body styles had enchantment. In the convertible, the "plus", more than obvious, was exactly in the fact of being a convertible. It was also the one with better access and the roomier. B) The engine, an inline four at rear, would condemn the behavior of the car in bends by moving aft and higher the center of gravity. Displacing 845-cm^3 only like the Gordini, it had a sporty yet limited temper. The low, 650-kg weight was very important for a reasonable performance. C) As the others Willys Renaults, it had rear grilles for air exiting.

coupes and, a lot less, the convertible's. The A108 in Berlineta version counted on this additional quality and it was more elegant than the coupe. However, with the aim of providing more room to taller people was the coupe's that, in practice, had the same body as the convertible, except for the non-removable hardtop.

The inline four-cylinder, small-displacement engine was longitudinally installed at the rear of the car, with the radiator right ahead of it.

The cooling air intake system was done through side intakes and underneath the car. The dimensioning of the system was critical, its efficiency highly compromised if the air ducts were not 100% unclogged.

To obtain a satisfactory performance out of the 845 cm^3 engine (there were souped-up versions that increased displacement to up to 1.000 cm^3) it was essential to precisely tune it up and to rev it up considerably.

At the wheel of the Interlagos, everything seemed minute, except three large-diameter circumferences: the rev-counter's, where the water temperature gauge was embedded; the speedometer's, which had the fuel gauge at bottom; and the wooden-rimmed steering wheel with the core in aluminum, that interfered with the legs. The styled "W", with two little checkered flags, explained very well what the sports car mission was.

For this purpose, the manifolds – both intake and exhaust – had to be accurately calculated and the side-effect of it was the emitting of pleasant sounds and tones that incited fast driving, besides giving life to the car's lines.

Four speeds proved insufficient for the gearbox to conciliate acceleration needs to higher cruising speeds. As the gears had to be short as to overcome inertia and since the car was not conceived for long distances, acceleration was privileged in detriment of sheer speed.

Although the center of gravity was very low, it was excessively biased towards the rear, where the powertrain was. Therefore, the Interlagos easily went through turns, yet it was extremely oversteering (the rear hanging out). These characteristics, together with the low weight, provided the ideal sporty driving – it allowed immediately resuming acceleration as of the apex of the curve.

Gear engaging was not precise, although it did not disturb driving. First gear was not synchronized, what ended demanding more skill from the driver in city driving – or patience, if not able to use the double-clutching technique to engage first with the car running, for it would be necessary to stop and start again.

The tighter the bends and the narrower the roads were, more juice the Interlagos could extract. If willingness and enthusiasm were strong enough and discomforts did not mixed up with charm, the Interlagos had plenty to offer.

INTERLAGOS

There were just two good reasons for owning a Willys Interlagos: charm and sports driving. Beauty and the immediate association with the racing cars have led many to choose the berlineta, although a convertible is always seducing. Regardless of version, it was a car for a very few. Only those who sought pleasure at the wheel, and could sustain a differentiated routine, were entitled to own one.

The small frontal area, of course, had a minute air resistance compared to that of a "regular" size automobile, almost regardless of what its coefficient of drag (Cd) was.

The very low body also forced a unique driving position – almost laid down. The seat cushion was extremely close to the floor and the back rest, adjustable in three positions: very laid down, almost laid down and laid down.

For being short, besides being nimble in urban situations and in small-radius turns, it collaborated to an even more singular driving position: the knees were well apart and very open.

For being narrow, when there was an escort aboard knees and shoulders went on touching each other. For a polite gear change an "excuse me" was a must.

Since floor was very close to ground and little distant from roof, entering and exiting the car was an exercise of flebility and mobility.

For all this, it was a restrict-use car, yet pleasant to drive when there were no other appointments.

Daily use

The Interlagos could only be daily used by people who had a lifestyle that included the automobile as an instrument of motoring and sheer enjoyment.

The first start in the morning was easy, as well as its satisfactory dynamic behavior for city traffic, after all it inherited all the Gordini's underpinnings, an economy car with a strong vocation for urban use.

To the characteristics of the Gordini it was improved with less weight and size, more nimbleness as a consequence.

To leat ahead of other cars at the traffic lights, to go through minute spaces and to promptly brake were part of the recipe of the car.

The basic design remained unchanged, but some details varied from one model year to another. The hubcaps were plain at first; in 1965, as in the photo, they became splined; and, in 1966, they were painted dull-black.

The only mechanical inconvenience present for most was engaging the non-synchronized first gear.

The difficulties of a more intense urban co-living were found in items related to comfort, which started by moving to enter the little car and continued through the not very comfortable seating, the driving position, the lack of room and the obvious limitation of carrying just one passenger besides the driver.

For all these reasons, the Interlagos would hardly be the first car of a household. It did better the task of being the car of a single person, whose lifestyle was that of owning an Interlagos. At the time it was translated as "playboy car".

On the road

The more straight and wide the road was, the worst for the Interlagos, which did not have top speed nor sustaining high speeds its biggest virtue.

To drive the Interlagos was all pleasure, as far as amid many curves and speed recovering. A short-radius, "tight" curve for other cars, was wide enough to draw up a line with the Interlagos.

Discomfort – which could be caused by long runs – went unnoticed in short hops, and the inconvenience of constant in-and-out of urban life would not be noticed either.

The luggage room of two people for a short motoring was reasonable.

To leave the São Paulo capital for a weekend at the coast, facing and overcoming the Sea Hill, was a opportune option. To take part in a cruising at the hottest points in these towns, a blessing.

The Interlagos and I

I only happened to have some contact with the Interlagos in the early 2000s, when traffic in big cities like São Paulo turned into pretty unfavorable characteristics to drive and even motoring with the Interlagos, except on weekends or in special times like during school vacations or at the end of the year.

The ever-jammed traffic made distances, when measured in time elapsed, very long for the Interlagos' discomforts.

The huge trucks – whose fender lines lay well above the roof of the car – went too fast in expressways (when not jammed), becoming menacing.

Taking the Interlagos on trips, it revealed itself brave although the roads exiting São Paulo city were most double-lane already and enabled (legally) 120 km/h top speed, just too high for the Interlagos. To remain on it the engine had to be revved to 5,500 rpm, an engine speed that could not be sustained for long, for water temperature would soon start to climb, to immediately going down after some "refreshment" on the gas pedal.

While the Interlagos has set presence in the streets during the 1960s, I was still very young as a child and all I can remember is that I was fascinated by that "little racing car" – but what child wouldn't be?

OTHER OPINION

The Willys Interlagos literally robbed the scene at the II São Paulo Motor Show, in October of 1961. Especially the berlineta version, which was really impressive by the pureness of the lines drawn by the studio Michelotti. A piece of art, one can say. Most incredible was the fact that Renault had been shortly in Brazil, since 1959, with the Dauphine, the Gordini not having been launched yet. Another shock was to see, for the first time ever, a car body made in fiberglass-reinforced plastic, entirely unmatched with a world of steel.

It was surprising to know that the engine was a minuscule 42 hp net, 845 cm³ four-cylinder engine, but a review by *Quatro Rodas* magazine (in April of 1963) concluded that that the small sports car was a good performer. It really was a great design from Alpine, which produced the car in France using the Dauphine's powertrain and rolling chassis.

TECHNICALLY CORRECT

It was difficult to modify the engine for more power and to assure reliability at the same time. Piston stroke was longer than desirable, 80 mm, which produced high mean piston speed. For example, at 6,000 rpm only the pistons would be traveling a 16 meters per second, too high a speed for the standards of the time. The stock engine also had too high a compression ratio, 9,2:1, for this reason it could only burn high-octane, premium gasoline. It happens that this fuel cost a lot more than regular gasoline and was not always available. If inadequate gasoline was used, detonation caused deep damages, such as piston seizure or a holed piston.

In face of difficulty of making the engine to rev more and thus winning power, the better solution was to increase displacement by bigger-diameter cylinders and pistons, in the case of this engine made easy because cylinder liners were removable from block. It was not necessary to bore the block out. There were 60-mm diameter kit that made displacement to increase to 904-cm³ and the 63-mm dia. kit, for 998-cm³ displacement.

Evidently orthodox recipes like increasing valve diameter, using a hotter camshaft and installing a larger carburetor were valuable.

The Achilles heel of the engine was exactly the removable cylinder liners, which depended on precise assembling considering the thickness of the sealing ring at the base of the liners. This aimed achieving the exact liner height-to-block for perfect liner sealing after the cylinder head was tightened in place. But a skilled and experienced mechanic could perform the right assemblage and then the engine lasted long, even in racing.

TECHNICAL INFORMATION OF WILLYS INTERLAGOS

VEHICLE	Convertible until 1965	Convertible 1966	Berlineta until 1965	Berlineta 1966	Cupê All
Type	Berlineta, coupe and convertible, rear engine and drive, 2-door, 2-passangers	*	*	*	*
	Chassis and body				
Type	Tubular chassis bonded to fiberglass-reinforced plastic	*	*	*	*
	Engine				
Type	Inline 4-cylinder, cast iron block and aluminum cylinder head, water cooled. Overhead valves (OHV)	*	*	*	*
Mixture formation	2-bbl staged 30-34 mm carburetor	*	*	*	*
Bore and stroke (mm)	58 x 80	*	*	*	*
Displacement (cm^3)	845 cm^3	*	*	*	*
Compression ratio	9.2:1	*	*	*	*
Maximum power (SAE)	53 hp at 5,600 rpm	*	*	*	*
Maximum torque (SAE)	6.8 m.kgf at 4,000 rpm	*	*	*	*
	Transmission				
Type	4-speed manual transaxle, non-synchronized first	*	*	*	*
	Brakes				
Type	Single hydraulic circuit, no powerbrake	*	*	*	*
Front	Drum	Disc	*	Disc	*
Rear	Drum	*	*	*	*
	Suspension				
Front	Independent, superposed arms, coil springs	*	*	*	*
Rear	Independent, swing axles and coil springs	*	*	*	*
	Steering				
Type	Rack and pinion	*	*	*	*
	Dimensions and capacities				
Wheelbase (mm)	2,110	2,100	2,100	2,100	2,100
Lenght (mm)	3,780	*	*	*	*
Width (mm)	1,450	*	*	*	*
Height (mm)	1,190	*	1,140	1,140	*
Ground clearance (mm)	160	*	*	*	*
Fuel tank (liter)	32	*	*	*	*
Curb weight (kg)	690	580	660	540	680
	Wheels and tyres				
Type	Steel wheels and cross-ply tyres	*	*	*	*
Tyre size	145-380	*	*	*	*

MEDIDA DA CORAGEM
22
Nervos, 160 km/h vertiginosos. Domínio. Desafio ao volante. Coragem para produzir o máximo. Willys-Interlagos Berlineta. Carro para quem quer chegar ontem. De ponta a ponta. O tempo em "suspense". Campeoníssimo. Estrutura tubular. Pouca altura; baixo centro de gravidade; grande distância entre eixos — ESTABILIDADE. Torpedo para competições.
Linha desportiva Willys. Côres que fascinam: bege-baisa-metálico, azul-metálico, cinza-metálico e vermelho-romano (exclusiva para o conversível). Alta qualidade. Veículos para gente moça. Potência disponível nos veículos W. I. 59 H.P. (até 140 km/h) a 5.600 r.p.m.
WILLYS
Produto da WILLYS-OVERLAND Fabricante de veículos de alta qualidade · São Bernardo do Campo · Est. de São Paulo
WILLYS
INTERLAGOS

(Europe)

Alfa Romeo Giulia gt

(1964 to 1968)

The goal was that the Brazilian auto industry would be installed. Therefore, some ways had to be opened beforehand. One of them was to make importing difficult.

Cars aimed to certain niches only, which were not covered by local products, kept being imported in small numbers and landed here at price short of inviting. However, those who wanted a high performance model, or with a higher degree of sophistication, would have to spend much more money, after all the Brazilian car was not supposed to be driven or was suitable for this public.

Those seeking for nimble and fast sports car, of medium size and engine displacement, would find options among cars of European origin only. During the second half of the 1950s until early next decade, the sports models of British origin, especially those of MG and Triumph brands, were favorites, yet right in the early 1960s those from Italy, the Alfa Romeos above all, fell in the grace of the Brazilian man and turned into the one that better represented this small and very important segment. The popularity of the brand was assured by Alfa Romeo berlina 2000, which was manufactured in Brazil by automaker Fábrica Nacional de Motores under FNM 2000 JK nameplate – from 1960 to 1964 – and later – until 1968 – without the JK suffix. Apart from it, the importer official racing team Jolly achieved great success with some Italian models, especially those of the Giulia lineup and, to a lesser extent, with the locally-made Alfa.

Alfa Romeo made use of bodies of previous years' designs for its less sophisticated and lower engine displacement versions. The Giulia gt 1300 had the Giulia gt's produced between 1964 and 1967. Designed by Bertone, the coupe is considered one of the best sports cars of the 1960s and 1970s. Its solutions were traditional yet sophisticated.

The Alfa Romeo Giulia gt, launched in Italy in 1964, was the sports coupe of the Giulia range. There were also, in addition to gt version, the four-door Giulia sedans in super and ti versions, and the convertible Giulias: the spider (1962 to 1965) and the Duetto (1965 to 1969).

The convertibles had their bodies signed by Pininfarina and the coupes, by Bertone, i.e., the two most important design wizards of all times.

The Giulia gt was a 2+2 coupe that, in practical terms, seated just two adults and two children or, at most, four adults for a minute elapsed time.

Applied technique and practical results

In a time European sports cars barely started using McPherson suspension layouts, independent rear axle as well and engine, transmission and driving wheels all coupled, the Giulia range featured more orthodox schemes, yet with technical sophistication and the use of noble materials.

Traditional, for an European sports car, were the front engine and rear-wheel drive layout; the1,600-cm^3 inline four-cylinder engine; the independent front suspension and the rear one by rigid axle, both on coil springs; the unitary construction; the separated manual gearbox, driveshaft and differential; and all others...

The sophistication came especially from the engine, with aluminum block; from the cylinder head with hemispherical combust ion chambers, also in aluminum and cross-flow; from the intake system by two 2-barrel side-draft carbure-

The double-overhead camshaft engine was brilliant. The fuel feed by two side-draft 2-bbl carburetors, was orchestrated by the gas pedal, playing together with the exhaust, a passion-making "music", at least for the make's lovers.

tors; from the exhaust header; and from the double camshaft design. The sophistication extended to the front suspension by unequal superposed triangles; to the five-speed gearbox in a time four was already appealing; and to the differential, whose case – like the gearbox's – was made in aluminum. Besides, the pedigree rose at the racing circuits could be apparent in: the hydraulic clutch actuation, which enabled a strong and progressive unit; the rear axle locating by two radius rods, an upper longitudinal link and a Panhard bar, all aided by an anti-roll bar, in order to avoid undesirable motions; the forged steel crankshaft; the seven-liter crankcase made in finned aluminum for oil cooling that could house a powerful, high-flow oil pump; the sodium-cooled exhaust valves; and disc brakes at the four corners.

With this recipe, the Giulia focused on known and proven solutions, skipping from novelties yet to work properly, although already showing a greater potential.

The blend of Alfa's ingredients was positive in respect of fast driving, a condition where the car dependable and reliable. To enjoy the best performance out of a Giulia was really pleasing.

By despising solutions like grouped engine, gearbox and driving wheels, McPherson front suspension and independent rear axle, the car performed below expected for becoming heavy and for not being able to deal with uneven pavement. Nevertheless, it compensated all of them with the absence of front wheel tramp when accelerating hard from standstill, usual in front-wheel drive cars of the time that had universal joints to allow the combination of steering and wheel driving and which were prone to fail frequently (in a future not far away they would be replaced by homokinetic joints that completely would eliminate the problem).

Some solutions, excellent for racing, presented side-effects in everyday use, like the aluminum crankcase that was exposed underneath the car. Involved by fresh air circulation caused by motion, it cooled the oil down before it went back to the lubrication circuit, what enabled to get the most out of the engine. However, any bump on the road could hit it, causing damages that would lead to oil leak and, therefore, could be responsible for its total loss if the driver did not care for watching the oil pressure gauge.

The steering box was of the traditional worm and sector type, but it did not escape from a "but": with re-circulating balls. It combined low steering effort and firmness in high speed in a balanced way.

The brakes, discs on four wheels, were much more powerful than it was usual at the time and performed well: braking was balanced, the running distance for decelerating or stopping was small and there was no fading, even after a lot of punishment.

Suspension was firm and the car's roadholding, exemplary, as long as road surface was not wavy. The ride, in spite of not being soft, could not be deemed harsh.

The engine worked happily in any speed, but showed a clear vocation for high revolutions. It was capable of reaching 6,500 rpm and, the bigger the demand, the better it responded. A remarkable feature was the water temperature gauge needle that never exceeded 80° C. The sound of the carburetors and exhaust – four into two – orchestrated gear changing, aided by the excellent rev counter, which was top star of a perfect instrument cluster

The five-speed gearbox was reference in precision and handling.

Seating was good for two occupants and luggage room, quite adequate for a sports car. To get in and out did not demand too much contortionism. Driving position – which forced arms to always remain more stretched than the legs, and put feet in a not very comfortable position as imposed by the pedals – would succumb to any ergonomy study, but it could be considered reasonable at the time.

Air venting was good, by the standards then.

Controls and instruments were matched for a car of its profile. Seats were reasonably convenient and provided good body support. Driving position, discussible respectful of comfort, was adequate for fast driving. The five-speed gearbox was perfect: engaging, gear ratios and even gearshift location served as reference.

This Alfa, in spite of all qualities, then proper of the cars of the brand, was not free from a "but" that was common to all Alfa Romeos: the compromising finishing.

Latches and handles worked poorly, fixation of "this and that" was not well done; cabin water tightness was bad, as well as the trunk's; exhaust easily broke loose and the electrical system, especially the part responsible for engine working – ignition, starting engine and alternator – was not trustworthy.

Temper

No choice of the Alfa Romeo Giulia was free from a "but".

So many "buts" indicated the Giulia made its choice: she opted for the sports temper, yet it did not forget that an automobile must be usable.

This qualifies it as an authentic grand-touring, a normal touring car, yet strongly compromised with pleasure at the wheel and with speed.

The temper of a true grand-touring.

Daily, urban driving the Giulia gt

Any Italian car, to be successful at its country of origin, could not bear exaggerated dimensions that made it unfeasible or even difficult to drive it in towns whose streets were too narrow, held a number of cars far greater than reasonable and, as a consequence, had an extremely congested traffic.

The Alfa Romeos of the Giulia range were successful in Italy, therefore they did not deceive on maneuverability and urban performance.

Just as they easily accelerated briskly at the green light and braked upon the coming red one, slowed down at intersections and convincingly recovered speed, they nimbly faced expressways. Controls were precise and, although steering and clutch were not exactly light, driving effort was small. The seats were comfortable and the gearshift, extremely smooth. These were all adjectives that would make it excellent for daily, urban commuting. However, the location of the pedals, typical of Alfa Romeos, and driving position, peculiar to Italian sports cars of that time, the required attention for the controls that should be precise, the space limitation and the bigger difficulty to step in and out, usual with sports cars, resulted in affecting the level of comfort. For who did not dispense a more sophisticated machine even for daily commuting, this was the higher price to pay for.

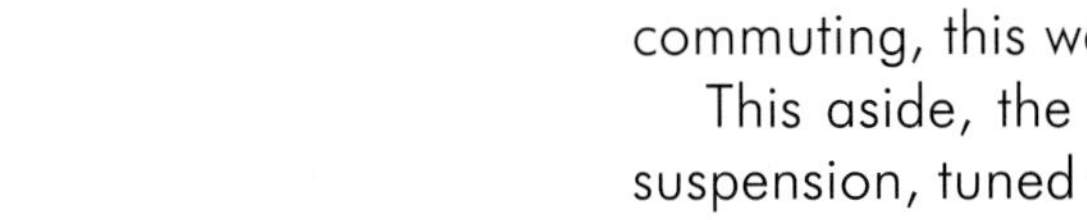

Externally, the major difference between the 1970 gt 1300 Junior and the 1966 Giulia gt was the badge.

This aside, the very uneven paving of our streets punished the little car. The suspension, tuned for higher speeds, did not spare the rest of the car as a whole. The car's structures resented the punishment: the fixation of the dashboard suffered, doors misadjusted, mechanical parts got loose and noises came along, evidencing that the car should be used with extra care.

Another point that demanded utmost attention was the very exposed crankcase. To avoid poor pavement was the most stressing obligation in urban co-living with the Alfa.

Always with the sporting vocation in mind, for city driving the Giulia could be considered excellent. The setup of the car, aimed to speed and fast driving, did not disrespect daily usage. Although it was not the ideal tool for going to the grocery shop, for example, it was capable of taking service without great discomfort. However, if its tasks were restraint to get to work and back, as well as night outings, the automobile would prove to be an excellent companion.

There were many "buts" as for daily commuting in city, but there were also qualities. In trips, the "excepts" vanished and virtues multiplied. The greater the diversity of road designs, more evident became its vocation for them.

On the road

If the "buts" insisted on sticking with the good predicates of the Giulia gt regarding urban use, on the road – no matter if stretchy or sweeping, good for high, medium or low speeds – they did not exist. They could even be listed:

1) In roads where speed did not vary much, the position of the gas pedal made the right foot to ache after some time.
2) Service was available in São Paulo and Rio de Janeiro cities and, in case of being stranded, the car would not resume just repaired by roadside mechanics, it required technicians.
3) The front seats – the only ones that could be used by adults – rendered excellent body support, but left to desire in softness and seating position.
4) The sound of the engine, enthusiastic for the first hour, after some time caused a certain stress.
5) The thermal insulation of the cabin was far from perfect.
6) And the suspension, with an accent for hardness, after a long time started to bother.

In spite of these few inconveniences, besides being a good speeder the Giulia was reasonably comfortable. Its pedals enabled fast motions; the mechanics was dependable; seats could not be classified as uncomfortable, nor the thermal insulation as mediocre and much less the suspension as extremely harsh.

Aboard an Alfa Romeo Giulia gt, one of the nice things of a São Paulo resident's motoring who decided to visit Rio de Janeiro city was the Dutra road. The diversity of possible situations seduced the driver of a Giulia. Yes, there was the possibility that an owner of one of these automobiles appreciated driving, otherwise it would be a wrong choice. Dedication to the steering wheel was the small gt's requirement.

The Giulia gt, in spite of the sporty accent, maintained a level of reasonable commitment to practicality. The trunk, for instance, provided sufficient room for the luggage of a couple or for everyday's shopping.

In the 1960s, Bertone, responsible for the Alfa Romeo Giulia gt, was one of the most respected automobile design studios. At the time, Giorgetto Giugiaro, a young designer, worked for Bertone and was the head of the design. Later, he opened his own business that would ear the same prestige. The design honored its origins.

Stretches that allowed to sustain high and steady speeds, the seeping sections that demanded roadholding, braking and speed recovering; moments of intense traffic and all kind of situations seemed to be the little car's specialty.

Headlights, as well as the windshield wipers, were sufficient and its controls, correct and well-located, besides the fact that even the defogger worked alright! It was a package that interested those who traveled.

Upon arriving in Rio de Janeiro, the Alfa – as with almost another imported sports car – could serve as an excellent wooing gear.

If the four hundred road kilometers were not sufficient and the heat and beauty of the Marvelous City weren't enough, the best thing to do was to go uphill to Petrópolis. Very sweeping and narrow, that was the road where the little Alfa could definitely enchant its motorist. Maybe the only action to take for this motoring was to go unaccompanied, for the risk of the male or female escort to get motion sick was enormous.

When the hill or beach drive ended, before facing the asphalt jungle São Paulo was, the driver, once more, could enjoy the car on the road.

In the 1980s, some few Brazilian automobiles would top the Giulia performance in sweeping roads. It's certain that they would do it with more comfort and dependability, but twenty years later only.

In the 1970s, the local industry launched automobiles – all large side family sedans – capable of being as or faster and of providing more comfort than the Giulia gt 1600, since on stretchy and wide roads, yet with lesser safety and less pleasure at the wheel.

In the 1960s, stretchy and wide roads not even existed in Brazil, as a matter of fact they were very scarce in the 1970s.

The Alfa Romeo Giulia gt and I

Between 1962 and 1975, the years Alfa Romeos of the Giulia lineup were imported to Brazil, a total of a little over one thousand five hundred units were brought in, among all versions and model-years.

The Giulia lineup inherited the space created by the Giulietta, whose models introduced Alfa Romeo to the medium-size segment, better yet, to medium-size sports cars, regardless of convertible, two-door coupe or even four-door sedan body types. In 2001, together with the MG Club of Brazil, I visited Italy and entered an antique car race in Monza. The rented model was a 1957 Giulietta ti. My colleague and I finished first in category and well classified amid superior categories' cars. The Italian Alfas had always been among my favorites, especially for racing.

For sure, in the beginning of the 1970s I was told that these cars were the best sports car in the world. I should be about 10 years old and an older chap, about 11, gave me the information. The car belonged to a family acquaintance but I cannot tell if it was a gt 1600 or a gt 1750.

Maybe sometime before that, in one of the drives my uncle liked to promote, I saw in a road freighter, near the Interlagos circuit, a racing model. It possibly was a gta, the racing version specially prepared by Autodelta, the official Alfa Romeo partner for the preparation of its racing cars.

To be honest, I do not recall any other reference of these cars, while they were on production, and I can't exactly say what time or model.

Years later, when I started to notice automobiles that were far away from my world, the cars that drew my attention were those from Alfa Romeo, the Giulia lineup in special. The brand was always part of my dreams, after all the car that bewitched me most in my childhood was the JK.

When I could afford a car with its own characteristics, a small and fast sports car, of the kind yet to be produced here, I bought a 1974 Alfa Romeo gtv 2000. It was 1984 then. The gtv 2000 was an evolution of the Giulia gt. Launched in 1972, it remained in production until 1977.

Undoubtedly, the 1974 gtv was much more evolved than the Giulia gt 1600 that in 1968 had undergone an upgrade, being then called Giulia gt 1750. They all had used the same body and the underpinnings of the last one – the 2000 – originated from, just a maximization, the ones used by the 1600.

Later on I purchased a 1968 Giulia Super. Its engine and solutions were identical to the gt 1600's.

In spite of not being very familiar with the gt 1600, I can say, by similarity, that the sports coupe of Alfa Romeo was one of the more fantastic medium-displacement grand-touring cars of all times.

Performance could still be considered excellent for Brazil of the 1980s, good for the 1990s and enough for early 2000's, however its "groan" that incited fast

The 2600 line is a direct descendant from the 2000 that originated the Brazilian Alfa Romeo, the FNM 2000. The Spider model had a made by Touring body, a very high-prestige carrozziere. In 1988, in an antique car race in Interlagos, São Paulo (SP), I surprised everyone by defeating larger displacement cars such as the XK 120 Jaguars. They were faster on the straights, but helped by radial-ply tires, the Alfa did better on the inside. In grids that mixed several categories, I had already won in mine, however that was the first time I crossed the finish line first, ahead of higher engine displacement cars.

driving has always exerted its magic. To drive a Giulia kept on enchanting, but its "buts" kept bothering.

With the Giulias I took part in all kinds of racing and, with a especially-tuned one, I achieved many wins and some championships.

Perhaps this may mean that everything I wrote about the Giulia might be suspicious, after all it is not free from passion, yet with a lot of knowledge.

The first Giulia coupe, the Giulia gy 1600, was launched in 1964. In 1968, with a new engine and some visual changes, it would be called Giulia gt 1750. In 1972, when it earned the 2,000-cm^3 engine, it was named gtv 2000. It was my first antique ever, purchased in 1984, and the one I used most. Later, in 1992, I developed another sample just for racing. I achieved many wins and titles in antique car races and championships. In the photo, in 1994, when I was taking part in the 12 Hours of Curitiba, a race open to contemporary cars. A very few cars completed the race in the track. Among them, the one of our team, my Alfa, a 20-year veteran. Even our pit neighbors celebrated!

ANOTHER OPINION

The Alfa Romeo Giulia has set presence in Brazil. The brand has always been admired here since the 1930s, at the time of the Gávea circuit races, in Rio de Janeiro. Especially for the 1937 race, when Italian Carlo Pintacuda, with an Alfa type 35, defeated German Hans Stuck and his powerful Auto Union type C V16, which had almost twice the Alfa Romeo's power. Then FNM 2000 JK came, the Brazilian version of the Alfa Romeo 2000 sedan and launched in 1960, and fully pleased everyone. Yet in the previous decade Alfa Romeos started to show around, but one of them would be dear some time later, in the 1960s: the Giulia gt. It was the synthesis of Italian design and engineering, a car clearly made for those who enjoyed driving exploring its potentialities.

TECHNICALLY CORRECT

The Alfa Romeos had always expressed engineer Vittorio Jano's (1891-1966) excellence of engine design, marked by aluminum, double overhead camshaft head with hemispherical combustion chambers with a center spark plug. The Giulia gt with its 1,750 cm^3, 102 hp at 5.500 rpm, aluminum block and cylinder head and two 2-bbl side-draft carburetors, has always excited older and newer generations, together with the five-speed gearbox, 175 km/h top speed, which was sweet to drive. The engine was pleasant to see, to listen and to use exploring all its power, with an additional advantage: it never break down. The Alfa Romeos have always been extremely reliable in endurance racing.

TECHNICAL INFORMATION OF ALFA GIULIA gt

VEHICLE	Alfa Giulia gt (1964 to 1967)
Type	2-door coupe for 2 + 2 passengers, front engine and rear drive
	Body and chassis
Type	Unitary, steel
	Engine
Type	Inline-4, cast iron block and aluminum cylinder head, water cooled. Double overhead camshaft (DOHC)
Mixture formation	2 2-bbl sidedraft 40-mm carburetors
Bore and stroke (mm)	78 x 82
Displacement (cm^3)	1,570
Compression ratio	9.00:1
Maximum power (SAE)	116 hp at 5,700 rpm or 102 hp (DIN) at 5,500 rpm
Maximum torque (SAE)	14.24 m.kgf
	Transmission
Type	5-speed manual, synchonized, and reverse
	Brakes
Type	Single hydraulic circuit, no powerbrake
Front	Disc
Rear	Disc
	Suspension
Front	Independent, unequal lenght superposed a-arms, coil springs
Rear	Rigid axle, locating rods, coil springs
	Steering
Type	Worm and sector with recirculating balls
	Dimensions and capacities
Wheelbase (mm)	2,350
Lenght (mm)	4,080
Width (mm)	1,550
Height (mm)	1,340
Ground clearance (mm)	110
Fuel tank (liter)	52
Curb weight (kg)	1,032
	Wheels and tyres
Type	Steel wheels and radial tyres
Tyre size	165-380

Junior 1.3/1.6 la Giulia che vince

La vostra GT Junior è identica per linea, arditezza sportiva e sicurezza alla GTA 1300 Junior che nel 1971 ha vinto il Campionato Europeo Turismo. Con qualcosa in più: la silenziosità, il conforto e le finiture di una macchina da grandi viaggi.

Alfa Romeo

(USA)

Ford Mustang

(1964 to 1967)

The Ford Mustang, launched in April of 1964, was one of the most significant automobiles of the 1960s. It has taken from the United States to the world a new automobile category: the pony cars. Lee Iacocca, then responsible for the Ford division, enounced the concept he claimed, in its essence, that the consumer was wishing to own a car with a sporty look, but he was not willing to give away the uncomplicated and practical use of a family passenger car.

Thus, worshiping this concept, the Ford Mustang was born. Success was stunning. No one could foresee that this new format could meet so strongly the expectations of so many.

The Mustang was conceived over the Ford Falcon platform, the brand's compact for the American market that made great success. Its design consisted of a proportionally exaggerated front section in relation to the remaining of the body, what made presume the presence of a large engine. However, big engines would only come after some evolutions, for when it was launched a basic six-cylinder was fitted to it and, by being North America, only the V8s enjoyed a superior *status*.

Hydraulic power steering, disc brake, V8 engines of several displacements and power outputs, convertible, fastback and hardtop coupe body styles, decoration with stripes and other embellishers, accessories that included sport wheels, hubcaps etc, did not take long to appear. High-scale sales made feasible new body, engine and equipment versions that set apart the most sophisticated models as of 1965 from the 1964 ½, quite basic when launched.

In spite of the sporting lines, the Ford Mustang should offer a behavior close to a family sedan's. For such, it used the platform of the Ford Falcon, the make's compact model. There was the option of a wide range of engines, including the powerful V8s that were used, and provided high performance, to larger and heavier models. When powering the Mustang, a sporty compact car-sized, they allowed acceleration equal to the fastest European models.

This Ford was one of the few novelties landed from abroad that achieved trespassing the barriers of the much closed, almost impermeable, Brazilian market. The locally-made automobile was extremely defended from the competing imports.

If in the land of Uncle Sam the Ford Falcon was considered – by its motorization or by its dimensions – a small car, in Brazil it was deemed as big. The same could be said about the Mustang.

Used technique and practical results

Except for the design and the unitary construction, in all other aspects the technical solutions of the Mustang respected the directives of almost all US-made automobiles: overhead valves V8 or inline-six cylinder engines up front; rear-wheel drive; standard manual transmission or optional automatic; drum brakes at four wheels or disc brakes (not vented) at front; steering by worm and gear with optional hydraulic assistance; front axle with helical springs, lower A-arm and transversal upper arm independent suspension; rigid real axle with semi-elliptical springs; and cross-ply tires. Even the body presented typically American solutions, like the enormous doors.

The Mustang behaved like a good touring car, yet there was space limitation. The sporting touch was provided by the transmission that, when manual, had four speeds; by the gear shift that, even when automatic, was floor mounted; and, especially, by the body silhouette and décor. The V8 "growl" – in spite of present, more or less muffled, in many luxury automobiles – also helped to compose the sporting aura.

To bring cars from abroad was not that easy and the few that entered here were carefully chosen. The Mustang belonged to the most wanted list, but it had to be a "V8".

Lots of torque and low traction. The tires of this Ford drew lines the asphalt in "Hollywood way" flying starts.

Motorization – that could be provided by high-output V8s – combined to the relatively low weight of a "compact", was the ideal formula for those wishing to accelerate very quickly from standstill. However, except for acceleration, equal to the greatest icons of its time, the car did not demonstrate bigger intimacy with high performance.

The body lines privileged the look and was uncaring about aerodynamics. To overcome air resistance, the Mustang provoked strong turbulence. As a result, in high speeds there was a strong noise, lost of driveability and waste of power.

Suspension, especially the rear one, was too rustic and limited, besides being calibrated more for softness than hardness. Only with a highly sophisticated assembly it could provide balance at speed without sacrificing comfort.

Brakes, especially when drum type, were not always that balanced. Weight distribution and suspension did not contribute to a safe braking.

Steering, when not power-assisted, was slow, requiring several turns for small wheel steering angles. With power steering, it was too light, favoring parking maneuvers and comfort in detriment of fast driving.

The cross-ply tires were also more suited for comfort than for performance.

Powerful engines, combined with mechanical assemblies that did not have great traction and roadholding capacity, were capable of providing the thrilling sensation of speed. Tire burning shows, in flying starts, braking and slides, controlled or not, gave life to exhibitionism the lines of the car showed off.

Internally, finishing materials were all synthetic; the instrument cluster focused more visual impact than reading, precision or level of information qualities; controls followed the American pattern that gave more importance to styling and rusticity than to quick and automatic handling; and so forth. This was the spirit!

Temper

Football, motor racing in oval tracks with lap information in average speed rather than clock times; action movies; whiskey, marshmallow and milk shake; soft drinks; hamburger and hot dog with ketchup; and scrambled eggs with bacon, are some of the icons of American identity.

Over there, power is more admired than ability: soccer; circuits with selective course design; poetic movies; Scotch whisky; fine bakery; pure mountain water; meat with special sauces; and croissant bread with butter e natural jellies, are not part of their culture.

To please most of the people, the automobile could not embody a different essence. As a rugby player, a bourbon, a sandwich or even a movie, a car must ensure the sensation of power. The best recipe was in the V8 engines, in the muscle cars and in the pony cars, not double overhead camshaft engines, super sports cars with aeronautical technologies or grand touring machines.

Just like what happens at the American schools, where geography and world history have little importance when compared to the local one, Ford also did not think of the consumers of other continents. The American market was the largest in the world, the most important and enough.

Regardless if in sports, in arts, in gastronomy, in cooking, or in the world of the automobile; regardless if strong or handy; regardless if to be in the Guinness Book of Records or to be understood, to be one of the best, talent is indispensable.

The Ford Mustang was a beast, yet it was the most talented of them.

Urban, daily driving with the Ford Mustang

The basic precepts for the creation of the Ford Mustang pointed to the consumer who wanted a car with a sporty look as well as the convenience of an automobile designed for day-by-day use, but within the American reality, entirely different from ours.

In Brazilian conditions, the Mustang presented strong limitations in everyday use.

Stepping into the car was not an easy task. Hardly there would be room so the doors could be fully open and the weight, when opening them, demanded muscles if the car was not on a leveled road.

Its controls and instrument cluster had no commitment to precision, but layout and design maintained a sporty look. The seats did not provide body support in bends, but were soft and comfortable.

The lines of the Mustang were elaborated with no compromise to aerodynamics, or functionality. Where an air intake should be, there was often "a false air intake". It seemed to have many things but they did not exist. Thanks to a good job, the look exhaled sportiveness.

To maneuver it was not easy at all. Visibility was poor, especially for the medium-height Brazilian, well below the American pattern's, and due to the exaggerated dimensions of the car in relation to our parking spots.

The car was poorly dimensioned for the country, for if by one side too big were its doors and outside dimensions, room for occupants and luggage was small, as well as limited was suspension travel to deal with our unleveled paving. All these inconveniences were common to sports cars, no matter if Europeans or Brazilian. Here, the Mustang was in equal terms regarding urban vocation. For sure it featured an advantage for a very smooth functioning, better than any other national car and equal to the most luxurious ones in the world. Its mechanics was robust and the only inconvenient laid in a certain pre-disposition to overheating. Simplicity was extremely welcome, after all our technicians were, by a major portion, unprepared. The most powerful versions had a 4-barrel carburetor. This sole item, which required utmost care, was itself a source of trouble.

On the road

The better the road, better yet for they who were aboard a Ford Mustang. The engine enabled sustained high speeds, yet to overcome air resistance above 120 km/h there were noises and some instability, even on the straights.

In spite of not being a specialist for turning, the Mustang could be quite fast, as long as there were no irregularities in the paving. It also did well in overtaking, for although the sequence of motions of the maneuver – change lane, accelerate, pull back and brake – caused a noticeable instability, the superior acceleration assured plenty of road room for the Mustang, in conditions other cars wouldn't dare to adventure.

The soul, the V8 engine, was the big difference. It was what unbalanced the game in favor of the Ford.

In spite of the simplicity, the best was to do not get away from the large urban centers, after all the arrogance of its lines intimidated the less skilled auto mechanics, used to the modest look of a Volkswagen or the rusticity o truck.

For a São Paulo City resident, to visit the family inland at a nice town like Ribeirão Preto, a shade over three hundred kilometers from capital, was a neat program. Even more neat for those who could go in a Mustang.

The road was quite straight, in spite of some twisty stretches. Near São Paulo City traffic was dense, yet overcoming the first one hundred kilometers, higher speeds could be attained.

Excluding the pleasures of motoring, success among relatives, friends and even anonymous ones was assured. If in São Paulo City who had one of these was already a king, at the inland he was a super sovereign. At evenings it would be infallible for wooing: even if the Mustang did not win the challenge of conquest alone, the squeal of spinning tires would suffice, conducted by the V8 exhausts, in a way its owner triggered envy of all the grown-ups.

The way home was the same. The rear seat could be used to hold some luggage, since it could not serve a passenger in a ride over half an hour and the trunk was minuscule. Yet the front seats were reasonably comfortable and did not provide good lateral support for the body, which was intensified if the car was being "piloted".

The badge of the galloping Mustang horse transmitted power, freedom and speed. The number referred to this sample's engine, a 289-cu. in, or 4,736-cm³ one.

The engine compartment did not hide, and did not intend to, that there was a jewel there. The engines were very simple, however very powerful thanks to size. The six-cylinder, very civilized, in a country of Simcas and Aero-Willyses, could be considered special already. Some "V8s" had "cavalry" enough to leap ahead of many a European supercar.

Driving position and the controls were typical of American cars: arms were proportionally more shrunk than legs, which was discussable, a matter of taste; the low seat cushion was not suitable for the average height of the Brazilians; pedals had nice layout; the headlight beam control, operated by the left foot, was inconvenient in models fitted with manual transmission due to the clutch pedal, especially in two-way sections and even in four-lane ones, for antiglare barriers did not exist then; the remaining controls didn't compromise, although they were not stalked at the steering column, close to the wheel.

However, any inconvenience on the road would go unnoticed. There was no fault that could not be hidden by the delicious V8 engine. The bigger the engine, the better the motoring and, even if the model was powered by inline-six, it provided a performance far better than any locally-produced car.

The Ford Mustang and I

During the 1960s, I don't remember having any contact with the Mustang "of tin and wheels", in actual size.

I knew the Mustang nameplate, I recognized one of these on the street, I admired it and knew that it was quite special an automobile. I certainly have watched movies where the Mustang served the purpose of identifying a character as he having good taste, or something like that, but no more than that.

I only came close to some of these real Fords after starting experiencing antique cars a bit more, by the 1990s. At that time the Ford Mustang began appreciating as antique and some models in special could only be purchased for a considerable amount of money.

Particularly, I have barely ridden in the 1960s Mustangs, perhaps somewhat on one or another good-tasting friend's, but that was all.

The engine compartment did not hide, and it neither intended to, that there was a jewel inside it. The engines were very simple, but due to size they were very powerful. The six-cylinder, quite calm, in a Brazil of Simcas and Aero-Willyses could be seen as special. Some "V8" had "cavalry" enough to leap ahead of many European super-machines.

ANOTHER OPINION

Very few cars had such an enormous success right at launching as the Mustang. The wave immediately reflected in Brazil under the format of a mammoth buying wish by people of the most variable age range. The main problem was how to get one, since importation had been suspended. Only those living abroad for more than two years and returning home could bring one with the luggage, or the diplomatic corps, allowed to do it. The solution was to look for it in one of these two sources, not rarely paying high for the self-indulgency.

TECHNICALLY CORRECT

The Mustang had nothing special in its underpinnings, for it derived from the Ford Falcon, a mere compact. It was powered by an inline six or a V8 engine, by far the choice of the entire Brazilian market. It might be a 164-hp 262-pol^3/4,300-cm^3 or the more usual 289-pol^3 (4,735 cm^3), gross horsepower in both cases. Only in 1972 the US shifted to net horsepower, leveling off at European standards. Yet the sound and the blast at driver's backs added charm to the car that inaugurated the pony car segment and has always been one of the most desired here.

TECHNICAL INFORMATION OF FORD MUSTANG

VEHICLE	Ford Mustang (1964 to 1967) "V8 302"
Type	Hardtop, Fastback and Convertible, 2-door for 2+2 passengers, front engine and rear drive
	Body and chassis
Type	Unitary, steel
	Engine
Type	V8, cast iron block and cylinder heads, water cooled. Overhead valves (OHV)
Mixture formation	1 4-bbl carburetor
Bore and stroke (mm)	101.6 x 72.9
Displacement (cm³)	4,728 cm³
Compression ratio	9.8:1
Maximum power (SAE)	225 hp at 4,400 rpm
Maximum torque (SAE)	32.5 m.kgf at 2,400 rpm
	Transmission
Type	4-speed manual synchronized or 3-speed automatic, and reverse.
	Brakes
Type	Single hydraulic circuit, no powerbrake
Front	Drum (disc optional)
Rear	Disc
	Suspension
Front	Independent, upper single arm and lower A-arm, coil springs
Rear	Rigid axle, longitudinal semi-elliptical leaf springs
	Steering
Type	Worm and sector (powersteering optional)
	Dimensions and capacities
Wheelbase (mm)	2,740
Lenght (mm)	4,647
Width (mm)	1,800
Height (mm)	1,310
Ground clearance (mm)	140
Fuel tank (liter)	61
Curb weight (kg)	1,352
	Wheels and tyres
Type	Steel wheels and cross-ply tyres
Tyre size	6.95-14

Well, they still have Lollobrigida . . . and Chateau Mouton Rothschild '59 and Balenciaga. But Europe no longer has a monopoly on this kind of four-wheeled flair and fire. Not with the Mustang 2+2 suddenly appearing on the scene. Just think, an unexpected low price and options you can't get in Modena and 6,000-mile or 6 months' maintenance and a ride like a little fat cloud and service at any Ford Dealer's.

Speaking of options, the basic V-8 has 289 cubes and 200 horsepower; the No. 2 version has a four-barrel carburetor and 225 hp. (but still with hydraulic lifters) and the solid-lifter High Performance jewel turns out 271 horses. Unless you want to go the kit route and that climbs all the way up to four Webers and 330 beasts (can you call 'em horses?).

More good news: front disc brakes are available, and for very little scratch. But the 2+2's fold-down rear seat, which opens up a ski-length luggage area right back to the trunk sill, isn't an option, it's there for free. And so are the bucket seats and floor-shift levers and the 200 cubic inches in the six-cylinder engine. And the looks. Don't forget the looks: that's what turns Main Street into the Via Veneto . . . and you into Nuvolari!

Best year yet to go Ford
Test Drive
Total Performance '6

FORD

MUSTANG · FALCON · FAIRLANE · FORD · THUNDERBIRD

A PRODUCT OF Ford MOTOR COMPANY

VW Karmann Ghia 1200

(1962 to 1966)

Built over the Volkswagen Sedan platform, from which it inherited all underpinnings, the Karmann Ghia, put into practice, was the same car as the Sedan, however with a well more charming design, capable of rendering it the *status* of a sports car, in spite of being a shy performer. As shy as the Sedan, that was no reference for it even as an economy car. As a matter of fact, the Sedan did not exceed in anything, neither in what was spelled out about its dynamic behavior nor in inside room.

The body of the sports car, as it could not be different, privileged beauty, not practicality and roominess. As for its construction, opposed to what was expected, did not foresee any light material, its weight even being slightly superior to the sedan's. In all, it featured a modest dynamic behavior, closely similar to that of an economy car, and there was the insufficient interior room typical of a sports car, which could not be deemed as an attractive package to begin with. Yet there was the enchantment provided by the elegance of its lines.

Introduced in Europe in 1955, the Karmann Ghia was jointly produced by Volkswagen with coachbuilder Wilhelm Karmann GmbH, the traditional partner that since the dawn of the brand transformed the Sedan into a convertible. Design was done by Italian studio Ghia, hence the model's nameplate. Volkswagen supplied the platform and the mechanics to Karmann, which turned it back assembled with the body it manufactured, to be finished and marketed then.

The Brazilian subsidiaries – Karmann Ghia do Brasil, in the case of body manufacturing – adopted the same process and, as of 1962, started producing

Whenever a jury is convoked to elect the most attractive cars of all times, the VW Karmann Ghia always come up among the more voted. Nine years before the Ford Mustang, in 1955, the Karmann Ghia already fomented the idea of an automobile with a sporty design and mechanics absolutely identical to a touring car's. Built on the VW Sedan platform, an European economy car, it reflected its main characteristics: easy to drive and inapt for higher speeds. It lost some of the Sedan body practicality. Yet it earned beauty and charm.

the Karmann Ghia coupe. In Europe it was also built a convertible version, which would be produced in Brazil, yet in small series, in 1969.

Out there, in 1962, the model was exhausted already. It had a design difficult to be retouched and updated, as it happens with many classics that are born nearly perfect.

The Karmann Ghia was a handsome car, really special, which worked fine and had much of the practicality of the most successful car in the world, the Volks, also called Beetle.

In a time larger cars were not fit for urban tasks, the Karmann Ghia, which performed them superbly and charmingly, what the most popular cars lacked of, was a successful recipe for a sports car. Since a sports car must pay more attention to sensations than fulfilling the basic mission of coming and going, and since beauty awakens our senses and feelings, the Karmann Ghia that was a hit in Europe and had invaded the most charming spaces in the United States, would conquer Brazil.

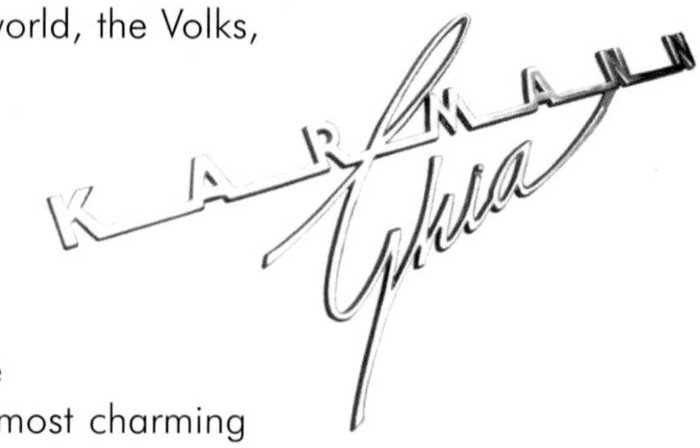

In Germany, Karmann was a traditional Volkswagen partner. Together, they produced the Volkswagen cabriolet, since the dawn of the make. When they associated to build a sports car, they used a Ghia design, hence the "Karmann Ghia" name brand. Here, in 1962, Karmann Ghia of Brazil repeated their mother company's partnership and the small sporty sedan began to be built.

It seemed perfect to be the second car of a couple. Following the dynamics of the time, the "master of the house" would use a larger car to go traveling or to work, safer and more suitable for such use. His wife, "the housekeeper", could perform the daily tasks with the sporting VW, very easy to be driven and featuring a simple and balanced operation. Going out on an evening, the Karmann Ghia would be the best choice. It provided more charm and the same *status* of a large car, with the same easiness of going on urban routes of a small car. It was the perfect use for the little car, since the couple did not have children or they were still small. The rear seat would not serve for more than that.

For singles, either man or woman, if roads were not part of everyday driving, this Volkswagen was also a nice option.

The Karmann Ghia had always been fitted with what VW had as best for other models' lineup. In 1967, the car gained the 1,500 cm^3 engine that was to power the Kombi also; in 1968 there some updating of details like fenders, taillights and other appendices; in 1970, following the launching of the four-door sedan the year before, the 1,600 cm^3 engine and front disc brakes, and so forth, until it was replaced by the Karmann Ghia TC, a liftback that did not have the same strength and even the room to re-edit the coupe's success.

Applied technique and practical results

The Karmann Ghia made full use of the traditional Volkswagen solutions of the time: horizontally-opposed four-cylinder engine, air-cooled and installed rearmost, with integrated gearbox and differential; torsion bar suspensions, in that the rear one featured swinging axle; platform-style chassis with separated body; worm and sector steering, as well as pedals and other controls layout; seat attachment and adjustment; upholstery details and all other, minor solutions.

The only big difference in relation to the Sedan was the body. Ground clearance was the same as the Beetle's, but since the body was much lower, the center of grav-

The VW 1200 engine ensured excellent working, but it was not capable of providing a compatible performance, even for a family sedan. In city driving, it fulfilled well its role, although it was a little noisier than desirable. For trips, it was dependable and wherever it arrived at, it would find competent service, should any repair be needed.

ity ended up displaced to a lower height, what represented a certain improvement in roadholding and driveability, which was also favored by the better aerodynamics. With a smaller frontal area, the Karmann Ghia was more apt to high speeds, although its engine was not capable of pushing or many kilometers per hour more, for it attained 125 km/h on a level stretch, 10 km/h more than the Volks.

The narrow rear track and the swinging axle, without the aid of a compensating bar, were not able do deal well with the bigger mass concentration over the rear axle, a known shortcoming of the Sedan, which however was attenuated thanks to the lower center of gravity.

The brakes, drums on the four corners, were sufficient; steering, for the standards of the time, could be considered smooth, although it did not steered enough; the four-speed all-synchromesh gearbox was easy to handle and gear ratios were adequate; controls were carefully spread, yet they were uncompromising; driving position, with arms and legs biased to the right, and the lesser visibility caused by the lower seating height in relation to ground, was somewhat tiring; but the finishing was adequate.

Temper

To plentifully use a Karmann Ghia it was necessary a routine that dismissed any transport obligation but your own, individual, private.

The intention was sophistication and unwillingness.

Advertisement communicated beauty, not performance, and the body design displayed a sporting aura, but it did not suggest it was fast. As for the engine, "the heart of an automobile", was identical to the Volks, an efficient popular car.

The Karmann Ghia lines incited freedom, while its "worker" underpinnings, for one side, assured the desirable peace of mind for a life with major compromises

Always in relation to the Sedan. When used in city, amid heavy traffic, it could entail higher claustrophobia: it was small inside; it had less glass area; it was lower; it had a more delicate look; and the common engine for the two car, was apathetic. Its occupants would feel more boxed in the cabin and oppressed by larger vehicles, besides being powerless to get away from them. Yet in the road, the scenery reverted: the moved down center of gravity and the smaller frontal area conferred to it, respectively, much better roadholding and quite higher top speed.

and, for the other, did not enable emotions, the search for a more daring behavior at the wheel, which give a bigger sense to a playboy's life.

Urban, daily driving

In 1955, Volkswagen, through a self, European language, came to satisfy a public avid for a sports-looking car, but not willing to giving away the economical and sound operation of one. The Karmann Ghia showed America the way that has lead to the Mustang, launched in 1964, a sporting car that shared the mechanical platform of a compact car. Compact is how the Americans called their more affordable cars, while Europeans classified theirs as economical, which were ranked subcompact by the American market. An American compact had the size of a large European or Brazilian car and, of course, was faster than

In the passenger compartment, the ambiance was not sophisticated at all, yet quite comfortable. Driver comfort was compromised by the position of the pedals, placed too far to the right. Two large-diameter meters drew attention in the instrument cluster – the speedometer and the clock. If the Karmann Ghia was really an orthodox sports car, instead of communicating time it would do so for engine speed and, as a minimum, would not dispense the temperature gauge.

an economical one, this one was more practical and suitable to be used in the Brazilian quotidian.

Freed from the compromise of carrying more than two people or to go shopping for the household, and with no major compromises in being versatile or practical, in daily use these limitations showed up.

The very low seats did not enable easy in-and-out and, in spite of the car's small size, doors demanded a reasonable room to fully open. Visibility suffered, too. The small glass area, added to the lower height, caused certain claustrophobia and made occupants feel somewhat oppressed, exposed to bumpers and other "weaponry" of heavy vehicles. All these sensations were common to other sports cars, yet more powerful engines compensated them, because of the sensation of power and ensured nimbleness.

To sum it up, the Karmann Ghia could be considered an excellent city car, adequate to daily commuting.

It launched and braked without showing any laziness amid the endless stop-and-go of urban traffic; it overcame the unevenness of bad paving without punishing the occupants and was not susceptible to it; it was very compact and easy to maneuver; it's controls were light; its operation was uniform and its mechanics, dependable; its finishing, free from major failures; and it had all the other virtues common to the Volks.

On the road

If the low profile of its body put it in disadvantage when compared to the Sedan regarding city use, on the road the ratio inverted. The smaller frontal area and the lower center of gravity contributed to a better driveability and nursed a little the instability caused by the bigger weight concentration at the rear that, to make matters worse, relied on an inefficient – regarding roadholding – swing axle rear suspension.

Some of the characteristics, inherited from the Beetle, condemned the Karmann Ghia as an option for those who took to the road often. There was no excuse for spending something equivalent to a large car, for one would have to co-live with low performance and poor roadholding, almost those of an economy car, or even with some important equipments, such as windshield wipers, as inefficient as the Sedan's. In spite of the shortcomings, it shared the Volkswagen's better service and superior dependability and reliability, important but not sufficient qualities for who had to spend hours in the road. The biased driving position, which did not bother in short runs, after a longer elapsed time started to punish the body.

Without concerning in sustaining high speeds, for small legs it provided an excellent service. To leave São Paulo to cruise in the state's coast, would be easy. On the way back, going uphill would be accomplished free from the ghost of engine overheating or any other failure.

At the coast, thanks to the materials used for its finishing and to its small size, the Karmann Ghia was a good companion. Besides not requiring major

For who owned a large car, the Karmann Ghia would be the ideal second car. In a time only the imports counted on power steering and power brakes, among other driving aids, it was an excellent option for evening outing and leisure moments. That's why it was a sports car.

attention regarding driving it, it was easy to park and to run short distances with vigor, its charm was ever present. It was good for wooing and always a plus to be appreciated.

The Karmann Ghia 1200 and I

Since the basic lines of the model have had small changes, I cannot be completely sure about the Karmann Ghia I had contact with, while it remained in production, if it was between 1962 and 1966 (1200 model) or after that (1967 to 1972, model 1500 or 1600). However, I seem to remember, it was the first one.

My parents had a friend couple, quite close, that had a son of my age. We were like cousins and his mother had a Karmann Ghia. Since we fit at the rear seat, it's quite probably that we were not more than seven years old.

Another thing I remember about this model is the clock. Its very wide needles and similarly shaped as the speedometer makes me believe that it was one of the first models.

I recall the fuzz it was to sit in it. At that age even discomfort was fun! Since that time the lines of the Karmann Ghia awakened my imagination and did please me. I supposed it was fast.

Time went by and, still a boy, I realized that its performance was very similar to the Beetle's. I was disappointed, but I kept admiring the small car even so.

I attentively followed the change of taillights design in 1968 and I was delighted when seeing the first convertibles. By the way, the powered scaled-down cars of this model were the dream of 10 among 10 boys. When I went down the road to the beach, what I enjoyed most was to "pilot" one. To sit in the cockpit and speed in "racing track" one of these was top. Many times I just stepped on the gas pedal, as to save money I divided the functions of accelerating, braking and steering with this friend, whose mother had a model in natural scale. These small cars did not go faster than a pedestrian in a hurry and the circuits were very short. However, it was by driving them that I and many kids started dreaming of becoming racing drivers and that its manufacturer, Gurgel, started his career of automaker. Years later he would enter History as the biggest manufacturer of genuinely Brazilian cars of all times.

For a long time, after phased out, the Karmann Ghia kept running. Its mechanics, identical to other "air" VWs, counted on service, what made easy by large the model's extra-life.

In the 1990s, I started ownership of a 1970 model-year, already with the 1,600 cm³ engine, a lot more fast and good-handling than the old 1200s and even the 1500s. The beauty of its lines pleased as much as 30 years before and the car kept dependable and low-maintenance.

The enchantment of a design and the right decision in producing a good idea showed their strength over time.

Its contours were elegant, no matter they were observed from. The two tiny grilles, besides giving some certain grace to front end, covered the cabin air intakes.

ANOTHER OPINION

The Karmann Ghia was one of these things that happened at the auto industry that can be considered a blessing. It was launched here long after in Germany, seven years later, yet still on time to be a player in the early phase of our auto industry. In a certain way, it soon assumed the character of as sports car for day commuting, hardly seen then and not so easy to find currently, since its toughness, production care and insensitiveness to heat were the same as the Beetle's. It was indeed a very elegant coupe and its body was quite efficient from the aerodynamic standpoint, for with the same 1,200-cm^3, 30-hp engine as the Sedan it attained 125 km/h, ten more than the Beetle. It was very pleasant to travel with, specially by the roadholding in high-speed turns, even impaired by the inefficient independent, swing axle rear suspension. In 1969 came the convertible, which conquered many hearts and until today highly coveted by collectors.

TECHNICALLY CORRECT

One of the best cars money could buy in 1970 was the Karmann Ghia, coupe or convertible, the result of an effective improving work on the model. The front suspension, equal to the four-door VW 1600's introduced the year before, had the ball-joint design instead of pins, the trailing arms were now supported by needle bearings in the axle housing, not bronze bushings, and the shock absorbers now had improved action for being attached at the end of the lower trailing arm, not in the middle of it anymore. Besides, the upper ball-joints were mounted on eccentric bushings, which enabled camber adjustment, non-existent before. And front axle lube service resumed to four nipples and needed to be performed each 10,000 km, *versus* ten nipples and 2,500 km intervals. Together with the new front axle came disc brakes, a vast improvement in safety, and the four-bolt wheel pattern instead of the five "star' one. At the rear, the same 50-hp engine of the four-door VW 1600, together with twin intake ports, the perfect basis for the many power soup-ups done by the independent engine tuners that followed. Rear track was enlarged by nothing less than 6,2 centimeters, providing a far better cornering behavior to the car, aided by Z-shaped compensating bar mounted over the transaxle. The two changes practically eliminated over-steer. The Karmann Ghia became even more desirable.

TECHNICAL INFORMATION OF KARMANN GHIA

VEHICLE	Karmann Ghia 1200 (1962 to 1966)
Type	2+2 coupe, 2-passengers, rear engine and drive
	Body and chassis
Type	Separated platform-type chassi and body; steel
	Engine
Type	Horizontally-opposed 4-cylinder, block and cylinder heads in light alloy, air cooled. Overhead valves (OHV)
Mixture formation	28 mm single bbl carburator
Bore and stroke (mm)	77 x 64
Displacement (cm^3)	1,192 cm^3
Compression ratio	6.6:1
Maximum power (SAE)	36 hp at 3,700 rpm or 30 hp (DIN) at 3,400 rpm
Maximum torque (SAE)	7.7 m.kgf at 2,000 rpm
	Transmission
Type	4-speed manual, fully synchronized and reverse
	Brakes
Type	Single hydraulic circuit, no powerbrake
Front	Drum
Rear	Drum
	Suspension
Front	Independent, superposed trailing arms and torsion leafs
Rear	Independent, swing axles and torsion bars
	Steering
Type	Worm and sector
	Dimensions and capacities
Wheelbase (mm)	2,400
Lenght (mm)	4,140
Width (mm)	1,634
Height (mm)	1,330
Ground clearance (mm)	152
Fuel tank (liter)	40
Curb weight (kg)	815
	Wheels and tyres
Type	Steel wheels and cross-ply tyres
Tyre size	5.60-15

Por que êste carro se chama Karmann Ghia?

Suas linhas foram idealizadas pelos desenhistas de Ghia, famoso "carrozziere" italiano.

Sua carroçaria, produzida por Karmann, um dos mais categorizados fabricantes europeus de carroçarias, num trabalho quase artesanal.

O Karmann Ghia é um dos mais belos carros jamais construidos.

Não é um carro de corrida.

É um carro de linhas esportivas, na categoria turismo, 120 km/h.

Sua mecânica é excepcional.

É Volkswagen.

O motor, refrigerado a ar.

A suspensão, por barras de torção.

É um carro de excepcional bom gôsto e de uma beleza sóbria.

Suas linhas avançam no tempo e estão sempre modernas.

É um carro para grandes ocasiões.

Combina com casas moderníssimas ou com tradicionais mansões e castelos.

Nada mais apropriado para levá-lo até ao iate e nunca um "mink" teve um ambiente tão perfeito quanto o interior de um Karmann Ghia.

E os mais austeros homens de negocios chegam de Karmann Ghia para suas reuniões comerciais.

O que v. deve fazer para ter um Karmann Ghia?

Passe num Revendedor Autorizado Volkswagen.

CHEVROLET
TEMP
COMB

From left to right: 1968 green Chevrolet Veraneio; 1960 gray Volkswagen Kombi and 1970 beige Rural Willys. The Veraneio derived from the Chevrolet Pick-Up, the light utility of cargo vehicle family. The Kombi made use of many mechanical components and solutions from the Volkswagen Sedan, a small car, of which it copied the wheelbase. The Rural came from the Jeep, an off-road work horse designed from a US Army order. The origins were very distant, as the final result was.

Mixed use utilitaries

(1957 to 1967)

Chevrolet Amazona (1962 and 1963) / Veraneio (from 1964 on), Volkswagen Kombi and Willys Rural

In the late 1950s/early 1960s, the pioneering implementation phase of the Brazilian auto industry, the launching of mixed use utilities was highly opportune. Their utilization was favored by the precarious conditions offered, both in use and maintenance, in several regions of the country, capitals included, as well as the fact that big families were more common. Also, there were more sons per household, mothers and fathers-in-law used to share the family motoring.

Since a few had a car, one that could hold a bigger number of passengers could become very useful.

It was also common to own a small business and a car that could serve both work and family.

The first model to have to "dual-purpose" and be launched here was the VW Kombi, by the way it was the second automobile made here. The first one was the DKW-Vemag station wagon which, so designed, also jointed the utility function with household transport, however highlighting the second purpose.

The Kombi, in fact, had multiple use applications. The body suggested so and it was suitable to work and, in spite of the underpinnings based on the Sedan, it did not look like a passenger car at all, neither hosted its occupants as such. In family transport, it did not treat passengers as goods, although the offered environment seemed more suitable for cargo loads.

The space solutions of the Kombi completely distanced it from the Sedan as an automobile; therefore, in spite of being a Volks descendant, in practical use it had little in common with it.

The Chevrolet Amazona was GM's the first step for a passenger transport car. In 1954, the Veraneio, with more of a touring car "accent" would replace it.

The Chevrolet Amazon originated from the caminhonete – as the pick-ups of the time were called in Brazil, later on they would receive the Portuguese form picape. The C14 line replaced it and soon after the utility version was called Veraneio.

Born from a light utility, therefore from a truck family, they could be considered as "little trucks" adapted – also – to passenger transport.

As the Chevrolet line was fitted for the C14 launch with a very efficient independent front suspension, the Veraneio – for this and other reasons – brought to its public that of family, big-size sedan users. Later on, in the 1990s, this kind of vehicle began to be considered as family utility.

As for the Rural Willys, it derived from the Jeep Universal, a vehicle born during World War II for military purposes that followed civilian life evidently working where there were no roads, just trails.

In 1960, the Rural Willys would earn roundish lines, in an attempt to escape somewhat from the work horse look. Until then, its front fenders did not even cover the fore part of the wheels. The skirt-and-blouse paint job and a few chrome works were the only attenuations.

The Kombi looked like a cobblestone sculpted on wheels. The luxe version, with skirt-and-blouse paint scheme, was better finished and holder of a unique sympathy. Its proposal was to serve as household transport.

For sure, the Rural inherited a vocation for bad roads and a certain inaptitude for the good ones.

In the 1990s, when they began being called sport utilities, the derivatives of off-road vehicles became highly popular, for they had their qualities for paved roads highly enhanced. The most successful ones were those branded Jeep, especially the Cherokee, therefore a direct descendant of the Rural. There were no sport utilities made in Brazil, they were all imported. Even the locally-made Chevrolet Blazer, which neared the concept, was close to family utility classification.

Just like in the passenger car world, the mixed use utilities may be classified in entirely different categories, including with more or less vocation for cargo, passengers or even kind of service.

The VW Kombi has been police car, it transported policemen. As for the Veraneio, it was the most authentic police vehicle, it actively participated in missions: it was used in pursuing and cell car, i.e., for carrying seized. By the way, the police Veraneio ended popularly called "the vehicle".

Both have worked also as ambulance: the Veraneio for the rich and the Kombi, for the poor.

The Rural also played, in more remote regions, ambulance and police "vehicle".

For severe load work, except for very rare exceptions, only the Kombi could fit.

Far from urban centers, the Veraneio served farmers and their families.

They usually ran over roads in extremely bad conditions, however always on road.

The Rural, by its turn, was used to go where roads did not lead to, or by people of lower economic *status* than the land owners.

But once at the country, the Veraneio accomplished the prestige automobile role, while the Rural accomplished the role of a medium-category automobile. In these sites the VW Kombi was also common, for load carrying.

Briefly, these were cars of quite different sizes that cannot be compared.
Each met a consumer's bracket needs.
They all were limited, however they all executed their tasks.

Each one's vocations

1. As a vehicle for more remote regions, without good roads, the Chevrolet Amazona and then the Veraneio and the Rural Willys.
2. As a transport vehicle where there were no roads, the Rural Willys, as long as 4x4.
3. As a vehicle for summer leisure, in a segment superior to others, the Chevrolet Veraneio utility. Yet in another time, in the immediate previous years, in as immediately inferior segment, the Amazona. Below, the Rural Willys and the Kombi shared the market.
4. For police vehicle or ambulance service, the Veraneio shared tasks with the VW Kombi in urban areas and with the Rural Willys in rural zones.
5. As a large car for family transport, the Veraneio was the only one that embodied the profile, which in many aspects was similar to the Aero-Willys', maybe even looking more like it than its direct competitors in their categories, the cars from the Simca and FNM 2000 lineups, which were quite distinct.
6. As a car for eight-passenger city mover or microbus, the Chevrolet Amazona, until 1964, when it was discontinued, and the VW Kombi. Originating from a truck lineup, the Chevrolet was tougher and more expensive.
7. As a urban parcel delivery vehicle, the VW Kombi and the Chevrolet Amazona, at the same time.

In remote zones

Pratically, in remote zones, the Veraneio could only be useful where a superior mobility under low traction conditions was not mandatory. Its ground clearance (minimum distance to ground) and toughness guaranteed traveling on bad roads. The same thing happened with the Rural Willys with the two-wheel drive version, which had the independent front suspension, much more civilized than the four-wheel drive's that was fitted with the same front rigid axle of the Jeep Willys and, therefore, had the same drawbacks in softness, comfort and roadholding. There was no direct competition between them, for the Rural was far inferior in price, performance and comfort. It they were automobiles, the Chevrolet would have a large car *status* and the Willys', that of a small one.

Where no roads existed

The Rural Willys, since it was four-wheel drive, did the same job as the Jeep Universal, whose platform and the entire mechanical ensemble it interited from. Not even its styling could hide the parenthood. Limited by the body, it served for passenger transport under these conditions and for this service, yet it did not reign absolute, for the Toyota Bandeirante, a vehicle whose proposal was above all that of an off-road utility, did the same job, more competently, yet less costly to purchase.

For summer leisure

The Chevrolet Veraneio, once again, did not have a direct competitor, since its price, performance and comfort was well above the Rural Willys' and the VW Kombi's. In the case of a fishing trip, the Veraneio would probably be the ideal car for passenger transport and fishing gear to the boat docked at a yacht club, while the Kombi and the Rural would carry – together with the fishing equipment – the boat to go sailing.

As police car, ambulance and other public services

From 1964 to 1990, Brazil was ruled by a military, totalizing régime. At that time, the police enjoyed high power and least popular sympathy. The Veraneio "went on duty" sometimes "civilian-dressed" and in other occasions, "on uniform". It was widely used for pursuing and as a cell car. It was the vehicle of all police forces. It was also ambulance, sewage crew's vehicle, power lines service vehicle etc. The VW Kombi held posts in the same corps; however it served as "microbus" for moving police or crews and as ambulance for least favored communities. When missions had to be done in some very remote area, it was Rural Willy's turn.

As a large car

The Chevrolet Veraneio performed and handled much like the Aero-Willys, in spite of differences in size.

For the price of a Veraneio it was possible to buy two Rurals. If they were touring cars, the Chevrolet would be classified as large, luxurious, while the Willys would be in the small car segment.

- The Aero's driving position was high and its steering required several turns for any maneuver. The same thing happened with the Veraneio, a "small truck" that, obviously, had these characteristics amplified in relation to the Willys' car. Since driving position was quite higher, its visibility was far better; however, due to bigger dimensions, maneuverability suffered.
- Both had six-cylinder engines, yet the Chevrolet's was larger, more advanced and powerful than the Willys', however it had to deal with more weight. Its suspension also did a better job, both in comfort and roadholding. Nevertheless, the high center of gravity (typical of a utility) ended up eliminating any initial advantage.
- The utility's design was more contemporary than that of the Aero. The Willys was an early post-war design and, in spite of the already body-integrated headlights, they were still kept embedded in the fender's prolonging after the junction between vehicle side and front section, while in the Chevrolet they already formed a unique visual next to front grille. Even being a utility, its lines were lighter than the automobile's.

Coming from a vehicle line for heavy cargo, the Chevrolet Brasil was tougher and safer than the VW Kombi that, for originating from a popular car, was less costly, light and nimble for urban tasks.

ANOTHER OPINION

It really was a propitious time for mixed-use utilities, given our highway network was smaller and mostly constituted by dirt roads. Besides, the economy was expanding fast then at that time and many businesses depended on the transport that did not exist.

It had happened about the same with the defeated countries in World War II, Germany and Japan. There was a huge lack of transport, for their industry had long been dedicated to war production in detriment of the civil one. We can say that these four utilities of the first phase were the ones that practically pushed business in Brazil.

TECHNICALLY CORRECT

They were not vehicles that can be called ideal, even considering the state-of-art then. The two Chevrolets were somewhat misfit in town due to size and had more of a truck ride than that of an automobile. The VW Kombi was nimbler in traffic, but its small engine developing just 30 hp (net) did not provide the expected acceleration and hill climbing speed, especially if fully loaded. Yet this would improve when the 1,500 cm^3 engine arrived in 1967.

The most suitable, as a whole, was the Willys Rural, the only to have all-terrain ability due to its part-time four-wheel drive. Those who already had to cross a muddy field know what it is like to count on four driving wheels. Nobody talked about off-road yet, just in mud, and there was plenty of it.

The Kombi fulfilled urban tasks with ease. The Rural played its role in more remote localities. On the road, driving them, both required extra caution.

PRICE TABLE OF MIXED USE UTILITIES[1]

	Model	1957	1958	1959	1960	1961	1962	1963	1964	1965	1966	1967	1968
VW	Kombi Standard					596	735	1,295	2,664	4,550.7	5,881	6,982	
	Kombi Luxe					676		1,455		5,110.7	6,605	7,839	
	Kombi Special						825	1,390	3,134				
	Kombi Bus						950						
	Kombi Van					570	704	1,230		4,323.6	5,343	6,294	
Willys	Rural 4x4					747	980	1,506	3,146	5,520	6,818	8,556	
	Rural 4x4 Luxe											8,656	
	Rural 4x2					697	908	1,370	2,857	4,978	6,148	7,703	
	Rural 4x2 Luxe										6,600	8,290	
	Pick-Up Jeep									5,169	5,863		
	Pick-Up Jeep 4x4					747	973				6,516		
	Pick-Up Jeep Body 2										6,153		
	Pick-Up Jeep Diesel 4x2										7,890		
	Pick-Up Jeep Diesel 4x4										8,440		
GMB	Amazona							2,466	4,918				
	S. Wagon 1416										12,740	15,383	

They were cars with entirely different proposals. In terms of prices, Kombi and Rural were not that distant. As for the price of a Veraneio, as the Rural advertisement would claim some time later, it was possible to purchase two Willys station wagons. The price of the Chevrolet was over 10% higher than local prestige cars and over 30% a large car such as the Aero-Willys. There was no sophistication or technology to justify so huge a difference.

PRODUCTION TABLE OF MIXED USE UTILITIES[2]

Make	Model Year ↓ →	1957	1958	1959	1960	1961	1962	1963	1964	1965	1966	1967	Até 1967	1968	Total
Willys	Rural	119	2,704	7,593	8,346	8,611	11,903	13,252	15,141	11,643	14,031	10,922	**104,265**	13,490	117,755
	Pickup				305	4,915	6,921	4,937	4,156	5,262	9,052	5,927	**41,475**	6,880	48,355
	Willys Total	119	2,704	7,593	8,651	13,526	18,824	18,189	19,297	16,905	23,083	16,849	**145,740**	20,370	166,110
VW	Kombi Utility	371	4,678	8,049	10,685	15,676	13,472	13,663	11,519	12,384	14,304	19,102	**123,903**	22,542	146,445
	Kombi Ambulance		122	151	164	152	594	316	325	158	159	138	**2,279**	268	2,547
	Kombi Van		19	183	450	487	497	449	534	572	635	981	**4,807**	1,202	6,009
	Kombi Pickup											957	**951**	2,871	3,822
	Kombi Total	371	4,819	8,383	11,299	16,315	14,563	14,428	12,378	13,114	15,098	21,178	**131,940**	26,883	158,823
Chevrolet	Amazona/ Veraneio			8	355	532	968	763	501	1,253	1,328	2,066	**7,774**	3,545	11,319
	Veraneio Ambulance										38	70	**108**	235	343
	Chevrolet Total	0	0	8	355	532	968	763	501	1,253	1,366	2,136	**7,882**	3,780	11,662
Mixed use	**Total**	**490**	7,523	15,984	20,305	30,373	34,355	33,380	32,176	31,272	39,547	40,163	**285,562**	**51,033**	336,595

Mixed use utilities total production volume was amazing. The Rural's 104,265 units easily rank it among the most sold vehicles. It had an attractive price and Brazil was a country under the industrialization phase that still depended on the inland economy, where roads did not always exist. The Rural-derived Willys Pick-Up also had a low retail price and had the ability to go far away from where asphalted roads existed. The Kombi, which remains in production until today, was one of the car that had interesting versatility and operational cost. Yet the Chevrolet Veraneio was derived from the Chevrolet Pick-Up, a light-weight and highly-priced utility that disputed market leadership with that from Ford, the F-100. Ford did not have a station wagon model, allowing the Veraneio to reign alone. It served both as touring car and working car, especially police and ambulance work.

1. Prices informed in thousands of Brazilian cruzeiros by *Quatro Rodas* magazine, January issue of each year.
2. Data according to documents supplied by Anfavea.

Chevrolet Veraneio (1964 to 1967) and Chevrolet Amazona (1962 and 1963)

With Amazona nameplate, in 1962 was launched the first multiuse national utility vehicle was launched, originating from a commercial vehicle lineup. General Motors, up to then, had only produced in Brazil cargo and collective transport vehicles.

The Chevrolet Brasil pick-up truck was the light utility of the series. It was a camionete, little truck in French, a word that later became graphed "caminhonete" in Portuguese.

That's how these vehicles were called for a good time, to finally become known as picapes, again Portuguese for pick-ups. That's what these vehicles are designed for, agile pick-up and delivery services. Over the Chevrolet Brasil pick-up chassis, and making use of its body from the cabin to front, a station wagon was built, i.e., a multiuse utility capable of carrying cargo or passengers with no physical partition for the space inside.

Seating capacity was nine, driver included, in three bench seats, in that it sufficed to unscrew the two rearmost ones to remove them.

Rear seats access was through a single door, identical to the front one, right side only.

The Chevrolet station wagon, originated from a family of work vehicles, showed the explicit proposal in its name – Veraneio (vacation leisure). The smooth lines for a car of the size, the efficiency of the suspension and the six-cylinder engine, much more modern than the Simca's and the Aero-Willys', contributed to its success.

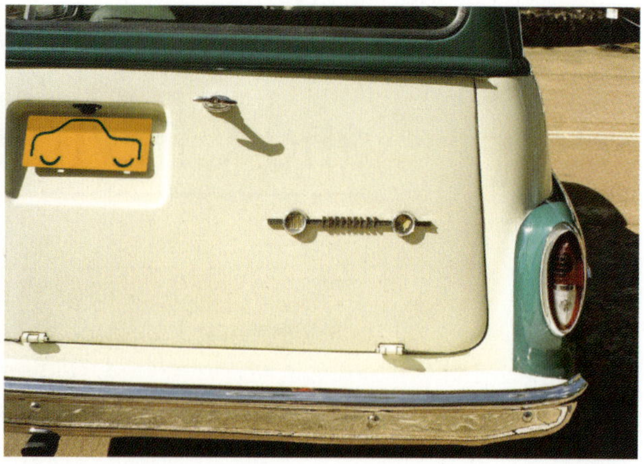

The Chevrolet Amazona, the Veraneio's forerunner, was quite more rustic. Its lines suggested a commercial, working vehicle, for people or cargo transport. The rigid axle front suspension with leaf spring assemblies confirm the veredict.

Access to the wooden-floored luggage compartment was done through a swiveling to-floor-level tailgate starting from the fixed rear window.

In addition to the crank-operated roll down windows on the three doors, there were sliding windows for those occupants seated at the outer ends of the seats.

The rear seats were quite thrifty and recalled more the seating of city buses of the time than those of an automobile.

The sliding windows, the poor floor finishing with wood-lined floor, as well as the seats with plain upholstery and looks, just three doors for a car with three rows of seats and details such as rustic handles and controls, everything added to the mechanical solutions, the design and the paint job typical of trucks of the time, ended up giving the Amazona the appearance of a vehicle for work more than for household transport. In fact, it filled much more the expectations for money-earning transport than a car for leisure.

Until the advent of the national car, the Chevrolet brand was one of the most popular. Its cars enjoyed solid reputation and excellent resale value. To benefit from this nameplate was a positive referential.

Many years after discontinued it was still used for school transfers in São Paulo City. It was deemed safer than the Kombi and a lot cheaper, simpler and roomier than the Chevrolet Veraneio, which it was succeeded by in the Chevrolet family and in its segment as a whole, in that until the end of the century no other vehicle of this kind, no matter the brand, was built countrywide.

The Amazon was a first step, however Chevrolet would get near the passenger car market with a model produced here, the Veraneio – Portuguese for summer leisure – whose nameplate suggested vocation for leisure.

After World War I, automobiles started to feature fender-embedded headlights. Following WWII, fenders became integrated to the bulk of the body.

As for utilities, fender integration to body took somewhat longer, yet the Chevrolet of Brazil utility lineup would adhere to it in 1964 only, when "C", the naming given to the utility model range the Veraneio belonged to replaced the Chevrolet Brasil series, that of the Amazona.

The Veraneio featured, besides body design evolutions, mechanical improvements that set it far away from the Amazona.

Besides the station wagon-like body, a few details only differentiated the Veraneio from the rest of Chevrolet's light commercial lineup. As for mechanical components, just the rear suspension changed, by adoption of coil springs instead of leaf spring assembly.

In spite of being used for service more than for summer leisure, the use of the utility was almost always aimed for personal transport. The Veraneio was not used for cargo service.

A third seat row was optional, however, if it was hardly ordered when buying the vehicle, it was even harder to see being used.

The lines of the C14 utility were delicate for a utility and the external dimensions, evidently, superior to those of a passenger car.

Adapted to the Veraneio, they assured bulk without losing smoothness.

Also smooth, always bearing in mind that the C14 belonged to a truck family, were suspension and powertrain. Adapted for the Veraneio, they became even more civilized.

Applied technique and practical results

Originated from a family of utilities, the Veraneio featured common, classical solutions of cargo transport vehicles or even buses'.

As it happened already with the C14 pick-up, the utility earned a very efficient independent front suspension respectful of softness and driveability, especially considering a vehicle with its proposal.

For better suitableness to passenger transport and providing them more comfort, the Veraneio rear suspension brought coil springs, seldom used for cargo transport for taking up space, besides higher manufacturing and maintenance costs.

The chassis independent from body was obligatory solution for cargo vehicles.

Heavier and less adequate to good performance in automobiles, it accomplished its mission in the Veraneio with honor.

The inline six cylinder, 4,275 cm^3 displacement engine, known here as Chevrolet Brasil, suitable for the brand's truck family, in the US was called 262

Chevrolet Engine Truck, the number referring to engine displacement in cubic inches. Its conception was widespread, with overhead valves (OHV). Convenient to load carrying, its torque developed in low engine speed range in detriment of good power output in the higher one. Its heavy crankshaft, suitable to maintain vehicle power once in motion, evidently was not cooperative for higher engine speeds.

It worked supported by four main bearings, which is not the best for a six-cylinder engine concerning reliability and vibration, but in a low-revving unit it did not compromise at all. The six-cylinder of the Opala, the first Chevrolet passenger car ever built in Brazil, had seven main bearings, for example.

Since the Veraneio was not a car for high speed, but practically "a station wagon for household transport", the combined work of engine, chassis and suspension was adequate enough.

The engine, a 4,275-cm^3 displacement, was an inline six with cam-in-block and overhead valves. Its crankshaft was too heavy, designed for duties that demanded plenty of power and capability of sustaining speed, in detriment of quick acceleration. It was not so modern as the one used by the mother company for its touring cars, that ran on seven main bearings, not four, which were known here as Chevrolet Brasil.

Yet the three-speed gearbox, most usual at the time, revealed inefficiency in spite of good gear engaging, yet it was full synchromesh. First it was very short, after all the launching of a vehicle of such a weight requires plenty of power; second it was also short in order to assure a reasonable performance in low vehicle speeds, and third, in spite of too short for higher cruising speeds, it was direct drive (output, or driveshaft speed, equal to input), as if it was a 1:1 gear set, therefore too distant from second gear (1.753 gear ratio), thus existing a large numerical gap between them that negatively affected acceleration. It lacked an in-between gear set and ratio that enabled better performance in twisting roads.

The steering wheel was too large in diameter and demanded several turns for any maneuver, resulting in a combination far from quick, but on the other hand it was quite lighter than the Veraneio's bulk and weight suggested.

At that time, power steering was an uncommon equipment and practically absent in work vehicles.

Professional drivers (of buses and trucks) deemed the equipment as dangerous. They alleged that, by being very light (and it was quite so at the time) it could lead to losing control at high speed, but prejudice really fell on an "unnecessary for men, sissy stuff'" equipment.

The utility body had four doors and luggage compartment access was through what later on (many year later, in the 1990s, in Brazil) became known as fifth door – a hatch that included the rear window and opened all way up from floor level.

The doors, except the driver's that could be locked from outside, could be locked internally only. The driver had to wait everyone to disembark in order to

A) A driver with less than 1,70 meters tall was not able to look over the steering wheel, but one over 1,75 m could not find position for legs and arms. The seatback was also low and the back had no support. In spite of these faults, the sensation of driving high, with a large glass area, with lots of room for the body and of being protected by plenty of steel, was truly pleasant.
B-C) The steering wheel was huge and turned six turns lock to lock, providing a good minimum turning radius, essential for a car so proposed. The dashboard, similar to other cars' of the utility lineup, was not sophisticated and provided information to a bare minimum.

lock the other doors and, after that, step out and lock his own. In all, it was quite an unpleasant exercise, for reaching all door locks he should "go for a walk" through the generous cabin.

Everything in the Veraneio was above the normal (horizontal) plan, one sitting quite high consequently, just like in a chair, the knees kinked at almost 90° angle. Floor was very far from ground, which forced climbing the car before sitting. Visibility was excellent, nevertheless the drawback was the center of gravity shifted way up, what is a complicating factor for roadholding turning and braking. The result not only became critical thanks to the excellent suspension performance, once brakes were far from exceptional.

Its space solutions, whatever they were, were compensated by the total volume that, for sure, would allow for better seats: the backrests were to low, they could cause certain discomforts.

CAR OF THE REPRESSION DAYS

The Veraneio was the preferred vehicle by the policemen, for:

- Its size imposed respect;
- It was truly reliable and it dispensed extra driving care, being able to go over tall curbs;
- Disembarking was easy. Even holding a gun, it was possible to get out quickly and continue on running. Accessing it was also convenient;
- No lack of room;
- Luggage compartment could be used for transporting the seized.

Temper

The Veraneio was a sturdy vehicle. It rendered the same sensation of power and sturdiness of a small truck, yet it provided the same comfort and performance of a large car. It also easily took any way ahead, what made it a good companion, especially for many continuous and uninterrupted kilometers on the road.

The Veraneio, as a whole, blended some of the appeal of a vehicle aimed to a family to the rusticity of one for work. The chromed hubcaps integrated and rendered some lightness to a wheel design fitted with tires typical of a utility.

Daily, urban driving

Hardly would the Veraneio be the right choice for daily use in a large Brazilian city, where streets and parking were never suitably dimensioned for a vehicle of its size.

However, except for parking troubles, the Veraneio could even be considered pleasant to be used in town, for its seating position with the driver seating up high rendered a certain impression of strength and protection, besides eliminating the claustrophobia sensation of regular passenger cars that makes occupants feel embedded in the middle of the car, of other cars and, especially, of buses and trucks. Also, visibility was excellent from the top.

In daily use, short commuting demands a constant get in-and-get out. Rusticity enabled a certain and pleasant carelessness in "opening and closing" doors, exactly the contrary to what happened when locking the car up, when an uncomfortable rite was necessary. The act of mounting ("climbing"), then sit and feel comfortable, was also more pleasant then with a car, which requires inverting the action by squatting.

Driver stature and physical bulk were decisive respectful of driving position and pleasure. Curiously, in spite of this kind of vehicle attracting many not-so-bulky men and especially women, conditions at the Veraneio's wheel did not favor them. Everything inside it had large dimensions and demanded ample actions, such as lot of turn for the steering wheel, the long pedal stroke or even the necessary movement to mount the car. People under 1.65 meters/5 ft. 5 in. tall for instance had their vision spoiled by the steering wheel.

The utility's size induced the idea of a muscle driver, also its image linked to a vehicle of the "mighty", specially for many of them being engaged in police service, sharpened the imagination in the sense of dominance and respect. No one inside a Veraneio felt like being an easy offense target in traffic.

Its mechanical sturdiness and the strength transmitted by the vehicle as a whole to overcome bad paving were other additives to the transmitted feeling of power.

In spite of seemingly having been designed for tall people, its maximum aft seat adjustment was small and people over 1.75 meters/5 ft. 9 in. tall hardly enjoyed a comfortable driving position.

Vehicles of its size would become popular among women years later, when power steering, besides other equipments, started to ensure effortless driving.

First start with a cold engine was not difficult at all and shortly afterwards the running of the car became stable.

The good torque of the engine and the easy shifting, low gearing favored urban driving.

Plenty of luggage room for shopping and easiness for laying down large volumes were undeniable Veraneio qualities that, however, for its bulk could not be considered as a choice of a car for urban, daily driving, in spite of accomplishing its mission.

On the road

The utility showed its real value on the road, not for performance or comfort, but especially for the vocation to eat up kilometers, for hours and hours, in any kind of road. The Veraneio was a true "arriver".

On good or bad asphalt-paved and not too twisty roads, cruising speed could be around 140 km/h, that is, its top speed. On hard dirt roads, a pace of some 110 km/h was usual. Yet on bad, narrow dirt roads, where low-ground clearance cars kept moving "crawling" avoiding bumps, the utility went straight on undisturbed.

At the "good" dirt roads its suspension exhibited the excellent balance between comfort and driveability. Of course, on asphalt the behavior was not that of a sports car, however, performance and comfort could be compared, and several times the utility did better, to the Aero-Willys', than the most sold Brazilian-made car and also capable of facing bad roads without showing fatigue.

For overtaking, it lacked one more speed on the gearbox, as well as in narrow and dense traffic roads the utility suffered due to its own weight and size.

As it so convened, the Veraneio was mostly seen in far inland regions, on roads with little traffic. On these, paving was very bad, however the scarce traffic permitted the Chevrolet to keep the momentum, the way it seemed it was designed to go. It did not have to slow down over bumps!

Some details brought the station wagon close to a touring car. A) In a time the most sophisticated national automobiles had the headlights embedded in the fenders, those of the Veraneio already integrated to the grille. B) At rear, the taillights were minute, yet they marked a visual identity.

The Veraneio and I

When it was launched in 1964, I was still very young, yet the model remained in production – with no structural change that could really modify its behavior

– until 1980, when it had the engine replaced by the Chevrolet 4100 that had powered the Opala since 1971.

During this lengthy period I did not underwent the experience of being "passenger", handcuffed or in a stretcher, in its rear compartment.

I did ride a lot in Veraneio, whether at the wheel or as passenger.

When I traveled to my uncle's farm in Mato Grosso and in Rio Grande do Sul states, our car was a Veraneio.

In these trips it was usual to stay day after day in all kind of roads.

One thousand kilometers was a customary journey, even at low average speed due to bad paving and to countless flat tires we had to change. My uncle's cars lacked better, or even none, maintenance, tires to begin with. Seven flat tires in a trip, if I recall well, was our record.

The three-speed gearbox with steering column shift was known as universal system. The shifter adopted by Chevrolet, as well as Chrysler's or Ford's, developed with time a worn out problem that resulted gearbox locking in first gear. An easy external fix, performed with the hood open, was enough to unlock. However, fixing the fault demanded a visit to the auto shop to replace nothing more than a bushing. My uncle preferred to go on unlocking the mechanism by ourselves each two or three times first speed was engaged.

Everything was very picturesque in our motoring with my uncle, including what we experienced on the road.

To begin with, he was not even 1.65 m/5 in. 5 ft. tall, had to use a cushion on the seat bottom for looking over the steering wheel.

As soon as the car moved from standing, he shifted into second gear. Before 30 km/h, third was the gear used, only to be disengaged when the engine was about to stall. This was also valid for overtaking.

On paved roads, the shoulder, even not asphalted, also served as track – it was used in turns.

All this happened when he was at the wheel, however he opted to go sleeping laying in the rear seat and, to my delight and his other nephew's, he used to handle over command to any candidate, generally not licensed to drive.

The first time I drove for more than an hour continuously in a road it was in one of those trips. I was 14 in 1975 and traveled around Mato Grosso state (presently Mato Grosso do Sul).

Another unique characteristic of my uncle was to keep going with the car where no one dared to, if not by foot or horseback. More than going by car, he did it with the Veraneio, which was not, nor intented to be a Jeep. Incredibly he always succeeded. On these occasions he used to regret not owning a Toyota Bandeirante.

The very straight and level roads of the Brazilian mid-west were covered by Veraneio, literally flat-out.

With his sapience, my uncle spelled out that going to the farms with the purpose of appreciating the sky and the stars was very pleasant, but to go there to work and to deal with all kind of people was entirely different.

I ended up loving the road and not the work in the country, as it was explicitly foretold in my uncle's speech. The proof of this is the fact that later on I had even traveled by Bandeirante to Mato Grosso do Sul with him, but after his death I never returned to the farms again. Yet to go traveling by Veraneio remained part of my life. I have bought one, 1968 model-year, in 2003.

ANOTHER OPINION

Both General Motors and Ford had not the green light from the Executive Group for the Auto Industry (Geia), which ruled out the implanting of this industry in the Juscelino Kubitschek administration, for producing automobiles. Geia wished that the two first manufacturing companies to install in Brazil, respectively in 1919 and 1925, focused on medium size trucks the country so needed. As automobile production increased in giant steps, the Brazilian GM looked for a way to join this market, hence the Amazona utility and soon later its successor, the Veraneio. These were mixed-use utilities, capable of carrying passengers and cargo. They reached sales success, for they were tough and good performers, with the advantage of seating nine people, driver included.

TECHNICALLY CORRECT

They were, to a point, rude vehicles, pick-ups with a body aimed for people transport. Yet the recipe was appropriate, at least for the gone 1960s. The huge mass provided a safety feeling to occupants, quite more than the light-weight Kombi.

The truck suspension made them suitable for police service, as it ended happening so, for they dominated this scenario. The six-cylinder, 4,275 cm^3 engine was acknowledged for its robustness qualities, it was almost indestructible, in spite of the crankshaft spinning on four main bearings only. The next generation had seven main bearings and was the powerplant for several years both in the commercial vehicles and the Opala and Omega car ranges.

TECHNICAL INFORMATION OF VERANEIO

VEHICLE	Chevrolet 1416 - Veraneio 1964 to 1967
Type	4-door station wagon for up to 8 passengers, with front engine and rear drive
	Body and chassis
Type	Separated; steel
	Engine
Type	Inline-6, cast iron block and cylinder head, water cooled. Overhead valves (OHV)
Mixture formation	40-mm single bbl carburetor
Bore and stroke (mm)	92.25 x 100.06
Displacement (cm^3)	4,271
Compression ratio	7.3:1
Maximum power (SAE)	149 hp at 3,800 rpm
Maximum torque (SAE)	32.1 m.kgf at 2,400 rpm
	Transmission
Type	3-speed manual, synchronized, and reverse
	Brakes
Type	Single hydraulic circuit, no powerbrake
Front	Drum
Rear	Drum
	Suspension
Front	Independent, upper single arm and lower A-arm, coil springs
Rear	Rigid axle, coil springs
	Steering
Type	Worm and sector
	Dimensions and capacities
Wheelbase (mm)	2,921
Lenght (mm)	4,847
Width (mm)	1,976
Height (mm)	1,776
Ground clearance (mm)	200
Fuel tank (liter)	70,5
Curb weight (kg)	1,940
	Wheels and tyres
Type	Steel wheels and cross-ply tyres
Tyre size	7.35-15

Êste é o outro Chevrolet. Seu nome é Veraneio.

Em primeiro lugar o conceito: um utilitário de classe, não só o melhor, mas o único. Agora o nome: Veraneio. Êste outro Chevrolet é incomparável em sua beleza sólida, em sua elegância prática, em sua completa segurança. O Veraneio é um Chevrolet de duas vidas, de duas caras. É bem visto a rigor ou a passeio. É o único utilitário brasileiro que faz tudo bem feito no asfalto ou na estrada de terra, no transporte de materiais ou na viagem com a família. Com 149 econômicos HP, exclusiva suspensão dianteira independente, Tração Positiva (opcional) e nôvo freio auto-ajustável, o Veraneio é um utilitário bonito e forte, sem concorrente. Faça uma visita ao seu Concessionário Chevrolet e experimente sem compromisso o Veraneio; êste outro Chevrolet.

CHEVROLET UM PRODUTO GENERAL MOTORS

GM BRASIL MARCA DE EXCELÊNCIA

VW Kombi 1200

(1957 to 1966)

The first vehicle to leave the assembly line of Volkswagen's subsidiary in Brazil was the Kombi passenger van, in 1957. Before Volkswagen, only Vemag, which in the previous year had launched DKW-Vemag Universal station wagon, produced automobiles in national territory. In spite of being called "peruas", the name for station wagon in Brazil, what the Kombi was not, they were vehicles with entirely different proposals: the DKW was a touring car with an enlarged luggage compartment and the Volkswagen, a vehicle for carrying up to nine people or light cargo, of up to 830 kilograms.

The Kombi success can be measured by its longevity. Platform and basic powertrain had been the same, in spite of having evolved. From launch date to 2005. It was the last Volkswagen vehicle in the whole world to be built with an engine descending from the first Sedan, in 1938. In 2006, it had its engine replaced by a water cooled one, yet it was produced with the same proposal and many of its early solutions.

From the shortening of the word Kombinationfahrzeug, which in German means combined-use vehicle, came the nameplate Kombi. Its format started to be known as mono-volume and its powertrain was a full loan from the Sedan, of

Looking to a rendering it was already possible to know what to expect from a Kombi: a lot of room and no roadholding. The shape was that of a minibus, as well as the treatment provided to driver and passengers was almost the same. There was room for up to nine passengers or 810 kg load, very close to the car's curb weight.

The luxury model had a two-color, skirt-and-blouse color scheme. Wheelbase was the same and overall length was just little bigger than the Sedan 1200's, which provided the Kombi an excellent mobility in city traffic. Versatile to the extreme, it performed delivery service or passenger transportation at low cost. Performance was one of its weak points, but the biggest faults were in safety and comfort.

which it also copied the wheelbase. However, its structure was unitary, quite different from platform type chassis separated from body like the Volk's.

The design of the axles followed the original Volkswagen concept, but there were differences. Up front, besides all parts being more reinforced, the steering linkage was quite different, resulting in equal-length tie rods, unlike the Sedan's unequal ones, something not recommendable. Therefore, there was a clear evolution in this point. At rear, suspension layout was the same swing axle with torsion bar, but at the outer end of each axle there was a reduction gear set to enable further increasing of overall transmission ratio and to increase ground clearance as well.

Another translation for Kombi, maybe a better one, would be versatile, a term that could be well more understood when observed through all possible uses for the vehicle and the easiness it could be adapted for this or that purpose.

The Kombi had three seat rows. The central one and the rear were attached to floor each by means of four removable oblong-head studs locked in the floor and respective wing nuts, which enabled quick and independent seat removal. The central could, if wished, be mounted facing rear to direction of travel. Access to these seats was through two doors on the right side that opened in inverted way one to the other and met when closed. Once without the central and rear seats, it was through this ample opening that the van was loaded.

The driver sit over the front axle and his boarding and other occupants' to the front seat was made through two large, conventional doors, whose windows were of the sliding kind.

Over the engine, at rear, there was a compartment allocated for small volumes, which could be loaded either through the rear doors or, more conveniently, through the tailgate, which included the rear window.

Applied technique and practical results

Those were basically the same solutions of the "Fusca" (Beetle), except for the unitary body construction, the differences in suspension and the design of the one-volume body, long and high.

Everything it preserved from the Sedan assured the same good urban behavior of an economical vehicle, while the body conferred a quite distinct use.

Exchanged to a multipurpose utility, the Volkswagen underpins exposed bigger limitations regarding comfort, performance, roadholding and safety than if used for a passenger car with sedan body, for which it already didn't excelled in any of these virtues. Nevertheless, in many tasks, it assured low-cost and competent operation.

The Kombi space solutions were pretty clever. Since the cargo were laid down on its floor, it was not necessary to dispend energy to raise them, opposite to what used to be when loading a pick-up truck.

There were two rear seat rows. It sufficed to unscrew four wingnuts per seat, to remove them. After removed, there was all the space dedicated to load. The two side doors provided excellent access and floor laid in a considerably lower height than the bed of a pick-up, making easier loading and unloading operations. With use the doors became noisy. Inside the Kombi there was huge air mass and almost no lining, in an ambiance extremely favorable to noise, heat and fire propagation.

Driving position, sitting ahead of the front wheels, high and with quite an upright back; close to steering wheel and windshield; with a practically horizontal steering wheel; and with the pedals – which sprouted from floor – operated from top down, was the most peculiar possible. More than weird, it was dangerous: in case of a frontal crash at foot height, these would be protected by the bumper only, and if the collision was in a higher point, the head would be shielded by the windshield only, while thorax, very close to steering wheel, would be hit for sure. Besides dangerous, it was uncomfortable: over the wheel, any and all bump was transmitted to the driver.

Driving position was singular, entirely different from that of a touring car. The large-diameter steering wheel was positioned almost horizontally; pedals sprouted from floor and were vertically operated, from top to bottom; the back laid almost upright; one sit over the front wheels, therefore subject to all kinds of jolts and completely unaware to the rear wheels' path; there was nothing ahead and so on. The instrument cluster with a sole meter, the 0-100 km/h speedometer, exposed no pretension for performance.

To make matter worse, the VW engine was noisy and placed inside the cabin, but is was not the sole source of noise: the rear doors, after a few thousand kilometers, developed plays responsible for "a symphony of rattles". Yet it helped the Kombi to be noisy and uncomfortable inside the lack of any thermo-acoustic insulation and the huge cabin volume. Both sound and heat propagate in air.

Suspension, brakes and powertrain as a whole had to be all very eclectic to deal almost 100% weight difference. Yes, the Kombi could be loaded with a weight that practically equaled that of curb weight. Besides weight variation, the cargo distribution changed. Since most of the underpinnings were inherited from the Beetle, it is admirable that it could accomplish its mission, however the drawbacks were not few.

The Kombi had the shape of a cube longitudinally cut in half: high, long and narrow. At naked eye it is easy to perceive the difficulty in keeping stabilized so shaped a vehicle. Besides center of gravity issues, the ample side area enabled that wind and turbulences compromised even more the delicate upright running of the Kombi.

In spite of it all, the Kombi was a success. No success resists to time for so long if not owning enough virtues for its shortcomings to be relegated to second plan. Then, it is expected that it had some of them, or at least some sizeable benefit, something unique.

The Kombi's great virtue was being able to fulfill work mission, in transporting cargo or passengers, in a practical and economical way. It had adequate performance in urban traffic, it was easy to park and carried very large and heavy volumes. On the highway, safety remained in a lower plan and even the low speeds its engine was capable of providing at maximum, should not be reached.

The Kombi always topped the roaster of most wanted car by thieves. In this 1960 one, a steering lock was installed, a very popular accessory at the time and that would not be admitted as factory equipment.

Temper

The Kombi was an excellent work horse, capable of performing many tasks more efficiently than with any other vehicle of its time, yet with no comfort or safety.

The Kombi was an employee, a worker that admirably accomplished his work, but it punished its boss with little comfort and threatening his safety.

Daily, urban driving

Hardly someone would option for a Kombi for daily family use. Not that it was huge or difficult to park, or that its controls were heavy and its fuel consumption was high.

The van was easy to drive and, except for gear engaging, somewhat vague, or by being difficult to estimate where the rear end was, in other aspects the Kombi was quite similar to the Sedan.

Comfort was what did not please at all.

On the road

The Kombi 1200, with just 30 cv, was too slow, unstable and unsafe, yet it was cheap to operate. Once driven with patience and responsibility, it, once again, fulfilled its missions.

The mechanics, reliable and well-known, helped in enabling the Kombi to travel for long distances and, if for the everyday household use it was occasionally seen, on the weekends it usually served the family and leisure.

A) In 1961, the Kombi taillight group would incorporate turn indicator. Up to then, the direction change was done by semaphores ("bananinhas"), rods embedded in the columns aft the front doors that popped up when actuated. B) The VW 1200 engine, with just 30 hp net, had to deal with an almost 100% weight variation, as it happened with suspension and brakes. The miracle happened, although with many deficiencies, in all situations.

The Kombi and I

In the first year of my life, my father was an entrepreneur. He did not drive the Kombi, but the fleet of delivery vans of his business had two of them, which one time or another were lent for home use.

Behind the front seat there was a metallic partition. At its center, there a stamped circumference to house the spare tire where there was a semi-circumference whose ribs designed a half sun on it. When I was a child, in the 1960s, I thought this detail was of very good tasting, fascinating. I rode in the Kombi, "enjoying all the space in the world", at rear, in the luggage compartment with the seats removed. Very few people, at the time, had in mind the danger that metallic partition represented in an accident, or even in a sudden stop.

A) As well as at the rear, in 1960 the Kombi did not have turn indicating, blinking lights. One of the first things I learned about the Kombi, yet in the 1960s, was that in spite of looking big, it was not mighty. In case of a frontal collision, the driver's feet would be hurt. B) As for the sliding windows, far less efficient than the usual ones, seemed more interesting.

At that time, it was not usual to keep home appliances and almost no other domestic hardware or clothing in a beach apartment. Therefore, on vacations, we usually went down to the coast, my sister and I, with my mother and all the vacation move, riding in a company Kombi driven by a driver employee. On the weekend my father went down to meet us, or with his own car and some remaining bits which failed to be transported in the Kombi, or with my mother's Beetle. In the second case he left the car with us and traveled back getting a lift.

I loved to travel by Kombi. Children do not know discomfort or danger, but they know how to use spaces, therefore, besides going out on vacation, I was traveling in a Kombi.

I figured that the Kombi was a robust car, after all it was big, however discussions with friends, not too much older, informed me about the danger of an automobile with no front end, that the Kombi was large enough, but it was light and turned over, besides powered by an engine that was equal to the Beetle's.

In spite of the deception, I kept enjoying the Kombi.

The Kombi evolved and I matured, I was no longer a child, went through adolescence, turned into an adult, but in a certain way I had never lost contact with the Kombi. Regardless of any time, I always saw myself making good use of its services.

They say that kids, since they are babies, are fascinated by wheels. It was not different with me. I thought that the Kombi's were the same as the Volks'. I was not capable yet to identify them by the shape of their windows.

ANOTHER OPINION

The Kombi may be considered a vivid legend in the Brazilian automotive scenario.

It's incalculable the number of small, medium and large companies that made full use of it for all kinds of services and the role it played at small businesses, like city marketers. Not less important was its people mover character, from first grade students to who needed to get to work. Even more incredible is that the Kombi is still among us, strong and healthy, after 50 years of being produced in Brazil, not to count the seven previous years of the imported/assembled phase, the undeniable proof of the excellence of its design. The Kombi may have a thousand faults, but its usefulness more than trade-off them all. Dutchman Ben Pon, who conceived it, probably never imagined that his idea reached so far in time.

TECHNICALLY CORRECT

The theoretically Volkswagen Sedan-derived Kombi's most amazing fact is its unitary construction, while its source of inspiration had separated chassis and body. In the early development stages, a similar construction was tried for the Kombi, but the platform-shaped chassis proved to be weak for the nearly 900-kg payload, failing in the firs tests. Because a new structural design was needed, Volkswagen set for the unitary construction solution, which was already emerging as solution for oncoming years. The Sedan itself, years before, could have been designed that way, but Ferdinand Porsche, its creator, had already a military body in mind, which was to become the Kübelwagen for the German army. For this reason, chassis and body had always been separated in the Sedan.

TECHNICAL INFORMATION OF VW KOMBI

VEHICLE	**Volkswagen Kombi 1957 to 1966**
Type	Mixed-use utility for up to 810 kg payload or people mover for up to 9 passengers, with rear engine and drive
	Body and chassis
Type	Unitary; steel
	Engine
Type	Horizontally-opposed 4-cylinder, block and cylinder heads in light alloy, air cooled. Overhead valves (OHV)
Mixture formation	28 mm single bbl carburator
Bore and stroke (mm)	77 x 64
Displacement (cm^3)	1,192
Compression ratio	6.6:1
Maximum power (SAE)	36 hp at 3,700 rpm or 30 hp (DIN) at 3,400 rpm
Maximum torque (SAE)	7.7 m.kgf at 2,000 rpm
	Transmission
Type	4-speed manual transaxle, non-synchonized first until 1960
	Brakes
Type	Single hydraulic circuit, no powerbrake
Front	Drum
Rear	Drum
	Suspension
Front	Independent, superposed trailing arms and torsion leafs
Rear	Independent, swing axles and torsion bars
	Steering
Type	Worm and sector
	Dimensions and capacities
Wheelbase (mm)	2,400
Lenght (mm)	4,280
Width (mm)	1,750
Height (mm)	1,940
Ground clearance (mm)	280
Fuel tank (liter)	40
Curb weight (kg)	1,040 Standard/1,060 Luxe/1,140 6-doors/970 van
	Wheels and tyres
Type	Steel wheels and cross-ply tyres
Tyre size	5.90-15

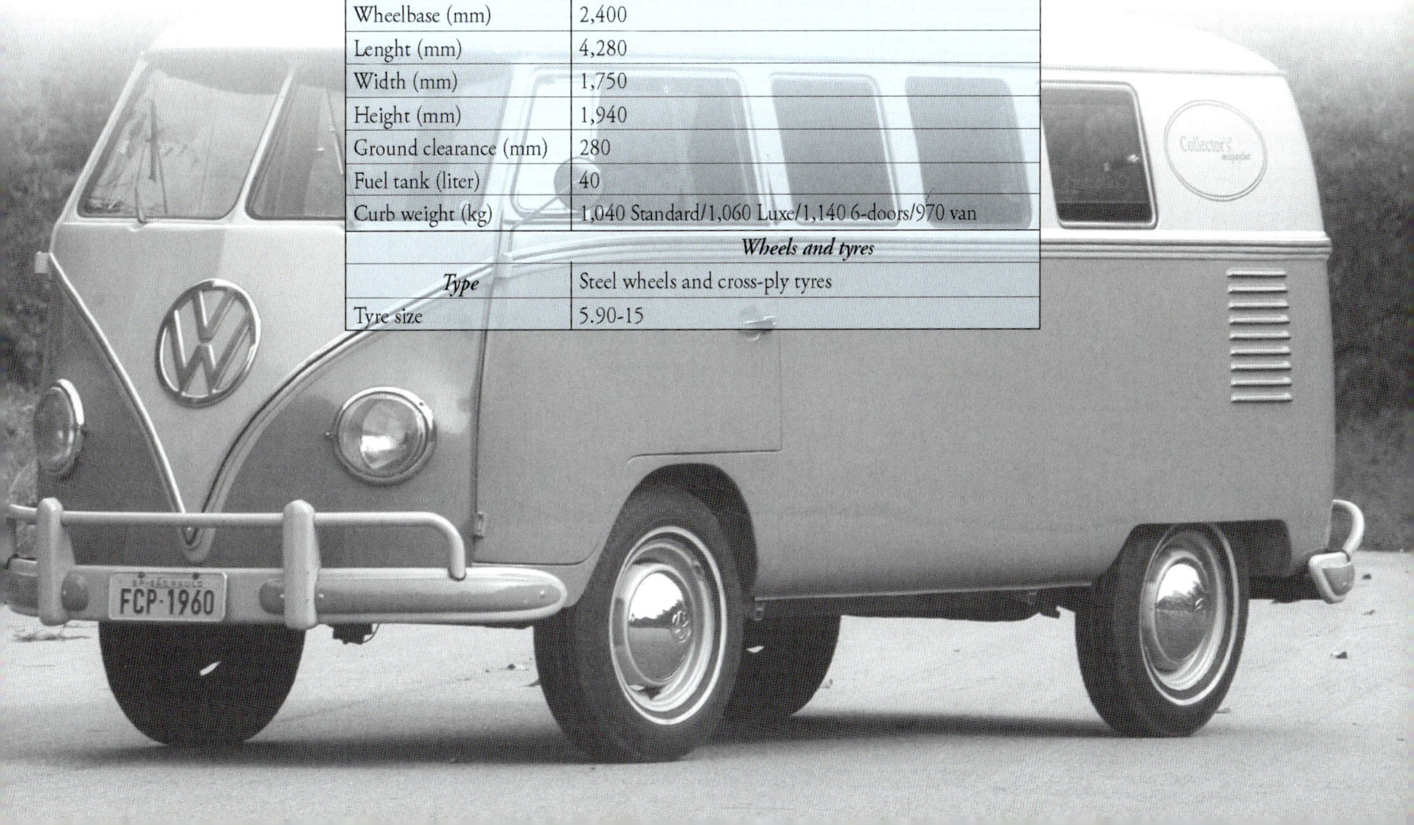

Volkswagen do Brasil S. A.

Onde cabe um Volkswagen, cabe outro Volkswagen.

Cabe.

Sai um Sedan, entra uma Kombi na vaga. A Kombi é sòmente 21 cm mais comprida do que o Sedan Volkswagen.

Experimente agora encostar uma camioneta qualquer nesse mesmo espaço.

Não cabe. Porque as camionetas convencionais são, no mínimo, meio metro mais compridas que o Sedan Volkswagen.

Então, a Kombi é menor do que as outras camionetas?

É menor, em comprimento.

É maior, em capacidade de carga.

A Kombi foi mesmo desenhada para ganhar espaço interno e economizar espaço externo.

O motor, que não ocupa mais espaço do que uma mala grande, foi colocado atrás, incorporado à carroçaria.

Isso foi o fim do cofre dianteiro, dos pára-lamas, da lataria supérflua.

E sobrou espaço para todo mundo.

Cabem 9 pessoas sentadas confortàvelmente. Dá para esticar as pernas, virar para os lados sem incomodar ninguém.

Conheça a Kombi por dentro e por fora num Revendedor Autorizado Volkswagen.

VOLKSWAGEN

o bom senso sôbre rodas

Rural Willys

(1958 to 1967)

In 1952, the Jeep Willys started being assembled in Brazil and, in 1957, its manufacturing had begun. Its derivative, the Rural utility, had commenced production in 1958, two years after assembling, therefore at the dawn of the national car. At the time, in a country without roads, the Jeep, a vehicle born to improvise ways, made all sense.

A station wagon derived from an off-road vehicle with a vocation next to it, certainly could be regarded as the recipe for success, as time made it clear. Roads took long to be built, especially paved ones, above all in localities distant from big urban centers, thus assuring longevity for the Rural, which was phased-out ten years after Ford took Willys over.

With four-wheel drive, the only limitation the Rural had additionally in respect for the Jeep was its body. The capability to paved roads continued to be minimal, as it occurred with the Jeep.

In 1964, a version with rear driven wheels only was introduced, in that besides being very short of mediocre, had a better dynamic behavior where four-wheel drive was unnecessary. With this layout, it was useful for utility, mixed use service:

With rounded edges and skirt-and-blouse paint work, the Rural looked more civilized, but it did not hide the direct parenthood with the Jeep utility. The four-wheel drive version had a dynamic behavior close to that of an utility. In 1964, a two-wheel drive only version was launched, fitted with independent front suspension. The new option aimed comfort and driveability. Its reactions ended more alike those of a mixed use utility, but kept it away from mud pools.

The 1958 model-year kept the square corners, as well as it preserved headlight location of the Jeep utility. The two-piece windshield and the split rear window were other indicators of its compromise with low cost.

a vehicle for light services, with vocation to go to far places and adapted for use by passengers.

The experience of using a Rural was a single one. No "ADN" test was necessary to conclude it was a Jeep, originated from a car conceived to war duties. It was tall, short and wide; its ground clearance was high and there were two doors only; it did not have running boards to "enable" rear seat access and to make it easy for the front ones; glass area was small; finishing was Spartan; the dashboard was as straightforward as the external look suggested; the finishing was rustic; nothing seemed to be designed to favor beauty; and everything suggested toughness. Nothing cozy, yet solid and robust!

Applied technique and pratical results

The engine was the same one of the Aero-Willys, a six-cylinder with camshaft in block and "F" head, i.e., intake valves overhead and exhaust on the side of the block.

For a passenger car like the Aero-Willys it proved to be inadequate, and when later on, even optimized, it powered the Ford Maverick, its limitations became evident. However, for a work horse it was suitable, in spite of not being fuel-efficient.

The engine has always been the same: a gas guzzler and unsuitable for peppy performance, however it did pretty well in heavy duties. Frankly speaking, no other would achieve the miracle of good fuel efficiency in a heavy vehicle, with no compromise at all with aerodynamics and gear ratios that privileged off-road tasks.

The brakes did not assure safety, balance or even reasonable braking distance in decelerations, but, incredible as it may seem, it would fit off-road work.

Trasmission was accomplished by a three-speed gearbox with floor shift, where the levers for the transfer case and low range gear were, bi-sided by the main lever. Low range could be engaged in association with four-wheel drive only. With this setting, the Rural was capable of overcoming obstacles and perform extremely heavy duties, yet it only fit to work far when from roads.

The four-wheel drive model's suspension, both front and rear, consisted of rigid axles with semi-elliptical leaf springs. The same evaluation of suspension performance rested to it.

The four-wheel drive Rural was a Jeep, a utility for off-road job, not a mixed use utility.

In spite of the same chassis and same body, as well as engine and finishing, the 4x2 model was quite more civilized and apt to perform multiple tasks such as people mover or carrying small loads, under several conditions. As opposite to the 4x4, it wasn´t suited to make its own road, or to work heavily out of it.

A) The 4x4 version retained the instrument cluster, the steering wheel and all other controls from the Jeep. B) Those of the 4x2 version had the Aero-Willys'. The provided information was the same, however readout quality, thanks to 4x4 dashboard layout, was superior, while the 4x2's had a better look.

The transmission of the 4x2 was basically the same of the 1964 Aero-Willys onwards. With column shift, gear engaging were not precise at all and if for an automobile like the Aero-Willys it did not please and later on in the Ford Maverick it ended up compromising it, for a car of the Rural's proposal this gear engaging feel fit perfectly. Exactly the same could be said about its suspension: in spite of not providing an even reasonable road-holding, it was one hundred percent in consonance with the station wagon looks suggested, which did not hide the parenthood with the Jeep Universal. The rear suspension was the same as the Jeep's, yet the front one was independent and coil sprung.

In all, the looks of the Rural did not suggest an automobile for high performance and much comfort: it just transmitted the sensation of toughness. The quiet posture was enhanced by the paint scheme, always of the "blouse-and-skirt" kind, with good-mannered combinations that always included white in the lower part.

Driving position also revealed that the car did not have compromise with high performance nor comfort. One sits high, with the almost horizontal steering wheel. Pedals rose from the very flat floor, assuring a quite erect posture for the driver: vertical back, arms and legs, always compounding an angle close to ninety degrees. The seat did not support the body, which the jolts of the suspension tried to expel, the hands firmly holding the steering wheel as a last resource. Since the accompanying person did not had a steering wheel and the panel was massive and with no reentrancy at all, the only relief was the fact that the station wagon was not able to go very fast.

A) The Rural's look was singular. Even after 1960, it remained very rustic, transmitting a sensation of power. B) There was room inside, but comfort was ruined by the suspension jolts and by the high, right-angled seats that were incapable of providing any side support. C) Volume distribution did not allow a better use of the luggage compartment.

Temper

When the station wagon started being optionally offered with 4x2 drive, it became, in fact, a mixed use utility.

Since in the times of the Rural there was no technology that managed to conciliate multiple tasks for one sole vehicle, without losing much this or that, and the Rural was an affordable option, there were a lot of sacrifices. As time went by, adopting more fine techniques, yet always very expensive, cars with its proposal ended up conquering the world.

The Rural could not harmonize the best of off-road with the reasonability of the touring car, but it was unique and pioneer.

Daily, urban driving

In conclusion, it is difficult to believe that the Rural could count virtues in urban circuits, however some characteristics, typical of an off-road vehicle, did please very much.

The first good sensation was the one that came from the indelicate manner to open and close the doors with, without having to care for subtleness. Then, to accommodate in the seat free from any preset position; to keep seated in a more elevated plan that, in addition to providing excellent visibility, assured the impression of strength, confirmed by its looks, also pleased.

But it was not just that: the rusticity of controls, carelessness with paving imperfections and the very low gear ratios, which provided prompt reaction and low speed acceleration, as well as the Spartan finishing that would not cause inhibitions to board with wet shoes or even rest it on the seat, allowed easiness and well-being.

Geralmente os carros são batizados com o nome da marca seguido pelo do modelo. A Willys, por vezes, invertia a ordem: Rural-Willys. A marca Jeep não foi aproveitada.

However, the cons were bigger: to enter the passenger cabin it was necessary to mount; the door easily misadjusted, requiring some force to shut it; steering and brake controls were especially heavy; gear changing was not precise; fuel economy was very poor; rear seat access was critical; rear side windows did not open; the finishing did not count on almost no sound deadening material, as well as the large volume of air in the cabin helped in propagating heat and noise; the stiffness of all motions provoked jolts and so on.

On the road

The presence of the station wagon grew in remote places. Proportionally, the farther from a great center a locality was, the larger the quantity of Rural station wagons around. Less existing paved roads, more the Rural was part of life of the community.

In spite of it all, the presence of the Rural was not that scarce in the Brazilian metropolis.

Many people dreamed of a car that could go in city and have enough room to carry the whole "team", with all the stuff, for a good fishing or a week end in the country.

Even fitted with conventional cross-ply tires, the wheels seemed to be "wearing boots".

To go traveling with the Rural required patience. It did not reach high speeds, it was unstable, braked poorly and, in spite of being roomy, was little comfortable. At 100 km/h on a level road, the engine noise already denounced that it was doing its best. Going up on long hills, the number "6" that indicated 60 km/h, was what was shown under the speedometer needle.

One of the statements in arithmetic notes that "the product of minus by minus is plus". This explains why it was better for performance of the Rural not contemplating high speeds, since it did not brake well; or, as roadholding was poor, it was better not being fast; or, if it did not safely contour turns, it was better that its driver did not even feel held by the seat; or, if its balance on wet was "equal to zero", it was better that its windshield wiper was inefficient and that its windows fogged; or, still, that its engine, which was suitable for heavy duty,

Its silhouette was brutish, but observed from a close distance, it was possible to note some details and curves that tried to confer more elegance to the whole vehicle.

was not reliable enough for keeping it in long distances with "pedal in floor". All computed inabilities did not encourage the driver to speed up and, slowly, it reached anywhere, especially where other cars couldn't. For such, the simple and known Jeep mechanics contributed.

"The slow horse reaches the mill".

One of the things that pleased in the Rural was its respect-imposing character. Hardly some automobile would try to take advantage of its bulk to dispute the same space.

The Rural and I

In spite of the rural vocation, as its name suggested, I recall seeing many of these station wagons around in São Paulo City, but my memory says that the first time I rode in a Rural was in Rio Grande do Sul state, when I visited an uncle that ran farms.

I was about ten years old and I can't tell if this car was new, however, since the Rural barely changed, it doesn't matter. I also don't know if it featured four-wheel drive. All I remember is its speedometer stuck to 10, when level, and that even going downhill it insisted in not reading above it. As for uphill, the speed suddenly dropped to 60 km/h. Another point that marked me was the difficulty I had, as a somewhat fat boy, in accessing the rear seat. I could only mount the car with a pushing help, a shame on me that helped me to share my uncle's preference for the Chevrolet Veraneio or even his "Fuca" (the Volkswagen sedan so nicknamed by the Southerns)

My experience with the Jeep lineup was deeper, but with the Rural it was just this one.

Access to rear seat was miserable. A somewhat fat child would certainly need help to access it.

Once, traveling through Mato Grosso state when I was 14, I had the chance to ride, for a few kilometers of a dirt road, at the wheel of a Pick-Up Jeep, the truck version of the Rural. It was the 4x2 version. With no cargo in the bed, that car really jolted! The shifter had such a play that it could not tell what gear was in and, if I remember, this was the only option to be used to leave the farm.

Years later and for a long time, in São Paulo inland, I used a long-wheelbase Jeep, called "Bernardão". It severely punished its occupants with jolts and did not admit high speeds, but nothing could stop it in off-road work.

ANOTHER OPINION

The Rural Willys was a passenger and luggage-carrying Jeep with more comfort than a Jeep, without dispensing the ability of facing any road in Brazil during the 1950s. It is the first ever history's sport utility, conceived for leisure, as much as a 'sport coat'. One can say without the risk of being wrong that it is the Jeep Cherokee's grandmother, a truly successful vehicle the world over since launched. The Rural Willys has been for a long time an extremely wished vehicle and the factory submitted it to several evolutions along the years. It has reached the extreme of making it suitable for a more civilized use, with rear-wheel drive only and independent front suspension on coil springs to enhance ride comfort.

In city, the sensation from seating higher than in other cars was welcomed. In paved roads, even if its engine performed better, only with a lot of goodwill it would be possible to attribute advantages to it. Far form asphalt the ride was bumpy, but it could go farther, far beyond an automobile could go.

TECHNICALLY CORRECT

Although the F-head six-cylinder, 2.6-liters engine was not an exponent in conception and efficiency, its 90-horsepower gross were sufficient for the whole, easy to drive above all. Power was plenty even at very low engine speeds, as it convenes to a sport utility with off-road capability, which is corroborated by the fact that the three-speed gearbox did not compromise in any way. It was a utility made to be driven at moderate speeds and, this fact observed, it did pretty well.

TECHNICAL INFORMATION OF RURAL

VEHICLE	Rural 4 x 2	4 x 4
Type	2-door station wagon for carrying up to 8 passagers, with front engine and rear drive	Four-wheel drive
	Body and chassis	
Type	Separeted; steel	*
	Engine	
Type	Inline 6-cylinder, cast iron block and cylinder head, water cooled. Overhead intake valves and in-block exhaust valves (F-Head)	*
Mixture formation	Single bbl carburetor	*
Bore and stroke (mm)	79.37 x 88.90	*
Displacement (cm^3)	2,638	*
Compression ratio	7.6:1	*
Maximum power (SAE)	90 hp at 4,000 rpm	168cv at 5,000
Maximum torque (SAE)	18.8 m.kgf at 2,000 rpm	*
	Transmission	
Type	4-speed manual, synchronized, and reverse	Non-synchro first; 3-speed + low range and reverse
	Brakes	
Type	Single hydraulic circuit, no powerbrake	*
Front	Drum	*
Rear	Drum	*
	Suspension	
Front	Independent, single upper arm and lower A-arm, coil srings	Rigid axle, semi-elliptical longitudinal leaf springs
Rear	Rigid axle, semi-elliptical longitudinal leaf springs	*
	Steering	
Type	Worm and sector	*
	Dimensions and capacities	
Wheelbase (mm)	2,654	*
Lenght (mm)	4,620	
Width (mm)	1,680	*
Height (mm)	1.95	*
Ground clearance (mm)	200	*
Fuel tank (liter)	66	*
Curb weight (kg)	1,488	1,586
	Wheels and tyres	
Type	Steel wheels and cross-ply tyres	*
Tyre size	6.45-15	6.45-15

um jovem (confiante) posa com a Rural

Retrato de formatura, sob o ponto de vista familiar. O caçula (êle tem futuro), os parentes, a casa em festa. E a presença da Rural "Jeep"... jovial sugestão de firmeza, solidez, estabilidade.

Rural "Jeep" — o veículo mais seguro que a sua tranqüilidade pode comprar. Tem a carroçaria de construção rígida, uma estrutura forte. O motor na parte dianteira, seu melhor pára-choque, diminui em 90% os riscos do motorista em caso de acidente. Maior visibilidade, em todos os sentidos: 5.000 a 6.000 cm² a mais de área coberta que nas outras camionetas. Portas mais seguras, freios mais eficientes (a relação freagem, pêso é bastante superior à dos demais). Com maior distância entre eixos, bitolas dianteira e traseira mais largas, a Rural "Jeep" faz curvas fechadas sem derrapar ou tombar.

RURAL Jeep®

UM PRODUTO WILLYS
VEÍCULOS DE ALTA QUALIDADE

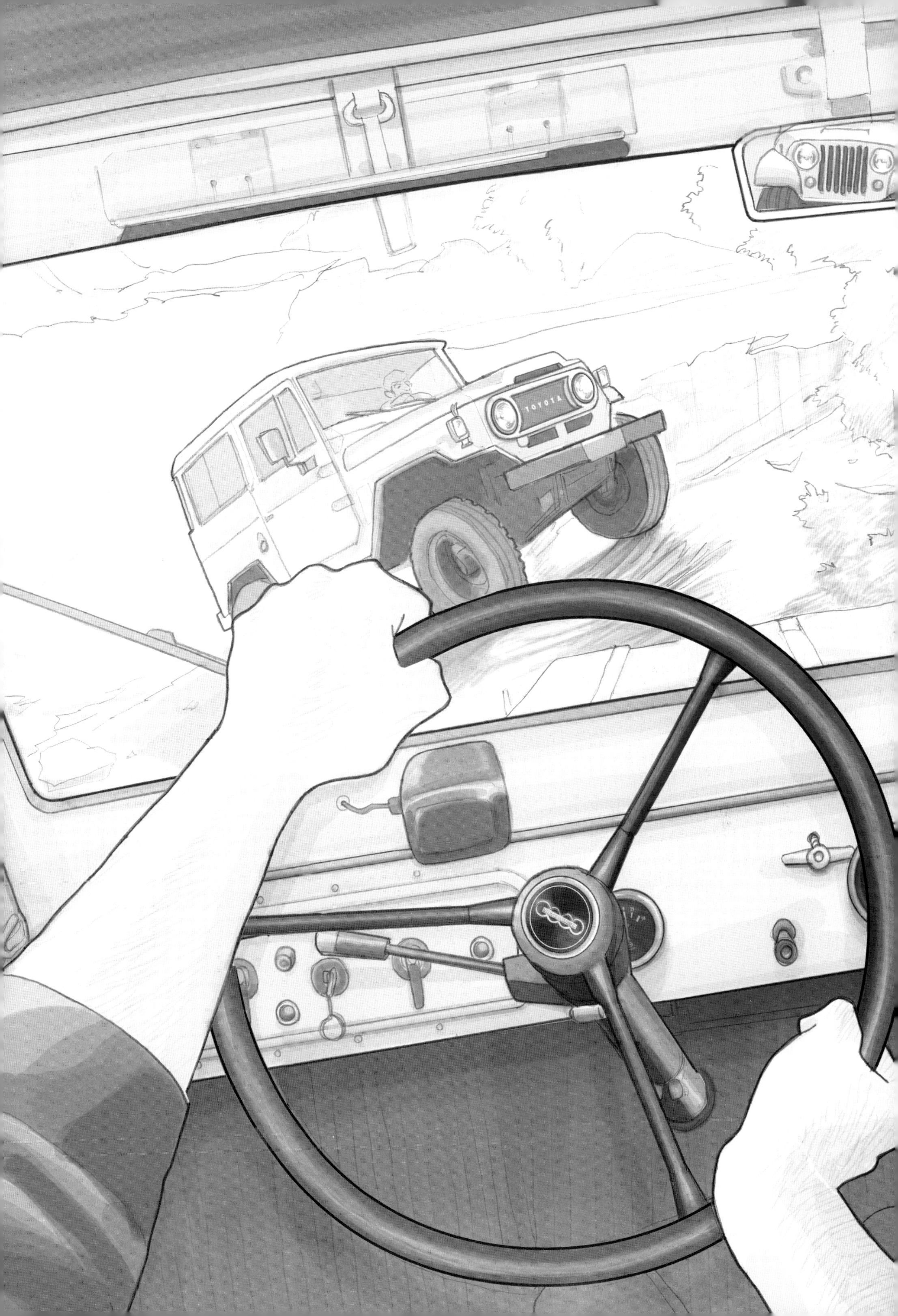
TOYOTA

These vehicles were conceived to work at Word War II. Once the conflict ended, the soldiers, enthusiastic with their performances, brought them to their countries. The first model to be produced, the Jeep, which Willys would keep on producing, became very popular, including in Brazil, a country that lacked roads, especially paved ones. In the photo queued up: at rear, a 1942 Jeep, the authentic for military use in the conflict; in the middle, a 1952 one for civilian use; and upfront, a "Sitting Duck" Dodge that during the war divided the task of weaponry and food transport, while the Jeep took care of troops deployments. Many of these vehicles are still active today, even more used as equipment for a sport, the Off-Road.

Off-road vehicles

(1958 to 1967)

DKW-Vemag Candango, Jeep Willys Universal and Toyota Bandeirante

In a country whose highway network was very far from meeting the real needs of transport and where the word "future" seemed to be in tune with "exploring", nothing more logical than the auto industry, which was settling here then, bringing work horses, for off-road use, far away from the paved ways of the great urban centers.

Willys had, during World War II, its existence assured through the production of the Jeep, a vehicle born to meet military needs during the conflict. Its performance had been so convincing at the war front that the word Jeep in Portuguese form – jipe – became a synonym of off-road vehicle.

Resulting from a US Army order, it soon became known as Jeep (the sound of "G" and "P", the initials for "General Purpose"). During World War II, Allied troops made full use of this four-wheel drive vehicle, which made a huge contribution for the success at the front. From then on, all cars with off-road ability ended being called "Jeep". With time, "Jeep" became a Willys trademark, which after the war would be produced, while the others (Jeeps) received new nameplates. In 1952, the model began assembling in Brazil and, in 1958, started being produced.

With a design similar to the Jeep, Auto Union would produce in Germany its utility that, as the Jeep, had four-wheel drive: the Munga – short for Mehrzweck Universal Geländewagen mit Allradantrieb, or multiuse vehicle for off-road use with all-wheel drive – that was born in 1954 by order of NATO, the North Atlantic Treaty Organization, the military power aimed to hold an eventual Soviet expansion, one of the symbols of the Cold War. Design followed the Jeep pattern, yet engine and other mechanical solutions originated from DKW cars. It was powered by the same two-stroke engine of the sedan and the station wagon, and four-wheel independent suspension.

The Toyota Land Cruiser was another Jeep inspiration and very efficient.

In Brazil, the Jeep Willys, soon after starting being produced, in 1957, began to be called Jeep Universal. From it derived a pick-up, the Willys Pick-Up, and a mixed-use utility, the Willys Rural.

In 1958, the Vemag company started producing of its utility, the DKW-Vemag jipe, and in 1960 re-christen it Candango, a migrant worker, to honor the workers that had built Brasília, inaugurated that year.

Toyota's Land Cruiser also happened to be manufactured here, as of 1962, under Bandeirante nameplate, what the original name meant in Portuguese. At first it was powered by the a six-cylinder engine of the brand, but soon it shifted to the Mercedes-Benz diesel, best suited for the kind of work it was designed for.

In 1954, the German army ordered to several local manufacturers a vehicle capable of joining NATO (North Atlantic Treaty Organization) forces, capable of fulfilling the same functions as the Jeep. Auto Union, with the DKW Munga, won the bid. The DKW Jeep, in 1960, was to be christened Candango and remain in production until 1963. It was braver and nimbler than the traditional Jeep. Besides being a working tool, it can be considered a leisure vehicle, the predecessor of the buggies.

They had much in common, especially four-wheel drive and quite a similar shape, almost as wide as long.

It was not surprising that there were similarities. The DKW was ordered by NATO to be a vehicle with the same abilities as the Jeep's, as well as the Toyota arose from the order made to a Eastern company, by the US Army, of a car with the Jeep's aptitude, for the Korea War.

None have ever gone "inactive", however, in peace time they had civil life, although the DKW had never been used in some light action or battle.

The Jeep Willys was the first to be produced and also the first to arrive to the Brazilian market. It was the most successful here, but not the one who had the largest longevity. It was phased-out in 1986, although it remained in production in the US, well evolved in relation to the Brazilian model.

The DKW-Vemag lasted little, it was dropped in 1962. The alleged reason was the lack of production capacity of transaxles to meet an economically feasible demand.

The Toyota was an ever lasting success. With the Jeep phase-out, it turned into the only utility available in the Brazilian market. During its life, to purchase one it was necessary to submit to long waiting lists, even if it was never cheap.

They did not directly compete. The Jeep served for inside work in the farms and for life at the country. It was not apt to provide any comfort or safety on highways. In spite of easily "overcoming" any road, born to "march", it did not "walk" smoothly on paved stretches.

The Bandeirante was more versatile and could face any challenge imposed by the Willys. The suspension was softer on tarmac and it was a utility with better handling, if this term could be properly used. The Diesel engine was an extra tool for heavy duty, but for the road it was just too noisy and transmitted an intense vibration. Really intense!

The US Army was searching for an Asian automaker capable of producing a thousand cars, in record time, with the same ability as the Jeep's, for operation in the Korea War. Almost as contemporarily as the Munga and with a quite similar history, in 1953 came the Toyota Jeep. In 1954 it would be renamed Land Cruiser, the model to be assembled in Brazil in 1959. In 1960, local content would climb to 60% and, in 1961, with Bandeirante nameplate, the Brazilian version would be powered by a Mercedes-Benz diesel engine. It was a sales success and remained in the market until 2001.

The DKW was more exotic. Despite being more fuel-efficient, it was not used much – also for not having been much produced – for work and, already as of the 1960s, it served as sports, leisure vehicle, like a dune buggy would do. At that time there were no dune buggies.

ANOTHER OPINION

It was a time when "off-road" had exactly this meaning, to drive where there was no road at all – only for absolute need, not for leisure or adventure, as it happen so as of the 1990s. But the off-road wave can be credited to the Camel Trophy, organized in early previous decade, a series of long annual events promoted by the R.J. Reynolds Tobacco, one of the leading cigarette makers. Incidentally, the first Camel Trophy, was run at the Amazon forest.

Thus, these three vehicles meant mobility for the country population, percentually larger than it is today, giving a push to agricultural and livestock economy.

Currently, off-road became a sport, the number of four-wheel drive vehicles substantially increased, including those high-performers such as sport utilities BMW X5, Mercedes-Benz ML and Porsche Cayenne.

The part-time 4x4 drive systems are steadily giving room to integral, full-time ones, like in these three Germans.

September/2007

TECHNICALLY CORRECT

These three utilities had in common the fact of featuring four-wheel drive. However, just the DKW had this system on full-time basis, it could not go two-wheel drive only. The three had low range gear, the Jeep Willys and the Toyota Bandeirante by floor-mounted lever and the Candango 4, by means of a handle placed in the dashboard, which was not very easy to use, it required some experience with it. It had to be pulled and turned ¼ of a turn to lock it in place and keep low range engaged. Since none had a central differential, is was usual for them to drag when maneuvering on dry ground, as if partially braked. For this reason, in the Willys and in the Toyota 4x4 operation was recommended for use in low traction surfaces only. In the DKW, the dragging effect could not be avoided, one had to co-live with this characteristic. On the other hand, only in this vehicle one could count on the advantages of independent suspension front and rear, always more comfortable than its peers', combined with the inexistence of differential housings at the axles, which made the DKW more apt to face critical muddy terrain. Apart from this, the Candango 4 had an exceptional roadholding, close to that of a sports car. It was so that the grandson of Ferdinand Porsche, when running the Audi company, had a VW Iltis (successor of the DKW utility) for a weekend and became so impressed with it that he ordered the development of an Audi 80 with that transmission layout. It was the birth of the Audi Quattro, in 1980.

September/2007

PRICE TABLE OF OFF-ROAD VEHICLES[1]

Make	Model	1957	1958	1959	1960	1961	1962	1963	1964	1965	1966	1967	1968
Willys	Jeep					548	726	1,113	2,350	3,956	4,418	5,794	
	Jeep Universal 6J-6 - 4-dr.						806				5,240	6,419	
	Jeep Universal 6J-6 - 2-dr.						778						
DKW-Vemag	Jeep Hardtop												
	Jeep Ragtop												
	Candango 4 w/ Top					559	747	1,410					
	Candango 4 w/o Top					550	733	1,370					
	Candango 2 w/ Top					504	676		2,994				
	Candango 2 w/o Top					500	6.656						
Toyota	Land Cruiser Hardtop					750	726						
	Land Cruiser Hagtop						860						
	Utility							1,400	2,951	5,522			
	Utility 4-doors									5,825		8,107	
	Utility 2-dr Hardtop											8,392	
	Utility Bandeirante										6,700	7,613	
	Station Wagon								3,685	7,111			
	S. Wagon 4x4										8,710	10,042	
	S. Wagon 4x2										8,150	9,395	
	Pick Up								3,638	7,021	8,440		
	Pick Up 4x2									7,111	7,890		

Undoubtedly, one of the Jeep Willys' great virtues was its price, which floated 10% up and down around a VW Sedan. And while the Toyota had the advantage of burning diesel, the Jeep was at least 20% less costly. As for the Candango, with DKW mechanical base, it followed the Willys in price, but it was short-lived.

PRODUCTION TABLE OF OFF-ROAD VEHICLES[2]

Make	Model / Year →	1957	1958	1959	1960	1961	1962	1963	1964	1965	1966	1967	Until 1967	1968	Total
DKW	Candango	8	1,174	1,968	2,481	1,582	615	20					7,848		7848
Willys	Jeep	9,156	13,099	15,626	16,738	16,032	21,005	12,411	10,714	9,096	14,039	7,971	145,887	7,138	153,025
Toyota	Utility			489	295	7	627	1,001	1,139	400	387	169	4,514	190	4,704
	Station Wagon							218	456	138	75	40	927	59	986
	Pickup							291	642	423	438	367	2,161	700	2,861
	Toyota Total	0	0	489	295	7	627	1,510	2,237	961	900	576	7,602	949	8,551
Off-road	Total	9,164	14,273	18,083	19,514	17,621	22,247	13,941	12,951	10,057	14,939	8,547	161,337	8,087	161,576

In number of sold units, only the VW Sedan surpassed the Jeep. When added to the rest of Jeep models, its derivatives, the number resulted even more impressive. At that time, between1957 and 1967, agriculture was still responsible for most of the national economic activity. The Jeep Willys was quite cheaper than Toyota's diesel-powered utilities, which had also all production sold before reaching the dealers. The DKW Candango, with an heterodox recipe, taking into account the period it was produced, occupied a significant space.

1. Prices informed in thousands of Brazilian cruzeiros by *Quatro Rodas* magazine, January issue of each year.
2. Data according to documents supplied by Anfavea.

Jeep Willys Universal

(1957 to 1967)

The Jeep did not need any road, it arrived to places no automobile would ever adventure to. It also served as a work tool. Rustic, with no luxury at all, it was easy-maintaining and did not require special care for handling it. Off the road, it could be followed by another Jeep model only and would loose for a tractor exclusively. As a trade-off, in places where paving existed, especially on roads, only a tractor would reveal more inadequate.

In 1940, shortly before the United States get involved in World War II, the US Army ordered a four-wheel drive vehicle, whose dimensions enable it to be air transported. Besides size, if parachuted it should resist ground impact.

The approved design came from Bantam, but the initial order of 15,000 units was split between Ford and Willys-Overland, which had bigger production capacity.

Without a proper name, it started being called "GP", the initials for general purpose. The sound of "G" and "P", when pronounced together, made Jeep. The name Jeep was not registered and, the world over, many armies have put orders – once the war was over – for a vehicle that had capabilities next to it. They were all christened Jeep, followed by the automaker name. However, some time later, Willys, which kept producing it for civilian use, took the brand as its property.

The Willys Jeep was fantastic for farm work, where it proved the virtues demonstrated at the war front. Its specialty was to arrive where no other car could go.

In the 1950s, there were very few roads in Brazil and almost all of them had no paving at all. Economy was essentially agricultural, therefore a car that could

make its own way and was powerful enough for heavy duty farm work, would have a sure success.

In 1952, the Willys Jeep started being assembled in Brazil and its acceptance was instant. Willys believed that there would be a great market for its products in countries like Brazil and bet on that.

In 1957, it started producing the local Willys Jeep with Jeep Willys Universal nameplate. From it the Rural would derive, at first a station wagon that differed from the Universal for having a closed, all-steel body, and the Pick-Up Willys, a Rural light truck.

Ahead of the tires, just the very high-mounted bumper. This design enabled the wheels to overcome tall obstacles with no other underpinning grabbing on anything. All body parts dispensed finishing that could confer more subtleness and that added any cost to manufacturing or repairing. Latches and locks with inside operation, or even embedded, were not in the menu as well.

Applied technique and practical results

The engine was the same six-cylinder that Willys would adopt in its Aero model range and in other Jeep's. In a time when all engines started having overhead valves, Willys put intake valves on it only, keeping the exhaust valves in the engine block. It was not an well approved recipe, but in a vehicle for off-road work, such an engine was quite acceptable, although it was far from being fuel efficient.

The Jeep was born with a four-cylinder engine, with side valves. Later, yet in the 1950s, it was powered by the six-cylinder similar to the Aero-Willys', displacing 2,600 cm³ and featuring overhead intake valves – the exhaust ones remained in the block. The models made in Brazil were powered by this engine that, although it had never been fuel-efficient, revealed adequate for work in low engine speeds.

The Jeep transmission was to become a pattern for this kind of vehicle. In normal conditions, where no extra traction was necessary, it worked fine with rear-wheel drive and three forward speeds and one reverse. However, if the terrain was slippery, there as a front differential that could be engaged through a transfer box. In this 4x4 condition top speed should not exceed 40 km/h (25 mph). If conditions demanded extra power like "wall climbing", there was a low range choice that limited top speed to 20 km/h and could be used together with 4x4 operation only. Gear changing was done by a conventional floorshift; those of four-wheel drive and low range gear, by independent levers, much shorter, also at floor.

The Jeep's suspension was the most rustic one could find: both front and rear were by semi-elliptical leaf springs assemblies, installed longitudinally, and rigid axles. The wheels were fit with mud-type tires, i.e., with transversal grooves that penetrated into and gripped soft and/or slippery ground.

The body was very wide and short, ground clearance was high enough and the wheels were close to the body ends. This format enabled excellent approach and departure angles: it was nearly always possible to meet an obstacle with the tire without any body interference; a good departure angle: when exiting a very steep slope, the rear would not easily hit the ground; and a sizeable ramp angle: it was possible to drive over high bumps without scratching or getting stuck.

The dashboard was as straightforward as the rest of the tub. Inserted in a "very massive" steel plate, the speedometer com trip counter, the temperature and the fuel gauges where the only meters. They were all grouped in one sole, big diam-

The transmission was operated through three levers. The bigger one was the kind of all cars with manual shift. It was the responsible for gear changing (three forward speeds and one reverse). The other two engaged four-wheel drive (normally, the car ran just with rear-wheel drive) and low range gear, to be used exclusively with four-wheel drive. In this condition, the vehicle was capable of towing a weight superior to its own, even on slippery ground. Thus geared, top speed was 30 km/h.

eter circular piece which contained also the warning lights for generator, oil pressure and high beams.

There was no detail, any decor, that tried to smooth out or render grace to the vehicle: the seat upholstery was plain; the dashboard was covered by the body color paint only and, besides the basic design of the meters, two plates attached it explained how engage four-wheel drive and low range; hinges and locks were apparent, as well as the sizeable screws; the top and the doors were in black canvas, the windshield frame was primary; its corners were sharp; there was no chrome finish...

Dashboard could not be simpler. It is not possible to affirm "simpler, impossible", for the models produced here later achieved this feat. Its instruments were alike the 1958 Willys Rural, presented in chapter about the mixed use utilities cars.

Carelessness did not resume finishing. The headlights were little potent and the windshield wiper, powered by a vacuum motor and poor sweeping, inefficient.

The driving position, which did not find any support in the seat, was uncomfortable: too tilted a steering wheel and pedals being hit vertically.

Heavy steering, with lot of play and little wheel turning, poor brakes and harsh gear changing with a non-synchronized first gear helped to complete a picture which was far from enchanting. However, no matter what, the Jeep was an efficient work horse.

Temper

Depending on where it is, in or out of water, a crocodile can be considered, respectively: dangerous, agile, strong and brave, or defenseless, slow, ephemeral and unprotected.

The Jeep could run on trails surfaced with mud, gravel, creeks or any kind of obstacle, as if all ways were like that. This virtue impressed at the front, during World War II, encouraging the soldiers to bring them to civilian world. In the 1980s, when they were still very useful in remote regions, a sport – called trail at first – became popular. The challenge was to arrive at the end of the trail, regardless of speed. The only competitors are in the way, the other entrants are no rivals, are peers. For drivers and crews, risks are low and use of a crash helmet, optional.

Tires were known as muddies. The grooves permitted that car to hold against the banks and the tread pattern was especially designed to keep traction on slippery ground. On asphalt they were inefficient and short-living. The car a whole was nimble, sturdy and brave when far from asphalt, exactly the opposed when on it.

Just like this reptile, the Jeep Universal, depending on where it was, in or off road, could be regarded, respectively, slow, imprecise and uncomfortable, or agile, strong and irreplaceable.

In spite of an ever ferocious look, the crocodile, by instinct, knows that it must not be aggressive when out of water.

Although its looks suggested that the Jeep Universal could be a valiant in tarmac, its sensitiveness at the wheel recommended cautiousness.

The Jeep was a machine, a work by Man that had the same temper of an animal, a work by nature.

Daily, urban driving

With no suspension system at all; engine aimed to run in constant speed; equipped with a gearbox that did not foresee gear changing while in motion; with heavy controls; with no luxury or any detail seeking beauty or comfort, tractors were the only wheeled vehicles capable of going farther than a Jeep Universal where there were no roads, yet they were absolutely unsuitable to road or city driving. With the Jeep it was possible to go traveling or wandering in urban centers, even in the larger ones, where they overcame, by large, the capabilities of any tractor, but not more than that.

Restricted to concepts and technological limits of the time, a tractor, as a work horse, did no need, nor could provide comfort. The commitment was with the efficiency it accomplished its tasks with. Through development, both in concepts and in technology, tractors improved in efficiency and started offering comfort to users, especially as of the 1980s.

The Jeep was born for warfare use and afterwards it started to be used in farm service. Since its design dates from the early 1940s, it is not surprising that there was no concern in providing good care to its occupants. As an urban transport mean, the fact to be able to run amid traffic was sufficient already.

The Jeep has brought a new vehicle concept, the off-road automobile that, in Brazil, was known as "jipe", after the name Jeep. It kept the charm and the pureness of the proposal, yet it could be excelled – especially where there were roads and/or paving – by some models for which it served as inspiration, chiefly by the British Land Rover utility and by Japanese Toyota Land Cruiser utility, which was manufactured in Brazil starting 1962 with Toyota Bandeirantes nameplate. The Jeep would lose in a direct competition, but it did the same service for quite a lower price.

On the road

Beginning with tire choice and vehicle shape, it could not be expected that the Jeep was capable of great feats on the roads. The fact that it was apt to travel

In difficult situations, the best thing to do was to engage four-wheel drive and count of the driver's skill. There were limits, however to reach them it required a lot of daring. Once stuck, additionally to own resources, to push it was the way out.

in speeds not exceeding 80 km/h by large was sufficient for its mission to be accomplished. In a time our roads did not allow much above it or even our base cars were not capable of sustaining higher average speeds, the Jeep performance could be termed as adequate.

The noise of its canvas top concealed and mixed up with mechanical ones: differentials and gearboxes "cried", while the engine emitted a sound that suggested power exhaustion, when kept at high, sustained engine revolutions.

Any hazard could be transformed in accident, if speed was too high. Its brakes, steering and suspension were not designed for speed, neither to render some comfort. Therefore, the respect to good manner rules had to be observed.

The Jeep was supposed to go from a working site to another, no more than that.

The Jeep and I

The Jeep was a popular character, even for children of predominantly urban culture, like me. Its different shape drew attention and incited imagination.

Little I knew about it, for when I was ten years old, maybe a little more, I wondered about something my dad sad on the road, after following one for some time: "Young people are irresponsible, they should not be driving a car like this that way". I was not aware that the Jeep was not suitable for high speeds!

When I was 14 years, in 1975, I started going to a farm, in São Paulo countryside, where the manager drove a 1968 Jeep, long-wheelbase model, also known as "Bernardão". This Jeep had a side mounted rear seat and maybe it was the only vehicle capable of jolting more than the regular Jeep.

Heavier, it could hardly exceed 80 km/h in the 10 km-long paved road stretch between the farm and the city that, as many cities of inland São Paulo, have a quite irregular topography. The paving was of cobblestones, therefore very slippery when it rained. The mud tires did not slip on mud, for they could dig in, but over wet and slippery stones that slipped more than ice skates. To go downhill sideways in one of those hills with the wheels locked and no steering, was a usual situation, so normal that the manager's expression did not reveal surprise, yet he could not hide fear.

In the farm, the Jeep went everywhere and I hardly saw four-wheel drive engaged. Once, when the gearbox locked with two speeds simultaneously engaged, once again the manager did not show any astonishment. He only asked us to rock – back and forth – the heavy vehicle until he could disengage and everything get

A) The towing bar upfront denounces that on the road it is more comfortable to take it towed. B) In water, one of its limitations was the gasoline engine, which requires a moist-sensitive ignition system. The occupants bounced quite too much, although they got less tired than if walking, the only feasible option.

back to normal. I also remember how difficult it was to do parking and return maneuvers with that car, the wheels steered little and it demanded lots of room.

I enjoyed driving the Jeep. By the way, I appreciated driving any motor vehicle on wheels. In these occasions, i felt great pleasure in steping on the gas pedal and notice Jeep's engine instantly showing its limitations and complaining about my attempts of getting a few more revolutions. The steering had an enormous play, but shortly got used to it, while other controls demanded effort but did not require any more expertise.

It was in this Jeep that I learned what a vehicle born to combat meant.

ANOTHER OPINION

The Jeep Willys was rustic in its own, but it has left its landmark in history. It was one of the vehicles that started motorizating of the Brazilians, when it started being assembled in Brazil in 1952. To get one those days was very difficult, you'd better have a "hot shot", as traffic of influence was called then, politicians that had power over the economic activity so to speak. But it was not a vehicle that provided any driving pleasure, for it was not made with this in mind. To own and to drive it could be termed as an obligation. Its only and maybe unique virtue, apart from off-road capability, was toughness. That´s why it was widely used in driving school.

Technically, the Jeep was quite primitive, as the road network in the early 1950s was. In 1952, the car began being assembled in Brazil and as of 1958, to be manufactured. Success was absolute. The production of the Willys Jeep lineup, until 1957, was shadowed by Volkswagen's only.

TECHNICALLY CORRECT

In spite of the simplicity inherent to its application, the Jeep Willys counted on a good and efficient part-time, four-wheel drive transmission. As such, it did not feature central differential, which restricted all-wheel driving to low traction ground like mud and sand.

Transmission operation was quite simple. A lever engaged the front axle, what was supposed to be done with a standing vehicle only. Another, shorter lever shifted to low range and on its travel there was a hidden neutral position which could serve as an anti-theft device. Factory instructions said that shifting from high to low range and vice-versa could be achieved with the Jeep standing still, but who had the knowledge and the skill managed to do it while moving, for the low range gear set consisted of an auxiliary two-speed gearbox.

TECHNICAL INFORMATION OF JEEP WILLYS

VEHICLE	Jeep Universal	Jeep 101 (Bernardão)
Type	Utility for off-road work, with front engine and four-wheel drive; 2 doors, canvas top	Utility for off-road work, with front engine and four-wheel drive; 4 doors, canvas top
	Chassi and body	
Type	Separated; steel	*
	Engine	
Type	Inline 6-cylinder, cast iron block and cylinder head, water cooled. Overhead intake valves and in-block exhaust valves (F-Head)	*
Mixture formation	Single bbl carburetor	*
Bore and stroke (mm)	79.37 x 88.90	*
Displacement (cm³)	2,638	*
Compression ratio	7.6:1	*
Maximum power (SAE)	90 hp at 4,000 rpm	*
Maximum torque (SAE)	18.8 m.kgf at 2,000 rpm	*
	Transmission	
Type	3-speed manual with low range, and reversa; non-synchronized first	*
	Brakes	
Type	Single hydraulic circuit, no powerbrake	*
Front	Drum	*
Rear	Drum	*
	Suspension	
Front	Rigid axle, semi-elliptical longitudinal leaf springs	*
Rear	Rigid axle, semi-elliptical longitudinal leaf springs	*
	Steering	
Type	Worm and sector	*
	Dimensions and capacities	
Wheelbase (mm)	2,057	2,565
Lenght (mm)	3,250	*
Width (mm)	1,500	*
Height (mm)	1,690	*
Ground clearance (mm)	203	*
Fuel tank (liter)	40	*
Curb weight (kg)	1,190	1,254
	Wheels and tyres	
Type	Steel wheels and cross-ply tyres	*
Tyre size	6.00-16	6.00-16

NÃO PRECISA DE ESTRADA
O 'JEEP' UNIVERSAL avança através de regiões inexploradas das florestas . . . transporta homens, ferramentas e abastecimentos aos lugares onde se abatem as árvores.
Fornece força locomotora nas profundezas da floresta.
Move equipamento pesado, arrasta troncos de árvores, remove do solo o raizame, quando munido de guindaste de cabrestante.
O 'JEEP' enfrenta qualquer tarefa — e leva-a de vencida — a despeito da lama, da aspereza do terreno e da ingremidade dos declives.
Willys-Overland Export Corporation
Toledo, Ohio, E.U.A.
O NOVO 'Jeep' Universal
construído por WILLYS-OVERLAND

Text
by Bob Sharp

Jipe DKW-Vemag (1958 and 1959) and Candango DKW-Vemag (1960 to 1962)

The DKW-Vemag utility, introduced in 1958, was the second one with all-terrain characteristic produced in Brazil. Its forerunner was the Willys Jeep Universal, whose production had started the year before. The DKW brand was still relatively new in Brazil, for in spite of the little station wagon being produced from November of 1956 on, it would accelerate production in the following year only, still on the F91 platform. For this reason, the coming of the DKW utility was followed by a certain surprise. In that same year the sedan and the new station wagon of a newer generation, the F94, wider and larger, were presented.

In Germany, the new Auto Union barely had started to produce DKWs after WWII, when the German Army set a bid in 1954 for a light military vehicle for liaison purposes and to integrate to Nato (North Atlantic Treaty Organization). Nato was a military force envisaged to hold up an eventual Soviet aggression. It was the dawn of the Cold War.

Auto Union, Porsche and Gutbrod took part in the bid and the winning vehicle was a DKW the factory called Munga, short for Mehrzweck Universal Geländewagen mit Allradantrieb, which means universal multi-purpose, all-wheel drive vehicle for off-road use.

Its look was not light, but when compared to other utilities of its time, the DKW transmitted a youngish manner. Its solutions were diverse: full-time all-wheel drive; independent suspensions; and two-stroke engine. The recipe was singular, however the ability to overcome obstacles was the same as the other utilities'.

It was a four-passenger utility with straightforward and straight lines that hid an efficient powertrain and a chassis with independent suspension on all four corners. The Willys Jeep had a strong opponent from then on.

Applied technique and practical results

The DKW utility was a bare vehicle. The ladder-type chassis entirely differed from the one used by the station wagon. A steel stamped body with four individual seats and four doors, the front ones opening rearwards also, was bolted to it. It was austere as so expected for a utility of those days, including the large steering wheel with three equidistantly-spaced spokes with a quite truck-like small horn button at the center.

Headlights were sealed beam units fit into housings outside the fenders and the flat windshield could tilt down forward flat. The canvas top was fixed, but soon an aftermarket model that could be folded down was available. As it was a steel top produced by the Carraço company.

Drew attention the short wheelbase of only 2,000 mm, even shorter than the Jeep Willys', which measured 2,032 mm. Front and rear suspensions were identical – the same parts! – and it followed the basic design of the station wagon's front end: lower A-arm and transverse leaf spring set that performed upper control arm function also, and tilted inwards hydraulic shock absorbers. A suspension that could be considered sophisticated for a utility.

Seats were relatively comfortable, driving position was superb and the steering was light yet quick, what made the DKW utility a very pleasant vehicle. Compared to the Willys, it was a sports car.

The engine was the same and minute three-cylinder two-stroke displacing 896 cm^3, 38 net horsepower unit from the station wagon. However, the cylinder hear

The two-stroke engine is not brilliant in the lower rpm range, therefore it should not fit to off-road conditions. In the case of the DKW, it required a different driving comparing to the Jeep Willys or the Toyota Bandeirante, nevertheless it fulfilled the mission.

The common denominator of utilities of the time was "simple". The Munga's dashboard offered information to a minimum and the upholstery (!) of the passenger compartment was entirely made in synthetic materials. The Munga, built by Auto Union in Germany, as well as the Candango in Brazil, was the same car. A curiosity, for those who had driven DKW-Vemag cars before, was the different shift pattern. The odd gears laid up front, as in most automobiles, but not the DKWs.

was different for not having the fan shaft housing, the fan lying right behind the large radiator installed in "normal" position as in most cars. Coolant circulation was by thermo-siphon.

The carburetor was a 32-mm twin-choke Zenith NDIX instead of the single throat Solex 40 ICB, which helped to bring power to lower engine speed range, as it suits this kind of vehicle, besides providing more reliability when driving in remote regions – a clogged jet did not cause the engine to stop dead. Also, the Zenith had a float that enabled the engine to keep working with the vehicle going up steep hills and/or strongly inclined laterally as well.

There was an extension in the cylinder head for the high-mounted generator for more protection when crossing wades. Since the ignition circuit breaker set remained low in the nose of the engine, its housing had a cover bolted by wing nuts and a rubber sealing for total waterproofing. This design would soon be extended to the whole lineup in lieu of the bare, circular rubber cap.

The four-speed gearbox with a non-sychronized first gear include a low range gear. It was a transaxle made by ZF of Germany (the same supplier for the automobiles') with a power takeoff for the rear differential propeller shaft. The most remarkable feature was the fact the four-wheel drive was full-time, not part-time as the Willys Jeep's. Even more remarkable was the absence of a center differential to compensate speed unevenness between front and rear wheels. The very short wheelbase enabled this solution, although at low speed maneuvering one could feel little vehicle braking due to tire scrub.

The long gearshift was floor mounted, but low range gear was selected via a handle placed in the middle of the dashboard. It had to be pulled all the way out and twisted one fourth of a turn to lock it in place. Total reduction in low first was 38,8:1, enabling the vehicle to overcome gradients of up to 100% (45 degrees).

Another "jeep" solution was the first exhaust silencer, a circular-shape box that became known as "banjo", in order to increase ground clearance, which would not be possible with the lengthy and cylindrical type of the station wagon, popularly called "cigar".

In 1960, the year the nation's capital Brasília was inaugurated, Vemag changed the name plate from utility to Candango. It was in the honour of the vast, anonymous contingent of so called employees that worked in the construction of the city. But it also resulted from the pressure Willys had been putting on Vemag claiming the exclusive right of using Jeep or jipe nameplate, which fell short of reaching court (jipe had been used by Vemag to name the utility since launch).

By 1969, the factory had had difficulties importing the transaxle and the rear differential from Germany and the Brazilian ZF subsidiary was not willing to produce them here on grounds of low production output. It would not be worth it. Vemag then decided to

The four-wheel independent suspension ensured a soft ride and its roadholding was quite superior, in any condition. Drivebility pleased. The lack of a central differential could be sensed and, when maneuvering, with the steering at full lock, the car seemed unable to move.

build the Candango with front-wheel drive only, using the Brazilian-made ZF transaxle. From them on there were Candango 2 and Candango 4. Beside identification badges, the Candango 2 had a better designed and nicer steering wheel and front seats became bench type. Both the "2" and the "4" had now a single choke Solex 40 ICB carburetor. But in late 1962 the DKW-Vemag "jipe" was forever discontinued.

Temper

There was absolutely no doubt about it: the DKW utility was much more nimble than its Willys competitor. Who happened to drive it could notice it at once. Even with 6.00-16 mud tires, its cornering behavior thrilled. It was more of a sports car than an all-terrain utility. To drive it fast on wet asphalt was exhilarating. The best part is that it was far from having a rough ride, a characteristic of the Willys Jeep.

Its real problem was the engine, because dealing with it was not an easy task. As it generally happens with two-stroke engines, palpable horsepower didn't come in before 1,200 to 1,500 rpm; it was necessary to understand it before driving it normally. But it could not be quickly learned. And things improved in the year after launching when the 900 engine was replaced by the 44 net hp, 1,000-cm^3 one.

There was also the issue of putting oil in the tank before refueling, something many people hated. One could not say to the attendant: "fill it up". How many liters the tank would take had to be guessed before hand in order to put oil accordingly. And it was not everybody that could stand the exhaust smoke on cold starts and neither the real unpleasant smell of the exhaust gases with a warmed engine (although the main cause of it was idle speed air-fuel mixture wrongly adjusted, something only a handful of auto mechanics could properly perform).

The blanks its body was made of did not feature folds or any finishing that lead to any additional cost. Headlights were not embedded. Like the others, it did not have latches.

Daily, urban driving

Its small dimensions, with an overall length of only 3.445 mm, combined with the very short wheelbase, made it very practical and convenient for city driving, although in those days traffic was quite lighter than it is today. The ride quality was very close to that of an automobile.

As a canvas top utility, it was far from ideal in rainy days, when the transparent plastic roll-up windows considerably reduced visibility. With the fold-down top of the aftermarket things did not improve, but in a warm summer evening, folding it down and completely swiveling the windshield over the engine hood was an indescribable pleasure. But who did not look for it at all and wanted a transport means that could reach any place, there was the steel top solution, which became very popular, although its weight affected performance somewhat and roadholding to a great extent, since the center of gravity became higher.

Although aimed for military purposes as much as the Willys, the fact is that the DKW was conceived in the other side of the Atlantic, by people with another idea in terms of vehicular behavior, and this become obvious when driving it.

The full-time four-wheel drive enabled to rocket from the green light with no wheel spin and even if it was not a powerful vehicle, it was always ahead of the pack. When traffic really slowed, to drive it in first low range gear made possible to crawl at 3 km/h only, the speed of a man walking normally – one of the reasons of the choice by the German army, to be able to go together with a platoon on foot.

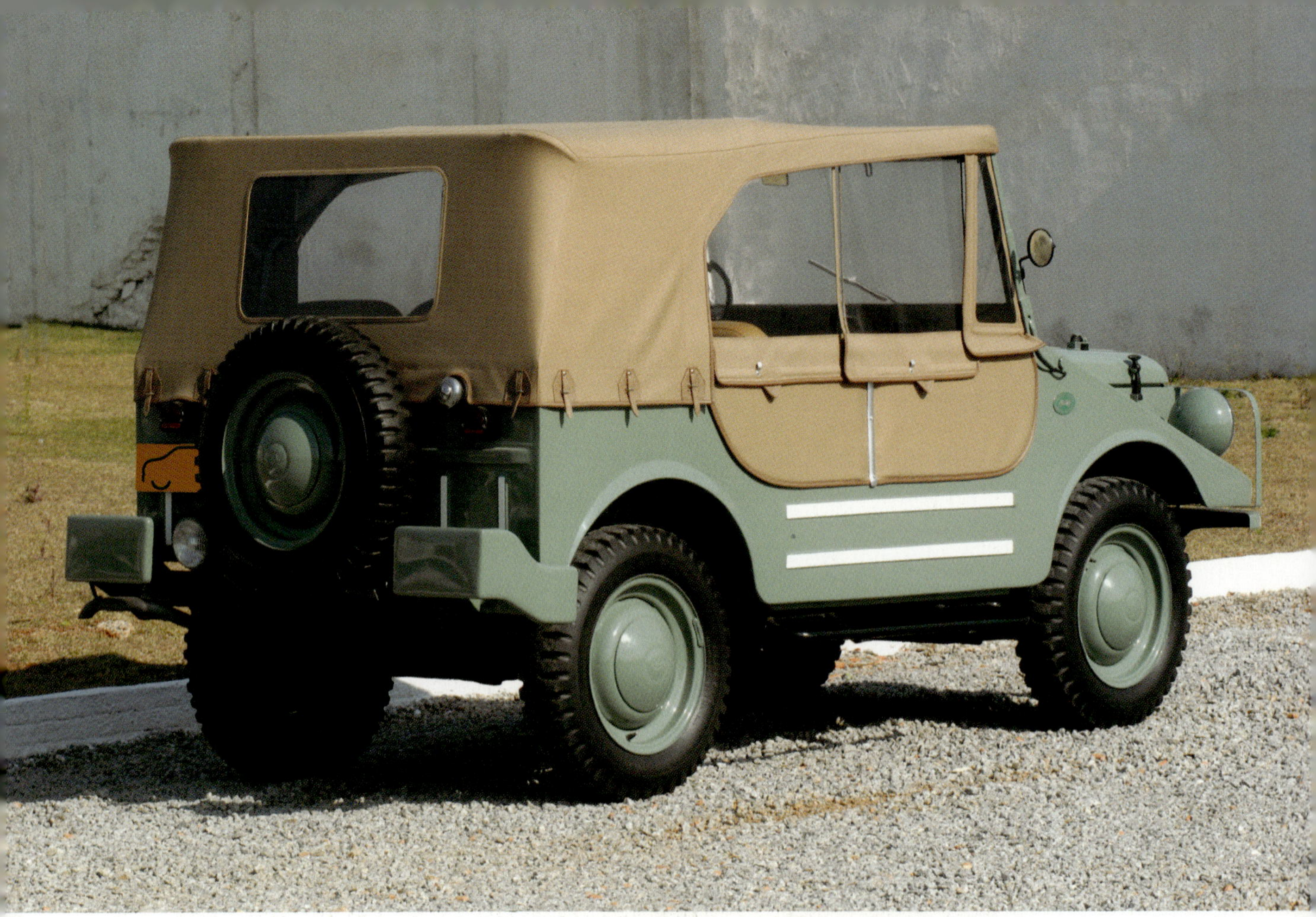

It was the smallest, the lightest and the nimblest of all utilities, besides being powered by a merrier engine. Its pack was much more suitable to paved roads. On the dirt, its mobility could be considered about the same, but the driver had to be skilled. When heavy duty came, it did not satisfy.

On the road

In spite of not being an asphalt cruiser, the fact is that its chassis "lashed" when the driver wished to travel at a faster, more vigorous pace. One forgot that it was on a utility. The drum brakes, with two leading shoes on the four wheels, were very good and confidence inspiring. With the 900-cm^3 engine top speed was 95 km/h, slightly higher (98 km/h) with the 1,000-cc one, but on the other hand it could be indefinitely sustained. The engine did not complain about it, but fuel economy considerably dropped, going down to 6 to 7 kilometers per liter in this condition. A more calm driving improved fuel economy to over 9 km/l. The utility's aerodynamics obviously did not help at all. And the fact it had no free-wheeling as the station wagon and the sedan had contributed for the DKW utility being not an example in fuel economy.

But when it came to a dirt road, dry or muddy, the DKW utility was matchless. When off-road, it was superb. The 28,2-centimetres ground clearance made all the difference. There were no differential housings integrated to the rigid axle, as in the Willys. The ability to go in difficult terrain was astonishing. Thanks to the full-time four-wheel drive, there was no worry in case the conditions suddenly worsened. At the worst, low range had to be engaged, so in spite of the owner's manual recommendation to do it while standing still, skilled drivers managed to engage low range with the vehicle moving.

When designed, for sure nobody guessed that its design could be considered light and youngish. However, it soon became appreciated by youngsters and ended as symbol of freedom. Years later the buggies would appear, and they had some quite similar details.

As a canvas top vehicle, it is sure that in highway speeds wind noise and drafts were inevitable, and traveling under rain was nothing short of a nightmare.

The DKW utility and I

Although I had driven the Candango several times, I never had the experience of owning one. The opportunity came in 1967 upon finding a low-mileage Candango 4 for sale, however garaged since 1963. At the time I was partner of a DKW-Vemag dealership in Rio de Janeiro and immediately we set

There was no room for luggage and the spare wheel was housed in an outside support, attached to the rear panel. The front suspension layout of the passenger cars was used both front and rear, therefore suspension was independent on the four wheels.

for completely overhauling it. We lifted the body to entirely paint it outside and underneath and to take the opportunity to replace all rubber pieces and blocs between it and the chassis. The mechanical conditions were very good except for the crankshaft, which had to be replaced due to noisy main ball bearings. It was quite easy at the time, even if the utility was already discontinued. The one and same crankshaft had always been the same, regardless of the DKW model.

Re-assembling the Candango obviously did not represent a major problem and once it was ready it looked brand new. Even the gearshift did not have any play. The seats' upholstery had resisted to time. Maybe the steel top it had was providential for that. Of course, the steel top was discarded and sold for any price and in its place we bought and installed a foldable canvas top. It turned into a beautiful utility, whose color was not the original light green anymore, but a tone of gray used by the Navy. Except for the canvas top and the body color, we decided to keep the Candango strictly original.

Soon the DKW utility started being disputed by the three partners of the company, for it was really funny to drive. With the top down and the windshield fully lowered over the hood, it was the military vehicle in its own, ready for a "battle". Pure enjoyment. One of my amusements was to take it to the sands of Ipanema Beach on evenings, reaching the water line. It was essential to engage low range and the effort the Candango was submitted to at the typical soft sand of the Rio de Janeiro beaches was considerable. Sometimes the engine started to detonate, demanding full attention to avoid piston seizure. But the problem was gone after we started fuelling it with premium gasoline instead of regular. Of course, in the following morning it would have a complete washing to remove any trace of sea water.

Another "art" I enjoyed was to demonstrate the ability of the Candango to climb stairs. Low range first and there it went, as if it was the most natural thing in the world. Or showing to people what it could do on turns. Nobody believed in what they were watching.

Everything – instruments, gearbox, brakes, including the parking brake, which consisted of a small drum on the propeller shaft shortly before the rear differential. The Zenith carburetor worked to perfection. We improved the skill of engaging low range with the vehicle moving, without gear clash. Passengers were stunned.

Therefore, the Candango 4, which belonged to the dealership, became part of the partners' lives. It was the replacement car when one of ours was being serviced and also the tractor to pull with a towing bar the racing DKW to the Jacarepaguá racetrack. There was nothing more charming, for our minds and for those who appreciate motor racing, than tractor and racing car being the same brand.

It was really a great companion.

ANOTHER OPINION

In the late 1950's, early 1960's, in inland Brazil, horse work was being replaced by the mechanical one. The pair of oxen or donkey back gave room to tractors and other agricultural machines, as well as the saddle and the cart had started dividing room with off-road vehicles – Jeeps and utilities.

The culture of the machine was being slowly introduced and the land worker needed to get acquainted with engines and gears.

In the urban context, the era of the automobile was present for long. The racing driver was the best picture that it had produced then. To race he wore boots and leather protection for the head, quite different from boots and hats – sometimes in leather – that the land worker wore for riding or working, but, even not by far, so different as the ability to deal with the machine.

The Vemag's utility was much more nimble than Willys' or Toyota's. It could overcome obstacles quite more easily, however it demanded more driver expertise and specialization of the service man. It was also outplaced for jobs such as pulling a trailer.

In the early 1970's the buggies had spread in the coastal cities. The forerunner of the idea that combined agility, lightness, wind in face and ability to go on sand was this notable utility powered by a two-stroke engine.

In the late 1970's, as motor sport, off-roading gained momentum. A few DKW utilities were on the road then. The Candango would have shown as unbeatable in practical terms: it was a quick and easy-going utility in any situation. (Fabio Steinbruch)

Fabio Steinbruch

TECHNICALLY CORRECT

The Candango had no self-locking differential. It means that if the wheels of the same side lost traction, the vehicle could not get out of a critical situation. However, there is no registry of this having occurred. Torque was split 50-50% front and rear and there was no way to change this distribution. Since the four wheels always pulled, at least two tires on the same side should have the same tread depth, or there would be tire scrub, slowing the vehicle down.

The low range mechanism was a mini gearbox placed where the sedan and station wagon free-wheeling device was. This was so because there was no room for it inside the transaxle case. Once the driver realized that it consisted of a small gearbox, it was sufficient to double-clutch for engaging took place with no difficulty at all while the vehicle was moving. The only trick was to get acquainted with the travel of the small handle, which was somewhat vague and did not allow to precisely know where neutral was. The gear ratio that influenced all forward gears and reverse was 1.604:1.

The Candango enclosed a lot of engineering in its bulk. Its performance in and off the road with the tiny 981 cm^3 engine (formerly 898 cm^3) was remarkable. Toughness was one of its greatest qualities, together with the straightforward mechanics. No wonder it was the choice of the German army.

In 1978, Volkswagen of Germany introduced the Iltis, a direct descendant of the Candango, with a small styling difference – the headlights became integrated to the fenders – and powered by a1,700-cm^3, 75 hp net horsepower engine from the Passat family. In lieu of the four-speed gearbox with low range gear set, a five-speed one with crawler first and reverse speeds. Second gear was used for normal launchs and the four-wheel drive became part-time. It was produced until mid-1990's. (Bob Sharp)

TECHNICAL INFORMATION OF DKW CANDANGO

VEHICLE	Candango
Type	Utility for off-road work, with front engine and full-time four-wheel drive with low range; 4 doors and canvas top
	Chassis and body
Type	Ladder-type chassis, separated; steel
	Engine
Type	Inline 3-cylinder, cast iron block and aluminum cylinder head, water cooled; two-stroke.
Mixture formation	2-bbl, 32-mm carburetor
Bore and stroke (mm)	74 x 76
Displacement (cm^3)	981 cm^3
Compression ratio	7.1:1
Maximum power (SAE)	50 hp at 4,500 rpm
Maximum torque (SAE)	8.5 m.kgf at 2,250 rpm
	Transmission
Type	4-speed with low range, non-synchronized first, and reverse
	Brakes
Type	Single hydraulic circuit, no powerbrake
Front	Drum
Rear	Drum
	Suspension
Front	Independent, lower A-arm and transverse leaf spring
Rear	Independent, lower A-arm and transverse leaf spring
	Steering
Type	Rack and pinion
	Dimensions and capacities
Wheelbase (mm)	2,000
Lenght (mm)	3,885
Width (mm)	1,520
Height (mm)	1,835
Ground clearance (mm)	225
Fuel tank (liter)	45
Curb weight (kg)	1,085
	Wheels and tyres
Type	Steel wheels and cross-ply tyres
Tyre size	6.00-16

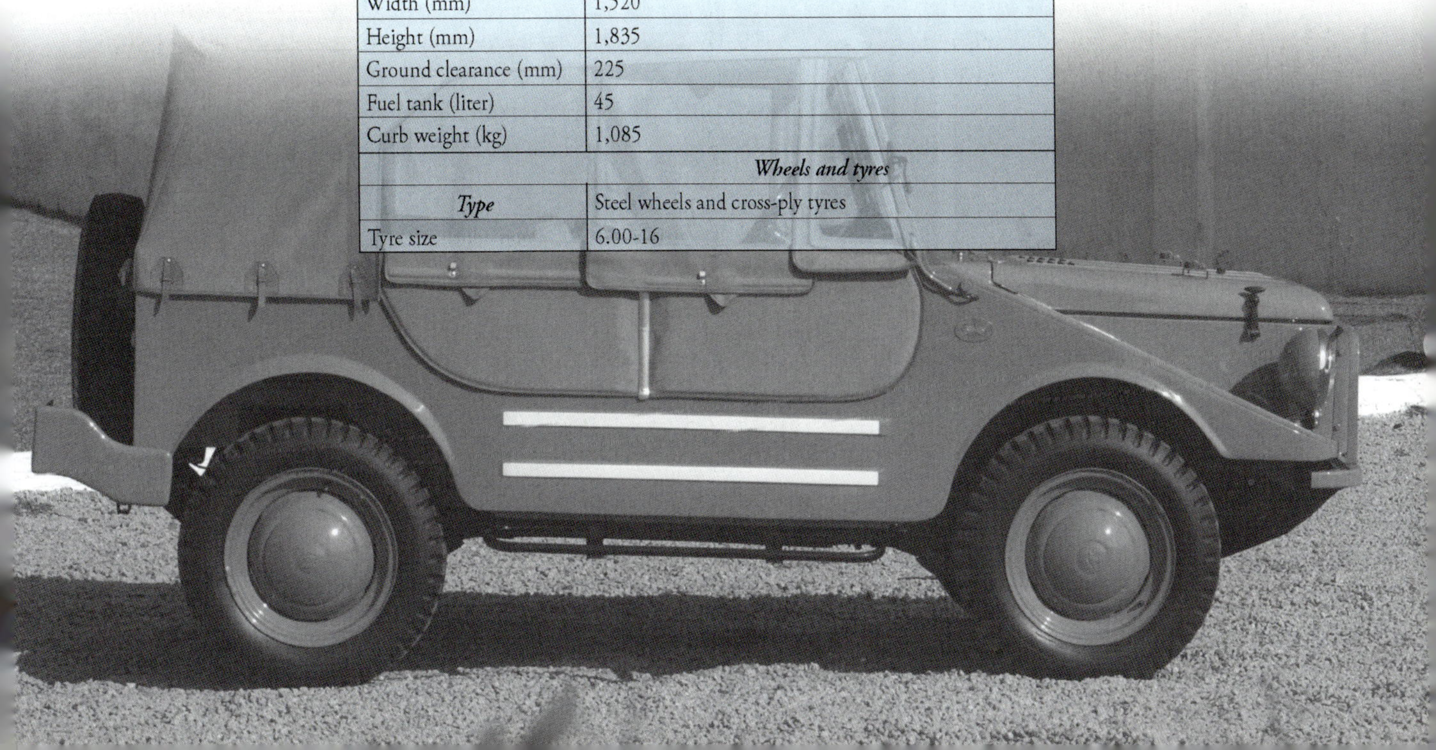

Candango
DKW-VEMAG

Para trás ficaram os obstáculos: aquêles trechos difíceis... a serra íngreme... areião... barro... quilômetros e quilômetros de estrada! E o que é mais importante: no CANDANGO DKW-VEMAG o motorista fêz viagem segura e confortável.

O moderno CANDANGO DKW-VEMAG possui tração nas 4 rodas. E também sòmente em duas, com reduzida - para uso em estradas menos difíceis e nas cidades. Ambos contam com o poderoso motor 1.000.

– o CANDANGO DKW-VEMAG atravessa cursos d'água de até meio metro de profundidade. O distribuidor protegido e a carroçaria blindada o fazem capaz disso.

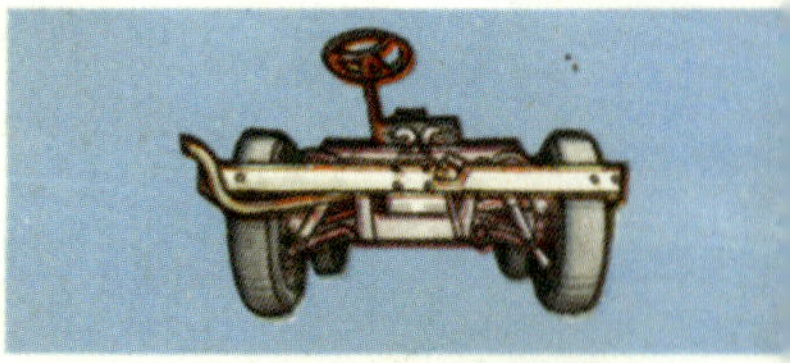

— o sistema de suspensão - exclusivo do notável CANDANGO DKW-VEMAG é independente nas 4 rodas. Proporciona mais estabilidade, segurança e confôrto.

VEMAG S.A. – Veículos e Máquinas Agrícolas

DKW-VEMAG
BRASIL

cin 159-96

Toyota Bandeirante

(1962 to 1967)

The land cruisers, searching for richness, departed from São Paulo towards the country's inland. In a way or another, they significantly conquered and expanded the Brazilian territory and its boundaries. This happened right at the beginning of the history of Brazil, in the early 1500s.

Toyota "Jeep" utility, in 1953, then Land Cruiser in 1954 – Land Cruiser incidentally was the name to be for its Brazilian utility, albeit translated into Portuguese and in singular: Bandeirante, a suitable name for its "jeep", a vehicle capable of making its own way, after the name. When it started being produced in Brazil, in 1962, the nameplate that resulted from the free translation did not loose the meaning conferred to the vehicle respectful of its true ability.

In the early 1980s, Toyota would turn into one of the biggest auto manufacturers in the world, especially of passenger cars'. Its history on wheels holds, at its very beginning, the manufacturing of off-road vehicles, the Land Cruiser representing its "business card" for many years.

Technical solutions and practical effects

The Toyota Bandeirante featured the classical solutions for off-road vehicles which were tested and proven, including the Land Cruiser that became known the world over.

The Toyota Bandeirante went a little farther, where others possibly could not go. Comfort and ability on asphalt were limited, however it ensured a somewhat better roadholding and convenience that the Willys Jeep. It had a cost! It's retail price was higher.

The format was born out of an almost square base, where parts superimposed: the fenders were not coupled to the remaining of the body; the hood did not embed either; the windshield was plain and framed by a straight-looking support; hinges and bolts were apparent; and so forth. Everything was quite "unfinished".

In brief: it had the shape, the looks and the finishing of all utilities. The suspension also followed the orthodox. Both in front and rear axles were rigid with semi-elliptical leaf springs, i.e., the more rustic possible.

Steering was by worm and sector, its parts always matched with lot of play. Quick and precise response was lost in exchange of no road roughness transmitting.

The gearbox had four speeds with a very short first – a true crawler. It was rear-wheel drive, however with the fitting of a transfer case, front wheels could drive too, then counting on four-wheel drive for typical off-road use in emergencies and low traction situations.

The engine solution found for the Bandeirante was the adoption of Daimler-Benz's Diesel, with all the characteristics for heavy-duty job that did not spare the occupants of noise and vibration even in Mercedes-Benz commercial vehicles, quite bigger and better structured than a light utility that weighed some 1,700 kg. In spite of discomfort, it featured Diesel character, well appreciated in a utility vehicle: lots of torque and absence of a ignition system, prone to failures and moisture-sensitive.

The Mercedes-Benz engine was one of the greatest differentials. Diesel-burning, it dispensed the electric ignition system, which enabled it to go through wades. The diesel's operational cost was lower and the better fuel efficiency resulted in longer range, something very important in regions with no roads and, even less, service stations.

The recipe for a utility was usual, yet it was outstanding for the better in balance and quality of the parts, as well as for the Diesel powerplant.

As for the body, it did not always resist the roughness of unpaved roads and to engine vibration itself. Unions getting loose and some surfaces showing cracks were quite usual.

Taking the Jeep Willys as a base, the Bandeirantes could be considered as:

- Fast – it was capable of sustaining speeds between 80 km/h and 100 km/h on asphalt and, in dirt roads, it could go at average speeds close to those of a passenger car.
- Comfortable – to go traveling a full journey through dirt roads, paved ones and where they not even existed, was an exercise of resistance for its occupants, yet possible. With the Willys, things were worse!
- Having a "soft" suspension.
- Featuring a well superior "roadholding". Also, "balance" during braking was far better, as well as the more "precise" steering.

When off the road, the utility character were undeniable, it could win any challenge and had the additional advantage of being able to go wadding thanks to the Diesel engine, with no ignition system.

Yet, another plus of the diesel-fueled engine was low fuel consumption that, additionally to low cost to drive, did not need a large fuel tank to provide an excellent range. It's worth remembering that where there are no roads, there are no refueling stations either!

Daily urban driving

To go around in a Bandeirante in a big city was a quite unusual option, nevertheless it was suitable for those who had a different lifestyle, with habits, itineraries, schedules and even singular wardrobe.

Those people that purchased the vehicle with the purpose of using it during the week in town and in the weekends to reach the beach or country house, certainly almost gave up and, or have transferred the home of the car to the country house, or just sold it. These Bandeirantes, those whose owners could not cope with the discomfort of the car (and not vice-versa) were the good samples to be bought for real, personal use. During certain times, when there were not enough new cars in the market, they could be accounted as a good capital inversion for the former owner, who certainly would not loose any money.

Finishing was Spartan, although when compared to others it seemed to be comfortable. The close-body version (there was also a ragtop one) ended becoming the more popular.

To be seated, one needed to mount the car. There were running boards for this purpose. In cold days, it was necessary to turn on a pre-heating system for one minute. While running, the Toyota exhaled a stinking black smoke, typical of the burning of the poor diesel fuel of the time, and emitted a loud noise diesel clack, besides vibrating quite a lot.

The first feeling rendered by the Spartan and rustic finishing – with seats, upholstery and everything else aimed to the practical – was not pleasant. Definitely, nothing was designed with comfort in mind.

Driving it in traffic it was slow, hard and heavy.

Its steering, besides featuring low precision, did not provide a turning radius sufficient for urban maneuvers.

The clutch was little progressive and the gearbox had firm and precise engaging. The gear ratios were not adequate to city speeds.

Driving position was quite unusual. It was not among the most comfortable and brake pedal effort was too high. Often, deceleration modulation could not be obtained.

The stamped-steel dashboard, with no lining at all, meant great danger in case of an accident. It was a common feature to all off-road vehicles at the time, as well as controls and instrument panel that were at the bare minimum.

Fine clothing did not match the finishing of the car and the perfume of diesel fuel, which would certainly mixture with the ones chosen by the occupants.

Sure, the Toyota was a work horse, not a luxury automobile. Yet it had conquered a specific urban public that evidently had differentiated compromises and loved the "country fashion" or just the rustic, always expressed by clothing and habits, too.

For ignoring any urban punishment, making it seem harmless because of its brute looks, fitted with true railroad rails as bumpers; for sitting its passengers at a higher level than in touring cars and for ensuing an image of not worrying at all about comfort, or no fear to face discomforts, the Bandeirante provided the very nice sensation of strength and power.

It was no target in traffic. Its image was far more "stone" than "glass".

On the road

Only those who had a specific work or looked for leisure traveled by utility. In this case, the utility had to be the Toyota. It was so that the most sold Bandeirante was the hardtop one, followed by the pick-up and, and far behind, the canvas top version. The later version was suitable for in-property work only, like the Jeep Willys.

Again, who wished to be the owner of a Toyota for town and for weekend outings to country or beach, ended giving up. The car would be sold or people would have to move.

Deep inland the country, the Bandeirante was quite a common car, no matter if on roads or in trails.

Many ran long journeys daily, and so high average speeds were not always possible.

After the land cruisers, the country's area enlarged dramatically and Brazil changed to continental dimensions. Road transport was adopted as the main modal. Its growth was even bigger during the pioneering phase of the auto industry. At that time, some country cities started being reached by recently-built dirt roads. Many were immediately paved, while others took quite longer to.

Besides the roads under construction, obviously there were places with no roads at all.

The only passenger vehicle capable of exiting the middle of a farm where its inside roadways were still being constructed, of running for many kilometers on non-paved roads, of attaining speeds close to passenger cars' in good roads and to be driven on asphalt for several hours to arrive in a large city, was the Bandeirante.

Therefore, in spite of not caring its occupants, it was unquestionable.

In the long asphalted stretches that began to appear, traffic was a bare minimum and required little acceleration or braking from an automobile. In spite of the Bandeirante being capable of attaining speeds of a little over 100 km/h, since there were no speed variations they could be maintained and, for such, roadholding was also sufficient.

In dirt roads, the Toyota absorbed well light roughness and was not that uncomfortable.

Yet where there were no roads, it was more comfortable than a tractor – the only transport mean capable of reaching far places as a Bandeirante.

The Bandeirante and I

The first glimpse of the Toyota utility that I have in memory is watching it on TV in an American series called Daktari, which was about daily life and adventures of a family of veterinarians committed to defend the animals in the African jungle.

I loved the idea of living in the jungle having a cross-eyed lion and a chimpanzee as pets. In spite of being interested in the central theme, the vehicles they used did not go unnoticed. They were the British off-road Land Rovers, almost homonymous of the Toyota, the name meaning "the ones that go all over the world", and a Toyota Land Cruiser pick-up.

The Bandeirante was a scarce presence in the big urban centers, however when I traveled, I met one sometimes.

In the mid-1970s I began to listen a lot about this utility. It was the "consumer dream" of my uncle that worked with farms in Mato Grosso do Sul state.

Only by late 1970s his dream would come true. Besides being very expensive, the waiting list to get one usually exceeded six months.

In the 1980s, this same uncle used to tell a very interesting "tale". It was about a man that died and went to heaven. Upon arriving there – after asking a few times but having no answer – St. Peter wrote down that Parkinson Disease caused his death. When reading the file, the man promptly corrected: "No! The thing is that I used to drive a Toyota".

The Bandeirantes I had contact with, as well as its stories, imagined or not, were with this uncle. In spite of not being manufactured in the pioneering time of industry, they kept the same characteristics.

I travelled a lot in these utilities, both as passenger as at the wheel. I have spent more than a day "jerking" aboard a sample, more than once. These were the best trips of my life, not so much for the comfort or performance, but more for where we passed by and for the stories we heard.

One of the curiosities of Physics I noticed was the existence of a unique voice frequency that, I don't know how, enabled conversation in the car and, even without having to yell, my uncle – whose hearing kept steadily deteriorating with the years and the trips – managed to communicate.

In a trip, while I slept drowsed by engine drone, I ended up hearing his muttering to my aunt, his sister. Those were subjects that they didn't want "children" (I was about 17) to hear

At that time there were humorists that recorded "K-7 tapes" with jokes. I remember one of them: "A hillbilly from São Paulo had his car stuck in a meadow, in neighboring Minas Gerais state and started to discuss with his friend about the car getting stuck or got stuck. After much quarrelling, they find a local peasant to whom they ask for an opinion. The man asks if the problem had happened with front or rear wheels. Since the four wheels were affected, the man decreed: "Then it got stuck".

I never understood what the joke meant until "got myself stuck" with a Bandeirante, in the Mato Grosso swamps. It was a typical urban-cultured, non-licensed beginner driver's mistake.

I had chosen the way that naturally gave continuity to the "road", not the detour. I did it wrongly but I had a lesson: if there was an alternative, that's where I should go by! The detour came later, for some reason!

From the "got stuck by me" car, the farm administrator stepped down and released the front wheel free-wheeling, which could only be done externally through two rotating knobs, one per wheel hub.

He walked back and, in "post-stuck person" *status*, got to the wheel, strongly rocked the vehicle alternating first and reverse. To my surprise, the car got unstuck.

Once again he got out of the utility, unlocked the front wheel hubs and returned to the car, which would continue to be driven by me and subject to other minor troubles.

Many kilometers I have rode aboard Bandeirantes in the 1970s and early 1980s. Time went by and Toyota accomplished its "land cruiser' mission of opening roadways at the farms; many main roads were paved and some routes had bridges built, enabling more smooth vehicles to take my uncle to the farms.

The Bandeirante remained for use within properties, fulfilling his mission of conferring the ability to govern business, after all, as Brazil's president Washington Luís said in the beginning of the 20th century, "To govern is to build roads". In a farm, administrating is to go through a quite similar phase: it is necessary to build accesses.

The Bandeirante seated five, with no luxury whatsoever, but without major crowding. Room for luggage was minimum.

For traveling purposes, he started using transformed Ford or Chevrolet diesel pick-ups that were a sales success in the 1980s. At the farms, he did not get back to tractors.

In the 1990s, imported models could provide a more reasonable comfort on the road, besides being able to reach almost the same spots as the Bandeirante.

ANOTHER OPINION

The Toyota Bandeirante reflects Japan's effort to build its automotive industry following the devastating World War II.

They have started with licensed designs, inspired in copies of what was manufactured the world over, but they knew how to leave the past behind and set for new flights. The Bandeirante is a plain utility yet fully suitable for heavy duty jobs. Its toughness is legendary and it worked fine to strengthen the Toyota brand in all markets of the world, Brazil included. The success of the Toyota Corolla as of 2002 has much to do with the heritage of this utility in terms of image.

TECHNICALLY CORRECT

The least unusual fact was Toyota having used an engine it did not produce for so long, in this case supplied by Mercedes-Benz of Brazil. Toyota has always built its own engines and it must have been difficult for them to admit that there was no way out in Brazil but to go ahead with this mixed solution. But they choose right, for the German originated-engines are tough, fuel efficient and above all dependable, what added value for work horse utility. The electric power companies preferred the pick-up version over any other brand or model for maintenance of rural power lines and the make became a synonymous of the vehicle, like "we are sending up a toyota right away, sir", as much as Kombi instead of van, Gilette for any safety blade and Lambretta, not scooter.

TECHNICAL INFORMATION OF TOYOTA BANDEIRANTE

VEHICLE	Toyota Bandeirante TB 25-L	TB 41-L
Type	Utility for off-road work, with front engine and four-wheel drive. Canvas top.	Teto rígido
	Chassis and body	
Type	Separated; steel	*
	Engine	
Type	Mercedes-Benz Diesel, inlilne-4, cast iron block and cylinder head, water cooled. Overhead valves (OHV)	*
Mixture formation	Inline injection pump	*
Bore and stroke (mm)	95 x 120	*
Displacement (cm^3)	3,400	*
Compression ratio	20.8:1	*
Maximum power (SAE)	78 hp at 3,000 rpm	*
Maximum torque (SAE)	19.6 m.kgf at 1,600 rpm	*
	Transmission	
Type	4-speed manual, non-synchronized first, and reverse	*
	Brakes	
Type	Single hydraulic circuit, no powerbrake	*
Front	Drum	*
Rear	Drum	*
	Suspension	
Front	Rigid axle, semi-elliptical longitudinal leaf springs	*
Rear	Rigid axle, semi-elliptical longitudinal leaf springs	*
	Steering	
Type	Worm and sector	*
	Dimensions and capacities	
Wheelbase (mm)	2,280	2,275
Lenght (mm)	3,830	*
Width (mm)	1,720	*
Height (mm)	1,950	*
Ground clearance (mm)	210	*
Fuel tank (liter)	47	*
Curb weight (kg)	1,610	1,725
	Wheels and tyres	
Type	Steel wheels and cross-ply tyres	*
Tyre size	6.50-16	*

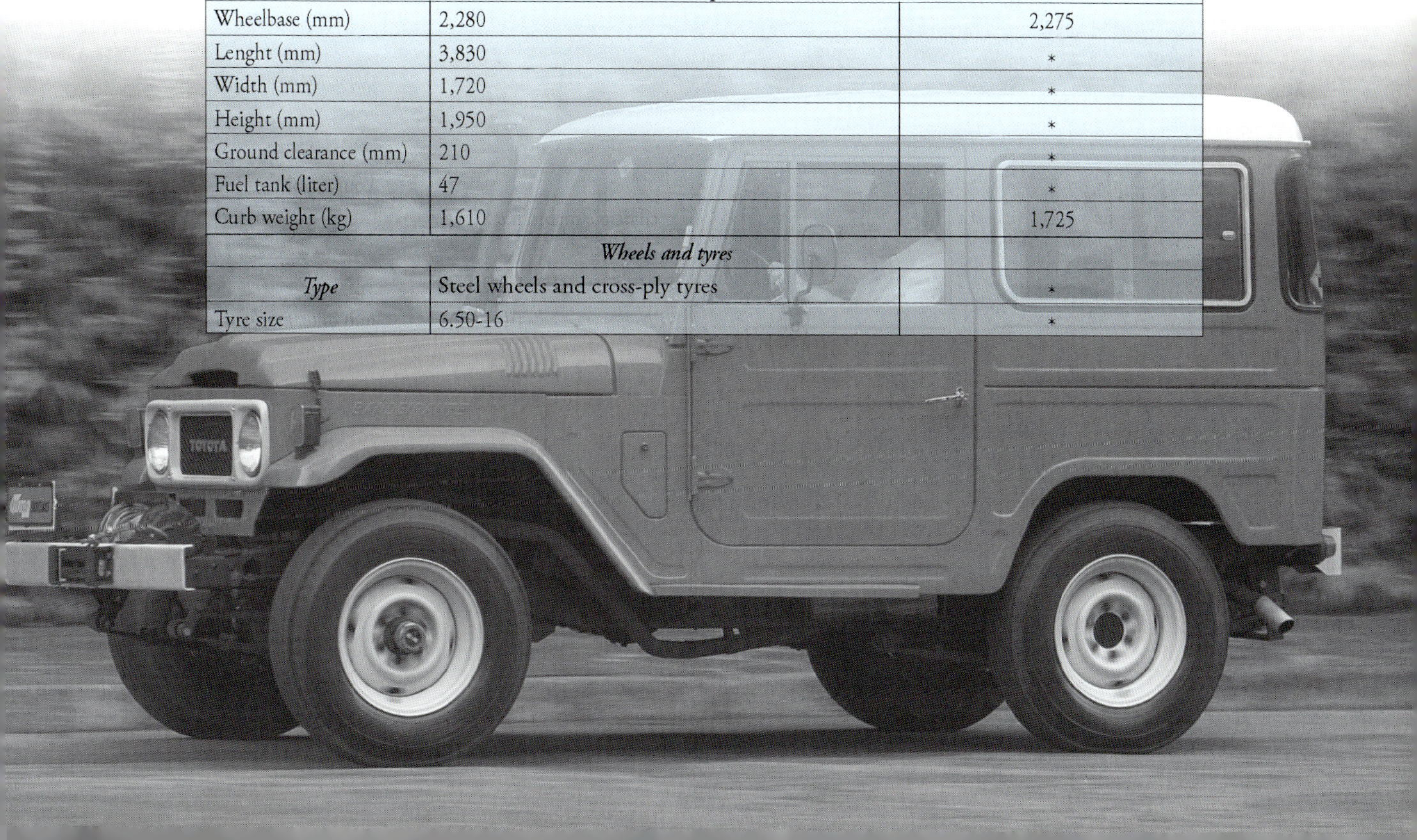

TOYOTA Bandeirante - Mod. TB41L - Tração em 2 ou 4 rodas

TAURUS 1010

também aos domingos

Valente no trabalho, a robusta Perua **TOYOTA Bandeirante** não descansa aos domingos. Enfrenta serras, areiões, lamaçais, em busca de um local aprazível onde seus ocupantes desfrutem de agradáveis momentos. E mesmo nas descidas mais íngremes seus nove ocupantes viajam tranqüilos, pois sabem que além de excelentes freios a Perua **TOYOTA Bandeirante** é dotada de motor Diesel de 78 HP, de alta compressão, que serve de seguro freio auxiliar. Inexistente em outros veículos de sua categoria, essa característica confere à Perua **TOYOTA Bandeirante** elevado índice de segurança. Vá conhecê-la no Revendedor **TOYOTA** mais próximo.

TOYOTA DO BRASIL S.A.

INDÚSTRIA E COMÉRCIO - São Bernardo do Campo - SP

Sources

Autoesporte Magazine, from 1964 to 1968 — Editora Fc.
Quatro Rodas Magazine, from 1960 to 1968 — Abril Cultural.
Alguns aspectos da história do automóvel no Brasil — Tempo e Memória.
ANFAVEA (Associação Nacional dos Fabricantes de Veículos Automotor) Product table informations.
Portal Best Cars Web Site, cars informations, at http://www.uol.com.br/best cars, consulted from 1997 to 2007.
Sandler, Paulo César. *DKW — a grande história da pequena maravilha*. São Paulo, Alaúde Editorial, 2006.
Sandler, Paulo César e Simone, Rogério de. *SIMCA — A história desde as origens*. São Paulo, Alaúde Editorial, 2005.

READ ALSO

DKW
The big story of the small wonder

Paulo Cesar Sandler

This book tells the rich DKW story and its path from Germany to Brazil. In the early 1950s, additionally to the Beetle, there was another automobile with German accent running in our streets and roads: the DKW. In the second half of the decade, its production in Brazil had started through a partnership with Vemag. At that time, it grew a true national pride by pioneering auto manufacturing in the country. Besides street and roads, the DKW also took to the racing circuits. Who experienced that period still remembers the deafening noise of these engines that excited so much and still do so the lovers of this car. This volume features more than 650 photos, some inedited, that portrays the arrival of the first national car to the road. A work that will fascinate collectors, admirers and the curious.

SIMCA
The story from the origins

Paulo Cesar Sandler and Rogério de Simone

The book begins telling the story of the factory at its country of origin – France, inviting the reader to follow the evolution of the brand since its foundation, in the 1930s, until the end of its activities, in the 1980s, having occurred in the middle of the way its coming to Brazil, in the late 1950s. The history of the Brazilian subsidiary, between 1959 and 1967, is illustrated with historical photos of the assembly line and of the launching of the main models such as the Chambord, Jangada and others. Among further interesting information, the book also tells the path of the brand in the racing circuits outlining the races throughout Brazil, with the main results as well, including the story of the legendary Simca racing team which was headed by the dearest, missing Chico Landi. Conceived with a superb graphic project and design, richly illustrated, it provides the reader with a voyage through time and the heroic universe of the pioneers of the Brazilian auto industry.

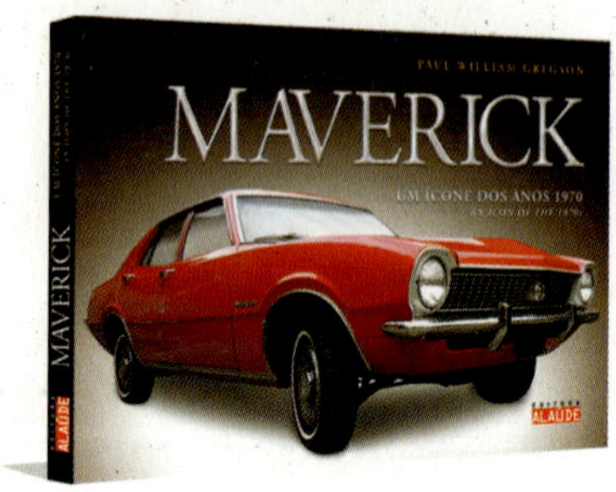

MAVERICK
An icon of the 1970s

Paul William Gregson

This work tells the story of one of the greatest icons of the Brazilian automotive industry. The author fully explores in a detailed way the path of the Ford Maverick both in Brazil and in the world, from launching to identity formation, additionally to its presence in the racing circuits. The historical aspect is complemented by the rich analysis of the marketing moment the national industry was going through when the Maverick arrived.

The historical focus and, at the same time, the richness of the images and technical information make out of this book an obligatory source of research for those interested in antique cars and in the Mavericks particularly. It is a reading that will draw attention from the layman as well whose sole interest is exclusively the search for quality information.

THE IMPLANTING OF THE AUTOMOTIVE INDUSTRY IN BRAZIL
From active importation substitution to passive globalization

Sydney A. Latini

The implanting of the auto industry in Brazil was a hallmark in the country's industrialization process By following a cautious program, it was the emblem of the importation substitution policy put into effect by the Juscelino Kubitschek administration (1956-1961), according to his Plan of Objectives. Through rigor in observing the rules set in the National Automotive Plans under GEIA's (Executive Group for the Automotive Industry) coordination, it triggered trust from national and foreign companies, who then invested in the manufacturing of vehicles and auto parts. The registry of this process' evolution and that of improving the instruments of economic policy as of World War II, with emphasis in the implanting of the automotive industry, was the proposal of the author, who witnessed its several steps and participated in many of them. Although written in first person-singular, there is no intention in being bibliographic, not even when episodes of his career coincide with the historical facts.